Thinking Through Cinema

Film as Philosophy

Edited by Murray Smith and Thomas E. Wartenberg

Blackwell Publishing

Contents

Blackwell Publishing, Inc.
350 Main Street
Malden, MA 02148 USA

Blackwell Publishing, Ltd.
960 Garsington Road
Oxford OX4 2DQ
United Kingdom

Library of Congress Cataloging-in-Publication Data has been applied for.

ISBN 978-1-4051-5411-6
ISSN 0021-8529

Preface

This volume brings together essays from a wide range of contributors, including both film scholars and philosophers, all of whom address the question of whether philosophy can take the form of, or be articulated through, film. The contributions canvas a wide variety of forms and periods of film as they present diverse answers to this question.

The idea for this volume was the result of a collaboration brought about through the generosity of the Leverhulme Trust. In the winter and spring of 2003, Murray Smith hosted Tom Wartenberg as a Visiting Leverhulme Professor in the Film Studies program at the University of Kent, Canterbury. During our many discussions, it became clear that, while we were both committed to the study of film in the light of philosophy, we had some fundamental disagreements about whether film could really function *as* philosophy and, if so, how. Realizing that many philosophers were now treating films as sources of philosophical insights, it seemed appropriate to provide an opportunity for a thorough-going discussion of this issue. We believe that this collection does just that. What is distinctive of the essays gathered here is the authors' methodological self-consciousness about the possibility that films might, in one sense or another, be philosophical.

Along the way, we benefited from the help of many people. Foremost was the support of Susan Feagin, the editor of *The Journal of Aesthetics and Art Criticism*, who has assisted us in the creation of this collection at every stage, from inception onwards. The project could not have taken on its ambitious form and scope without her advice, insight, and backing. Thanks also to the board of *JAAC* for greenlighting the project. At Blackwell Publishing, Jeff Dean, philosophy acquisitions editor, was enthusiastic about this project from its inception, and Anne Jones, senior editor of journals, has helped steer us through the many shoals we have inevitably encountered. Rachel Falkenstern at *JAAC* and Aimee Chevrette, the journals production editor at Blackwell, have provided expert, scrupulous, and patient assistance with the editing and design of the volume. We thank all of these people for their efforts. We also thank those supportive of our undertaking at the University of Kent: the members of the Film Studies, Philosophy, History and Theory of Art, and Drama programs, especially Sarah Cardwell, Elizabeth Cowie, Katie Grant, Michael Grant, Frances Guerin, Andrew Klevan, Richard Norman, Sean Sayers, Tony Skillen, and Matthew Walter.

This book was originally published as the *Journal of Aesthetics and Art Criticism*, Vol. 64:1 (Winter 2006), on behalf of the American Society for Aesthetics.

M.S. and T.E.W.

MURRAY SMITH AND THOMAS E. WARTENBERG

Introduction

From Astruc who thinks philosophers would have to film.

Maurice Nadeau [has claimed]…"If Descartes lived today, he would write novels." With all due respect to Nadeau, a Descartes of today would already have shut himself up in his bedroom with a 16mm camera and some film, and would be writing his philosophy on film: for his *Discours de la Méthode* would today be of such a kind that only the cinema could express it satisfactorily.

Alexandre Astruc[1]

I've thought of my film work as a kind of philosophy.
Michael Snow[2]

After decades in the shadows, the philosophy of film has arrived, borne on the currents of the wider revival of philosophical aesthetics. But there are a variety of different ways that the relationship between film and philosophy can be understood. The most general conception takes as its subject film as an art form, posing a variety of questions that parallel those asked by philosophical aesthetics about other art forms: What is the nature of cinematic depiction? Is there anything special about the realism often claimed for film? Can a film be authored in just the same way as a poem or novel? There is, however, one question that has become very prominent in philosophical discussions of film: To what extent can film—or individual films— act as a vehicle of or forum for philosophy itself? This is the domain of "film *as* philosophy," and forms the focus of this collection.

The flourishing of philosophical attention to film since the 1990s should not obscure its long germination prior to this period of rapid growth. A great deal of philosophical writing on film has been pursued under the guise of "film theory"—that voluminous body of writing on the general principles and questions thrown up by the medium of film, written by filmmakers, film critics, film scholars, art historians, literary

theorists, and semioticians. One of the earliest extensive treatises on the nature of film was written by Hugo Münsterberg, Professor of Experimental Psychology at Harvard University. In *The Photoplay: A Psychological Study* (1916), Münsterberg inaugurated philosophical reflection on film and his work has come to be regarded as the first classic of film theory.[3] Münsterberg, however, was not concerned with film *as* philosophy, but rather with a philosophical and psychological characterization of film as a distinct art form. This concern with characterizing (and legitimating) film as an art was the major preoccupation of classical film theory.

Nevertheless, in the hands of some early and classical film theorists, the debate over film as an art form gave rise to a question, or cluster of questions, which bear a strong resemblance to the debate over film as philosophy. For any theorist who held that art required a strong conceptual component, the ability of film to render ideas—and not merely to record a moving image of the world—was key to the claim that film was indeed a medium of art. The most important of such theorists was the Soviet filmmaker, theorist, and all-round force of nature, Sergei Eisenstein. Central to Eisenstein's claim concerning film's ability to embody concepts and arguments was his own conception of *montage*, one that enveloped more than the traditional notion of editing. In both his theoretical writings and filmmaking practice, Eisenstein sought to demonstrate how film could render ideas visibly, most overtly in his explorations of what he termed "intellectual cinema."[4]

Eisenstein was not alone, especially in the "silent" era, in his preoccupation with establishing the "intellectual" capacities of film. However, while arguments of this sort continued to

Cavell vs Deleuze

appear in later film theory and criticism—as it does, in a strikingly emphatic way, and cast very specifically in terms of *philosophy*, in the work of Alexandre Astruc who is quoted at the outset of this introduction—on the whole the issue became considerably less prominent in the sound era. To a large extent, the battle had been—or had been perceived to have been— won; there is never any real doubt in the work of the French film critic and theorist André Bazin, for example, that films are capable of all the sophistication of classical works and forms of art, thematically and stylistically, albeit in the specific forms of complexity afforded by the medium of film.

If it does not derive directly from the distant precursors we have discussed so far, from where does the current surge of debate around film as philosophy come? Two more immediate sources suggest themselves. The first is the work of the American philosopher, Stanley Cavell. In a series of books, Cavell has outlined his own distinctive understanding of film that, although deeply influenced by Bazin's conception of film as an imprint of the world itself, makes the philosophical potential of film much more salient than it was for Bazin.[5] More recently, Stephen Mulhall has adapted and extended Cavell's approach to the study of contemporary popular filmmaking, in the process if anything strengthening the claim that at least some filmmaking ought to be recognized as "philosophy in action" in the fullest sense.[6]

The second proximate source of contemporary debate on the idea of "film as philosophy" derives from the Continental tradition, in particular the work of the French philosopher Gilles Deleuze (along with other theorists, such as the psycho-analytically-oriented philosopher Slavoj Žižek). Where the emphasis in the Cavellian tradition lies on the ability of film to embody philosophical thought, albeit in distinctive ways, on recognized philosophical problems—skepticism and personal identity, for example—for Deleuze, the philosophical interest of film lies in its purported capacity to generate new philosophical concepts and problems.[7] Moreover, while Deleuze does discuss individual films, his emphasis is often on the way these individual films are said to realize features and implications of the technology of film itself. Henri Bergson's use of the metaphor of cinema in his philosophical writings on

time—the starting point for Deleuze's exploration of cinema, and now widely discussed in the literature inspired by Deleuze—might be seen as a founding example of treating the technology or "apparatus" of cinema, rather than the individual film, as a vehicle of philosophy.[8] Although the contrast is not absolute, it is hard to deny that a notably different weighting is given by the Cavellian and Deleuzian trends to the medium in general, and the particular film, respectively.

I. THE VERY IDEA OF FILM AS PHILOSOPHY

What exactly does it mean, then, to assert the possibility of film as philosophy? There are a number of different ways that this can be interpreted. The weakest version is the assertion that films have a philosophical content, in the sense that films inevitably make certain philosophical assumptions, a claim that few would dispute. A stronger interpretation holds that films can make a philosophical claim or point. Even more substantial is the idea that films actually philosophize, the most controversial rendering of the idea that films have an important relationship to philosophy.

How one approaches the claim that films can count as philosophy depends to a certain degree on one's understanding of philosophy itself. On the one hand, if philosophy is regarded as an academic discipline with a highly specific methodology—as many professional philosophers now do conceive it—it seems quite implausible that a film could be capable of instantiating that methodology. After all, as an essentially, or at least typically, visual medium, film seems very different from the verbal forms of discourse that constitute traditional philosophy. On the other hand, if philosophy is regarded as the attempt to think systematically about fundamental issues of human existence, it seems more plausible to regard film as capable of embodying such acts of reflection. For if philosophy names a range of concerns that are the common property of every thoughtful human being during at least some moments of his or her life, why should not films mobilize those concerns in ways that would count as philosophy in this sense? As Stephen Mulhall has noted, "a person's way of working can intentionally have a philosophical dimension without his being professionally identifiable as a philosopher. Einstein's questions about physics are at least as much philosophical as scientific; so why must we reject the possibility of a film director's endeavors as being similarly both philosophical and cinematic?"[9]

We clearly are not in a position to settle the question of what philosophy itself is and therefore to use an agreed upon conception of philosophy as the basis for discussing what it means for films to be philosophy. So in thinking about this issue, we will try to remain neutral about the nature of philosophy itself, taking as minimal a position as possible on the question of what philosophy is. Still, there is a great deal that can be said at a general level about the possibility of film as philosophy. For example, let us consider why someone might think that a film can be a work of philosophy. One fact that can be appealed to is the actual practice of philosophers, many of whom, in writing about specific films, have claimed that they contain philosophical insights. If you look at any volume of the journal *Film and Philosophy*, as Dan Shaw does in his contribution to this collection, you will find a variety of essays that purport to unpack the philosophical content and presuppositions of specific films. Since professional philosophers have a claim to being good judges of philosophical content when they see it, their very practice provides a reason for thinking that films can have philosophical content.

Another factor is the testimony of filmmakers. Various filmmakers have claimed their films to be animated by philosophical interests, as the quotations from Alexandre Astruc and Michael Snow at the beginning of this introduction attest. Although we might be critical of filmmakers' ability to be good judges of whether their films really are philosophy, their own words do provide support for the idea of film as philosophy.

In recent years, there has also been work by professional philosophers that attributes to some works of literature the status of philosophy. Martha Nussbaum's essays on the novels of Henry James were pivotal in getting philosophers to see that novels can make a significant contribution to our understanding of ethical issues.[10] If works of literature may count as philosophy, then why not film? But this connection raises more questions than it answers about film as philosophy, for Nussbaum claims that James's novels furnish philosophical insights by virtue of the very detailed and fine-grained examples they present. It might be argued that a standard film—one that lasts around two hours—necessarily lacks the sort of density and detail that a book of several hundred pages possesses; or that the form of such films inhibits the careful and sustained reflection on such detail as they do possess. So, does not the very argument for certain works of literature counting as philosophy also explain why films cannot be treated in the same fashion?

Here, the opponent to the idea of film as philosophy might continue by noting that there is something about film *as a medium* that makes it inhospitable to philosophical content. In particular, film's nature as a visual medium might be taken to preclude it from acting as a vehicle of philosophy. On the view that philosophy requires explicit argumentation, it might be thought that films could not meet this standard.

It is important to acknowledge that there is, nonetheless, a trivial sense in which a film can be a work of philosophy. Relying on film's ability to transcribe reality, one could simply film a philosopher reading a paper out loud. If the paper is a work of philosophy, so, it could be argued, is the film that records its oral presentation. But the supporter of the idea of "film as philosophy" will not be satisfied with this example, for the philosophy contained in the film is in no way dependent on the medium of film itself. For the claim that films can be philosophy to be in any way significant, the philosophy contained in the film must somehow be presented in a way that depends on some feature of film as an artistic medium.

This is just where Paisley Livingston enters the argument. In his essay, "Theses on Cinema as Philosophy," Livingston takes on what he calls "the bold thesis" that film is able, because of its nature as a medium, to make a unique contribution to philosophy. He presents a dilemma to advocates of the bold thesis that involves the possibility of paraphrase. If the purportedly distinctive contribution to philosophy made by a film can be paraphrased, then it is not unique; if it cannot be, then how could it be a contribution to the discursive discipline of philosophy? The lesson that Livingston draws is that we should be more modest in our expectations about what film can contribute to the discipline of philosophy.

Thomas E. Wartenberg takes the opposing point of view in his contribution, "Beyond *Mere* Illustration: How Films Can Be Philosophy." Wartenberg considers the dichotomy frequently made by philosophers of film between a film's merely illustrating a philosophical issue and its making a more substantive contribution to the discipline, arguing that it rests on an undertheorized notion of illustration. He presents a range of different examples of pictorial illustrations of written texts in order to support his claim that an illustration can be as central to the meaning of a text as its written counterpart. Using the example of Charles Chaplin's comic film *Modern Times* (1936) and Karl Marx's *Economic and Philosophical Manuscripts of 1844*, he shows how a film that illustrates a philosophical theory can actually make a contribution to the philosophical discussion of that theory by providing specific concrete interpretations of some of the central claims of the theory.[11]

In "Film Art, Argument, and Ambiguity," Murray Smith argues that there are significant differences between the aims of philosophy and the aims of film art that make it implausible or misleading, in most cases, to see the latter as "philosophy in action." Taking the case of the Steve Martin comedy *All of Me* (Carl Reiner, 1984), a film whose narrative bears an uncanny resemblance to a philosophical thought experiment, Smith argues that the roles of the thought experiment in the narrative film, on the one hand, and the philosophical essay, on the other, are quite distinct. Although conceding that many films may embody philosophical ideas in some modest sense, and that certain unusual types of filmmaking may live up to the idea of "philosophizing," Smith is skeptical of stronger claims for the philosophical status of most narrative filmmaking. In taking this position, Smith alludes to Cleanth Brooks's famous essay on "The Heresy of Paraphrase," in which Brooks warns against setting the cognitive or truth-claiming dimension of a poem (or any work of art) "into an unreal competition with science or philosophy or theology."[12]

II. POPULAR AMERICAN FILM: ENTERTAINMENT AND ENLIGHTENMENT

A paradoxical feature of a great deal of recent work on film as philosophy is that the films that most philosophers have taken to be candidates for making a distinctive contribution to philosophy are the ones that *appear* least likely to have philosophical content: popular narrative films. Although it intuitively makes sense to attribute philosophical content to the types of film discussed in the next two sections of this collection—European art films and avant-garde films—popular narrative films, whether Independent or Hollywood productions, just do not seem the sort of works that are capable of making a deep philosophical point. After all, such films are designed to please a broad audience, rather than to probe philosophical ideas. They aim to entertain rather than enlighten. Or do they?

Surprisingly, many recent philosophers have adopted the counterintuitive position that it is just such popular films that are capable of yielding philosophical insight. In so doing, they have followed the lead of Stanley Cavell, who argued in *Pursuits of Happiness: The Hollywood Comedy of Remarriage* and other books that Hollywood films of the 1930s contained philosophical insights on a par with the works of great philosophers such as Kant and Emerson.[13]

Responding to the dismissive attitude toward such films that he took to be dominant among film scholars, Cavell argued that the "comedies of remarriage" embodied the philosophical trope of skepticism about other minds, the philosophical doubt that one can know what someone else is really feeling or thinking that has been a staple of post-Cartesian philosophical reflection. The humorous and charming stories of these films belied their profound investigations into our anxieties as human beings, according to Cavell. To make his case, he relied on the works of the great philosophers to unpack the significance of the films he analyzed. Cavell's provocative juxtaposition of, for example, *The Critique of Pure Reason* with *It Happened One Night* (Frank Capra, 1934) provoked the expected outrage and dismissal on the part of both philosophers and film scholars.[14] Nonetheless, his innovative argument paved the way for many younger philosophers to investigate how popular narrative films might function as vehicles of philosophical insight.

This section contains a variety of essays, each of which explores the possibility that popular

narrative film can have philosophical significance. Beyond this connecting thread, they
approach the question of what gives a film philosophical significance in different ways and
address a variety of distinct philosophical
issues, from love to personal identity and the
nature of racism.

The section begins with Richard Allen's
"Hitchcock and Cavell," which, while sympathetic to Cavell's broader perspective, uses the
films of Alfred Hitchcock as a test case for the
validity of Cavell's claim that film has an intrinsic relationship to philosophical skepticism.
After providing a synthetic overview of central
themes in Cavell's own philosophy, Allen
argues that Hitchcock's films do not embody
the philosophical skepticism so central to
Cavell, so that doubt is shed on the validity of
Cavell's enterprise of seeing film as an embodiment of this specific philosophical trope.

In "The Paradox of the Unknown Lover: A
Reading of *Letter from an Unknown Woman*,"
Lester H. Hunt argues that Max Ophul's 1948
film presents a conception of romantic love that
is original and should be taken seriously by philosophers. This well-known film has been the
subject of a great deal of philosophical interest,
but philosophers have not seen it as presenting a
view of love we should endorse. But this is just
what Hunt claims. According to him, the film
presents an account of love as involving a
unique sort of knowledge about the object of
one's love. This epistemic aspect of love, he
believes, has not been generally acknowledged
in philosophical accounts of love, so he finds
the film to have made a contribution to our philosophical understanding of that significant
emotion.

In "Spike Lee and the Sympathetic Racist,"
Dan Flory explores how Spike Lee lures white
audience members into a serious confrontation
with their own racist attitudes. Flory's argument
begins with the fact that many of Lee's films
include sympathetic white characters who nonetheless express and enact racist attitudes—most
notably Sal in *Do the Right Thing* (1989). Flory
argues that Lee uses such characters to push
white audience members to acknowledge an
uncomfortable possibility: that they, too, harbor
racist attitudes. In this way, Flory claims, Lee is
making an intervention into our philosophical
understanding of racism by presenting viewers

with that most traditional of Socratic philosophical challenges: "to evaluate the contents of
their souls" (Flory, p. 77).

"Transparency and Twist in Narrative Fiction
Film," by George Wilson, focuses on a formal
feature of a number of recent films: the presence of a narrative "twist" that requires viewers
to reassess their own understandings of the
films' narratives. Films that have this feature
proceed relatively unproblematically until a
final twist reveals that viewers have been misled about what has taken place. Wilson argues
that previous accounts of the nature of fictional
narrative have overlooked the precise nature of
the deceptive shots on which such films rely.
Wilson characterizes them as "impersonal yet
subjectively inflected" and shows how their
presence complicates the claim of transparency—the idea that films and photographs
prompt us to imagine seeing the objects that
they depict, and that the narrational form of
most popular filmmaking trades on this feature.
Wilson thus elucidates a kind of formal, narrative complexity that apparently "lightweight"
films can exhibit, a complexity that both parallels and, in particular instances, might support
philosophical complexity. The essays on *Being
John Malkovich* (Spike Jonze, 1999) and *Eternal Sunshine of the Spotless Mind* (Michel
Gondry, 2004), discussed below, provide good
examples of this possibility.

The final three contributions in this section
all focus on aspects of the question of personal
identity. This is a topic that has been the focus
of philosophical interest since the ancient
Greeks first noticed how difficult it was to provide a convincing account of it. Many science
fiction films have played with this idea as well.
What is interesting to reflect on is how new
technologies—both of human reproduction and
of filmmaking itself—may have given this issue
a new immediacy that is reflected both in contemporary filmmakers' focus on it and in these
three essays discussing it.

Stephen Mulhall's "The Impersonation of
Personality: Film as Philosophy in *Mission:
Impossible*" amplifies the argument made in his
recent book, *On Film*, that films can actually
philosophize.[15] Here, Mulhall's concern is a
film series that is, in some sense, a remake of
the famous television series, *Mission: Impossible* (Bruce Geller, 1966–73). In analyzing the

films, Mulhall finds them to be investigating broadly the same set of philosophical ideas he identified as the concern of the *Alien* tetralogy[16] (the central case study in *On Film*): the nature of human identity and embodiment, as well as the nature of film itself. In addition, Mulhall argues that the *Mission: Impossible* films embody a reflection on the   tionship between television and film as two paradigmatic artistic media.

Daniel Shaw's contribution, "On Being Philosophical and *Being John Malkovich*," begins with a survey of different attempts by philosophers to attribute philosophical content to a film. Drawing on the journal he edits, *Film and Philosophy*, as well as other writings about film by philosophers, Shaw categorizes different ways philosophers have taken films to be philosophical, providing useful means for conceptualizing different philosophical positions on the relationship between film and philosophy. Shaw then turns to *Being John Malkovich* as an example of a film that he believes to be genuinely philosophical in that it furthers our understanding of a philosophical issue. In making his case, Shaw compares the film's understanding of human personality to that articulated by Friedrich Nietzsche in *Beyond Good and Evil*.[17] Rather than presenting a completed theory of human identity, Shaw holds, both the film and Nietzsche's text present a challenge to "our simpler and more comforting notions of who we are, as well as [an] undermining [of] accepted philosophical definitions of personal identity" (Shaw, p. 117) that qualifies both as examples of genuine philosophy.

Chris Grau's "*Eternal Sunshine of the Spotless Mind* and the Morality of Memory" investigates the morality of the practice of memory erasure depicted in the 2004 film directed by Michel Gondry. Grau argues that the film embodies a critique of this practice that cannot be made sense of by utilitarian theories of morality. To explain our negative emotional response to aspects of the practice depicted in the film, Grau appeals to both Kantian and virtue-based ethical theories, claiming that each provides an explanation of certain features of our reactions. In a sobering appendix, Grau shows that this is not just an exercise in fantasy, for the issue of memory erasure is actually being raised by certain current clinical practices. The film provides us with the ethical

resources, Grau claims, to begin to assess these problematic techniques.

III. CONTINENTAL FILM, CONTINENTAL PHILOSOPHY

The idea of a significant relationship between philosophy and the tradition of European art cinema is less obviously problematic than the idea that popular films might be vehicles for substantial philosophical insight. As the name implies, "art" films are typically characterized by an ostentatious ambition and high cultural address, sometimes in the form of allusions to philosophy, a tendency with its origins in the determination of various European national cinemas to differentiate themselves from (what is perceived as) the "pure entertainment" of Hollywood and kindred forms of popular filmmaking around the world. (Of course, the essays on popular filmmaking in this collection challenge just this apparently clear distinction between art and entertainment, but that the distinction exists as an orthodoxy, implicit in the very idea of a special field of "art cinema," is beyond dispute.) Each of the essays in this section explores the philosophical ramifications of significant directors in the art cinema tradition.

András Bálint Kovács examines Michelangelo Antonioni's classic trilogy of the early 1960s in "Sartre, the Philosophy of Nothingness, and the Modern Melodrama," arguing that the films are part of a wider trend in European cinema in which the influence of Sartre's existentialism is evident. Kovács notes Sartre's stature at the time and the extent of his influence among European intellectuals and artists. Kovács also reminds us that, somewhat unusually for a twentieth-century philosopher, Sartre wrote novels and plays to expound his philosophical ideas, along with more traditional philosophical texts. Antonioni's films may be best understood, on this view, precisely as "films of ideas," or philosophical dramas; films whose storylines, structure, and style are expressly designed to express philosophical concepts and elicit our reflection upon them. The strange melancholy and inability to act that afflicts the characters in Antonioni's *L'eclisse* (1962), for example, is best understood as a dramatization of the abyss of "nothingness" that, according to Sartre, opens up for those who embrace the possibility of acting freely, a shadow accompanying the potential of liberation from custom, habit, and traditional metaphysical myths.

In "Cinema and Subjectivity in Krzysztof Kieślowski," Paul Santilli explores the metaphysics implicit in the films of the Polish director, finding in them a reflection on the tension between—in Kant's terms—the phenomenal and the noumenal dimensions of human existence. Drawing on the work of Žižek, Santilli argues that Kieślowski exploits the success of film in the representation of phenomenal appearance, precisely, if paradoxically, to intimate the idea of a noumenal reality to which we have only indirect and imperfect access. The essays by Kovács and Santilli thus complement each other. For Kovács, Antonioni's films exploit film's capacity to capture in meticulous detail the sensuous surface of existence, while insinuating a "worm in the heart of being" that drains it of metaphysical value. For Santilli, by contrast, Kieślowski's films use the "hyperphenomenal" quality of film to evoke just the kind of transcendent realm that, for Sartre, is unavailable to the authentic, modern human being.[18]

Katherine Ince explores the work of novelist and filmmaker Catherine Breillat in "Is Sex Comedy or Tragedy? Directing Desire and Female *Auteur*ship in the Cinema of Catherine Breillat." Through her career Breillat has made a series of unflinching films on the politics of sexuality and gender, and not least the politics of the depiction of gender. Ince places Breillat's work in the context of feminist philosophy, in particular the writings of Luce Irigaray, exploring the vital influence of Freudian and Lacanian psychoanalysis on them, and their critical extension by Judith Butler. (It is worth noting in this connection that Breillat's films have also been discussed by film scholars as knowing, self-conscious responses to the substantial body of feminist film theory on the representation of gender in cinema.) Ince argues that Breillat's films reflect on the various ways the adoption and maintenance of sexual identity can be represented as comedy or tragedy, in a variety of senses of each of these terms. Far from embodying an essentialist philosophy of sexuality, as it might seem, Ince argues that Breillat's films playfully dismantle the "tragic" conception of sexual identity evident in the writings of Lacan, and instead offer a vision

of sexuality as a fundamentally "constructed"—contingent and culturally variable—phenomenon.

IV. FILM AS "THEORY": THE AVANT-GARDE

The final group of essays pursue the idea of an explicit and strong relationship between film and philosophy in a different direction. Here, the focus is on films from the avant-garde tradition—films that, like art films, aspire to high cultural status, but that, unlike art films, circulate in art galleries and museums rather than in cinemas, and take their cue as much or more from painting, sculpture, and music as from the literary arts. Three of the essays take as their focus a particular type of avant-garde film known as the "structural film," a form that emerged in its mature form in the 1960s and is characterized by its emphatic reflexivity: structural films are often described as films about the nature of film and filmmaking. It is this reflexive character that makes them akin to philosophy, insofar as philosophy itself is characterized by a self-conscious attitude and interrogatory stance, questioning that which is usually taken for granted. As we have already noted, Michael Snow, once described as the "dean" of structural filmmakers,[19] describes his filmmaking as "a kind of philosophy." In this respect, structural films might be regarded as "philosophy" in just the way that Arthur Danto treats Marcel Duchamp's *Fountain* or Andy Warhol's *Brillo Box* as works of philosophy.[20] For just as Duchamp's inverted urinal poses the philosophical question, "Just what constitutes a work of art?" so structural films ask, "Just what is a film?" Perhaps not surprisingly, it has also been argued that structural filmmaking is a kind of "theoretical" filmmaking.[21]

It is also true, however, that structural films largely disdain the type of narrative form that, as we have seen in the discussions of popular and art films in this issue, acts as the supporting spine for the philosophical theses or ideas embodied by them. Instead, structural films are more apt to adopt puzzling, oblique, and cryptic forms, often making little or no use of language (in the form of dialogue or titles) and depending solely on visual and nonverbal sonic representation. From this point of view, such films pose a special kind of challenge to those who would claim them as philosophy, distinct from (and perhaps more difficult than) the issues facing those discerning philosophy in narrative forms of filmmaking.

Jinhee Choi frames her "Apperception on Display: Structural Films and Philosophy" with reference to the essay by P. Adams Sitney that first proposed the category of structural film-making and claimed that such films aim to render human self-consciousness or "apperception."[22] In the course of the essay she examines some skeptical arguments advanced by Noël Carroll against the idea that these films should be regarded as instances of theory, and proposes alternative ways such films might make a "philosophical contribution," stressing the ideas of revelation and suggestion rather than argument. She goes on to examine a particular structural film in detail, Kurt Kren's *TV 15/67* (1967), considering how it suggests new hypotheses regarding the nature of film, and exploring the relationship between this philosophical (or "cognitive") dimension of the film and its overall aesthetic value.

In "Philosophizing Through the Moving Image: The Case of *Serene Velocity*," Noël Carroll examines Ernie Gehr's classic structural film from 1970, and in so doing modifies the skeptical stance—discussed by Choi—that he had adopted in earlier essays toward the idea that a film could be a work of philosophy or theory. Carroll argues that, in spite of the absence of language in the film, *Serene Velocity* embodies the idea that motion is an essential feature of film, and (echoing Danto's claim on behalf of Duchamp's "readymades") that the film does so in advance of the first traditional philosophical articulation of this idea.[23]

In his essay "The Substance of Cinema," Trevor Ponech also takes the body of structural filmmaking as his central example, but Ponech's goal and his stance toward the films differs markedly from that of Carroll and Choi. Reviewing recent (and strongly contrasting) arguments from Gregory Currie and Carroll on the nature and definition of cinema, Ponech uses a number of structural films in order to support a definition of the cinematic that differs from both Currie's and Carroll's, based on what he terms the "stroboscopic visual display." But Ponech is not inclined to treat the films that he discusses as works of philosophy in any strong

sense. Instead, he views them "as vehicles for their makers' philosophically pertinent ideas about cinema's nature" that supply philosophy proper with "concrete as well as conceptual resources that we can mobilize to debate and refine our ontological hypotheses" (p. 187). From Carroll through Choi to Ponech, then, we move from a strong to increasingly circumspect claims regarding the extent to which particular films might count as instances of philosophy.

The focus of Whitney Davis's essay, "The World Rewound: Peter Forgács' *Wittgenstein Tractatus*," is an avant-garde film of more recent vintage. Made by the Hungarian film-maker Peter Forgács, *Wittgenstein Tractatus* (1992) is not a structural film (although the combination of formal precision and enigmatic import certainly recalls many structural films). But the film is of evident, special significance for the theme of this collection in that it is one of the very few films—and the only such film discussed in depth in the essays collected here—that enters into an explicit, direct, and sustained dialogue with a recognized philosophical text, the *Tractatus Logico-Philosophicus* by Ludwig Wittgenstein. The *Tractatus* is one of the central texts of twentieth-century Analytic philosophy. As the title implies, the film is to be approached and understood as a rendering of the philosophy of that text. What is more, Davis argues that the film exploits specific features of film that allow it to embody or realize Wittgenstein's proposal: "What *can* be shown *cannot* be said" (4.1212). In this sense, the ambition of the film is to be much more than a visualization of key ideas in Wittgenstein's early work. Instead, according to Davis, the film gives expression to an understanding of the world that, on Wittgenstein's argument in the *Tractatus*, eludes verbal statement. In this sense, the film might be regarded as a philosophical complement to the *Tractatus*, rather than an illustration or dramatization—or some other secondary elaboration—of it.

The essays included in this collection, then, take a variety of different positions on the question of whether film can be philosophy. Varying from strong endorsements to clear denials of the possibility—and a range of other options in between—these essays all share a deep interest in the relationship between philosophy and film. We hope that readers of this collection will themselves be inspired to reflect on this question, one that we see as moving onto centerstage in discussions of the philosophical significance of film as an art form.

MURRAY SMITH
School of Drama, Film and Visual Arts
University of Kent
Canterbury
Kent CT2 7NX
UK

INTERNET: mss@kent.ac.uk

THOMAS E. WARTENBERG
Department of Philosophy
Mount Holyoke College
South Hadley, MA 01075
USA

INTERNET: twartenb@mtholyoke.edu

1. Alexandre Astruc, "The Birth of a New Avant-Garde: La Caméra-Stylo," in *The New Wave*, ed. Peter Graham (New York: Doubleday, 1968), p. 19.

2. Michael Snow, interview with Scott MacDonald, in *A Critical Cinema 2: Interviews with Independent Filmmakers*, ed. Scott MacDonald (University of California Press, 1992), p. 76.

3. This work was recently republished in *Hugo Münsterberg on Film*, ed. Allan Langdale (New York: Routledge, 2002).

4. See, for example, "The Dramaturgy of Film Form" (1929) in *Eisenstein: Writings 1922–1934*, ed. Richard Taylor (London: BFI, 1988), pp. 161–180.

5. Stanley Cavell's first book on film was *The World Viewed: Reflections on the Ontology of Film* (New York: Viking Press, 1971).

6. Stephen Mulhall, *On Film* (London: Routledge, 2002).

7. Gilles Deleuze, *Cinema 1–2*, trans. Hugh Tomlinson and Barbara Habberjam (University of Minnesota Press, 1986 and 1989).

8. Henri Bergson, *Creative Evolution*, trans. Arthur Mitchell (New York: Modern Library, 1944), ch. 4.

9. Stephen Mulhall, "Ways of Thinking: A Response to Andersen and Baggini," *Film-Philosophy* 7 (2003),

available at <http://www.film-philosophy.com/vol7-2003/n25mulhall>.

10. Martha Nussbaum, *Love's Knowledge* (New York: Oxford University Press, 1990).

11. Karl Marx, *Economic and Philosophical Manuscripts of 1844* (New York: International Publishers, 1964).

12. Cleanth Brooks, "The Heresy of Paraphrase," in *The Well Wrought Urn* (London: Methuen, 1968), p. 164.

13. Stanley Cavell, *Pursuits of Happiness: The Hollywood Comedy of Remarriage* (Harvard University Press, 1981).

14. Cavell, *Pursuits of Happiness*, pp. 71–110.

15. See note 6. The first *Mission: Impossible* film, directed by Brian De Palma, is from 1996; the second, released in 2000, was directed by John Woo.

16. *Alien* (Ridley Scott, 1979); *Aliens* (James Cameron, 1986); *Alien*[3] (David Fincher, 1992); *Alien Resurrection* (Jean-Pierre Jeunet, 1997).

17. Friedrich Nietzsche, *Beyond Good and Evil*, trans. Walter Kaufmann (New York: Random House, 1966).

18. Santilli, "Cinema and Subjectivity in Krzysztof Kieślowski," *The Journal of Aesthetics and Art Criticism* 64 (2006): 148. The idea here is that while film captures the phenomenal world with extraordinary fidelity, as a representation of the phenomenal world it is twice-removed from the noumenal world. The tension that Santilli identifies is thus exacerbated by distinctive qualities of film as a medium.

19. P. Adams Sitney, *Visionary Film: The American Avant-Garde* (New York: Oxford University Press, 1974), p. 412.

20. Danto first discusses the impact that Warhol had on him in "The Artworld," *Journal of Philosophy* 61 (1964): 571–584. Danto elaborates this argument in various works, including most notably his *The Transfiguration of the Commonplace: A Philosophy of Art* (Harvard University Press, 1981), in which he writes of the "profound philosophical originality" (p. vi) of Duchamp's work.

21. Scott MacDonald writes of a "theoretical" type of filmmaking in *A Critical Cinema 1: Interviews with Independent Filmmakers*, ed. Scott MacDonald (University of California Press, 1988). The idea of structural filmmaking (along with some other kinds of avant-garde filmmaking) as a form of theory is advanced in detail in Edward S. Small, *Direct Theory: Experimental Film/Video as Major Genre* (Carbondale: Southern Illinois University Press, 1994). The notion "direct theory"—theory rendered directly by means of film—has been recently adopted as the theme of a conference on the work of Swedish filmmaker Olle Hedman. Materials related to this conference can be found at http://www.kk.kau.se/filmv/index.html.

22. Sitney, *Visionary Film*, ch. 12.

23. Which Carroll ascribes to—who else?—Danto. See Arthur C. Danto, "Moving Pictures," *Quarterly Review of Film Studies* 4 (1979): 1–21.

PAISLEY LIVINGSTON

Theses on Cinema as Philosophy

Can films make creative contributions to philosophical knowledge, and this by means exclusive to the cinematic medium? Although it may be tempting to offer a positive response to this question, a bold "cinema as philosophy" thesis of this ilk is difficult to defend. A better option, I contend, is to accept a more modest conception of the cinema's role in the development of philosophical insight. Films can provide vivid and emotionally engaging illustrations of philosophical issues, and when sufficient background knowledge is in place, reflections about films can contribute to the exploration of specific theses and arguments, sometimes yielding enhanced philosophical understanding.

In the first section of this essay I briefly identify key components of a type of bold thesis about film's exclusive contribution to philosophy. In Section II, I outline what I take to be a ruinous dilemma facing advocates of such a thesis. In Section III, I sketch an alternative based on some of the illustrative and heuristic roles films can be made to serve.

I. CONSTITUENTS OF A BOLD EPISTEMIC THESIS

Key conceptual constituents of a type of bold thesis about cinema as philosophy (bold epistemic thesis) include: (1) a conception of which sorts of *exclusive* capacities of the cinematic medium (or art form) are said to make a special contribution to philosophy and (2) claims about the significance and independence of the latter contribution.

With regard to (2), a modest and uncontroversial claim is that films sometimes express or give rise to well-known philosophical questions and ideas. Clearly, this much is achieved by some of the squire's ruminations in Ingmar Bergman's *Det sjunde inseglet* [*The Seventh Seal*] (1957). A stronger claim is that there are films that do not merely illustrate previously published philosophical ideas, but realize historically innovative philosophical contributions. (An achievement is historically innovative only if it is new relative to the history of the relevant tradition.[1]) An even bolder contention would be that a film can provide a historically innovative contribution to knowledge regarding some philosophical topic, doing so in a significantly independent or autonomous manner, that is, the contribution would not be dependent on a subsequent paraphrase.

I turn now to (1), or the constraints a bold epistemic thesis places on the specifically cinematic means by which a suitably important philosophical achievement is to be realized. Although in a broad sense any feature of a motion picture is "cinematic" by virtue of being a feature of a film, this is not what philosophers and film theorists have had in mind in using the expression "the specificity of the cinematic medium," nor is such a broad and all-inclusive notion a component of the bold thesis about cinema's exclusive epistemic value.[2] What, then, does the latter rule out with its conception of the exclusive capacities of the medium?

Consider a film comprised of a single medium-long shot of a philosopher giving a genial talk on personal identity or some other philosophical subject. We may be tempted to say that this film would not enhance philosophical knowledge by virtue of devices exclusive to cinema. This would be true even if the audio-visual depiction of the philosopher's gestures and intonation contributed to the philosophical points being made, as the film does not provide any information that the philosopher's lecture did not provide. It might be concluded, then, that only if the film did not rely primarily on the philosopher's use of the linguistic medium could its contribution to philosophy be *exclusively* cinematic. Instead, the cinematic medium's exclusive capacities involve the possibility of providing an internally articulated, nonlinguistic, visual expression of content, as when some idea is indicated by means of the sequential juxtaposition of two or more visual displays or shots (so-called Kuleshov effects being an oft-mentioned example). More generally, the category of specifically cinematic stylistic devices or modes of expression is usually taken to include montage or editing, camera movements and selective focus within a shot, and correlations between the soundtrack and moving image (for example effects involving "off-screen sound").

The same assumption finds additional justification if one's focus is not on the specificity of the cinematic medium, but on the characteristic and exclusive features of the cinematic art form. Static cinematic recordings of theatrical events may contribute greatly to the performing arts by providing valuable documentation of bygone performances, but they are not generally acclaimed as contributions to the art of cinema, for the latter must manifest a skillful use of the medium's expressive capacities in addition to exploiting its recording capacity. Thus, filmed operas are contributions to the art of cinema only if they solve specifically cinematic artistic problems, such as that of providing a visual complement to the operatic overture (a shot of the curtain constituting the "degree zero" stylistic option).

What I am calling the bold thesis is a conjunction of strong claims with regard to points (1) and (2), namely, the idea that films do make historically innovative and independent contributions to philosophy by means exclusive to the cinematic medium or art form.[3] Different versions of this schematic thesis, as well as various weaker options, will be considered in what follows.

II. A DILEMMA FOR THE BOLD THESIS

What is wrong with the contention that a film's philosophically innovative contribution can be made by exclusively cinematic devices? Quickly, the dilemma takes the following form.

First Horn of the Dilemma. To accept a narrow (and prevalent) conception of the cinema's specific representational devices, while arguing for an innovative and independent philosophical contribution, leads to an insoluble problem of paraphrase.[4] That problem itself takes the form of a dilemma. If it is contended that the exclusively cinematic insight cannot be paraphrased, reasonable doubt arises with regard to its very existence. If it is granted, on the other hand, that the cinematic contribution can and must be paraphrased, this contention is incompatible with arguments for a significantly independent, innovative, and purely "filmic" philosophical achievement, as linguistic mediation turns out to be constitutive of (our knowledge of) the epistemic contribution a film can make.

Second Horn of the Dilemma. To accept, on the other hand, a more plausible, yet less narrow, conception of the cinema's exclusive capacities leads to a trivialization of the thesis that cinema can contribute to philosophy. Suppose, for example, that we allow that an exclusive and valuable feature of the cinematic medium is its "recording and representational" capacity, the idea being simply that the cinematic apparatus can be used to make shots of items in front of a camera (and microphone), which representations can then be used to provide an artificially generated "detached display" that visually (and sometimes aurally) depicts those items.[5] Only the cinema can provide moving images of past events, and such images can be informative in ways other representations cannot. (This contention need not rest on an extreme realist or "transparency" thesis, according to which there is a natural, counterfactual dependence between the contents of the cinematic representation and the actual objects represented. Rather, we need only recognize that an accurate verbal transcription of what a philosopher said in a lecture does not give us all the information provided by a motion picture recording of that lecture, as the latter can convey visual and aural information regarding the speaker's delivery.) Such a conception of the cinema's representational capacities will be compatible, then, with the observation that audio-visual recordings of a philosopher's lectures are an exclusively cinematic resource. It follows that the cinema can make an exclusive contribution to philosophy by providing vivid audio-visual representations of genial philosophical conversations and lectures. Yet this tepid result serves as a *reductio* of the idea of yoking this very broad conception of film's capacities to the bold thesis about the medium's (or art form's) contributions to philosophy.

To expound on this dilemma argument a bit more, we may return to the first horn and ask how linguistically mediated arguments can describe or otherwise demonstrate the existence of a philosophical contribution that *in principle* transcends the expressive capacities of linguistic media. If the "properly cinematic" contribution to philosophy can be referred to but not stated with words, proponents of a bold epistemic thesis have to fall back on appeals to an indescribable cinematic *je ne sais quoi* that they believe they have experienced, in the hope that others may have a similar experience and come to agree that philosophical insight or understanding has been manifested in a film. Yet here is where reasonable doubts arise. Although it may be plausible to report that an experience of a work's montage or motion picture style has given rise to a vivid, visually mediated recollection of some previously known philosophical thought, it is fair to ask whether such appeals to experience can offer good grounds for believing that a significantly new idea or argument has emerged. If such a claim is made, it is only reasonable to ask for an articulation of the important ideas in question. If such a request is thought unfair or question-begging, it should be noted that the situation is not simply a dialectical standoff between advocates of two contrasting claims, that is, between those who believe in ineffable cinematic insights and those who happen to have doubts about their existence. The problem here is not essentially a social one, but that of providing reasons or evidence for belief in a philosophical insight, be it for oneself or others. The burden of proof rests on the shoulders of anyone who comes to suspect that there exists a new and controversial source of philosophical knowledge. He or she should be able to give reasons in support of the belief that appeals

to verbally indescribable experiences or entities should exert a significant influence on philosophical opinion on such subjects as personal identity, freedom, meta-ethics, moral dilemmas, or epistemology (all of which are topics that have been central to the cinema and philosophy literature). Here we chart the gap between the cinema's various pedagogically useful illustrations or evocations of previously published philosophical reasonings, and the bold claim that in its ineffable, exclusively cinematic form of expression, some work of cinema has significantly advanced philosophical knowledge in a way supporting some suitably strong version of the cinema as philosophy thesis.

If it is allowed, on the other hand, that cinematic insights can be paraphrased, other problems for the bold thesis become salient. I take it that a paraphrase of something is the result of an attempt to provide an interpretative statement or thinking through of that item's meanings. To convey an interpretation of some item's philosophically relevant meanings, one must employ linguistically mediated philosophical background assumptions and arguments.[6] Thus, if our aim is to provide an interpretation of René Descartes's *Meditations*, we must relate what we take to be the text's linguistic meanings to assumptions about the philosopher's intentions and philosophical background, or to other relevant philosophical works and arguments (such as St. Augustine's arguments against skepticism). It seems plausible to assume that similar considerations hold for philosophically-oriented interpretations of the meanings of a picture or a film. So that even if specifically cinematic devices, such as montage, were essential to a film's philosophical content in the sense that this content could not have been fully articulated in another medium, the successful *philosophical* function of that device remains importantly dependent on linguistically articulated background thoughts that are mobilized in both the creation and interpretation of the film's philosophical significance. In the absence of such background ideas, questions about personal identity, free will, the possibility of knowledge, and so on could not be cogently pondered by either the filmmakers or spectators. The same point holds, *a fortiori*, for more sophisticated argumentations about a film's implications for such topics. It follows that sufficient evidence for any claim that a film has achieved an historically innovative expression of philosophical insight crucially depends on the activity of an expositor (who could in principle be the filmmaker), which entails in turn that taken on its own, the cinematic display's contribution *to philosophy* can be neither independent nor historically innovative—as the bold thesis would have it.

I shall briefly illustrate some of these points with reference to a few examples. In his 1943 film, *Vredens Dag [Day of Wrath]*, Carl Theodor Dreyer used various specifically cinematic means to express ideas pertaining to ethical and epistemic issues. For example, by means of a cleverly designed montage sequence, he leads spectators to the brink of inferring a causal connection between a young woman's words of hatred and the sudden affliction that brings about the death of her elderly husband, a pastor in seventeenth-century Denmark. The question whether she could have demonically "wished" her husband to death is implicitly raised by Dreyer's montage, and subsequently in the story, such a causal connection is publicly drawn by the pastor's relatives, the result being that the young woman is accused of witchcraft and condemned to be burned at the stake. Many aspects of the film, however, are designed to raise doubts about the accuracy and justice of such harsh and ill-founded judgments. There are ample reasons to conclude that Dreyer worked with the ambition of having his audiences generalize such anti-scapegoating reflections, particularly with regard to relevant affairs in the film's initial context of reception, Nazi-occupied Denmark. Arguably, it is the cinema-specific montage that most effectively leads the spectator to the point of mistaking coincidence for causation, thereby vividly setting the thematic agenda. Yet it is not the use of montage alone that enables the viewer to pursue these reflections about causation and accusation in any philosophically interesting manner, and it is clear that this particular, genial employment of cinematic technique only acquires a determinate meaning in the context of a work that makes extensive use of such nonspecifically cinematic means as dialogue and characterization. And to come to the crucial question for the bold thesis, does the film's treatment of philosophically-relevant topics manifest any historically innovative insights? It is impossible to address

ourselves reasonably to such a question in the absence of a specific interpretative proposal along those lines, and this fact indicates that a linguistic interpretation is a necessary constituent of a philosophical acknowledgment of any such contribution. Yet this is fatal to the bold thesis, which requires that a film's epistemic contribution to philosophy be paraphrase-independent and historically innovative, and not parasitic on either the filmmaker's or the spectator's linguistically articulated interpretation of the film's content.

A second example can be evoked more quickly. In *The Seventh Seal*, the knight Antonius Block (Max von Sydow) enters a church and sees a hooded figure standing on the other side of the iron grid of a window to another chamber. Mistaking this figure for a priest, he begins to confess, revealing his fears, doubts, and his ardent desire for direct and certain knowledge of God, as well as the strategy he intends to use to trick Death in the game of chess they are playing. Behind the grid, however, stands not a sympathetic priest, but the allegorical figure of Death, the knight's opponent in the game. Once the knight has betrayed his secret strategy, Death turns to reveal himself, and the knight realizes his mistake. Alert spectators, however, may have earlier noticed the knight's strategic error, since it was already underscored visually by the very appearance of the iron grid separating the knight and the hooded figure. With its eight-by-eight configuration of squares, this

FIGURE 1. Chessboard symbolism in the confession scene in *The Seventh Seal.*

iron grid, and the shadows it casts on the adjacent wall, strikingly resemble a chess board. Thus Bergman visually makes the point that the game goes on even when the knight thinks there is a truce. It is also possible to interpret this imagery as amplifying some of the larger points in Bergman's film. Instead of offering absolution, the ritual of confession is only another moment in the hopeless, strategically rational thinking in which the knight is caught. (Throughout the film, his unhappy reasoning is contrasted to the grace enjoyed by the intuitive, visionary juggler, Jof.) If we bring in additional background information, Bergman's chessboard imagery in this scene can be understood as contributing to a more general, anti-liturgical opposition between the vain and violent institutional forms of what Søren Kierkegaard called "Christendom" (epitomized by witch burnings, processions of flagellants, doomsday speeches, and so forth), and the Pauline "God is love" theme that punctuates Bergman's corpus. But to enlarge philosophically on Bergman's Protestant response to Christendom would require reference to sources and arguments (such as Martin Luther, John Calvin, and Søren Kierkegaard) extending far beyond what the spectator is given by the cinematic display.

My central point here is that a philosophically-oriented interpreter of a film must take up the task of importing a well-defined *problématique* if aspects of the film's thematic and narrative design are to resonate with sufficiently sophisticated and well-articulated theses or arguments. There may, of course, be films where some of this work has already been done by the filmmaker. (The one film I know of that explicitly provides some of the relevant bibliography is Pier Paolo Pasolini's (1975) *Salò o il centroventi giornate di Sodoma* [*Salo or the 120 Days of Sodom*], where a reading list appears in the title sequence.) Another interesting case is Alain Resnais's *Mon oncle d'amérique* [*My Uncle from America*] (1979), which cuts back and forth between shots from an interview with Henri Laborit and scenes from a series of interlaced fictional stories that may be taken as both exemplifying and challenging Laborit's sociobiological propositions.[7] It is likely, however, that the latter do not take us to the cutting edge of current debates, so that new philosophical insight based in part on an interpretation of this

film would require engagement with more recent theories. In any case, an interpretative context must be established in relation to which features of the film are shown to have some worthwhile philosophical resonance.

To sum up, if the bold thesis rests on a narrow conception of cinema's specificity, the upshot is an insoluble dilemma of paraphrase. Either the properly cinematic insight, narrowly construed, cannot be paraphrased, in which case its existence is doubtful, or it can and must be paraphrased, in which case it is on its own insufficient to the philosophical task assigned to it by the bold thesis.

If, on the other hand, a broader conception of cinema's exclusive capacities is opted for, the epistemic thesis is trivialized, as audio-visual recordings of philosophical lectures are included.

What other options are there? As the bold epistemic thesis is a conjunction of exclusivity and epistemic requirements, three main alternatives can be considered: (1) giving up on exclusivity while maintaining strong epistemic requirements; (2) maintaining exclusivity while giving up on strong epistemic requirements; and (3) giving up on both the exclusivity and strong epistemic constraints. In the next section I shall advocate the third option.

III. CINEMA IN THE CONTEXT OF PHILOSOPHICAL INQUIRY

To begin with the exclusivity requirement, what good grounds can be given for limiting the philosopher's interest in cinema to any of the restrictive notions associated with the expression "the specificity of the cinematic medium or art form"? Such notions are dubious in any case, as it is unlikely that a successful argument can be made for any restrictive list of the medium's exclusive functions. Instead, it is more plausible to recognize film's remarkable capacity to quote, re-present, or "nest" a wide range of other media and expressive devices, including verbal discourse, pictures, bodily gestures, theatrical decors, the expressivity of the human face, music, various cultures' communicative codes or symbol systems, and so on.[8]

Yet even if one did develop a strong argument for some restrictive notion of the specificity of the cinematic medium or art form, a philosopher may, but need not, approach a cinematic work as a work of cinema or, in other words, seek to understand and appreciate it *qua* cinematic art or *qua* manifestation of a particular medium. To appreciate a film as a work of art adequately one must ask how successfully its themes have been expressed or embodied by its style and by devices specific to the medium.[9] Some philosophical raids on movies' philosophical contents have the otherwise undesirable characteristic of being very poor instances of critical appreciation. In an effort to bring "cinema as philosophy" back in line with what is generally perceived as sensitive or even moderately competent film appreciation, one insists that attention must be focused on medium- and art-form-specific devices, on the stylistic "how" as a necessary means to the thematic "what." A problem with this line of thought, however, is that it underestimates the practical difficulty of simultaneously pursuing what are two rather distinct ends. One goal is that of providing a critical discussion of a film that best elucidates and assesses its artistic value and use of the cinematic medium. A distinct goal is that of asking whether and how the film expresses or gives rise to thoughts contributing genuinely to some philosophical debate on a specialized topic. Attentive critical appreciation of a particular work of art rarely requires the importation of the requisite philosophical background with its complex array of terms, positions, arguments (and, at times, formal notations). To do so is to employ the work, and most commonly, aspects of the story the work can be taken as conveying, as an illustration; whereas to engage in careful appreciation of the individual work is distinct from the properly philosophical goal of exploring and constructing more general arguments. The two goals are not logically incompatible, but it is at least rhetorically very difficult to pursue them simultaneously.

I turn now to the weakening of the second major component of the bold thesis, namely, its expectations with regard to the philosophical significance of cinema's contributions. My recommendation here is that the bar should not be set too high. There is no good reason to spurn or belittle the pedagogical functions to which films can be put in the philosophical curriculum. The appeal of the medium, as well as the affective and persuasive force films can have, help make cinema an effective complement to a philosophical *pensum* comprised of difficult writings by philosophers. The stimulation of students' imaginative engagement with philosophical issues, which engagement in turn heightens motivation for renewed encounters with the items on the reading list, is probably the single most valuable contribution the cinema can make to philosophy.

An alternative to the bold thesis need not, however, contend that cinema's contributions are exclusively pedagogical. Films may also have a heuristic role in the context of ongoing investigations within a number of avenues of philosophical inquiry. Thinking about the issues raised by a cinematic (or other) work of fiction could help a philosopher come up with some new hypothesis or argumentative strategy, perhaps by giving rise to creative imaginings about patterns of behavior or interaction. As David K. Lewis points out, sometimes we already have the evidence we need but do not appreciate its significance, and a fiction can play a crucial role in helping us to think about this evidence correctly.[10] Clearly, however, there are abstract problems in philosophy of logic and metaphysics that are not likely to be illumined with reference to cinematic storytelling; on the other hand, as the stories films convey generally deal with people's unusual problems and efforts to solve them, it may be expected that pondering such matters can help shed light on a range of topics pertaining to agency.

In one category of cases, the argument for films making heuristic contributions via theoretically-oriented interpretation is easier to make. If the research topic pertains to aesthetics or to the philosophy of art (and especially the philosophy of film!), ruminations over the specific style and themes of a given film may yield insights with regard to some well-framed question under discussion in the field. This would be the case because the filmmakers have detailed, specialized, insiders' insight into the relevant topics and have shown genuine creativity in expressing theoretically interesting attitudes about their own craft.

For example, if we are interested in issues related to filmmaking and "creativity under constraints," we would do well to investigate Lars von Trier's and Jørgen Leth's *De fem* benspænd [*The Five Obstructions*] (2003), which provides fascinating examples and insightful commentaries on relations between rules and creativity.[11] In this film's story, a character named "Lars von Trier" (played by Lars von Trier), acting on what he describes as benevolent motives, challenges his former film school teacher, "Jørgen Leth" (played by himself), to create new versions of Leth's 1967 film, *Det perfekte menneske* [*The Perfect Human*]. Leth is to make these versions while obeying rules and orders that Trier imposes on Leth in a putative effort to help him develop artistically. Yet it also appears that Trier's choice of rules is designed to make the task highly difficult and uncomfortable for Leth. As the story unfolds, we see how Leth struggles with the shackles Trier has devised, but manages to come up with artful solutions to the artistic and moral challenges they involve. (The four short films Leth makes are nested in *Five Obstructions* along with segments from *The Perfect Human*, so spectators are allowed to appreciate Leth's results directly.) Leth returns and screens each finished film for Trier, who then subjects them to critical commentary. As Leth sometimes bends and even ignores Trier's rules, Trier scolds him and tries to make the next set of rules even more harsh and difficult for Leth to follow (for example Leth, who says he "hates" animated films, is ordered to make an animated version of his earlier work). Finally Trier who seems frustrated that Leth has somehow eluded him, takes over the making of the fifth film himself, writing a text that purports to sum up the whole affair. Leth is then required to read this text in the first person as though it constituted his own critical commentary, and he thereby ends up becoming Trier's *porte-parole*.

The upshot is a remarkable and complex film that not only forcefully illustrates well-known distinctions (such as Jon Elster's distinction between imposed and chosen constraints), but that also explores the relatively uncharted gray zone in which artistic constraints are negotiated in a shifting mixture of cooperative and competitive relations. In politics, Elster tells us, people want to bind others' choices.[12] This is true in the arts as well. People sometimes want to be helped along by constraints others provide, as long as these are not too inflexible. As Mette

Hjort has argued, the constraints within which artists work can be "multiply motivated," and some of these motives and choices of constraints involve creative responses to the sociopolitical and economic conditions under which films are made.[13] It is hard to imagine an adequate theoretical understanding of such matters being developed without careful attention being paid to the insights expressed by artworks and artists, including filmmakers.

IV. CODA

G. W. F. Hegel warns that it is a mistake to value an art form in terms of its ability to serve external ends, such as "instruction, moral improvement, or political agitation," as these ends "are pursued and achieved still more effectively by other means."[14] Part of Hegel's thinking here seems to be that an art form such as poetry has its own intrinsic value, and thereby ought not to be evaluated in terms of instrumental rationality (in the same passage Hegel evokes the "free heights where poetry lives for its own sake alone"). Perhaps Hegel's thought was that to assess art *qua* art cannot in any case be a matter of appraising its instrumental rewards. Yet insofar as our experiences of art have various instrumental values, Hegel's secondary worry about the rationality of choosing artistic means to nonartistic ends remains relevant. Can his drastic conclusion in this regard be forestalled? Is it always suboptimal to try to use an art form to advance knowledge?

One tack would be to assail Hegel's apparent assumption about optimality, which might be restated as the thesis that it is only rational to value a work of art as a means to some end if we have good reason to believe that it is the most efficient means to that end. Yet we must be careful here. If we in fact believe a more efficient means to our goal is available, would it not indeed be irrational to pass it by?

Another option is to widen the scope of the assessment. The relevant choice is not between only doing philosophy via film interpretation, and conducting philosophical research uniquely by more familiar means. Explorations of films' illustrative and heuristic values are rational when undertaken alongside other means of pursing philosophical goals and, as I have suggested above, the most effective versions of such explorations are those that draw on those other means, by bringing in and reflecting over sophisticated philosophical background assumptions. In short, inquiries into films' epistemic values can be a rational strategy insofar as they provide a useful complement to the overarching project of philosophical pedagogy and research.[15]

PAISLEY LIVINGSTON
Department of Philosophy
Lingnan University
Tuen Mun
Hong Kong

INTERNET: pl@ln.edu.hk

1. Margaret A. Boden distinguishes between historical and psychological creativity as follows: An idea is P-creative if it is valuable and "the person in whose mind it arises could not have had it before"; to be historically creative, the idea must be not only P-creative, but must never have been thought of before. I have weakened this latter condition, and doubt that P-creativity is necessary to historical creativity. See Boden, "What is Creativity?" in *Dimensions of Creativity*, ed. Margaret A. Boden (MIT Press, 1994), p. 76. For discussion of this and other accounts of creativity, see Berys Gaut and Paisley Livingston, "Introduction," in *The Creation of Art: New Essays in Philosophical Aesthetics*, ed. Berys Gaut and Paisley Livingston (New York: Cambridge University Press, 2003), pp. 1–32.

2. For some pertinent background, see Noël Carroll, "The Specificity of Media in the Arts," *The Journal of Aesthetic Education* 14/15 (1984–1985): 127–153; reprinted in *Theorizing the Moving Image* (Cambridge University Press, 1996), pp. 25–36. I document and criticize Christian Metz's early, disastrous emphasis on the specificity of the cinematic medium in "Disciplining Film: Code and Specificity," *Cinema Canada* 97 (1983): 47–57.

3. In their editorial comments, Murray Smith and Thomas Wartenberg usefully asked me whether the bold thesis is a straw man. Even if no film theorist fully espouses the bold thesis, the bold thesis is conceptually salient and worthy of consideration. I believe some actual theorists come pretty close to promoting the bold thesis, though I will not try to provide any extensive documentation here. Consider, for example, Jean Epstein's views in *L'intelligence d'une machine* (Paris: Jacques Melot, 1946).

4. Such a problem surfaces repeatedly in discussions of art and knowledge, though not in the precise form it is given

here. For surveys, see my "Literature and Knowledge," in *A Companion to Epistemology*, ed. Jonathan Dancy and Ernest Sosa (Oxford: Blackwell, 1992), pp. 255–258, and Berys Gaut, "Art and Knowledge," in *The Oxford Handbook of Aesthetics*, ed. Jerrold Levinson (Oxford University Press, 2003), pp. 436–450.

5. Noël Carroll, "Towards an Ontology of the Moving Image," in *Philosophy and Film*, ed. Cynthia A. Freeland and Thomas E. Wartenberg (New York: Routledge, 1995), pp. 68–85.

6. This basic assumption about interpretation finds a clear statement and justification in Jerry R. Hobbs, *Literature and Cognition* (Stanford: Center for the Study of Language and Information, 1990). There is, of course, a looser sense of "interpretation" that also covers musical and other performances. My remark focuses on critical interpretations, not performances. See Jerrold Levinson, "Performative vs. Critical Interpretation in Music," in *The Interpretation of Music*, ed. Michael Krausz (Oxford: Clarendon, 1993), pp. 33–60.

7. For some discussion of this example, see Seymour Chatman, *Coming to Terms: The Rhetoric of Narrative in Fiction and Film* (Cornell University Press, 1990).

8. In film semiology, the "heterogeneity" thesis was stressed by Emilio Garroni, *Semiotica ed estetica. L'eterogeneità del linguaggio et il linguaggio cinematografico* (Bari: Laterza, 1968). For a definition of 'nesting' and discussion of examples, see my "Nested Art," *The Journal of Aesthetics and Art Criticism* 61 (2003): 233–246.

9. For background, see Gary Iseminger, "Aesthetic Appreciation," *The Journal of Aesthetics and Art Criticism* 39 (1981): 389–399, and Stein Haugom Olsen, "Criticism and Appreciation," in *Philosophy and Fiction*, ed. Peter Lamarque (Aberdeen University Press, 1983), pp. 38–51.

10. David K. Lewis, "Postscripts to 'Truth in Fiction,'" in *Philosophical Papers*, vol. 1 (Oxford University Press, 1983), pp. 276–280.

11. For explorations of this topic, see Jon Elster, *Ulysses Unbound: Studies in Rationality, Precommitment, and Constraints* (Cambridge University Press, 2000); for critical comments, see Jerrold Levinson, "Elster on Artistic Creativity," in *The Creation of Art*, pp. 235–256.

12. Elster, *Ulysses Unbound*, p. ix.

13. Mette Hjort, "Dogma '95: A Small Nation's Response to Globalisation," in *Purity and Provocation: Dogma 95*, ed. Mette Hjort and Scott MacKenzie (London: British Film Institute Press, 2003), p. 35. Hjort goes on to relate the Dogma movements' "Vow of Chastity" constraints to Wittgenstein-inspired rule-following considerations. I thank her for bringing *Five Obstructions* to my attention.

14. G. W. F. Hegel, *Aesthetics: Lectures on Fine Art*, vol. 2, trans. T. M. Knox (Oxford: Clarendon, 1975), p. 995.

15. Thanks to Neven Sesardic for comments on a draft of this essay, and to Murray Smith and Thomas Wartenberg for helpful editorial suggestions.

THOMAS E. WARTENBERG

Beyond *Mere* Illustration: How Films Can Be Philosophy

The last decade has seen significant growth in the amount of attention that philosophers have paid to film. Whereas the philosophy of film used to be a small subfield of aesthetics practiced only by a few specialists, now philosophers with many different interests and specialties are using film as a means to address a broad range of philosophical topics.

One very specific instance of this development is the number of books and articles written by philosophers that address the Wachowski Brothers' 1999 film, *The Matrix*, and its two sequels, *The Matrix Reloaded* (2003) and *The Matrix Revolutions* (2003). By my count, there currently are two monographs authored by philosophers, three collections of essays, and innumerable articles in journals.[1] Although the quantity of material generated by philosophers in relation to this film is unusual, I cite it as an indication of the tremendous attraction that films now exert on philosophers.

One interesting feature of this trend is that popular films—both Hollywood and independent—have been the subject of most of this recent philosophical activity. Previously, both the European art film and the avant-garde film were the types of films that seemed the likeliest vehicles to inspire philosophical reflection. Intuitively, it makes sense that philosophical discussion would be prompted by heady, difficult films like Ingmar Bergman's *The Seventh Seal* (1954), which raises the sorts of existential issues traditionally the concern of philosophy, or an abstract, structural film like Michael Snow's *Wavelength* (1967), whose entire 45-minute length is composed of a single, slowly zooming shot. But now, following the

example of Stanley Cavell, the philosopher's gaze has shifted to popular fiction films, and it is these films, usually taken to be mere vehicles for mass entertainment, that are claimed as sites of philosophical reflection that yield significant insight into perennial philosophical concerns.[2]

Despite this flurry of interest, there has been only minimal sustained reflection on the theoretical issues surrounding the use of film to discuss philosophical topics. In particular, philosophers have not generally asked whether films can themselves count as works of philosophy or, even, whether there is something peculiarly philosophical about the films they have chosen to discuss.[3] Prior to the publication of this collection, instead of proceeding with explicit theoretical discussions of the legitimacy of using film as a vehicle for philosophy, the general tendency has been for philosophers to use film as a springboard for discussions of subjects of philosophical interest while paying only scant attention to the theoretical issues generated by this practice.

What makes this particularly surprising is that, on the face of it, there are many features of film that militate against it yielding philosophical insights. For example, certain formal features that distinguish films from philosophical discussions cast doubt on the assimilation of film to philosophy. Although philosophy is a purely verbal discipline—whether written or oral—film is an essentially visual medium. Treating film as philosophy might seem to deny the role of this obvious fact. In addition, philosophy is generally characterized by explicit argumentation while those recent films that have been of most interest to philosophers present narratives, stories. One might wonder whether a narrative can establish the sorts of general truths that philosophers take to be the goal of their enterprise.[4]

An additional stumbling block in developing such an account is the fundamental difference between the goals of filmmaking and philosophizing. While philosophy is a practice guided by the desire to attain truth, films are normally made to engage their audiences. Although this is certainly true of popular films, such as those made in Hollywood where entertainment—not to mention profit—is the dominant aim, even alternative filmmaking practices strive to engage, if not entertain, their more specific audiences. This might make it seem that treating films as philosophy does not make sense, given that films have a fundamentally different agenda from that dominant in philosophy itself.[5]

These differences certainly highlight difficulties facing the project of using film as a source of philosophical enlightenment. However, I do not think they are decisive. In what follows, I will give a defense of the practice of treating certain films as instances of philosophy and, in so doing, explain why the putative differences between film and philosophy do not entail that films cannot provide philosophical knowledge.

Since a full justification for taking film as a source of philosophical insight is a task much larger than is possible in the scope of a single essay, I will not attempt it here, or even undertake a direct refutation of all these objections.[6] Instead, I want to buttress the case for film as a vehicle for philosophical reflection by exploring one viable form that philosophizing on film can take: that of illustrating a philosophical claim or theory. Generally, philosophers of film have tended to dismiss "illustration" as a legitimate means whereby films can make a contribution to philosophy. I shall show this to be a mistake, for at least certain cinematic illustrations of a philosophical theory or claim do make a contribution to the philosophical discussion of a problem or issue.

I

As a first step in presenting my argument, I examine two recent attempts to justify taking

films seriously as sources of philosophical insight. My reason for doing so is to show not only that these attempts have serious deficiencies in their justification for claiming that films can be or do philosophy, but also that they accept a dichotomy between illustrating a philosophical claim and actually doing philosophy.

Christopher Falzon presents a defense of treating film as philosophy in his provocatively entitled book *Philosophy Goes to the Movies: An Introduction to Philosophy*.[7] Falzon is aware that there are many philosophers who are skeptical of his undertaking. Referencing Plato's "Parable of the Cave," Falzon acknowledges that there has been "a deep philosophical prejudice against the visual image as an avenue to philosophical enlightenment."[8] Here, Falzon admits that the attempt to view film as a source of philosophical insight may be doomed from the start because of film's inherently visual nature. After all, many philosophers, from Plato onward, have opposed philosophy, considered to be a source of rational conviction, to visual images, believed to beguile viewers with an appeal to their credulity via the emotions. From such a point of view, it would seem that film lacks the capacity for philosophical thought.

Falzon dismisses this objection because he believes that films are capable of genuine philosophical insight. To make his point, he distinguishes the use of films to "illustrate" philosophical positions from his own exploration of the philosophical "content" that he attributes to the films themselves. He explains that he does "not only turn to films in order to help *illustrate or illuminate* philosophical themes. To identify philosophical positions, themes, or questions that are being presented or worked through in particular films is also to understand something important about what is going on within these films, to say something about *their intellectual and philosophical content*."[9] Falzon's point is that films themselves traffic in philosophical ideas, that these are part of what they are about.

My first reservation about Falzon's discussion is that he does not explain what justifies his treatment of films as more than illustrations of philosophical themes that have already been articulated by philosophers themselves. Although he clearly asserts that films make a larger contribution to philosophy than merely "illustrating or illuminating" philosophical ideas, he does no more than make the claim that films "present and work through ... philosophical positions, themes, or questions," and does not justify the validity of this crucial assertion.

This is a problem because, while few would deny that some films have philosophical content, it is not clear that they should so readily accede to Falzon's claim that films develop philosophical views of their own. One could acknowledge, for example, that many of Woody Allen's films are vivid presentations of certain ideas from Sartre's philosophy without also holding that the films thereby *are* a form of philosophy, "philosophy in action," to borrow Stephen Mulhall's useful if ambiguous phrase.[10] Falzon has provided us with a reason for thinking that the films themselves are, at most, presentations in visual form of already worked out philosophical ideas. But if this is so, by his own lights they would not count as themselves actively philosophizing.

Now Falzon does attempt to justify his attribution of philosophical content to films by citing what he takes to be an important commonality between film and philosophy: their mutual use of *images*. Central to his strategy in this regard is an acknowledgment of the presence of images within philosophy itself, for this allows him to dispute the claim that film's similar reliance on images undermines its potential for philosophy. "Despite a lingering Platonic tendency to disparage the image in their 'official' pronouncements, philosophers have always resorted to a multitude of arresting and vivid visions to illustrate or clarify their position, to formulate a problem or to provide some basis for discussion. Philosophy is full of strange and wonderful images and inventions of this sort."[11] Although Falzon notes that one could argue that images are essential to the task of philosophy—despite philosophers "official" pronouncements to the contrary—he does not wish to defend this claim. Rather, as he puts it in a clever turn of phrase, "my interest in images is not so much the role of the image in philosophy as in the philosophy we can discern in the image."[12]

Earlier, as we have seen, Falzon denied that films were merely illustrations of already worked out philosophical positions. But now, in linking film to philosophy, he focuses on the roles that images have in philosophical texts and, he tells us, among the things these images do is to *illustrate* a philosophical position. Are we now to take it that this counts as an instance of genuine philosophical thought whereas it was previously contrasted with it? Falzon seems not to notice that he has contradicted himself.

Even more importantly, Falzon does not provide an account of when the presence of an image in a philosophical text counts as an element in a philosophical argument or discussion and when it is merely a propaedeutic, an aid to our understanding. Although it may be true that some images, such as those contained in Plato's "Parable of the Cave," play a necessary role in a philosophical argument, others do not.[13] After all, Immanuel Kant's striking image of the understanding is generally not regarded as part of his argument for the *a priori* necessity of the categories, the central claim of the "Analytic" of the *Critique of Pure Reason*.

We have now not merely explored the territory of pure understanding, and carefully surveyed every part of it, but have also measured its extent, and assigned to everything in it its rightful place. ... It is the land of truth—enchanting name!—surrounded by a wide and stormy ocean, the native home of illusion, where many a fog bank and many a swiftly melting iceberg give the deceptive appearance of farther shores, deluding the adventurous seafarer ever anew with empty hopes, and engaging him in enterprises which he can never abandon and yet is unable to carry to completion.[14]

Kant's imagery here, though quite graphic, does not make a philosophical contribution to his argument, even if it helps a reader understand its general thrust. Falzon has not supplied a criterion adequate for distinguishing such useful but dispensable images from the ones that should be deemed necessary to a philosopher's general argument.

The issue, then, is whether there is a way to distinguish the non-essential imagery to be found in philosophical texts from those that play necessary role in a philosophical argument. To investigate this problem, I want to look more carefully at an example Falzon cites: Plato's "Parable of the Cave." In what sense is the parable more than *merely* an illustration of Plato's metaphysics?

Plato presents the "Parable of the Cave" in *The Republic* (514a–517c). Because it is too long to quote in full, I will intersperse quotations from Plato's text with my own summary of his presentation of the parable. Throughout, we need to be careful to think about the parable's contribution to Plato's overall argument in *The Republic*, for we want to see why it is more than just a handy way of illustrating his metaphysics.

Socrates begins by asking his interlocutors to "imagine men to be living in an underground cave-like dwelling. ... Light is provided by a fire." One group is held prisoner by the other. "Between the fire and the prisoners ... there is a path across the cave and along this a low wall has been built, like the screen at a puppet show. ... See then also men carrying along that wall ... all kinds of artifacts ... some of the carriers are talking while others are silent." These artifacts cast shadows on the cave's wall, shadows that the chained prisoners take to be real rather than the objects themselves.

There is some justification for claiming that this much of the parable constitutes an illustration of Plato's metaphysics of Forms. The analogy that Plato draws between the prisoners' mistaking shadows for real things and our taking physical things to be real when they are merely appearances of the underlying reality of the Forms constitutes the parable as an illustration of Plato's ontology.[15]

However, the parable does not stop there, but continues. Plato envisions one of the prisoners escaping his bonds: "Consider then what deliverance from their bonds and the curing of their ignorance would be. ... Do you not think he [the freed prisoner] would ... believe that the things which he saw earlier [the shadows on the cave wall] were truer than the things now pointed out to him [the physical things that cast the shadows and that he now sees]?"[16] Plato goes on to discuss how difficult it would be for one unaccustomed to anything but firelight to see things in sunlight and how such a person would be regarded as mad when he returned to the cave to tell his fellow prisoners what he had seen.

This latter half of the parable is even more important to Plato's argument than the first, for it explains why people would not immediately embrace the theory of the Forms on the assumption that it is, in fact, the correct metaphysical account of reality. The parable explains people's resistance to accepting Plato's metaphysics by comparing them to the cave's prisoners, who have been misled about the nature of reality since their birth. Although the parable concerns just those individuals, it attempts to justify a more general claim: that people who have been habitually misled about reality will not immediately accept the correct view once it is presented to them. If Plato's argument is successful, then it will not count against his metaphysics that people refuse to accept it when they first are presented with it, for the parable explains why this is so.

In this latter aspect, the "Parable of the Cave" is a thought experiment. A thought experiment functions in a philosophical argument by presenting readers with a hypothetical case. They are then asked to endorse a general conclusion on the basis of their reaction to this case. The thought experiment mobilizes people's intuitions about certain ideas or concepts so that they can see why a general claim is true.[17]

Thought experiments are one instance in which a narrative yields a philosophical truth. Even though a thought experiment tells a particular story, the truth that it establishes is general, for it does not rely on the specific details of its story. Instead, the story is used to illustrate a general truth that the reader is supposed to be able to accept by means of his or her reflection on the thought experiment's narrative. The question of whether films can be thought experiments—and hence capable of doing philosophy—is one that is worth pursuing, but I cannot do so here.[18]

What then emerges from our look at Plato's parable that is applicable to the question of whether films can be philosophy? We have seen that the presence of (literary) images in philosophical texts does not automatically justify Falzon's claim that films can also be philosophy because they involve (visual) images. In particular, I argued that the philosophically distinctive use of an image was as a thought experiment, something that Falzon's own discussion obscures. Although this can help us think about the possibility of philosophy on/in/through film, Falzon has not provided us with adequate guidance for so doing.

II

So let me turn now to Stephen Mulhall, another philosopher who explicitly endorses the claim that films can be philosophy. His book, *On Film*, despite its very general title, is a study of the four films that make up the *Alien* tetralogy, supplemented by discussions of other films by each of the directors of those films. Mulhall claims that the *Alien* films *actually philosophize*. In explaining why he believes this, Mulhall cites what he sees as the general topic or focus of the films, viz., "the relation of human identity to embodiment."[19] This issue, Mulhall claims, "has been central to philosophical reflection in the modern period since Descartes," a claim that he takes to support his view of the films as engaging in philosophical reflection.[20] The reason for this, he tells us, is that "the sophistication and self-awareness with which these films [that is, the *Alien* tetralogy] deploy and develop that issue ... suggest to me that they should themselves be taken as making *real contributions* to these [that is, philosophy's] intellectual debates."[21]

This suggestion is intriguing, but I also find it a bit puzzling. There is no doubt that much of post-Cartesian philosophy in the West has been concerned with understanding what it is to be human and, in particular, what role our bodies play in structuring our sense of our own identities. But this concern may also be found in cultural forms besides philosophy, such as painting and literature. To choose but one example, there is a rich history in Western art of depictions of the Crucifixion. Given their subject matter, all such depictions will involve the idea of human embodiment—as well as a great deal more, such as the relationship between suffering and redemption. But do they, as a result of this concern, also deal with human identity in a way that is philosophical? And, even if they do, does this mean that they therefore should be seen as actively philosophizing and specifically in a manner that enriches the philosophical discussion of embodiment? I have no doubt that paintings and other artworks can have philosophical interest, but their focusing on aspects of our embodiment does not ensure that they have made "real contributions" to the specifically philosophical debates about that issue.

Consider, for example, any painting of the Crucifixion, such as Andrea Mantagna's

Calvary (1457–1460), located in the Louvre.[22] Jesus is depicted flanked by the two others crucified with him, each of whom appears to be screaming in agony in contrast to Jesus, who may already be dead. These bodies rise above a crowd of onlookers who include Roman soldiers and Jesus' disciples. With its direct depiction of the bodies of three nearly naked males, there is no doubt that this painting is concerned with human embodiment and may even attempt to show that physical suffering can be mitigated by faith. But that does not justify the claim that the painting thereby *contributes* to the specifically philosophical discussion of the role of the body in constituting human identity. What Mulhall owes us, but fails to provide, is an explanation of how a cultural form other than philosophy itself—and, of course, it is film that is the real issue both for him and for us—can make a substantial contribution to the specifically philosophical discussion of an issue such as that of human embodiment.[23] Even though his discussions of the *Alien* films are insightful for showing how the monster itself, for example, raises issues about sexuality, reproduction, and gender, he never clarifies what he takes to be the film's specifically philosophical contribution.[24]

In distinguishing his view of these films from alternatives that do not grant them the status of actually being (works of) philosophy, Mulhall winds up endorsing a similar dichotomy to that we saw at work in Falzon—one between actually doing philosophy and merely illustrating philosophical ideas: "I do not look to these films as handy or popular illustrations of views and arguments properly developed by philosophers; I see them rather as themselves *reflecting on and evaluating* such views and arguments, as thinking seriously and systematically about them *in just the way* that philosophers do. ... They [the films] are philosophical exercises, philosophy in action—film as philosophizing."[25] There is much in this short passage that calls for comment, but I shall concentrate on only one issue: the validity of Mulhall's dichotomy between "handy or popular illustrations" and "thinking seriously and systematically." This dichotomy suggests that there is a domain of serious and systematic philosophical thought—to which the films he is interested in belong—and one consisting of handy or popular illustrations of the views developed by philosophers that does not count as involving serious and systematic thought.

There are many ways one might undermine the validity of this dichotomy. For example, one might ask what Mulhall means when he qualifies thought as *serious*. If he means to contrast the serious with the humorous, for example, then the equation of philosophy with serious thinking seems an error. After all, not all philosophical thought need be "serious" in this sense, as Derrida has argued. And as Nietzsche asserted that philosophy needs to learn to dance, maybe it also makes sense to propose that it needs to laugh. There is a famous story about the late Sidney Morgenbesser that is relevant to this point. When an earnest young man delivering a paper at a Columbia University lecture made the assertion that English allowed for double negatives but not double positives, Morgenbesser piped up from the back of the room, "Yeah, yeah." The humor of this counterexample enhances its philosophical punch. Philosophy can be humorous and still insightful, so there remains the question of what Mulhall's use of the adjective "serious" means.

Equally problematic is Mulhall's putative identification of philosophy with *systematic* thinking. Although some philosophers, such as Immanuel Kant and G. W. F. Hegel, emphasized the systematic nature of their work, there is an alternative tradition of philosophizing that denies the possibility of systematicity. I am thinking here of, among others, Søren Kierkegaard, Friedrich Nietzsche, and Ludwig Wittgenstein, all of whom opposed the systematic impulse. It would therefore seem that the contrast Mulhall attempts to draw between "serious and systematic thinking" and "handy or popular illustration" is fundamentally flawed.

III

So let us look more carefully at the contrast, common to Falzon and Mulhall, between genuine philosophizing and merely illustrating a philosophical theory or claim. I know of no philosophic study of the role of illustrations and this is not the place to develop one.[26] All I can hope to do is make some initial steps toward a more serious and systematic study of what is involved in something being an illustration.

A first claim to note is that an illustration is always an illustration of something, so that an illustration will always refer to something other than itself. If this is correct, then a mark of "illustration" is its intentionality, its reference to something beyond itself.[27]

There are various different types of things that can serve as illustrations of other types of things. For example, we often tell stories to illustrate points that we have made, as when I tell my son about how I was a victim of teasing as a child in order to get him to see that the best way to handle such annoyances is by ignoring them. Also, as Falzon notes, philosophers are wont to use imagery to illustrate their theories, as when Kant claimed that the understanding was an island surrounded by a threatening sea. But one especially prominent form of illustration is that of a picture illustrating a written text. Although this is clearly different from using an image to illustrate a philosophical point, I want to look carefully at such pictorial illustrations in order to see whether this type of illustration can provide us with some insight into what is problematic about the "mere illustration/serious thought" dichotomy.

To begin, let us consider an illustrated version of a classic novel, such as Mark Twain's classic book, *The Adventures of Tom Sawyer* (see Figure 1).[28] The illustrations in such a book are mere supplements to the text, designed to make the text more accessible to readers, especially those who are young. It keeps their interest in the story by showing them a rendering of what the text says and providing concrete images of the book's protagonists, such as Tom and Aunt Polly, and the various situations in which they find themselves. But the text itself is not substantially enriched by the illustration, which is, we might be inclined to say, *merely* an illustration of the preexisting text. We do not think that our imagining of Tom and Huck is either constrained or enabled by the nature of a particular illustration of them.

This is not the only type of illustration we find in children's books. Consider the case of *Alice's Adventures in Wonderland* by Lewis Carroll (see Figure 2).[29] John Tenniel's illustrations are more than simply "handy and popular illustrations" of the book, attempts to keep the

TOM GAVE UP THE BRUSH

FIGURE 1. Illustration of the famous fence painting scene from *Tom Sawyer*.

attention of young readers or listeners. They were part of the book in its original publication and are now taken to be an integral part of it.

We can explain this fact by saying that these illustrations are *iconic* representations of the book's central characters.[30] Unlike the *Tom Sawyer* case, they do not just provide us with one example of how we might imagine the fictional characters of, say, Alice or the Mad Hatter. Rather, our imaginings of such characters are determined by the illustrations. There is a sense in which it makes sense to say that our imaginings of Alice and the Mad Hatter are as much the result of the illustrations that picture them as they are of the words that describe them. If this is true, Tenniel's illustrations are as essential a part of the book as Carroll's text.

This suggests that we should be wary of assuming that illustrations are less important or significant than the texts they are designed to illustrate. In cases like that of the *Alice* books— the *Harry Potter* books might be another

FIGURE 2. Iconic illustration of Alice by John Tenniel from *Alice's Adventures in Wonderland*.

instance of this type—the illustrations are integral to the text. The fictional world constructed by the book depends on both the text and its illustrations.[31]

Now someone might reply that the text still retains priority because the same text might have been published without illustrations or with different ones.[32] Since both of those books—the real one and its imaginary counterpart—count as instances of *Alice's Adventures in Wonderland* by Lewis Carroll, this shows that the illustrations are really a supplement to the text proper.

Even though it is true that we might have had a book called *Alice's Adventures in Wonderland* with no or other illustrations than those it does have, this does not show that the present book is not constituted as much by the illustrations as by the written text. Because the illustrations have become iconic for the various characters, the imaginative activity involved in reading the text-cum-illustrations is now simply part of what that book is.

Let us pause in our discussion of different types of pictorial illustrations in order to consider pictorial illustrations of philosophical texts. There are a few, but a very few, that I can think of, and they are more diagrams than full-fledged illustrations. Edmund Husserl illustrates his theory of time as "running off" by means of a diagram whose point is even harder to grasp than the claims of the text it is meant to illustrate.[33] Arthur Danto also provides a diagram in his influential article, "The Artworld," to show how the properties taken to be necessary for something being a work of art change as new theories of art are developed.[34] In addition, some secondary works use pictorial illustrations in their attempt to render philosophical texts more accessible to students and others. A recent book on *The Matrix*, for example, includes an illustration of the "Parable of the Cave"—or, at least, the cave itself.[35] Illuminating as it might be, this illustration seems more like the illustration of *Tom Sawyer* than the *Alice* books, for its link to the text of which it is an illustration remains contingent. I, for one, prefer my own darker, more ambiguous imagined scene to the antiseptic and ordered one presented by this illustration.

Returning to our general discussion of different types of pictorial illustration, I want to point out one domain in which illustrations, although still connected to the texts of which they are illustrations, achieve a presence that is even more significant than that of the texts they illustrate or, to speak in a more tempered mode,

equally important to their texts. What I have in mind are the illustrations in birding books, such as Florence Merrian Bailey's *Handbook of Birds of the Western United States* (see Figure 3).[36] Birding books contain prose descriptions of individual bird species—including physical markings, vocal characteristics, and locations—together with illustrations of the relevant species. The goal of such books is to assist people in identifying birds. As such, the illustrations are integral to the books' purpose, for they convey a great deal of information that is not ascertainable from the text alone. In particular, they give a sense of what the bird might look like when it is seen flying. The reason for this is that birders rely on the drawings to show them the aspects of the birds they need in order to identify them in the field. I am told that most birds are identified by their "jizz," their appearance as they disappear from view. Drawings are

FORSTER TERN

FIGURE 3. Drawing of a Foster Tern from *Handbook of Birds of the Western United States.*

sometimes able to depict this, but photographs cannot. The role of some of the illustrations in Bailey's *Handbook* is to present birders with accurate images of these jizzes, that is, illustrations of birds that birders can use to identify the type of bird they are seeing.[37] Without these illustrations, birding guides would not achieve their purpose of helping people identify birds with which they are not familiar. The illustrations of such texts are crucial to their fulfilling their purpose and, as a result, cannot be regarded as "a mere supplement" to the texts that they illustrate.

Since the illustrations in such texts are an integral part of them, the fact that something is an illustration does not entail that it is subordinate to the written text for which it is an illustration. Indeed, at least in the case of birding guides, illustrations are a fundamental element whereby the text is able to realize its purpose.

As an aside, it is worth remembering that a philosophical anticipation of this view can be found in Kant's claim, made in the "Aesthetic" of the first *Critique*, that constructions are an essential part of geometrical proofs. Whereas many modern accounts of geometry treat it as a purely axiomatic system, Kant thought that constructions—because of their stimulus to the imagination—play an essential role in the proof of geometrical truths. Clearly, this is not the occasion to decide whether Kant is right about geometry. Nonetheless, I want to mark that claim as related to the one I have been advancing: that certain "illustrations" are essential to the texts they illustrate.

This discussion of the nature of illustrations, then, shows that it is a mistake to conclude that, just because something is an illustration, it is not original or illuminating. Although I have focused on pictorial illustrations of written texts and this is only one type of illustration that a text can receive, my argument shows that one cannot generally treat illustrations as simply means for understanding the texts they illustrate.

If this is correct, then it is a mistake to conclude, as Falzon and Mulhall do, that just because a film illustrates the view of a philosopher that it is not itself "philosophy in action," that is, a genuine instance of philosophy on/in/through film. Although we are not in a position to assert that illustrations of philosophical positions on film can count as instances of philosophy itself, Falzon and Mulhall have not given us adequate grounds for rejecting the idea *tout court*.

To add more support to this idea, it is worth recalling that most philosophers philosophize without making original contributions to the discipline. Philosophy journals are filled with essays that are clearly philosophical but few count as substantially advancing the discussion of the philosophical topics they address. Additionally, historians of philosophy are clearly doing philosophy, even though they rarely make original contributions to philosophy itself, but instead contribute to our understanding of its history. Have not Falzon and Mulhall simply set the bar too high by claiming that films that illustrate philosophical theories in interesting and illuminating ways are not genuine instances of philosophy on/in/through film?

IV

Does our reflection on the concept of illustration and, more specifically, on the relationship between visual illustrations and the texts they illustrate shed any light on the question of whether films can philosophize? I think it has and, to show this, I want to consider a film that many might think of as merely an illustration of a philosophical text and, indeed, a comic rather than a serious illustration at that, Charles Chaplin's 1936 masterpiece, *Modern Times*.

I will only consider the opening scenes of the film, although there are other portions of the film that might be equally interesting to investigate. The reason for this is that these scenes provide a humorous but philosophically significant illustration of Karl Marx's theory of alienation.

The film opens with a serious thought: that workers in a modern factory are like sheep being led to a slaughter. How does the film convey this thought? It uses a technique developed early on by Russian filmmakers such as Sergei Eisenstein: the juxtaposition of two seemingly unrelated images in a *symbolic montage*. The impact of such a juxtaposition was theorized as the "Kuleshov effect," for the two images, when juxtaposed, acquired a meaning over and above that contained in each image considered in isolation. So the film begins with a shot that is easily recognizable as one of sheep being forced up a chute that leads to a slaughterhouse (see Figure 4). It then dissolves to a shot in which factory workers ascending a subway staircase crowd one another in a way very similar to that of the unfortunate sheep (see Figure 5). These two shots in juxtaposition produce the thought contained in neither: that the workers are like the sheep, that they, too, face an ignominious end.[38]

Although this opening sequence is not, or not yet, an illustration of a philosophical theory, it contains a serious thought, makes a serious assertion. Does this qualify it as philosophy? Should it?

Rather than answer these questions at this point, I want to look at the following scenes from the film in which we see Charlie in the factory that the workers were going to in the opening shots, for these scenes provide an illustration of one important claim of Marx's theory.

In the *Economic and Philosophical Manuscripts of 1844*, Marx theorizes the alienation of workers in a capitalist society. One aspect of that alienation is that the workers are dehumanized, becoming tools of the very machines that are supposed to satisfy their needs.

What constitutes the alienation of labor? ... The fact that labor is *external* to the worker, i.e. does not belong to his essential being; that he therefore does not confirm himself in his work but denies himself, feels miserable and not happy, does not develop free mental and physical energy, but mortifies his flesh

FIGURE 4. Sheep being led to the slaughter in *Modern Times.*

FIGURE 5. Workers emerging from the subway in *Modern Times.*

and ruins his mind. ... The machine accommodates itself to man's *weakness*, in order to turn *weak* man into a machine.[39]

The claim that I want to explore is the final one Marx makes in this passage: that machines turn men into machines in a capitalist economic system. Although we all have an intuitive sense of what it means for a person to be turned into a machine, this locution is pretty imprecise, more of a metaphor than a literal claim made about the conditions of the working class. What would it mean, after all, for a person quite literally to become a machine?

I want to suggest that one instance of the "serious" philosophical thinking that is embodied in *Modern Times* involves the complete visualization of Marx's metaphor, a visualization that makes that metaphor more concrete. That is, my claim for the film as an instance of the philosophical on film is that it provides us with a specific interpretation of the mechanization of the human being Marx attributes to capitalism.

When we see first Charlie (Charles Chaplin) in the factory, he is working on an assembly line. The assembly line was an important innovation that made the modern factory possible. It was developed around 1913 by Henry Ford in Highland Park, Michigan. It is important to realize this because Marx's analysis applied to a different factory structure. One could ask whether Marx's claims about the alienation of workers fit the new manufacturing structure of the modern assembly line.

From this point of view, we can see *Modern Times* as, among other things, a rumination about how the assembly line turned men into machines, thereby adapting Marx's theory to specific context. Charlie is a worker on an assembly line in a hyper-modern factory with a range of advanced surveillance techniques that employ the newly deployed technology of television. Charlie and his two co-workers work on a conveyor belt that then takes the pieces they have worked on into a purely mechanical system. Charlie is to tighten two bolts, and his two co-workers then each hammer one of the bolts as they pass by on the conveyor belt.

Clearly, Charlie's job is boring and yet demanding. This becomes apparent when he has to sneeze, and then has to rush to where the pieces he has failed to tighten have moved, pushing into his co-workers and nearly getting the belt shut down, an event that would bring disciplinary action. These features of the production process show that humans have become, as Marx puts it, appendages of the machines, for the workers must accommodate their own needs to the pace and demands of production. Still, this does not yet allow us to see how it turns a man into a machine.

The film illustrates the mechanization of the human body by the assembly line when it shows Charlie's arms continuing to rotate in the tightening motion even when the assembly line is shut down. One example occurs at lunchtime. Charlie nearly sits on a bowl of soup that his co-worker (Tiny Sandford) has poured and so has to pass the soup to him. But his arms and entire upper body continue to twitch in that tightening motion, causing him to spill the soup on his massive co-worker.

Although this scene is funny, it is much more than that. Although Marx claimed that workers' bodies became machines, he did not provide a detailed account of what about factories do this, nor how such mechanization is registered on and by the human body and the human mind. Part of the achievement of the film is to present a specific view of how such mechanization takes place, particularly in the new context of the assembly line. The view of the human body that the film presents, while perhaps not realistic, does convey the toll that the assembly line takes on its workers. And the idea that the human mind also becomes mechanical is itself a

stroke of comic genius. All of this becomes even more evident later in this sequence.

The mechanization of Charlie's body—now presented in tandem with the destruction of his mind—is vividly dramatized in the film by his continuing to use his wrenches on objects other than those he is supposed to. Especially as a result of a speed-up on the line, Charlie cannot control his own arms, nor can he maintain an awareness of the distinction between the line and the balance of his life-world. As a result, he mistakes other patterns in the world that are similar to those of the two nuts he has been tightening and, with his ever-twitching, wrench-laden arms, tries to tighten those "nuts" as well—even when they are buttons on a woman's dress or the noses of the factory bosses (see Figure 6). Neither a verbal description nor a still photograph can convey the humor in these routines, even as a serious point emerges: the pace and repetitiveness of the work Charlie is forced to do has turned him into a veritable bolt-tightening machine, whose arms continue to tighten bolts even when there are no bolts to tighten and whose mind is so fixated on bolts that he assimilates all the visual information he receives to the pattern they form, finding it in unexpected, and hence humorous, places.

It is worth emphasizing that the film's depiction of human mechanization has two elements to it. To the more obvious idea of a body becoming mechanical, *Modern Times* adds the notion of a mind so rigidified by routine that it also becomes a mere mechanism, seeing only

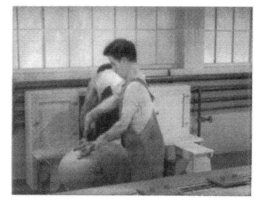

FIGURE 6. Charlie mistakes a woman's dress for a machine part in *Modern Times*.

evidence of patterns it has been required to search for and recognize. Both these elements in the portrayal of the mechanized human being are very creative and, I think, philosophically significant.

The point of all this is to say that a film that is an illustration of Marx's claim that (the bodies and minds of) workers in a capitalist economic system become machines is the locus of some deep thinking—albeit it comical rather than serious—on the nature of the human being and the deleterious effects of capitalism on it. In particular, *Modern Times* interprets and updates Marx's claim about the mechanization of the human to the factory system through a series of comic riffs. But while those riffs are true gems of the silent comic's art, they work because they manifest sustained reflection of how the inhumanity of the assembly line registers itself on the human being in a visually apparent manner.

I can imagine someone objecting to my account of *Modern Times* by saying that its portrayal of the mechanized human body is not very profound, so that even if the film is attempting to make a philosophical point, it is not a significant one. To this, I can only respond by saying that, for me, the film opens up a way of thinking about the human body as machine-like that Marx's claim on its own does not. In addition, the film's portrayal of assembly-line work as mentally decapacitating strikes me as an innovative addition to Marx's claim.

Still, the objector might persist, even if you are right about that, viewers do not watch the Chaplin film for its philosophical insights, but for its humor. Although you might be able to squeeze some philosophy out of its portrayal of the assembly line, we are not interested in the film for that, but rather for Chaplin's amazing antics.

Here, I can only agree that Chaplin's comic riffs are an important source of our interest in *Modern Times*. But I would go on to point out that the humor of the sequence I have been discussing is intimately bound up with the thought that the human being is functioning as a machine, mechanically. So the objector's distinction between Chaplin's antics and the point I claim the film conveys will not stand up, for the two are intrinsically bound together in this film. As I see it, you cannot separate the film's serious thinking about alienation from its comic

portrayal in order to deny that the film involves a philosophically significant contribution.

v

I began this paper with the observation that popular narrative films had recently become frequent objects of philosophical attention. In presenting the beginnings of an account of this phenomenon, I have critically examined two recent attempts to justify seeing films as contributing to our reflection of philosophical questions. I found those accounts to be flawed because of their reliance on an inadequately theorized dichotomy between doing philosophy and merely illustrating it. After a cursory initial investigation into the notion of pictorial illustration, one that undercut the validity of the thinking-illustrating dichotomy, I showed how *Modern Times* could be both an illustration of a philosophical theory and yet also a site of deep thinking on the mechanization of the human under capitalism. Although this example does not exhaust the ways in which films can be philosophy, I think that it lays to rest some skeptical doubts about the validity of the recent trend of seeing philosophy in the moving image.[40]

THOMAS E. WARTENBERG
Department of Philosophy
Mount Holyoke College
South Hadley, MA 01075
USA

INTERNET: twartenb@mtholyoke.edu

1. William Irwin has edited two anthologies on the film, *The Matrix and Philosophy* (Chicago: Open Court, 2002) and *More Matrix and Philosophy* (Chicago: Open Court, 2005). Other anthologies are *Philosophers Explore the Matrix*, ed. Christopher Grau (Oxford University Press, 2005) and *Taking the Red Pill*, ed. Glenn Yeffeth (Dallas: Benbella Books, 2003). Single-author books are Matt Lawrence, *Like a Splinter in Your Mind* (Oxford: Blackwell, 2005) and Jake Horsley, *Being the One* (New York: St. Martin's Press, 2003). There are a number of other books dealing with the film's spirituality and the list of philosophically inspired books keeps growing.

2. Stanley Cavell's interest in popular fiction films predates the current trend. See, for example, his *Pursuits of Happiness: The Hollywood Comedy of Remarriage* (Harvard University Press, 1981).

3. In this paper, I will use a number of expressions as if they were equivalent. I will talk of films "philosophizing,"

"being sites of philosophic reflection, insight, knowledge," "being philosophy," and so on. A discussion of these various locutions is necessary but cannot be undertaken here.

4. This question is raised, albeit in slightly different form, by Bruce Russell, "The Philosophical Limits of Film," *Film and Philosophy* 3 (2000): pp. 166–167.

5. This consideration does not force us to conclude that film and philosophy are irrevocably at odds. Instead, what it shows is that no general account of film as inherently of philosophical value can succeed. It certainly is possible that there are films that are not amenable to an interesting philosophical interpretation, but this merely justifies the conclusion that only certain films—those that we see as seeking to make a philosophical point—will have a legitimate claim on us as viable sources of philosophical enlightenment.

6. I hope to address these objections more fully in a manuscript tentatively titled, *Screening Philosophy*.

7. Christopher Falzon, *Philosophy Goes to the Movies: An Introduction to Philosophy* (London: Routledge, 2002).

8. Falzon, *Philosophy Goes to the Movies*, p. 4.

9. Falzon, *Philosophy Goes to the Movies*, p. 6, emphasis added.

10. This is not to deny that there may be *some* philosophy in Woody Allen's films. For example, *Crimes and Misdemeanors* might count as a counterexample to the claim that "crime does not pay," but it would be a mistake to limit the philosophic content of his films to those few instance of genuine philosophy in them. See Russell, "The Philosophical Limits of Film."

11. Falzon, *Philosophy Goes to the Movies*, p. 4. Falzon seems here to conflate the *literary* images employed within a philosophical text with the *visual* images that compose a film.

12. Falzon, *Philosophy Goes to the Movies*, p. 5.

13. I will discuss this "image" in more detail in a moment. It is worth noting that there is one dialogue where there is something like a visual image, namely, the *Meno*, in which a slave boy is asked to consider a geometrical construction. Falzon does not discuss this, nor would it serve to bolster his argument.

14. Immanuel Kant, *Critique of Pure Reason*, trans. Norman Kemp Smith (New York: St. Martin's Press, 1929), §§A235-36/B294-95. In *The Philosophical Imaginary* (Stanford University Press, 1989), Michele Le Doeuff argues that images generally play a role in justifying a philosopher's position and justifies her claim using this very example. While her view would support the idea that filmic illustrations of a philosophical position should be counted as instances of philosophy itself, I do not wish to base my argument on the acceptance of her controversial thesis.

15. One might doubt that this analogy really constitutes the parable as an *illustration* of Plato's metaphysics. I will simply assume here that this is the case.

16. Plato, *The Republic*, trans. G. M. A. Grube (Indianapolis: Hackett Publishing Company, 1974), p. 168.

17. There is a growing literature on thought experiments in philosophy. See, for example, Tamar Szabó Gendler, *Thought Experiments: On the Powers and Limits of Imaginary Cases* (New York: Garland Publishing, 2000).

18. I pursue this point in "Philosophy Screened: Viewing *The Matrix*," *Midwest Studies in Philosophy* 27 (2003): 139–152, as well as "Film as Argument," forthcoming in *Film Studies: An International Review*. See also Noël

Carroll's contribution to this collection for a similar argument in the context of nonnarrative films.

19. Stephen Mulhall, *On Film* (London: Routledge, 2002), p. 2. Mulhall's terminology of films actually *philosophizing* is problematic in its assumption that anything other than human agents are capable of philosophic activity. I will take up this point later in my discussion. Nonetheless, I will adopt Mulhall's terminology during my discussion of his claims despite this serious reservation about its coherence.

20. Ibid.

21. Ibid., emphasis added.

22. To view a photograph of the picture, go to <http://www.artchive.com>.

23. Mulhall has been criticized for this by Nathan Anderson, "Is Film the Alien Other to Philosophy? Film as Philosophy in Mulhall's On Film," *Film-Philosophy* 7 (2003), available at <http://www.film-philosophy.com/vol7-2003/n23anderson> and by Julian Baggini, "Alien Ways of Thinking: Mulhall's On Film," *Film-Philosophy* 7 (2003), available at <http://www.film-philosophy.com/vol7-2003/n24baggini>. Mulhall fails to elucidate this issue in his response, "Ways of Thinking: A Response to Andersen and Baggini," *Film-Philosophy* 7 (2003), available at <http://www.film-philosophy.com/vol7-2003/n25mulhall>.

24. There could be a film that just consisted of a philosophical essay being photographed so that one could read it, but this would hardly constitute an example of philosophy in a film in the sense intended.

25. Mulhall, *On Film*, p. 2, emphasis added.

26. Arthur Danto makes some interesting comments in this regard in "Illustrating a Philosophical Text," in his *Philosophizing Art: Selected Essays* (University of California Press, 1999), pp. 100–105.

27. Jasper Johns famously plays with this idea in his paintings such as *Flag* (1954–55) or *Number 9* (1969) for the paintings do not simply illustrate or represent the things of which they are illustrations or representations, they *are* those things as well. My statement is not meant to claim that the subject of an illustration must actually exist, but only that illustrations are representational.

28. There are many illustrated versions of the book. The image used here comes from Mark Twain, *The Adventures of Tom Sawyer* (New York: Harper and Brothers Publishers, 1922).

29. Lewis Carroll, *Alice's Adventures in Wonderland* (New York: MacMillan and Co., 1877). Illustrations by John Tenniel.

30. I owe this formulation to Angela Curran (personal communication).

31. In both these cases, there is the additional issue of the relationship between the books and the films based on them, a question that I must leave to one side.

32. This is not just a philosopher's objection. In the case of another set of iconic illustrations, those by E. H. Shepherd for A. A. Milne's *Winnie the Pooh*, the first published Pooh Story was accompanied by illustrations by J. H. Dowd rather than Shepherd when it appeared in *The London Evening News* on December 24, 1925.

33. Edmund Husserl, *The Phenomenology of Internal Time Consciousness* (University of Indiana Press, 1964).

34. Arthur Danto, "The Artworld," *Journal of Philosophy*, 61 (1964): 571–584.

35. Lawrence, *Like a Splinter in Your Mind*, p. 5.

36. Florence Merriam Bailey, *Handbook of Birds of the Western United States* (Boston   New York: Houghton

Mittlin Company, 1902). Virtually any birding guide can be consulted to confirm my point, so long as it contains drawings or sketches rather than photographs. More recent birding guides have more illustrations that confirm my claim.

37. I owe this point to Stephen Davies (personal communication).

38. It could be argued, though I will not do so here, that this scene contains not only a philosophical thought, but a philosophical argument. The topic of visual arguments has had extensive discussion. See, for example, the essays in *Arguing, Communication, & Culture*, vol. 1, ed. G. Thomas Goodnight (Annandale, VA: National Communications Association, 2001).

39. Karl Marx, *Early Writings* (New York: Random House, 1975), pp. 326, 360.

40. An earlier version of this paper was presented at the Institute for the Advancement of Philosophy for Children at Montclair State University. I want to thank the audience there as well as Angela Curran, Megan Laverty, and Alan Schiffmann for their helpful criticisms and suggestions.

Film Art, Argument, and Ambiguity

The proposal that the medium of film, or individual films, might not only be the subject of philosophical study, but the vehicle of philosophical activity, has recently come to the fore in, for example, several essays by Tom Wartenberg, and in Stephen Mulhall's *On Film*.[1] Mapping out his position in the opening pages of that book, Mulhall writes:

I do not look to these films [the *Alien* quartet] as handy or popular illustrations of views and arguments properly developed by philosophers; I see them rather as themselves reflecting on and evaluating such views and arguments, as thinking seriously and systematically about them in *just the ways* that philosophers do. Such films are not philosophy's raw material, nor a source for its ornamentation; they are philosophical exercises, philosophy in action—film as philosophizing.[2]

Mulhall is concerned here to stress the seriousness with which he makes the claim that films can be philosophical. I take it to be relatively uncontentious that, in some broad sense, a film can be philosophical. This is hardly surprising if we regard both film (as an art form) and philosophy as extensions of the human capacity for self-consciousness, that is, of our capacity for reflection on ourselves. Seen in this light, philosophy arises from something about us that is, if not exactly "everyday," then is certainly central to ourselves. If this is true, then philosophy is not something merely abstract, a rarefied and exotic practice set over against the meat and potatoes of life itself, but just a part of life itself. If we accept this view of the philosophical enterprise, then there is nothing controversial in the claim that philosophy and the arts in general, including film and literature, inhabit the same territory. Indeed, Mulhall has gestured in just this direction in stating that he has "a sense that there's some kind of open border between philosophy and literature."[3]

But Mulhall's thesis in *On Film* is bolder than this implies in two respects. First, if we are to take Mulhall's statement from the opening of *On Film* at face value, it is not enough to say that some filmmaking and philosophy inhabit the same territory, as one might imply in suggesting that a film has a philosophical theme or tone. Rather, Mulhall wants to argue that films can inhabit the territory of human self-reflection *in the same way* as philosophy—that films can be "philosophy in action." And what is that "way" or "mode" that a film, as much as a philosophical text, can embody, on Mulhall's account? This is the question that will preoccupy me in this essay.

Second, it is important to note the type of film that Mulhall puts at the center of his discussion: the Hollywood narrative film, complete with all the usual trappings—stars, spectacle, and, above all, stories. Mulhall is thus not pursuing two other salient possibilities within the "film as philosophy" debate: the idea that certain films might embody *moral* philosophy in the way that Martha Nussbaum and others have argued that certain novels do (such as, perhaps, Mike Leigh's *Vera Drake* (2004)); or the idea that there might be a "film of ideas" genre, cousin to the "novel of ideas," which explicitly strives for philosophical value (for example, Chris Marker's *Sans soleil* (1983)). Mulhall takes on the most challenging possibility of all in proposing that some big-budget, popular entertainment films—movies—philosophize in just the same way as a traditional philosophical text.

There are broadly two ways in which film-making can be aligned with philosophy in its more traditional forms—call them the *reductive* and the *expansive* strategies. The reductive strategy involves showing how all the various things we might think a film to be doing (for example, engaging us through storytelling) can be shown to coalesce around a specific, narrow conception of philosophical activity. To be really persuasive, this strategy needs to "reduce" the key activities of a film to the philosophical without creating the sense that those activities are thereby travestied or mistakenly described and, ideally, by showing that those activities are *best* illuminated by casting them in terms of philosophical activity. The expansive strategy takes the opposite tack. Rather than showing how a film's design might fit some very specific criteria of membership in the category "work of philosophy," the expansive strategy begins with a looser, more inclusive conception of philosophy. This creates a philosophical context in which many activities that, on the face of it, do not look very philosophical—like filmmaking—turn out to be philosophical, or at least to have important philosophical dimensions. One particular tactic sometimes employed as a part of the expansive strategy is to break down the work of philosophy into various constituents so that we see both the breadth and variety of activities that "doing philosophy" might entail, as well as seeing how film might perform some of these activities very effectively some of the time.[4]

For the most part, Mulhall employs the expansive strategy; that is the import of his "open border" metaphor. Traffic between the domain of "real philosophy" and any adjacent realm of self-reflective activity does in fact exist and should be embraced, so Mulhall implies. But the metaphor cuts both ways—note that Mulhall does not claim that there is no border, and so maintains the idea that there is something distinctive about philosophy that marks it off from other forms or products of self-reflection. And when it comes to characterizing "philosophy in action," Mulhall's strategy looks more reductive than expansive. In the quotation with which I began, Mulhall states that films are capable of thinking "seriously and systematically," and are able to reflect on and evaluate the "views and arguments" of philoso-phers ("in just the ways that philosophers do"). It is hard to avoid the conclusion that Mulhall believes that films, when acting as vehicles of philosophy, embody arguments (albeit, presumably, of an implicit and informal nature) in support of theses ("views").

Is this a reasonable construal, given that Mulhall speaks only of films thinking "seriously and systematically"? Surely, it might be said, there are ways of thinking seriously and system-atically other than in the form of argument. Be that as it may, Mulhall himself brings the concept of "argument" into the equation by writing of the "arguments" of philosophers and by then insisting on an identity between the activity of some films and the activity of philosophers as traditionally conceived. It is also notable that Julian Baggini, in a sympathetic review of Mulhall's book, strives to characterize philosophy without recourse to the concept of argument, but finds the term irresistible (referring to it sev-eral times in his attempts to capture the sense in which we are to understand a narrative film as a potential form of philosophy).[5]

The trouble is—a narrative is not, literally speaking, an argument.[6] Of course, the idea that a narrative might imply an argument, or in some other way act to realize an argument, is an ancient idea. It is implicit in the assumption that certain narratives carry "messages," "morals," or "lessons," in the sense that these "morals" are like the conclusion of an argument. Some critics and theorists have spelled out this intui-tion more explicitly: André Bazin, for example, wrote that the "thesis implied" by *Ladri di bici-clette [Bicycle Thieves]* (Vittorio de Sica, 1948) "is wondrously and outrageously simple: in the world where this workman lives, the poor must steal from each other in order to survive. But this thesis is never stated as such, it is just that events are so linked together that they have the appearance of a formal truth while retaining an anecdotal quality."[7] What distinguishes Mulhall is the strength of the claim he wishes to make with respect to the potential argumentative "force" of narrative form. But the precise relationship between narrative and argument remains impressionistic and undertheorized. What is needed is an analysis of how a narrative can deliver the basic constituents of argument—premises, a pattern of inference, and a conclusion.[8]

I. FICTION AS THOUGHT EXPERIMENT

If the analogy between narrative and argument appears to be too strained or too vague, the expansive strategy opens up the possibility of identifying alternative links between philosophy and narrative filmmaking. For example, in an essay concerned with the extent to which and the ways in which fictional narratives can be vehicles of knowledge, Noël Carroll argues that such narratives very often function as either *counterexamples* to some philosophical argument, or as *thought experiments* conveying a philosophical thesis or implication.[9] A thought experiment, in the words of Tom Wartenberg, asks a reader "to consider a certain possibility that she might not have considered before, a possibility that is often at odds with her established patterns of belief and action. Once this possibility is entertained as a real possibility, then the reader is confronted with the question of what justifies her customary belief rather than the possibility put forward in the thought experiment." The thought experiment is, in Wartenberg's resonant phrase, a device for challenging the "tenacity of the habitual."[10] Carroll goes on to note that since philosophy has freely conjured up fictional counterexamples and thought experiments throughout its history—René Descartes's evil demon, Hilary Putnam's brain in a vat, Robert Nozick's experience machine, and so on—it cannot without contradiction deny that fictional narratives may deliver knowledge: "in the great and ongoing quarrel between philosophy and poetry, philosophy cannot win without undermining itself."[11] Or, to put it in terms closer to Mulhall's, philosophy cannot deny that fictional narratives may be vehicles of philosophical insight, or "philosophy in action." Putting Carroll's point in Mulhall's terms, however, involves closing a gap—between knowledge in general and philosophical knowledge more specifically—that may turn out to be problematic. But to tackle this question now would be to jump the gun; we need to approach it more circumspectly.

One might go a step further than Carroll and think of fictions in general just *as* thought experiments. But if we do so, we will realize that unlike the fictions posed as thought experiments by philosophers, artistic fictions— including fiction films, comic books, popular and literary novels, and short stories—are, relatively speaking, immensely detailed and elaborate.[12] This difference raises the suspicion that the thought experiment serves different purposes in philosophy and artistic storytelling, respectively. Just what is all that detail *doing* there?!

Carroll's identification of the thought experiment as something straddling the domains of philosophy and narrative art, then, allows us to ask whether the *role* of the thought experiment in each domain is the same. At this juncture, an example will help us. In an essay on the nature of personal identity and the role of the body in relation to it, Bernard Williams concocts the following thought experiment (with a nod to a similar thought experiment proposed by Locke).

Suppose a magician is hired to perform the old trick of making the emperor and the peasant become each other. He gets the emperor and the peasant in one room, with the emperor on his throne and the peasant in the corner, and then casts the spell. What will count as success? …The requirement is presumably that the emperor's body, with the peasant's personality, should be on the throne, and the peasant's body with the emperor's personality in the corner. What does this mean? In particular, what has happened to the voices? The voice ought to count as a bodily function; yet how would the peasant's gruff blasphemies be uttered in the emperor's cultivated tones, or the emperor's witticisms in the peasant's growl? A similar point holds for the [facial] features.[13]

Williams is concerned here to take one view of personal identity, in which the body plays no essential role in the individuation of persons, and confront this view with an imagined scenario—a thought experiment—that reveals, or at least suggests, deep flaws in that conception of personal identity. Williams only needs to elaborate and extend the basic premise of the thought experiment over a few sentences in order to reveal the conceptual confusion on which (he argues) the dualistic conception of personal identity—of the self as a disembodied soul—rests. The thought experiment here plays a variety of roles, including a rhetorical role— by shifting mode briefly from more abstract argumentation, Williams engages the reader's attention through variety and through the gently absurd humor of the scene he asks us to imagine. But the *primary* role of the thought experiment is *epistemic*: Williams wants us to think clearly and precisely about the nature of personal identity and the role of the body, and he uses the story of the emperor and the peasant as a way of exposing a confusion that needs to be addressed if we are to arrive at a clear, if complex, account of personal identity.

All of Me (1984), a romantic comedy directed by Carl Reiner and starring Steve Martin, is based on the same premise as Williams's thought experiment. Martin plays a lawyer, Roger Cobb, who is instructed by his boss to deal with the legal affairs of a rich client, Edwina Cutwater (played by Lili Tomlin). Cutwater is dying and has engaged a guru to transport her mind into the body of a willing transplantee, Terry Hoskins (Victoria Tennant)—whose own mind will in turn "transmigrate" into the universe as a whole. Cobb's main legal task is to revise Cutwater's will so that Terry Hoskins becomes her sole inheritor—the logic being that, once the mind switch has occurred, Cutwater simply repossesses her own estate, now "housed" in a new and healthy body. However, at the moment of mental transplantation, a mishap results in Cutwater's mind entering *Cobb's* body, which is then "cohabited" by Cobb and Cutwater—Cobb retaining control of the left side of his body, Cutwater taking control of the right side of "her" body (for the most part).

Immediately following the transplantation, Cobb struggles to comprehend what has happened to him, while Cutwater stretches her new limbs. This is the scene in which the physical comedy implicit in the thought experiment takes hold. Cobb's body flails around as both Cobb and Cutwater attempt to assert control over it. Martin performs the idea of Cutwater's presence in Cobb's body through a parody of prissy femininity—falsetto voice, swinging hips, angled hand on hip, and so forth (Figure 1). The humor here undoubtedly connects with the philosophical issue raised by Williams, especially when he asks: "[H]ow would the peasant's gruff blasphemies be uttered in the emperor's cultivated tones, or the emperor's witticisms in the peasant's growl?" For the only way Cobb's body can give expression to Cutwater's mind and character is through

FIGURE 1. Bodily cohabitation.

caricatured gesture. In other words, if we look to the film for an implied answer to Williams's question, concerning the prospects of a displaced mind expressing itself in an alien body, that answer is: "crudely, and with difficulty." The comedy of the scene is thus intimately related to the incongruity of Cutwater's mind in Cobb's body (indeed, there is even an echo of Williams's emperor/peasant contrast—Cutwater is an aristocrat, Cobb the son of a barber, and an unaccomplished lawyer). This is compounded by the situation into which "Cobb-Cutwater" is thrust—no sooner has this new entity mastered the art of walking than s/he has to negotiate a visit to the men's room. In passing, we should also note that this scene establishes a convention whereby whenever Cobb looks in a mirror, he sees not his own body, but Cutwater's (that is, we see Lily Tomlin, playing Cutwater, in mirror reflections of Cobb). This occurs first when Cobb catches sight of Cutwater as he looks into the wing mirror of a car, and is then confirmed in an extended exchange in the restroom between Cobb standing before a urinal and Cutwater reflected in the mirror above it (Figure 2).

The film also develops a subplot concerning Cobb's philandering boss, Burton Schuyler (Dana Elgar), who is being sued for divorce. Under pressure within Schuyler's practice and seeking to become a partner, Cobb is compelled to take on the role of defense attorney representing Schuyler. In one scene, we see Cobb in court during proceedings. But there is a problem. Distracted by the presence of an additional mind within his body, Cobb has been up most of the night preparing legal arguments. Now

FIGURE 2. Body and soul.

exhausted, he has fallen asleep. Or rather, Cobb's "mind" has fallen asleep, but Cutwater's mind is still awake—in other words, Cobb's body is awake but is animated at this point only by Cutwater's mind. Called into the proceedings by the judge, Cutwater is compelled to *perform* Cobb's masculine gestures, using Cobb's body. Once again, this proceeds through caricature. Where in the earlier scene Martin effected a parodic rendering of femininity in order to give expression to Cutwater, here he executes a burlesque of masculinity in order to represent Cutwater's imitation of Cobb—a performance incorporating a broad swaggering gait, tobacco spitting, crotch scratching, and a boot stuck on the prosecuting attorney's desk. Comic capital is again extracted from the awkward "fit" of a mind in an alien body. Across the two scenes, then, we have considerable elaboration of the basic thought experiment: instead of a simple switch of minds, we have two minds in one body; and in the courtroom scene, we see the "displaced" mind (Cutwater's) mimicking the "home" mind while the latter is unconscious.

These are the scenes in which the parallel with Williams's thought experiment is most salient. But other aspects of the film resonate with the problem of the bodily dimension of personal identity, drawing out the social implications of that dimension of identity. Cobb's closest friend in the film is a blind, black sax player, Tyrone Wattell (Jason Bernard) (Cobb moonlights as a jazz guitarist, playing alongside Wattell). In the course of some comic repartee, Wattell calls Cobb a "honky mook." Cobb retorts that Wattell really should not use such

language—not least because, Cobb jests, Wattell is white. We can see that Wattell is in fact black, and the whole exchange is a playful one. But it exposes a curious aspect of Wattell's experience—although he is black, he himself has no access to, nor evidence of, that part of his physical being from which the social notion of "blackness" builds. It might as well be a fiction as far as he is concerned. So here we see a kind of disconnection between bodily identity and "interior" identity.

Cutwater also speaks of a disjunction between her inner self and her bodily identity. In explaining the motivation behind the transplantation scheme, she describes a childhood and a lifetime of physical infirmity, and thus an inability to give expression to (what she feels to be) her vivacious and life-affirming character. Her body simply will not live up to the desires and values that, on her account at least, constitute the core of her personality. So if, in the case of Wattell, the visible aspect of bodily identity is only experienced in a remote and abstract way, here the body is represented as an impediment to the realization of the self, rather than simply as a constitutive part of it. In both cases, there is discord, rather than integration, between the inner self and the bodily self. Thus, different facets of *All of Me* have contrasting implications with respect to the role of the body in personal identity. While the central line of action concerning mental relocation underlines the "positive" significance of the body to personal identity—the body as expressive vehicle of identity—other strands of the plot play up the way in which the body may block the expression of or otherwise problematize certain aspects of identity.

After various twists and turns, including the accidental transplantation of Cutwater's mind from Cobb's body into a bucket of stable water, Cutwater's mind is eventually successfully relocated in Terry Hoskins's body. This sets up a fitting conclusion for a romantic comedy. Cobb has lusted after Hoskins's body throughout, while growing unexpectedly fond of Cutwater during her "stay" in his body. The transplantation of Cutwater's mind into Tennant's body thus apparently grants Cobb his ideal synthesis. In the final scene, Cobb and Cutwater (now embodied by Tennant) dance. But there is one more twist. With its final gesture, the film reverts to the convention whereby Cutwater's mind becomes manifest through her original body whenever the new host is seen in a mirror. Following Cobb and Cutwater/Tennant onto the dance floor, the camera pans away from them after a few seconds in order to pick up their reflections in a mirror. As the film ends, then, instead of seeing Cobb dance with Cutwater/Tennant, we see him dance with Cutwater/Tomlin (Figure 3).

This is a paradoxical conclusion. On the one hand, the film seems to insist on the centrality of a particular body (Tomlin's) to Cutwater's mind (it is hard to imagine Tennant dancing with just the kind of free-form playfulness that characterizes Tomlin's movements). On the other hand, the film has established, via the mirror convention, that Cutwater's mind (or "soul," we might very well say here) persists in

FIGURE 3. The soul as body.

its original form even as it inhabits another body, the original mind being manifest in the mirror views. The paradox thus resides in the fact that Cutwater's persisting soul can *only* be represented by her body! The film seems committed, then, to both dualism and monistic physicalism. You might even say that it rests on the *paradox of personal identity*: personal identity both requires, and yet is independent of, the body. Or at least, *All of Me* gives expression to inconsistencies in our assumptions about personal identity that this paradox, as I have stated it, summarizes and condenses.[14]

II. DRAMATIC IMAGINING, DRAMATIC PARADOX, AND AMBIGUITY

It might seem that in discovering this paradox in *All of Me* that I have acceded to the very contention—that mainstream films can philosophize—that I have been questioning. But this would be to mistake what, precisely, is at stake in the debate and in the account of *All of Me* that I have advanced. What is at stake here is not whether the film has a philosophical theme, or philosophical implications, or that the film can be used to introduce just the kind of philosophical conundrums regarding personal identity that Williams analyzes. I am not seeking to deny any of these possibilities. Rather, the question I am asking is: What is the *film* doing with the scenario that it shares with the thought experiment in Williams's essay? Is the film's project in some important sense a philosophical one?

Let me answer this question by comparing my account of the film with both the commentary on the film provided by Christopher Falzon and with the sort of stance that we can imagine Mulhall taking toward it. Falzon's goal is to introduce various philosophical concepts and arguments via films. *All of Me* is one of the films he draws on to introduce dualism; Falzon interprets the film as straightforwardly assuming a dualistic worldview.[15] One can see why he might think this, given the fact that it is fictional in the film that minds can move from body to body (via metal bowls and buckets of water, no less). But the burden of my analysis of the film has been to show that it is not *straightforwardly* dualistic.[16] The awkwardness of fit between a mind and an alien body resonates with

Williams's thought experiment, designed to expose the problems with dualism, as does the fact that Cutwater's continuous-but-displaced inner self is represented by her bodily being (her body, face, and voice). Making the film the *primary* object of analysis, and capturing such nuances in the "thinking" of the film, aligns my interpretation of *All of Me* more closely with Mulhall's approach, as Mulhall is eager to go beyond the use of films as "handy" illustrations of philosophical concepts. But this returns us to the following question: Is the complexity of narrative filmmaking manifest in a film like *All of Me* best described and analyzed in terms of "philosophizing," or are there other more apt ways of capturing such complexity?

Unlike Williams's essay, the film uses the thought experiment primarily as a vehicle of comedy. The primary goal of the film is to elaborate the *comic ramifications* of its "philosophical" premise. If we were to judge the artistic value of the film, the most apt criteria would be *comic complexity* and *ingenuity*. Put schematically, the priority of the epistemic and the artistic (in this case, comic complexity) are flipped, relative to their roles in Williams's essay. So the film has an epistemic dimension—we might well be brought to reflect on personal identity by the film and learn something from it—but it is subsidiary to its comic imperative. This subordination of the epistemic to the artistic is surely the main reason why narrative films based on philosophical themes, like *All of Me*, will often compromise the "logic" of the philosophical problem that they dramatize. A filmmaker working with a comic priority will normally opt for those features (of plot and stylistic design) that maximize the comic rather than the epistemic value of the film. Thus, *All of Me* may not be conceptually watertight, but it is very funny. As that sage of Hollywood, Sam Goldwyn, might have put it: "Pictures are for entertainment—if I wanted to make a philosophical point, I'd publish an essay in *Proceedings of the Aristotelian Society*."[17]

In saying this, however, I do not want to be understood as suggesting that the relationship between artistic value (and its various instantiations in comedy, tragedy, horror, and so forth) and epistemic value is a mutually exclusive one. The conveying of knowledge or prompting of conceptual thinking is certainly an important part of the artistic value of many genres; in some cases, like that of documentary filmmaking, the epistemic value of a film may be absolutely central to the artistic value of the film. There is more to be said on the *way* in which the epistemic dimension of a work of narrative film art relates to its aesthetic dimensions: the way that it subsists as part of the overall fabric of the work. The preliminary point here, however, is to highlight the relative importance of the epistemic and the artistic (the comic, in this case) in works of different sorts. Thus a work of philosophy and a work of art will, typically, rank these priorities differently; philosophical insight and the creation of comedy are both facets of both Williams's essay and *All of Me*, but they are weighted quite differently, and thus function differently, in the two cases. But it is also true, as I have just suggested, that the relative significance of the epistemic and various artistic values will vary among different kinds of artworks.

We can deepen our understanding of the different role played by the thought experiment in philosophical argument, and artistic narrative, respectively, through the contrast proposed by Richard Moran between *hypothetical* and *dramatic imagining*. To imagine something hypothetically is to pose the possibility of some counterfactual in a spare and abstract way. Dramatic imagining involves elaborating and ramifying the bare counterfactual in one or more ways. We might imagine experiencing the events "from the inside," that is, as a witness or as a participant, rather than merely imagining *that* the events occur; Moran writes that dramatic imagining "involves something … like genuine rehearsal, 'trying on' [a] point of view, trying to determine what it is like to inhabit it."[18] Or we might imagine the ever-widening circle of possible consequences that follow from the basic thought experiment, that is, the initial set of explicitly stated counterfactuals. As I have already implied, this second form of dramatic imagining is evidently important for a film like *All of Me*, but the first form may be significant too, insofar as some of the comedy depends on, or will be most fully appreciated through, our ability to imagine what it feels like to be in a certain sort of absurd or humiliating situation. One consequence of such dramatic imagining is that we are much more likely to be engaged emotionally than we would be if the same scenario were imagined in hypothetical fashion.

The nature and relevance of this contrast could easily be misunderstood. The point is not that philosophical thought experiments require *no* elaboration; rather, philosophical thought experiments seem to require relatively little elaboration.[19] This quantitative difference points us toward a different kind of imagining at stake in the two practices, and supports the argument advanced here that the philosophical thought experiment, on the one hand, and the artistic thought experiment, on the other, are geared toward different tasks. Mulhall's rejoinder might be that there is no reason why a filmmaker might not be both a comic *and* a philosopher, just as Einstein might be regarded as both a physicist and a philosopher.[20] Some philosophers are, after all, pretty funny, and *All of Me* is not unique in deriving comedy from philosophical ideas. Once again, though, the point is not to deny the evident possibility of overlap between a philosophical and an artistic (here, comic) project, but to ask whether there is not some tension between the goals of philosophy and the goals of art, and that for this reason we find that, typically, a film or a text will organize these goals hierarchically. Most works will manifest in their design an overriding, dominant goal even as they may instantiate secondary goals, or enlist the techniques and forms we associate with these secondary goals as means to securing the primary goal, as we have seen in the case of Williams's use of humor as a means of exposing the incoherence of dualism.[21]

The particular artistic properties that characterize *All of Me* will not, of course, be found in every work of art. We would not expect or want to find comedy in a tragedy or a horror fiction (not, at least, as the "defining" emotion of such works). But if we move up one level of abstraction, we begin to find properties with greater reach across the arts and across particular works of art—properties like complexity, ingenuity, inventiveness, density, ambiguity, and profundity. And while we can imagine finding these same properties in works of philosophy, it is not clear that we would value them in just the same way in a work of philosophy as in a work of art. Something like *ambiguity*, in the New Critical sense of the term, lies at the heart of this vital

but elusive contrast between philosophy and art. In part, this arises from the concreteness and particularity of art, as distinct from the abstract, conceptual character of philosophy.[22] The epistemic content of a work of art does not enter into it, and is not conveyed to us, in such a philosophical manner. The meaning and experience that works of art typically create is one characterized by sufficient complexity and indirection that it resists restatement—or "paraphrase"—in clear and unequivocal terms. In other words, no matter how "philosophical" the theme of a narrative, to the extent that it is designed as an artwork it is apt to put a spanner in the philosophical works. As Cleanth Brooks, one of the architects of the New Criticism, put it: "When we consider the statement immersed in the poem, it presents itself to us, like the stick immersed in the pool of water, warped and bent. Indeed, whatever the statement, it will always show itself as deflected away from a positive, straightforward formulation."[23] Few criticisms are more apt to strike terror into the heart of the philosopher than the assertion that such-and-such a proposition is "ambiguous," while in the world of art, that term is more apt to be used as a term of praise.

Brooks often used the idea of "paradox" (along with ambiguity and irony) in order to describe the form of poetry, and to distinguish such form from "rational statement."[24] Paradox, in this sense, comes to mean the unification or holding-in-balance, within the form of an artwork, of contrasting attitudes or meanings. The "paradoxicality" of *All of Me*, then, might be seen in these terms, as a "dramatic" rather than strictly philosophical, conceptual phenomenon. Instead of interpreting the film's treatment of the bodily dimension of identity as a symptom of its philosophical inconsistency, that paradoxical treatment might be seen (and valued) as a compact dramatization of our conflicting intuitions about the place of the body in personal identity. The film provides us with a comic-dramatic image of our understanding of personhood and the body. That is something we are likely to value in a work of art, but not value in a work of philosophy (or, at least, not in the same way or to the same degree). To recall a criterion I proposed earlier, we might ask ourselves whether a narrative film like *All of Me* is best illuminated on the basis of this artistic conception of "paradoxicality" or on the basis of more strictly philosophical models of argument, thought experiment and paradox?

In "The Heresy of Paraphrase," Brooks argued that the danger posed by the "heresy" is that "we bring the statement [of a poem] into an unreal competition with science or philosophy or theology."[25] This is precisely the danger of Mulhall's argument. Mulhall is motivated to defend popular film from the familiar charge that it necessarily lacks sophistication, and especially conceptual sophistication, and so Mulhall is driven to argue that at least some popular films can be assimilated wholesale to philosophy. But is not Mulhall's position colored by the ancient view that the worth of art will always pale in comparison with the worth of philosophy? A different path is open to us if we recognize and challenge this assumption. We can, and should, take popular films seriously—but as works of art, rather than as works of philosophy. After all, in the larger scheme of things, comic artistry is probably as important to human flourishing as philosophy. What it means to take popular filmmaking as an art seriously, of course, is still another matter.[26]

MURRAY SMITH
School of Drama, Film and Visual Arts
University of Kent
Canterbury
Kent CT2 7NX
UK

INTERNET: mss@kent.ac.uk

1. Stephen Mulhall, *On Film* (London: Routledge, 2002); Thomas E. Wartenberg, "Experiencing *The Matrix*," *Midwest Studies in Philosophy* 26 (2003): 139–152. For a parallel treatment of "opera as philosophy," see Philip Kitcher and Richard Schacht, *Finding an Ending: Reflections on Wagner's "Ring"* (New York: Oxford University Press, 2004).

2. Mulhall, *On Film*, p. 2, emphasis added.

3. Quoted by Julian Baggini, "Alien Ways of Thinking: Mulhall's *On Film*," *Film-Philosophy* 7 (2003), available at <http://www.film-philosophy.com/vol7–2003/n24baggini>. Baggini quotes from "Post-Analytic Philosophy: In Conversation with Stephen Mulhall," in *New British Philosophy: The Interviews*, ed. Julian Baggini and Jeremy Stangroom (London: Routledge, 2002), p. 241.

4. See, for example, Thomas Wartenberg's treatment of illustration, in "Beyond *Mere* Illustration: How Films Can Be Philosophy," *The Journal of Aesthetics and Art Criticism* 64 (2006): 19–32.

5. Baggini, "Alien Ways of Thinking."

6. See Jerry Fodor: "*The Ring* isn't … an enthymeme, a paradox or a dilemma. It isn't any kind of argument at all," in "What Wotan Wants," review of *Finding an Ending*, by Kitcher and Schacht, *London Review of Books*, August 5, 2004, p. 8.

7. André Bazin, *What is Cinema?* vol. II (University of California Press, 1971), p. 51.

8. Noël Carroll offers an analysis of narrative in terms of what he terms the "narrative enthymeme," where the intelligibility of a narrative depends on an often implicit presupposition or premise that the narrative goes on to bear out. However, the generalizations embodied in these presuppositions are commonplace, often serving ideological ends, and insofar as they are ideological, they will be (among other things) "epistemically defective." The model thus offers little direct assistance to those who hold that popular narratives can forge philosophically groundbreaking thinking. See Carroll, "Film, Rhetoric, and Ideology," in *Explanation and Value in the Arts*, ed. Salim Kemal and Ivan Gaskell (Cambridge: Cambridge University Press, 1993), pp. 215–237.

9. Noël Carroll, "The Wheel of Virtue: Art, Literature, and Moral Knowledge," *The Journal of Aesthetics and Art Criticism* 60 (2002): 3–26.

10. Wartenberg, "Experiencing *The Matrix*," p. 145.

11. Carroll, "The Wheel of Virtue," p. 19.

12. David Gooding describes thought experiments as "sparse, carefully-crafted narratives," likening them to jokes, in "Thought Experiments," in *Routledge Encyclopedia of Philosophy*, ed. E. Craig (London: Routledge, 1988). Of course, the level of detail evident in an artistic fiction will vary immensely according to genre and the style of particular authors. The fact of that variety, however, does not undermine the overarching contrast that I propose between the artistic fiction and the philosophical thought experiment.

13. Bernard Williams, "Personal Identity and Individuation," in *Problems of the Self: Philosophical Papers 1956–72* (Cambridge: Cambridge University Press, 1973), pp. 11–12. Locke's thought experiment concerned the transfer of the "soul" of a prince into the body of a cobbler, though Locke draws precisely the conclusion that Williams disputes: that bodily identity is not a necessary condition of personal identity. Williams's thought experiment is thus a *counter-thought experiment*. John Locke, *An Essay Concerning Human Understanding*, ed. Peter H. Nidditch (Oxford: Oxford University Press, 1975), II.xxvii.15.

14. My interpretation here treats the conclusion of the narrative as a matter of the internal logic of the film, whether conceived generically, thematically, or philosophically. But it is likely that another, "external" factor was important in determining the form of the final scene—star power. Martin and Tomlin were undoubtedly the two major stars in the film, and so by convention the film needs to end with the depiction of their romantic union, rather than the union of Martin and Tennant. (Or, more strictly, the film needs to end with the romantic union of Cobb and Cutwater represented by Martin and Tomlin rather than by Martin and Tennant.) I do not mean to suggest that such external considerations will necessarily undermine the artistic, including epistemic and even philosophical, goals of Hollywood filmmakers. This ending has been prepared for by the mirror motif and, more broadly, by the very casting of Tomlin into the primary and authentic female romantic role in the film. Art and commerce need not be antithetical. But equally, it

will not do simply to ignore these external factors in the shaping of films. It is always a question as to how far the filmmakers of a given film have managed to channel the force of such external factors toward their own internal, artistic ends.

15. Christopher Falzon, *Philosophy Goes to the Movies: An Introduction to Philosophy* (London: Routledge, 2002), pp. 51, 62–63.

16. Falzon's commentary on the film *Suture* (David Siegel, Scott McGehee, 1993) suggests that that film, unusually and quite self-consciously, is premised on a more thorough-going dualism, as contrasted with the various, complex, and sometimes conflicting intuitions that find expression in *All of Me*. Falzon, *Philosophy Goes to the Movies*, p. 64.

17. What Sam Goldwyn actually said was: "Pictures are for entertainment, messages should be delivered by Western Union." Allegedly.

18. Richard Moran, "The Expression of Feeling in Imagination," *The Philosophical Review* 103 (1994): 105. See also Tamar Szabó Gendler, "The Puzzle of Imaginative Resistance," *Journal of Philosophy* 97 (2000): 55–81.

19. Immediately following the paragraph in which he sets out the thought experiment concerning the emperor and the peasant, Williams explicitly states: "The point need not be elaborated…" Williams, "Personal Identity and Individuation," p. 12

20. Stephen Mulhall, "Ways of Thinking: A Response to Andersen and Baggini," *Film-Philosophy* 7 (2003), available at <http://www.film-philosophy.com/vol7-2003/n25mulhall>.

21. Another objection might be that *All of Me* is not a good or fair example to test Mulhall's argument. Is a cute little Hollywood comedy really a robust enough example to raise questions about the philosophical potential of filmmaking in general? In fact, in terms of the kind of "filmic philosophizing" that Mulhall has in mind, the film is a very apt example. *All of Me* is precisely the sort of film that Mulhall focuses on: a studio picture designed within a clear generic framework (comedy in the case of *All of Me*, horror in the case of the *Alien* films) that sustains its sophistication through the narrative values for which Hollywood is famed. And the film has a direct generic relationship with screwball comedy, one of the favored genres of Mulhall's major influence, Stanley Cavell.

22. For a discussion of this contrast see the exchange between René Wellek, "Literary Criticism and Philosophy," *Scrutiny* 5 (1937): 375–383, and F. R. Leavis, "Literary Criticism and Philosophy: A Reply," *Scrutiny* 6 (1937): 59–70. Leavis argues staunchly for the importance of the concreteness of art—as exemplified by poetry—and the significance of its contrast with philosophy in this respect. Hegel's definition of art as the unveiling of "*truth* in the form of sensuous artistic configuration," which he distinguishes from the purely conceptual form of "truth" as it is manifest in philosophy, is a canonical example of the contrast. G. W. F. Hegel, *Aesthetics: Lectures on Fine Art*, Vol. 1 (Oxford: Clarendon Press, 1975), trans T. M. Knox, p. 55.

23. Cleanth Brooks, "The Heresy of Paraphrase," in *The Well Wrought Urn* (London: Methuen, 1968), p. 172.

24. Brooks, "Heresy of Paraphrase," p. 172. Although Brooks was writing of poetry, his analysis freely draws on analogies with the other arts, including painting, architecture, and drama; extending his analysis to narrative filmmaking thus does not violate the spirit of the argument.

25. Brooks, "Heresy of Paraphrase," p. 164.

26. My thanks to audiences at the 2003 ASA conference in San Francisco, and the Philosophy Work-in-Progress Seminar at the University of Kent, especially Tom Wartenberg, Alan Thomas, and Edward Harcourt, for comments on earlier versions of this essay.

II. POPULAR AMERICAN FILM: ENTERTAINMENT AND ENLIGHTENMENT

RICHARD ALLEN

Hitchcock and Cavell

Stanley Cavell's philosophy and Alfred Hitchcock's films share a distinctive feature: they are both concerned with the relationship between doubt and romance. Cavell is a thinker who has forcefully articulated the idea that the narrative of heterosexual romance is a place where philosophical doubt or skepticism enters into the everyday or the ordinary. For Cavell, skepticism is the central problem that is confronted in the lives of protagonists who seek to enter into and sustain a relationship of intimacy, and classical Hollywood cinema is a privileged place for staging the relationship between heterosexual romance and skepticism. In the history of cinema, it is Hitchcock who has most consistently charted the vicissitudes of romance in relationship to the representation of doubt about what characters within the romance and the spectator, alongside those characters, see and hear. Furthermore, Cavell himself has written an essay on Hitchcock's film *North by Northwest* (1959) as an exemplification of what he calls "Comedies of Remarriage" that play a significant role in the articulation of his philosophy.[1]

Yet I shall argue in this essay that it is precisely because Hitchcock's films share Cavell's concern with the relationship between doubt and romance that they call into question his presupposition of the bond between skepticism and romance, and the manner in which he uses texts to illustrate and illuminate it. Cavell's philosophy is based on two interrelated claims. First, our relationship to other people and the world is

not one of knowing. This is what Cavell calls "the truth of skepticism."[2] Second, romantic love and, in particular, marriage, is the place where we best learn to live with "the truth of skepticism," where we overcome or succumb to its corrosive effects. Although romance in Hitchcock's films is a place inhabited by doubt that tests the capacity of a protagonist to understand the true intentions of his or her romantic partner, and the world of Hitchcock's films from *North by Northwest* to *Psycho* (1960) seems governed by a sense of arbitrariness and incipient chaos, Hitchcock's films do not demonstrate "the truth of skepticism," for the protagonists of his works, together with the audience, typically arrive at certainty about what it is that they see and hear. Although the protagonists of Hitchcock's works, and even the audience for a time, may be uncertain about the motivation of other characters, these doubts are not essentially irresolvable, they do not provide evidence of an inescapable skepticism that informs everyday interactions. By at once making doubt explicit and typically resolving it, Hitchcock's films call into question Cavell's assumption that the portrayal of romance in popular American cinema and in Hitchcock's films, in particular, dramatizes "the truth of skepticism."

In suggesting that Hitchcock's films provide a counterexample to the claims made by Cavell, I hope to establish the broader point that Cavell's interpretations of the works of popular culture fail to provide "evidence" for the truth of his philosophy and, insofar as the truth of his philosophy depends on the interpretation of texts, that truth is open to question. Of course, I do not expect Cavell or his followers to be persuaded by the putative counterexample to his philosophy provided by Hitchcock's films. For it seems to me that Cavell's assumption that "the truth of skepticism" is portrayed in the vicissitudes of romance is probably an intellectual presupposition of the kind that Ludwig Wittgenstein after Goethe called an *Urphänomen*, "a preconceived idea that takes possession of us."[3] By captivating the mind of the person who adopts it, the *Urphänomen* is claimed to underlie all phenomena, regardless of anything that might count as evidence against it. Cavell implicitly presupposes that the explicit representation of doubt and its resolution in texts, such as those of Hitchcock, are secondary to the radical doubt or "the truth of skepticism" that he perceives to underlie the human condition and that is dramatized in the romance. In this sense, citing Hitchcock's treatment of doubt in romance as a counterexample to Cavell's philosophy will do nothing to dislodge the conviction of Cavell and his followers in the truth of that philosophy. However, the grounds for the truth of Cavell's philosophy cannot be convincingly based on the interpretation of texts, despite the appearance of "evidence" that his discussions of texts seem to provide, if nothing could qualify as a counterexample to those interpretations.

I. CAVELL, SKEPTICISM, AND ROMANCE

Cavell writes that skepticism "is a place, perhaps the central secular place, in which the human wish to deny the condition of human existence is expressed."[4] By skepticism, he means the familiar philosophical argument that "we can never know with certainty of the existence of something; call it the external world, and call it other minds."[5] What is "the condition of human existence" that human beings wish to deny and why do they wish to deny it? Broadly speaking, by "the condition of human existence" Cavell seems to mean human mortality or "finitude." The wish or impulse to deny human mortality seems to arise out of the very fact that

to be human is to be aware of one's mortality. For it seems, for Cavell, that human beings are inevitably drawn to conceive of their embodied nature as a constraint or limitation that they seek to overcome or deny. Skepticism, for Cavell, is thus an expression of this wish to transcend our mortal coil. Why? The skeptic claims that human beings possess a seemingly direct, unmediated, and therefore indubitable awareness of our own sensations, thoughts, and feelings. By comparison, the external world is known only through our perception of it. Since in any given case we may be deceived about what it is that we perceive—for example, we may wrongly infer that the stick that appears bent in the water really is bent—how can we be sure that the external world exists? Furthermore, since the sensations, thoughts, and feelings of another can be inferred only through our perception of what he or she does and says, the existence of these sensations, thoughts, and feelings is also subject to doubt. If we can mistakenly infer that someone is in pain when they are not, how can we even be sure that his or her behavior is expressive of something called a mind? Thus it seems that, for the skeptic, the condition of human embodiment that makes possible our orientation in the world and interaction with others is experienced as a limitation or constraint that would have to be transcended in order to achieve certainty. Thus, for Cavell, skepticism expresses human beings' inability to transcend their condition of embodiment. Since awareness of embodiment as a constraint is a condition of being human, skepticism, for Cavell, is itself an inevitable consequence of the human condition. In this sense, Cavell is a skeptic.

However, what the skeptic overlooks in his or her pursuit of certainty is the manner that human expressive behavior in general and the skeptic's expressive behavior in particular are embedded in human community. For Cavell, what makes someone's behavior *pain* behavior, as opposed to, say, the expression of pleasure or an empty gesture, is the fact that other people recognize and respond to that behavior as providing criteria for the existence of pain, for example, by expressing sympathy. Cavell calls this recognition or response "acknowledgment." Acknowledgment is a form of attunement with others and characterizes the way we exist with others in the world in a manner that is not based on knowing. The skeptic thus seeks to replace the only relationship to the world and to others that is available to him or her—attunement with the behavior of others that recognizes or acknowledges that behavior as human behavior or as expressive of mind—with something else, namely, certainty. By seeking certainty in the existence of the other and thereby coming to doubt that existence, the skeptic withholds his or her response to the other; he or she refuses to acknowledge, for example, pain behavior as expressive. Skeptical doubt thus expresses a failure of acknowledgment.

To withhold, or hedge, our concepts of psychological states from a given creature on the ground that our criteria cannot reach to the inner life of the creature, is specifically to withhold the source of my idea that living beings are things that feel; it is to withhold myself, to reject my response to anything as a living being: to blank so much as my idea of anything as *having a body.*[6]

There is not only confusion but also a tragic pathos in the skeptic's position. The skeptic seeks certainty in the existence of the other in order to affirm his or her own membership in the human community. However, by repudiating the idea that the behavior of others is expressive behavior, the skeptic repudiates the conditions of his or her own existence in the world with others that depends on the acknowledgment by others of his or her own behavior as expressive behavior. For it is only through responding to the behavior of others as expressive behavior, for example, by sympathizing with someone who is in pain, that I call on my own behavior to be affirmed as my behavior, as expressive of my self. By withholding his or her response to the other, the skeptic renders himself or herself unknown to and isolated from the other. The skeptic thus ends up tragically misrecognizing the condition of human finitude, one that is shared with others, as a condition of isolation or of expressive silence. In so doing, the skeptic creates the very conditions of existence that he or she purported to derive from reflection on those conditions of existence. Yet, at the same time, it is this very fact that allows the conclusion of the skeptic to be contested. For the skeptic can be brought back from his

or her condition of skeptical isolation through the acknowledgment that his or her response to the human condition, however extreme, is nonetheless a human response, that the skeptic's behavior, too, may be acknowledged as human behavior.

For Cavell, the drama of skeptical denial and acknowledgment is played out most intensely in the relationship between an individual and a privileged other, in particular (though by no means exclusively) the other privileged in a romantic relationship, exemplars of which Cavell discovers in the works of Shakespeare and popular culture alike. The reason that Cavell focuses on this privileged other in his philosophy is that if I am inclined to disavow attributing minds to human beings and hence to disavow their humanity (their autonomy from me) and hence my humanity (my autonomy from them), the best case for testing my theory would be "a given other who exemplifies all others for me, humanity as such."[7] This best case then becomes at once for the skeptic the occasion for the rejection of the humanity of the other—their autonomy and uniqueness—through their metaphorical or literal annihilation (which reciprocally entails the annihilation of the self), as in Shakespeare's tragedies such as *Othello*, and, at the same time, an occasion for the most forceful and articulate assertion of human possibility and renewal through the creation of a relationship between equals, as in the cinematic genre Cavell identifies as Comedies of Remarriage.

Cavell characterizes the Comedy of Remarriage in terms of a founding myth in which "[a] running quarrel is forcing apart a pair who recognize themselves as having known one another forever, that is from the beginning, not just in the past but in a period before there was a past, before history."[8] They discover sexuality at the same time as they enter the social world, which is a complementary discovery marked by marriage "as if the sexual and social are to legitimize one another." But there is trouble in the paradise of marriage: "call it its impotence to domesticate sexuality without discouraging it, or its stupidity in the face of the riddle of intimacy." Disappointment engenders a desire for revenge in which the woman leaves the man for a simpler soul who is a father substitute. Archetypically, Cary Grant is traded for Ralph

Bellamy. "The man must counter by showing that he has survived his yielding and by finding a way to enter a claim," and he does this by allowing that he is not in complete control, that "he is able to wish, and consequently to make a fool of himself." This enables the woman to reawaken her desire and accept the man once again, thereby renewing the human conversation and the society it stands for. Skeptical doubt is thus at once experienced—yielding a sense of separateness that degenerates into isolation—but it is at the same time overcome because the condition of human separateness comes to be accepted and accommodated through mutual affirmation or acknowledgment.

As this brief discussion of Cavell's philosophy of skepticism suggests, not only is his conception of skepticism distinctive in its conclusion that our basic relationship to the world is not one of knowing, but it is distinctive in the way he privileges what analytical philosophers call "other minds skepticism" over skepticism about the external world in his formulation of the role in which skepticism plays in human life. This emphasis in part stems from his focus on the role of behavioral criteria in establishing the terms on which we can acknowledge or fail to acknowledge the mental state of another. But Cavell also argues that, in a key sense, skepticism about other minds is central to explaining skepticism about the external world because it allows us to understand the way skepticism about the external world involves a failure to acknowledge the world's claim on us, a failure to open ourselves to what it expresses in a manner that is akin to the failure of one human being to acknowledge another. This is not the place to examine Cavell's romantic conception of self-world relations in detail; rather, I simply want to point out the implications of the explanatory privilege given to self-other relationships in Cavell's understanding of skepticism. For this privilege is what, in part, enables Cavell to focus on, as it were, the human dimensions of the skeptical drama, that is, the question of the recognition and denial of the humanity of the other, rather than the more recognizable themes of philosophical skepticism that revolve around the grounds for believing the evidence that is given to our senses.

I have described how skepticism, for Cavell, at once informs and is contested in human relationships; but what explains the skeptical impulse to deny the condition of human existence, what are the origins of this impulse? Although Cavell admits that "there is no (single) motive" underlying "the human denial of the conditions of humanity," he requires a quite general explanation to support his theory.[9] This general explanation seems to be provided by psychoanalysis. Although Cavell never systematically outlines his debt to Freud, a psychoanalytic characterization of human motivation informs his work. Cavell's interpretation of Freud suggests that the impulse toward skepticism is essentially an unconscious one that stems from imaginary conditions of infantile omnipotence and the relationship that this condition bears to the onset of sexual desire as the drive to attach oneself to something that is irretrievably lost. This fantasy of imaginary identity with and hence certitude in the other and the world, from which the subject has fallen, produces a denial of difference and otherness that leaves the subject fixated in a solipsistic isolation. For Freud, and hence for Cavell, the vicissitudes of (hetero)sexual desire engenders the central, most expressive, figuration of this sense of loss, and the place where that sense of loss is dramatized in ways that are different for men and women. But romance is also, for Cavell, the central place where the relationship of love between human beings is nurtured. Romance is where that loss can be most fully acknowledged, reconciled, and domesticated or made ordinary. The relationship of love is essentially therapeutic, as the Comedies of Remarriage suggest, for it is the place where human isolation is redeemed and made livable because it is acknowledged as a condition that is shared. "Sexuality," Cavell writes, "is the field in which the fantasy of finitude, of its acceptance and its repetitious overcoming, is worked out; the way human separateness is turned equally toward splendor and toward horror, mixing beauty and ugliness."[10]

The idea of skepticism as issuing from an unconscious impulse to deny the condition of the human provides the universal explanation of why human beings' relationships to others and to the world is not one of knowing with certainty, where the paradigm of certainty is the fantasy of the absolute presence of the other to the self that psychoanalysis accords the imaginarily omnipotent infant. Everyday certainty pales by comparison to this kind of certainty, which is perhaps why Cavell sometimes writes not that our relationship to the world is not one of knowledge in the form of certainty but that "certainty is not enough."[11] But Cavell's interpretation of psychoanalysis not only yields the kind of universal explanation of the impulse to skepticism that Cavell requires, it also provides a genetic explanation for why other minds skepticism should take privilege over external world skepticism in the explanation of skepticism and for the priority thus accorded to the idea of acknowledgment. For in psychoanalytic theory, the genesis of the relationship that the infant bears to the external world in general lies in the relationship that the infant bears to his or her mother, that is, to his or her real and imaginary presences and absences. The sense of "externality" from the infant that is accorded the "external" world results from the failure, from the perspective of the infant, of his or her needs being fully met. Maturity requires the "acknowledgment" of the externality of the external world, of its claims on me, just us it requires acknowledgment that the significant other, for which the mother provides the paradigm, is external from me, that is, an autonomous human being.

Psychoanalysis also plays an implicit role in Cavell's diagnosis of the gender-based asymmetry of skepticism. For Cavell, in Shakespeare's *A Winter's Tale*, Leontes emotionally withdraws from Hermione on account of his anxiety about the paternity of her child, which is also an anxiety about his potency, his capacity to satisfy her. Since Hermione is immune from this kind of doubt she is punished for her immunity. Conversely, Cavell discovers in certain Hollywood melodramas, in particular, in *Letter from an Unknown Woman* (Max Ophuls, 1948), a different, female form of skepticism that concerns doubt over the identity of the father of one's child and manifests itself in the obsessive desire of the woman to be loved by the father of her child or the man she would like to be the father, which is accompanied by corrosive self-doubt about her own worthiness. The origins of both kinds of doubt can be traced to the fantasy of castration as it is described by psychoanalysis. In the perception of sexual difference, the fantasy of wholeness and its loss is projected on and dramatized in the heterosexual

relationship with asymmetrical consequences. The boy is led to fear the woman's difference, her apparent incompleteness due to a lack of a penis, and compensates by idealizing or effacing her, rather than acknowledging her difference and with it his own potential incompleteness. The girl is led to seek compensation for her apparent lack and/or incompleteness by idolizing the male and seeking the gift of his baby, rather than embracing and accepting her own finitude. Thus the original skepticism that is derived from the child's fantasy of omnipotence comes to have a male and female inflection.[12]

This is not the place to enter into an assessment of Freud's theory. Regardless of its truth, psychoanalysis provides a picture of the human condition that supports Cavell's conception of the role of skepticism in human life as well as his account of the gender asymmetry of skepticism. But Freud scarcely supports Cavell's picture of the therapeutic role of love. What is the source of Cavell's countervailing picture to that of human skepticism, the picture of human relatedness exemplified in the relationship of marriage? As Stephen Mulhall has pointed out, there is a close parallel between the relationship to God as it is conceived by Christians and Cavell's ideal conception of marriage.

In Christian thought, our unending sequence of particular sinful acts reveals that human beings are possessed of a nature which disposes them to sin and prevents them from escaping their bondage by using their own resources; what they need to attain their new nature is a fully acknowledged relationship with a particular person—one through whose words divine grace is made accessible, one who exemplifies the further, unattained but attainable human state to which God wishes to attract every individual, whilst respecting her freedom to deny its attractions and spurn his grace. In Cavellian thought, the unending sequence of specific manifestations of skepticism in modernity reveals that human beings are possessed of a nature in which the skeptical impulse is ineradicably inscribed; what is needed if it is to be combated is a fully acknowledged relationship with a particular human other—one whose words have the power of making us ashamed of our present frozen and fixated state, one who, by exemplifying a further attainable state of the self, attracts us to it whilst respecting our autonomy.[13]

Cavell suggests that Descartes in his philosophy sought to recover from the threat of skepticism, in particular, from the thought that he may be utterly alone, by proving the existence of God: "It follows that if that proof is not, or is no longer, credible to us—as it has not been credible in respectable philosophy since its apparent annihilation in Hume's *Dialogues on Natural Religion* and in Kant's *Critique of Pure Reason*—then the question of metaphysical isolation is in principle torn open."[14] Skepticism is thus a standing threat to human beings not simply because of the presence of human sexuality and the skeptical fantasies it engenders, but because those skeptical fantasies are no longer assuaged by the concept of original sin that opens a way to the relationship with God that would compensate for secular, skeptical disappointment. In a world that no longer has a relationship with God to combat the human sense of metaphysical isolation, the skeptical impulse comes to the fore with a renewed force in a manner that is diagnosed by psychoanalysis but also represented by it. After all, for Freud, religion itself was a species of illusion. The distinctive contribution of Cavell's philosophy is to rekindle the redemptive aspect of religion in the wake of Freud's diagnosis of skepticism by reclaiming the romantic origins of psychoanalytic thought: the idea that, rather than form the nucleus of skepticism, childlike intimations of immortality can be redeemed in everyday interactions with people and things if we are sufficiently alive to them and the claims they make upon us. Speaking of Wordsworth's "vision splendid" that "fades into the light of common day," Cavell writes that "Wordsworth's construction is to replace the ordinary in the light in which we live it, with its shades of the prison-house closing upon us young, and its custom lying upon us deep almost as life, a world of death, to which we are dead—replace it accordingly with freedom ('heaven-born freedom'); and with lively origination, or say birth; with interest."[15]

II. HITCHCOCK, KNOWLEDGE, AND ROMANCE

Hitchcock's stylistically self-conscious body of work ranges from buoyant, optimistic, romantic thrillers such as *The 39 Steps* (1935), *Young and Innocent* (1937), *To Catch a Thief* (1955), and *North By Northwest*, to dark, even pessimistic, works such a *Shadow of a Doubt* (1943), *Vertigo* (1958), and *Psycho*. Generations of critics have wrestled with the apparently contradictory nature of Hitchcock's achievement. Some, like Lesley Brill, have argued that Hitchcock's vision is essentially comic, that his preoccupation with artifice and masquerade contribute to a fairytale-like atmosphere in his works in which flawed human beings are redeemed by the "miracle" of romance.[16] Others have elaborated on the "therapeutic" nature of Hitchcock's romances. For example, Cavell himself has analyzed *North by Northwest* as an exemplification of the Comedy of Remarriage.[17] Eve Kendall (Eva Marie Saint) and Roger Thornhill (Cary Grant) are not married, but their encounter on the Twentieth Century Limited secures the foundational myth of the marriage (it functions as their honeymoon). Eve's subsequent duplicity literally threatens Thornhill's life. Yet Thornhill miraculously survives this radical statement of what Cavell would understand as the heroine's skeptical withdrawal from him and, through his survival, is transformed into an agent who can redeem Eve and foster her rebirth. Paula Marantz Cohen has discerned in the films of the mature Hitchcock a species of gender revisionism in which an emotionally detached male character is forced to confront his feminine side through his encounter with the woman. For example, in *Rear Window* (1954), L. B. Jeffries (James Stewart), an emotionally distant bachelor who takes satisfaction in voyeuristically spying on his neighbors, is forced, by dint of witnessing a man—Lars Thorwald (Raymond Burr)—murder his wife, to confront his own feelings toward and relationship with Lisa Freemont (Grace Kelly).[18] Although Cohen does not refer to Cavell, it is relevant in this context that Thorwald takes his name from Torvald, the hero of Ibsen's play, *The Doll's House*, which in turn provides a model for Cavell's "Melodrama of the Unknown Woman" in which a woman finds her identity by leaving her man. In *Rear Window*, this solution is avoided by, as it were, sacrificing Mrs. Thorwald to Mr. Thorwald so that Jeffries can witness the injustice and so foster a recognition and appreciation of the female by the male.

At the same time, romance in Hitchcock's films is plagued by duplicity, deceit, and deception. Here, Hitchcock's emphasis on artifice and masquerade seems to undermine rather than support the establishment of romance, as if the fictiveness of romance exposed it as a species of illusion, a façade. Many of Hitchcock's films, for example, *The Lodger* (1926), *Rebecca* (1939), *Suspicion* (1941), *Shadow of a Doubt*, and *Psycho*, turn on the question: "How do I know that the man I love is not a murderer?"[19] Many others, such as *Notorious* (1946), *Vertigo*, and *North by Northwest*, turn on the question: "How do I know that the woman I love is not a whore?" Pervasive doubt about the motivation of the hero in Hitchcock's work is sustained through narrative ambiguity combined with visual metaphor and expressionism that to a greater or lesser extent provides evidence for the spectator to share the doubt that is entertained by the heroine as to the intentions of the hero, or to counter the apparent certainty that the heroine expresses in the hero's innocence. The story of Hitchcock's film *Suspicion* centers on the question of whether the man to whom the heroine is married intends to murder her, and Hitchcock invites the audience to share the suspicions of the heroine. In *The Lodger*, the behavior of the Lodger (Ivor Novello) causes us to suspect he is a Jack the Ripper, called the Avenger in the film, and this suspicion is reinforced by the numerous visual touches that suggest that he may have nefarious designs on the heroine, Daisy (June), despite her steadfast belief in his innocence.

The classic Hitchcock formula to which many, though not all, his films conform is the wrong (or wronged) man narrative in which the hero of the romance is mistaken as a killer. There is also, less frequently, the wrong (or wronged) woman narrative in which the heroine of the romance is sometimes mistaken as a whore. Sometimes the two narratives combine, as in *North by Northwest*. But the wrong man (or woman) formula creates a narrative situation in which the romance is often forged from circumstances of deception or doubt, and it does not emerge unscathed from the circumstances in which it is forged. Hitchcock's films can be broadly divided into three groups. There are those works in which the hero's innocence is transparent from the beginning, though not

always to the heroine. This is the classic formula of the romantic thriller that Hitchcock perfected in his British sound films, such as *39 Steps*, and returned to in *North by Northwest*. There are those films in which the figure of the murderer emerges from his gentlemanly disguise, and redemption through romance is precluded, such as in *Psycho* and *Frenzy* (1972). However, the majority of works lie in between. They retain a fundamentally ambivalent attitude toward the romance, either through narrative and stylistic ambiguity, such as in *The Lodger*, *Suspicion*, *The Birds* (1963), and *Marnie* (1964), or by strategies of a narrative doubling that color the protagonist with the qualities of his or her alter ego or render the comparison an unfavorable one to the hero or heroine, such as in *Rebecca*, *Shadow of a Doubt*, *Notorious*, *Strangers on a Train*, or *Rear Window*. In this way, politically sensitive critics such as Robin Wood have suggested that Hitchcock's films subvert the ideology of romance they ostensibly adhere to.[20]

Clearly, there is in Hitchcock's works a pervasive thematic relationship established between the threat to romance and the ability of the protagonists of his films to discriminate the motivations of another on the basis of what they see. But does this thematic link between romance and doubt support a Cavellian interpretation of Hitchcock? That is, to pose the argument simply, is it plausible to conceive the success of romance in Hitchcock as an exemplification of attunement with others in a manner that is not based on knowing or, alternatively, to conceive the failure of romance as the triumph of skepticism? There is a further aspect of Hitchcock's films that seems to align them with Cavell's philosophy. This is the role of faith in cementing the romance in Hitchcock's work, a faith that seems to fly in the face of rational grounds for doubt. As Lesley Brill has written of Constance Peterson (Ingrid Bergman), the heroine of one of Hitchcock's most romantic films, *Spellbound* (1945):

She maintains her belief [in the hero] in the face of assurances to the contrary from all her colleagues, the police, the courts, and even her old teacher and emotional father Brulov. Love, as usual in Hitchcock movies, sees deeper than the most brilliant empiricism....Constance's first name underlines the importance of her unflagging faith in her lover's innocence; her second name, Peterson, may contain a faint biblical allusion with similar reference to faith and grace.[21]

Romance in Hitchcock embodies a secularized version of faith that is the residue of Hitchcock's Catholicism and, often, as in *Spellbound*, this faith informs the "therapeutic" aspect of the romance.[22]

Conversely, where the miracle of romance is made impossible, faith itself is corrupted or betrayed. In *Shadow of a Doubt*, the heroine, Young Charlie (Teresa Wright), yearns to transcend the banal, stifling world of ordinary small-town Santa Rosa by "magically" summoning her legendary larger-than-life uncle who represents all the romantic possibilities her youthful imagination can conjure up. To all appearances, Uncle Charlie (Joseph Cotton) is the perfect gentleman, but his gentlemanliness turns out to be a dandified surface that conceals a corrupted core. Although he is officially proved to be innocent of the crimes he was suspected of, Young Charlie, because of her spiritual proximity to Uncle Charlie, discovers the truth about him. The ring he has given her that seals their incestuous-romantic union is inscribed with initials that reveal its origins. It was placed on the dead finger of a murdered widow before it was placed on her own. Although Young Charlie has developed a romantic involvement with the cop who is pursuing the Merry Widow Murderer, the relationship pales by comparison, the world of the ordinary has lost its enchantment. In *Vertigo*, the hero, Scottie Ferguson (James Stewart), trusting the evidence of his senses, is drawn to fall in love with an illusion—Judy Barton playing Madeleine, the wife of Gavin Elster, possessed by her ancestor, Carlotta Valdes (Kim Novak). But once the deceit is exposed, and Scottie survives his breakdown, the promise of romance is still tantalizingly possible when he "magically" reencounters Judy. Provided that Scottie still believes in his fiction and does not insist on finding out who Judy really is, the ordinary can become reenchanted, as it is for a moment in the seedy hotel room when the newly reformed couple make love. But Scottie tragically persists in knowing for certain, and because he persists in knowing for certain, the

possibility of romance is shattered, and he ends up, in effect, killing the thing that he loves.

However, the "faith" that is portrayed and sometimes betrayed in Hitchcock's films is not something that is opposed to or acts in place of knowledge. On the contrary, what justifies faith in Hitchcock or leads to disenchantment is precisely that a character arrives at a condition of knowledge. The role of faith in Hitchcock's films is not confirmation of an underlying skepticism that can be expressed in the formula that our basic relationship to the world is not one of knowing. Though it may sometimes be blind, faith characteristically enables knowledge to be attained. Constance Peterson in *Spellbound* certainly manifests a faith in John Ballantyne (Gregory Peck) that flies in the face of all evidence, but it is also a faith that leads her to mobilize all her formidable professional skills to solve the riddle of who committed the murder of which Ballantyne has been accused, and confront the true killer. Even when faith is shattered by knowledge, it is faith that makes knowledge possible. In *Shadow of a Doubt*, when Charlie does indeed discover the evil nature of Uncle Charlie, it is only the special relationship that she has attained with Uncle Charlie that makes her subsequent knowledge possible. Faith is a different thing from ordinary knowledge in Hitchcock because it involves a particular kind of sympathy toward or attunement with the other. But this kind of attunement with another is not, pace Cavell, something that replaces a knowledge that is always subject to doubt, rather, it is a capacity for attachment that, though it may blind us, can also lead us to penetrate the veil of appearance and reveal the deeper truths about human motivation—truths about the human capacity for good or the human capacity for evil. Hitchcock, although he is, like Cavell, preoccupied with doubt and deception, is thus not, like Cavell, a skeptic. Hitchcock's secular version of faith does not play the Cavellian role of acknowledgment; it is not a solution or response to skepticism.

Hitchcock's films are also informed by the gender asymmetry diagnosed by Cavell as different forms of skepticism. Hitchcock's films are populated with male characters that William Rothman refers to as Hitchcock's "Wrong Ones," who are portrayed as dandies and rogues.[23] These are characters who are unable to love. Uncle Charlie in *Shadow of a Doubt* believes that the world is an illusion, and this betrays his difference from Young Charlie, who seeks an emotional connection to the others rather than a withdrawal from the world: "You're a sleepwalker. Blind. How do you know what the world is like? Do you know that the world is a foul sty? Do you know that if you rip the fronts off houses you'd find swine?" His disenchanted view of the world finds its realization or expression in his revulsion toward women, "horrible, fat, faded, greedy women." The philosophy of *Psycho*'s Norman Bates, another killer of women, is that "we're all in our private traps, clamped in them. And none of us can ever get out. We scratch and claw, but only at the air, only at each other. And for all of it we never budge an inch." He seems to personify Cavell's idea of the madman as skeptic or the skeptic as madman. These dark characters have their echoes in the Hitchcock hero—personified, in their different ways, by James Stewart and Cary Grant—who must overcome a certain emotional isolation or detachment to secure a romantic partnership with a woman.

In Cavell's philosophy, the opposite of the man who is emotionally withdrawn from and hence hostile to the world is the woman who loves too much, who exhibits a blind faith in her relationships to others. She is the subject of Hitchcock's gothic melodramas, such as *Rebecca* and *Suspicion*, and in a less formulaic way, *Shadow of a Doubt*. In these female-centered narratives, it is woman's faith in the man's virtue that sustains the romance in the face of evidence that points to the contrary, though it is possible, too, that faith is merely wish fulfillment. Joan Fontaine, in *Rebecca* and *Suspicion*, plays a heroine paralyzed by insecurity and self-doubt who is swept off her feet by the man of her dreams to a home away from home. The question at stake in both films is whether her anxieties about her new husband are products of self-doubt or whether in fact she has good grounds to worry about his motivations and intentions. In *Rebecca*, her anxieties are in part justified, though because of self-doubt she misunderstands their source. Maxim (Laurence Olivier), her husband, did not love Rebecca, he hated her and as a consequence killed her. In *Suspicion*, Fontaine's character worries that her husband wishes to murder her. In part her doubts are justified but in part they are

not, in a manner that leaves it undecidable, in the end, whether she redeems the hero through her faith in him or whether she will die for love, as she does in the novel by Francis Iles (Anthony Berkeley), *Before the Fact*, from which Hitchcock's film was adapted.[24]

As we have seen, Cavell uses the term 'skepticism' to describe the isolation from or over-identification with the other that defines these characteristically male and female responses, where "skepticism" is interpreted as a failure of "acknowledgment," a failure to attain a realistic sense of shared finitude that issues from a deluded quest for certainty. But as I have suggested, Hitchcock, though he is preoccupied with doubt and deception, is not a skeptic. It is thus misleading to interpret the vicissitudes of faith as a manifestation of the skeptical impulse. In the case of the woman who loves too much, her attachment to her husband is a prelude to or makes possible knowledge, even as she struggles against self-doubt and self-delusion. *Suspicion* leaves the heroine's recognition unresolved, but in both *Rebecca* and *Shadow of a Doubt*, as I have already suggested, the heroine achieves knowledge. Furthermore, it is a knowledge that is all the more profound because it results from a struggle to wrest the truth from a perception of the world as the heroine would wish it to be.[25] The relationship between faith and knowledge that characterizes female characters in Hitchcock's films contrasts with that of male characters. Uncle Charlie is a misanthrope; he lacks faith and the capacity for love. Even the more noble male characters in Hitchcock suffer from a lack of faith, from sour grapes that infect their capacity to sympathize with another. For example, Devlin (Cary Grant), in *Notorious*, allows his jealousy and resentment of Alicia Huberman (Ingrid Bergman), who plays the role of the wronged woman, to contaminate his feelings toward her and jeopardize their relationship. This lack of sympathy for the other tends to render the male (as opposed to the female) quest for knowledge coercive, because it arises not from a predisposition to sympathize with the other but out of self-interest. The coercive effects of knowledge are especially apparent in those films where the hero is a cop, or self-appointed detective, investigating a woman, as in *Blackmail* (1929), *Vertigo*, or *Marnie*, or where he is seeking to unmask the figure of the dandy or rogue, as in *Murder!* (1930) or *Notorious*.

Hitchcock's films thus resonate with a number of Cavellian themes: the link between the theme of doubt and romance; the idea of love as a secular form of faith and its impact on knowledge; and the asymmetry between male and female in their capacities for attunement with the other. His films thus seem to provide an ideal test case for Cavell's view of the relationship between skepticism and romance. However, as I have argued, Hitchcock's treatment of these themes cannot be satisfactorily accommodated within the framework of Cavell's philosophy because Hitchcock, unlike Cavell, is not a skeptic. Although in Hitchcock's cinema, doubt, duplicity, and deception infect human relationships, Hitchcock's films do not demonstrate the "truth of skepticism." On the contrary, often there is a point at which the protagonist of a Hitchcock film and the spectator alongside him or her arrives at a state of certainty that may support either the affirmation of romance or disillusionment with it. The affirmation of romance or romantic disillusionment in Hitchcock's works does not mean that the characters have learned to live with their skepticism or succumbed to it, but that doubt or uncertainty has been overcome. In conformity with the method of Cavell's own philosophy that uses texts as confirmation or evidence of the philosophical propositions he wishes to make, I thus propose Hitchcock's films as a counterexample to the claim made by Cavell's philosophy about "the truth of skepticism" and the role played by this purported truth in the enactment of romance. The dramatization of doubt, faith, and romance in Hitchcock's work encourages us to view the claims of Cavell's philosophy and the method he uses to support those claims with a skeptical eye.[26]

RICHARD ALLEN
Department of Cinema Studies
New York University
New York, NY 10003
USA

INTERNET: richard.allen@nyu.edu

1. Cavell's disciple William Rothman has offered what he understands to be a Cavellian interpretation of Hitchcock in his book *Hitchcock: The Murderous Gaze* (Harvard University Press, 1982). However, Rothman uses the inspiration of Cavell not to reflect on the relationship between doubt and romance in Hitchcock's work, but on the idea of authorship in film. Thus I will not be addressing Rothman's interpretation of Hitchcock in this essay.

2. Stanley Cavell, *The Claim of Reason: Wittgenstein, Skepticism, Morality and Tragedy* (New York: Oxford University Press, 1979), p. 7.

3. Ludwig Wittgenstein, *Remarks on Color*, ed. G. E. M. Anscombe (University of California Press, 1977), pt. 3, § 230. Cavell's ideas are also characterized in these terms by Malcolm Turvey in "Is Scepticism a 'Natural Possibility' of Language?: Reasons to be Sceptical of Cavell's Wittgenstein," in *Wittgenstein, Theory and the Arts*, ed. Richard Allen and Malcolm Turvey (London: Routledge, 2001), p. 118.

4. Stanley Cavell, *In Quest of the Ordinary: Lines of Skepticism and Romanticism* (University of Chicago Press, 1988), p. 5.

5. Cavell, *The Claim of Reason*, p. 37.

6. Cavell, *The Claim of Reason*, p. 83.

7. Cavell, *The Claim of Reason*, p. 430.

8. Stanley Cavell, *Pursuits of Happiness: The Hollywood Comedy of Remarriage* (Harvard University Press, 1981), p. 31. The remaining quotations in this paragraph follow on pp. 31–32.

9. Cavell, *In Quest of the Ordinary*, p. 57.

10. Cavell, *The Claim of Reason*, p. 492.

11. Stanley Cavell, "Knowing and Acknowledging," in *Must We Mean What We Say?* (New York: Cambridge University Press, 1976), p. 258.

12. This paragraph is indebted to Stephen Mulhall, *Stanley Cavell, Philosophy's Recounting of the Ordinary* (Oxford: Clarendon Press, 1994), pp. 204–206. Cavell's conception of gender here is an essentialist one. Even though Mulhall argues that one could conceive male and female skepticism as different inflections of the human character, heterosexuality is still assumed.

13. Mulhall, *Stanley Cavell*, pp. 292–293.

14. Cavell, *In Quest of the Ordinary*, p. 186.

15. Cavell, *In Quest of the Ordinary*, p. 75.

16. Lesley Brill, *The Hitchcock Romance: Love and Irony in Hitchcock's Films* (Princeton University Press, 1988).

17. Stanley Cavell, "North By Northwest," in *Themes Out of School: Effects and Causes* (San Francisco: North Point Press, 1984), pp. 152–172.

18. Paula Marantz Cohen, *Hitchcock: The Legacy of Victorianism* (University of Kentucky Press, 1995), pp. 99–113.

19. The idea presented in Hitchcock's films that men are incipient murderers of women and women are incipient "whores" has led feminist critics to conclude that his films are either implicated in or about male misogyny (or perhaps both). See, in particular, Tania Modleski, *The Women Who Knew Too Much: Hitchcock and Feminist Theory* (New York: Routledge, 1988).

20. Robin Wood's *Hitchcock's Films Revisited* (Columbia University Press, 1989) in fact combines two contrasting interpretations of Hitchcock in one study: his early "therapeutic" view of Hitchcock first published in 1965 and his later reassessment of the director's work and, implicitly, his

own early critical writings on it, from the standpoint of Marxism and feminism.

21. Lesley Brill, *The Hitchcock Romance*, p. 279.

22. I thank Rahul Hamid for the idea of "secular Catholicism" in an unpublished paper entitled "Hitchcock as a Catholic Director."

23. Rothman, *Hitchcock: The Murderous Gaze*, p. 53.

24. Francis Iles, *Before the Fact* (London: Gollancz, 1932).

25. The role of deception and doubt in *Rebecca* is explored by Robert J. Yanal in "Rebecca's Deceivers," *Philosophy and Literature* 24 (2000): 67–82.

26. I am grateful to Malcolm Turvey for his penetrating criticisms of an early draft of this essay, and to the editors for their comments on the manuscript.

LESTER H. HUNT

The Paradox of the Unknown Lover: A Reading of *Letter from an Unknown Woman*

Let man fear woman when she loves: then she makes any sacrifice and everything else seems without value to her.

Friedrich Nietzsche, *Thus Spoke Zarathustra*

I

I think I can assume that it long ago became unnecessary to defend the Max Ophuls and Howard Koch film *Letter from an Unknown Woman* (Universal-International, 1948) against the impression that it is merely a well-wrought specimen of some Hollywood genre or other, such as "women's picture" or melodrama. Robin Wood and George Wilson have shown that though this remarkable work conforms (at least superficially) to certain genre requirements, there is a good deal more to it than that.[1] Stanley Cavell has gone so far as to name a new genre after it.[2] Still, though the film itself no longer requires defenders, I do see a need to come to the defense of its principal character. If *Letter* were simply a typical "women's picture," this would imply that it aims at a very strong sort of audience identification with the character of its protagonist, Lisa Berndle (Joan Fontaine). In the course of arguing for an interpretation of the film as transcending its origins as a genre film, Wilson points out various ways in which the film is actually critical of Lisa's position. He claims that the point of view of the film is that Lisa's view of Stefan Brand (Louis Jourdan) is "deluded," that it is based on "an hallucination of the actual man." If it is true that Stefan, as the title of the film suggests, does

not know Lisa, it is also true, according to Wilson, that she does not know him. The conception of love embodied in the film, he argues, is Stendhal's crystallization theory, according to which love by nature attributes nonexistent perfections to the love-object.[3] It seems to me that, as marvelously insightful as Wilson's discussion of *Letter* is in other respects, on this particular point he comes very close to standing the truth on its head. What I will do here is offer an interpretation of the film that is much more favorable to Lisa. In so doing, I will also be arguing that the film comes much closer to fulfilling the above-mentioned genre requirement—audience identification with the female protagonist—but that it is no less interesting for that.

First, I should say a few words about the structure of the film to serve as a frame of reference for what follows. Though early reviews found *Letter*'s flashback structure "a bit difficult to follow at times," its temporal shape is actually very clear-cut.[4] It begins and ends with short narrative sequences that take place in the present (that is, circa 1900), in Vienna. I will call these two sequences the Prologue and Epilogue. In the Prologue, a dark carriage draws up to Stefan Brand's apartment. We learn that Stefan, who is coming home at two in the morning, has an appointment at dawn, a duel with an indignant husband. It is an appointment he has no intention of keeping. He finds that a thick letter has come for him while he was out, a letter from Lisa, whom Stefan does not at first remember. She is, as we eventually find out, the wife of the indignant husband about whom we have already heard. Stefan begins to read the letter. In the Epilogue, the letter's consequences, at once redemptive and horrible, are revealed to us and the dark carriage pulls out again, bringing the events full circle.

Between these two sequences in the present come several other sequences depicting Lisa's life at various times in the past as Stefan reads about them in her letter. The first, which takes place at least fourteen years ago, depicts some of Lisa's first encounters with Stefan in her childhood and adolescence. This material, together with an episode depicting Lisa after she and her mother have moved from Vienna to Linz, I will call Act I. Act II, set ten years before, depicts Lisa's second encounter with Stefan and its immediate consequences (mainly, the birth of their son) when she was a young model in Vienna. Act III, set at least two days before, when Lisa was a wife and mother (the mother of Stefan's child, though the wife of another man), depicts Lisa's catastrophic encounter with Stefan at the opera, together with antecedent and consequent events. The joints between each of these sequences (including the joint between the episode in Linz and the rest of Act I) are bridged by shots in the present, showing Stefan reading the letter or viewing enclosed photographs. These are essentially elaborate reaction shots, showing Stefan's pity, regret, and horror as he views the world disclosed by Lisa's letter.

In the next two sections of this essay, I will collect various apparently meaning-bearing elements of the film without making a great many elaborate comments (yet) on what they might mean. Then, in Sections IV and V, I will put forth a claim that brings all these elements together into a coherent whole. *Letter*, I will argue, presents an interesting philosophical idea—to the effect that love actually makes a certain sort of knowledge possible—and, surprisingly enough, makes a challenging case for this idea.

II

One thing about the meaning of *Letter from an Unknown Woman* that is announced already in its title is that it is about knowledge and ignorance. More exactly, it is about knowledge and

ignorance of people. This, however, barely conceals a paradox, since the unknown woman, as it soon turns out, was a lover of Brand's: she was his unknown lover. How can a lover be unknown? A paradox, in this sense, is something seemingly contradictory or impossible that is nonetheless asserted as true and known to be true.[5] The themes of ignorance and of paradox are gently but insistently sounded throughout Lisa's letter, from its very first sentences. She begins with an avowal of knowledge and, at the same time, a confession of ignorance: "By the time you read this letter, I may be dead. I have so much to tell you and perhaps very little time. Will I ever send it? I don't know." The ignorance she confesses, as I will later have cause to emphasize, is about herself. She immediately makes another confession: "as I write it may become clear that what happened to us had its own reason for being beyond our poor understanding." Here, the confession of ignorance is linked to a promise, or a proffered hope, to create knowledge: it may become clear. Clear to whom? we might ask. Her act of writing might create knowledge, and for all we know at present it may be knowledge for her as well as for him. Then comes a paradox: "If this reaches you, you will know how I became yours when you didn't know who I was or even that I existed" (p. 35).[6] Throughout the letter, she repeatedly warns the reader that he will find what she says difficult to believe or understand. She ends with a series of crashing paradoxes, beginning with the most astonishing of all of her paradoxes: that, after the awful events she has recounted, she still loves him, and seemingly without regrets: "If this letter reaches you, believe this—that I love you now as I have always loved you. My life can be measured by the moments I've had with you and your child. If only you could have shared those moments, if only you could have recognized what was always yours, could have found what was never lost. If only" (p. 135). If only he could have shared—what? The moments she spent with him! If only he could have found—what was not lost in the first place! I will not have space here to resolve all of *Letter*'s paradoxes, but I will eventually try to resolve the one on which many of them are based, the paradox of the unknown lover.[7]

Letter is a film that rather obviously has what, for want of a better word, one might call leitmotifs—elements, often but not always visual ones, that are repeated from one scene to another in ways that are meaningful (despite the fact that they are often, at least initially, mysterious). Most obviously, the film is distinguished by the presence of diegetic *music*—the characters seem to be forever playing music, listening to it, talking about it, or simply going about their business while others play it. There are a number of different *journeys*, especially by train. There are a number of scenes in which *curtains* figure prominently in one way or another. Finally, there is a leitmotif obviously related to one of the meanings that curtains might have—a number of characters, in one way or another, perform the function of stagehands. Again, I will not be able to discuss all these here, but I will say a few words about the last two before setting forth an idea that ties them together.[8]

Curtains. The first curtain, or curtain-like object, occurs early in the middle of Act I. The voice-over narration of Lisa's says, "Then came a great day for me," and we see a dark, blurred image that quickly turns out to be a shot of Lisa beating a very large rug (p. 47). She pulls the rug out of the way, revealing the courtyard behind it, as if parting a curtain to begin a drama.[9] The courtyard then does become the scene of a little drama, which we understand to be conveyed by Stefan's reading of the letter. In it, Lisa helps Stefan's mute servant John (Art Smith) as a secret stratagem to gain entrance into Stefan's apartment, where she examines his beautiful objects and musical memorabilia. Act II has the most elaborate variations on the curtain motif. It begins in Madame Spitzer's fashion shop with a shot in which the camera peers through curtains into a small booth where a model is being helped by an assistant into a dress (p. 97). It then pans to another booth in which Lisa is framed by curtains. The next shot begins with Lisa entering through curtains into the display area of the shop to model a stunning Travis Banton outfit for appreciative customers. This shot dissolves to another one showing Lisa later in the day bending over a task at a desk in Madame Spitzer's. Hearing a knock at the window above her, she sees two young soldiers smiling

down at her. She immediately reaches up to pull both sides of the window curtain closed, thus ending the little show they were enjoying. This action, like her pulling down the carpet in Act I, reminds us of what the principal function of curtains is. They part to reveal, and they close to conceal. In such cases they control what is seen and, thus, what is known.

Sometimes, curtains are used to frame things, directing our attention or marking something as particularly worthy of it. The next appearance of curtains in Act II is a rather elaborate instance of framing. The first shot of the scene in which Lisa and Stefan dine in an elegant restaurant begins with the couple framed by curtains in a private booth (p. 123). As Stefan chatters charmingly to Lisa about her lobster bib, the camera very slowly tracks toward them until the curtains are no longer visible. Shortly afterward, the waiter (in a rather curious gesture) partly, not fully, closes the same curtains. Then as if it cannot resist viewing what the couple is doing, the camera very, very slowly tracks forward again (p. 128). It is then that Lisa elicits from Stefan what might be his most sincere and authentic act of self-revelation, in which he discusses his development as an artist.

The final elaborate use of curtains is, once again, in Act II and at the beginning of a scene. The scene in the hospital maternity ward begins with a shot of a nun approaching the camera in a dark corridor. The camera follows her into a large dark room, confronting a wall of black curtains. She parts them slightly, peeks discreetly inside, quickly snatches a sheet of paper hanging from one curtain, and moves on. She moves through the curtains and, as we follow her, we see that the room is a sort of dark labyrinth of small spaces closed off by identical black curtains. The nun spots an open curtain, looks inside, and closes it. Eventually, she passes Lisa's space, and we hear a nun asking prying questions about her baby's father, which she is refusing to answer. Here, rather obviously, the curtains serve to conceal things from view, as fits a scene of suffering and shame, though the prying and peeking of the nuns suggest that the curtains' function is a little more complex than this: that they not only close to conceal but part to reveal and expose.

Stagehands. Like "curtains," the "stagehands" leitmotif appears early. It begins at the beginning, immediately after Lisa's voice-over narration says, "when you didn't know who I was or even that I existed." We see a dark blurred image (p. 11). As the image resolves into the interior of a moving van, we hear, "I think everyone has two birthdays, the day of his physical birth and the beginning of his conscious life" (p. 36).[10] We feel rather as if we were witnessing the beginning of Lisa's conscious life. We see a man beginning to wrestle a large harp, of the sort played in symphony orchestras, out of the van. Simultaneously, we see Lisa for the first time. Her head and shoulders are intruding into the van through a window on the left edge of the frame, in an attitude in which we will often see her: staring in wonder (Figure 1). In one of Ophuls's celebrated moving-camera sequences, the camera then tracks and pans to follow Lisa as she moves, still staring, past piles of art objects and leather-bound books, up the twisting staircase, to what will soon be Stefan's apartment. All around her, the moving men bustle like stagehands—shouting orders, requesting help, complaining—arranging the props and scenery for a drama that is about to begin.[11] In the most conspicuous activity, a group of irritable men with a block and tackle are struggling to hoist a grand piano past the narrow stairs to the second floor. The moving men disappear after this scene, but during it we meet two other characters, one at the bottom of the stairs and one at the top, who will carry on the same sort

of function, managing props and scenery in a drama in which they know they are not the objects of interest. One is the concierge of the little apartment building who repeatedly greets Stefan as he enters the building. ("Who is it?" "Brand." "Good evening Mr. Brand.") The other is Stefan's ubiquitous, self-effacing (indeed, perfectly silent) butler John, whose sole function is to manage Stefan's beautiful possessions and—like Fritz, the maitre d' at the café that Brand frequents—to facilitate his complex comings and goings.[12] The scene with the moving men, presented as it is as the prelude to the drama that follows, carries with it a sense of the contrast between a beautiful drama and the sharply contrasting backstage goings-on without which the drama could not take place. The same is true of the Act II scenes at Madame Spitzer's, with its contrast between the sewing and fitting rooms in the rear and the elegant display area where Lisa models for admiring customers, and, more obviously, of the faux train ride in the Prater, with the scrolling scenery powered by an old man on a bicycle contraption.

The last elaborate appearance of characters performing the function of stagehands (unless we count the two seconds who, having appeared in the Prologue, return in the Epilogue) is the nun who walks through the maternity ward's labyrinth of curtains, making mysterious little adjustments. It is noteworthy that the scenes in which curtains appear prominently also tend to be the ones that feature the bustling activities of these theatrical menials. A minor occurrence of the later leitmotif is the out-of-frame voice in the lobby of the opera house, calling out, "Second act! Curtain going up!" The general impression given by these intertwining leitmotifs of curtains and bustling theatrical support staff is to make us aware of the presence of controlled revelation and theatrical display.

Before I discuss how this sense contributes to the meaning of the film as a whole, I will need to say something about the two central characters.

III

Figure 1. Lisa stares in wonder in *Letter from an Unknown Woman.*

Lisa and Stefan are obviously two very different people. However, there is one, somewhat less obvious, way in which they are alike.[13] It comes to the surface in the dialogue between them on their evening together in Act II. During their dinner at the restaurant, Stefan comments on the wine he has ordered, saying that it is from the "first vineyard you see when you come down the other side of the Alps. The Italians say it's such a good wine because the grapes have their roots in the valley and their eyes on the mountains" (p. 78). To some extent, of course, we are supposed to take this comment as charming banter, as a remark that he might well have said to many other women. But it anticipates another comment he makes about climbing mountains—*and* coming down from them—and this suggests that we should also take it as something more. Later that evening, when an image of the Matterhorn scrolls past the window in their faux train ride in the amusement park, Stefan reveals that he has climbed the real Matterhorn. Lisa asks him: "When you climb up a mountain, what then?" He responds: "Well, you come down again." When she asks him why he likes to climb mountains, he says, "I suppose because no matter how high you climb there's always a higher one." She adds, "and you like to imagine that the other one is even more wonderful." He agrees (pp. 86–87). As she suggests, this recalls an earlier comment of hers, with which he had also agreed, that the reason he prefers to come to the Prater in the winter is that "if it's spring, there's nothing to imagine, nothing to wish for" (p. 82). Now he adds a comment that is much truer than he realizes: "You know far too much about me, and I know almost nothing about you" (p. 87).

These exchanges are subtly revealing about both characters in a number of ways. For the moment, I will comment on only one of these. From the beginning, we have been aware that Lisa is in some sense profoundly *idealistic*. That is, there are certain values that she holds, to which she is devoted. In her case, the values involved are Stefan and the greatness she sees in him.[14] She is, we might say, a seeker. The same is true of Stefan, though in his case the values seem to be multifarious. Lisa touches on an important aspect of Stefan's idealism when she tells him, "Sometimes I felt when you were playing that…you hadn't quite found—I don't know what it is—what you're looking for." This is rather a hazardous thing to say to an

accomplished artist. His response—"How long have you been hiding in my piano?"—is expressed with evident sincerity. The remark has hit home. One of the values to which Stefan has been devoted is artistic. Another aspect of Stefan's idealism appears, ironically, in the scene in which his behavior is arguably the furthest removed from the ideal, in the final encounter in his apartment after the opera. Seeing Lisa looking at a small statue of a bust of a woman on the table, he says: "You remember the Greeks built a statue to a god they didn't know, but hoped some day would come to them. Well, mine happens to be a goddess.… For years, I never woke in the morning but I said to myself, 'Perhaps today she will come and my life will really begin.' Sometimes it seemed very near. Well, now I'm older and I know better" (pp. 125–126). I think this remark, like his earlier comments about mountains, has to be taken as a genuine self-disclosure. Like Lisa, he is in a way (or at least once was) intensely committed to values. They differ in what those values are. Stefan's values are both artistic and erotic, while Lisa is virtually all *eros*.

Another difference, and a critical one, suggested by some of the exchanges I have just quoted, is the staggering asymmetry in what these two characters know about each other. As Stefan says with unwitting penetration, Lisa knows entirely too much about him. Everything she says about him is true, and some of it is *penetratingly* true, while virtually everything he ever says about her is either false or true in a way that he cannot grasp. Lisa is far from being a star-struck fool. The many hours she spent as a girl listening to him practice were not a mere emotional indulgence: she has reflected on them and gained insight. In particular, she clearly sees the point that they have in common. When Stefan, who seems baffled by her insightfulness, suggests that she has been hiding in his piano, he is here, as elsewhere, closer to the truth than he realizes.

Where Lisa is concerned, Stefan is often right by accident, or more right than he knows. The first thing he says to her in Act II, when he finally notices her standing vigil across the street from his apartment, is, "I've seen you before" (p. 73). We know that he has seen her many times before, throughout the years that transpired in Act I, but he is only aware of having seen her a few nights ago, and on this very spot. When he tells her, "You're a very strange girl," his ignorance is underscored, not only by the fact that he says it twice, and when saying it the second time does not remember having said it before, but even more obviously by the fact that we know that she is *much* stranger than he realizes (pp. 80, 128). He has no idea wherein her real strangeness consists.

In addition, when Stefan hazards an opinion about Lisa, he is often obviously wrong. When in the carriage ride in Act II he stops to buy roses, and the flower woman asks, "Red roses?" He answers with perfect assurance, "No, red is the wrong color. A single, white rose, that's perfect!" When he gives Lisa the flower he asks, "Did I guess right? Is it your color?" She pauses and says, "From now on, it will be" (pp. 80–81). Partly because he is so sure that he has guessed right, the audience is aware that he has not. In Act III, when he sees her looking absent-mindedly at the statue of the unknown goddess, he says, "She fascinates you too!" The audience is painfully aware that the statue is not what is on her mind at that moment at all. It is, as always, he that fascinates her, but he is again quite unaware of that.

However, though Stefan's insight regarding Lisa is pitiably weak, his judgments about himself are impressive. In the exchange in the restaurant, the one that is highlighted by some complicated interplay between the camera and a set of curtains, he says, "Well, the truth is I've had rather an easy time of it. People accepted my music very quickly, perhaps too quickly. Sometimes it's easier to please others than oneself" (p. 79). Years later, in the Act III encounter in his apartment, he explains to Lisa why he no longer gives concerts. It was after a concert he had given, "like all the others, not better, not worse," he says, "I happened to look in the mirror…The young prodigy was no longer so young, certainly wasn't prodigious" (p. 127). In the Act II scene in the restaurant he comments on an early review comparing him to the young Mozart, he says "I was—very young. There was that much resemblance" (p. 78). Seen in context, this does not sound like false modesty at all. Throughout the film, his comments on himself have the same sort of insightful objectivity, without the flattering soft focus that human self-appraisals generally have.

This is actually one more way in which Lisa is precisely the reverse of Stefan. I can find only one statement she makes about what sort of person she is, as opposed to reporting specific things she does or feels, and it is stunningly mistaken. In the carriage ride home after encountering Stefan at the opera, she says: "I've had no will but his, ever." Her husband's comment, "That's romantic nonsense!" is almost an understatement (p. 113). As George Wilson has said:

If *Letter* has established any one thing it is the iron will of this woman to pursue the love of Stefan Brand and possess it on her own terms. (In her letter, commenting on her refusal to identify Brand as the father of her child, she writes, "I wanted to be the one woman you've known who never asked you for anything.") As emerges shortly, she is determined to give up everything to regain this man.

As Wilson goes on to point out, it is Brand who has no will of his own, not Lisa.[15] This is one of the things that Stefan is coolly objective enough to comment on himself, usually with self-deprecating humor. When, in Act II, he walks up to Lisa across the street from his apartment as he is coming home, he says to her, "Well, I almost never get to the place I start out for anyway" (p. 74). At this point he turns and (now accompanied by Lisa) he walks in (as the audience can clearly see) the direction opposite to his initial one. Within minutes, he and Fritz at the café are concocting excuses for his missing the evening's rehearsal with the orchestra and a date with another woman: actions once undertaken but now abandoned. In Act III, in front of the opera, when Lisa asks him if he has stopped playing, he says: "Oh, it's not quite as final as that. I always tell myself I'll begin again next week, and then when next week comes, it's this week, so I wait for next week again" (p. 111). His remark about climbing mountains—"well, you come down again"—is in the same vein: the events in his life, one might say, always seem to lack the quality of *finality*. Indeed, the events in the film itself, as Stefan reads the letter, constitute another enterprise taken up and then dropped. Just prior to the beginning of the Prologue, Stefan has gone through the actions that constitute the overture to a duel: accepting a challenge, appointing seconds, agreeing to meet them at a specific hour. He then almost immediately begins to make arrangements to skip town: another project interrupted. It is at that point that, unexpectedly, he is handed the letter and he begins to read it. Now, for the moment, he has forgotten to leave town. The letter is an interruption of an interruption.

The ways the two principal characters in *Letter* are alike and different are striking and potentially meaningful. They are alike in that they are both idealists: they are both intensely committed to a personal vision of the good. However, there are enormous and potentially critical differences between them. They are different in terms of what they know: Lisa knows Stefan, and Stefan knows himself. They are also different in terms of what they do not know: Stefan does not know Lisa, and Lisa does not know herself. Finally, they are different with respect to action: Lisa possesses a powerful will and is (for better or worse) quite capable of conceiving actions and carrying them through to completion. Stefan seems to lack such capacities. Some of these features of these characters serve an obvious function in making the film work as classical Hollywood narratives are conventionally supposed to work. Stephan's accurate self-understanding prevents us from dismissing him as a self-indulgent swine. This is important because, given that this is a "women's picture," we are supposed to sympathize (not merely empathize) with Lisa, and we cannot do that if we think that she is devoted to an utter scoundrel. The same function of underwriting sympathy for Lisa is served by her insightfulness regarding Stefan. However, some of the features I have just surveyed require us to look beyond the requirements of traditional genres to the deeper human significance of *Letter*. To show this, however, I will need to turn my attention for the moment to other matters.

IV

If someone asks you if you know a certain person—someone, let us suppose, named Fred—what is it that qualifies you to say, "Yes, I do"? Ordinarily, you are satisfied if you can correctly match a name "Fred" with a face, or if you have interacted with Fred at some point in the past. It may be, however, that knowing someone appears this simple because there are other conditions we can safely ignore, not because they are not necessary but because we can assume they are satisfied. Perhaps the human capacities that enable us to satisfy them are ones that we ordinarily suppose are always quietly at work, humming away somewhere. We can do this without being consciously aware of what these conditions are. In such a case, it might take an unusual set of circumstances to expose such conditions and make us aware of what they are. This, I think, is the possibility that *Letter* raises for us. It is one of the things that make it philosophically interesting.

Suppose that you interacted with Fred on several occasions in the past, but each time did not remember him as the person you met the last time. Obviously, this is the possibility that *Letter* asks us to entertain. In these circumstances, would it be true to say that you know Fred? The criteria we ordinarily apply do not seem to be sufficient to answer this question. What does this film have to tell us about it?

One thing is quite obvious: *Letter* does make it intuitively plausible to say that in such circumstances one does not know the person, regardless of what our ordinary criteria would be. It is hard to imagine someone saying, quite seriously, that the film is mis-titled on the grounds that Stefan did know Lisa. Though in some sense he knew her on three separate occasions, though he indeed "knew" her in what used to be called the biblical sense of the word, he nonetheless did not know her. This, however, seems merely to restate the paradox with which I began, that of the unknown lover. I will return to this problem shortly. Before that, I would like to say a few words about what *Letter* has to say about two other matters: what human capacities are presupposed by knowledge of others and what sort of process can provide this sort of knowledge. By the time I have done this, the paradox will have unraveled.

The film conveys a suggestion about the psychological preconditions of knowledge of other people, and it does so by means of the symmetrical characters of Lisa and Stefan. Once we formulate the nature of Stefan's failure as I just have, the reason for that failure becomes obvious. For the particular failure involved, as we have seen, consists in the failure to relate moments of experience widely separated in time and refer them to a single object supposed to be the occasion of them all. This would require at least one capacity that seems to be poorly developed in Stefan's case, namely, persistence. His way of life involves gliding from one experience to the next, each being complete in itself. There is a deep truth in the comment we overhear someone making about him at the opera: "Perhaps he has too many talents." Multiplicity is indeed Stefan's problem: his way of life splits experience into an unordered array of self-contained moments. Lisa's way, of course, is just the opposite. Her attention is fastened on a single object with an unshakable grip. The precondition of knowing others that is lacking in Stefan's case is, if anything, overdeveloped in hers. This of course explains her insightfulness about him.

She has exactly what Stefan lacks and needs. What she has, though, is something that can be communicated to him. It can be communicated by means of language, though language of a certain sort. What she needs to do is to recount certain individual experiences he has already had, and which in *some* sense he already knows, in such a way that they are now related to one another as parts of a meaningful whole. The relations, the whole, and the meaning will be what he lacked before. This function of assembling elements drawn from experience in such a way as to give them meaning as a whole is one way to describe what an *artist* does. Again, the sort of recounting she must give—in which a series of events is described in such a way as to exhibit them as being related to one another in ways (by cause and effect, for instance) that can be perceived as meaningful—is precisely what a *narrative* is. To create narrative art is, in a way, exactly what Lisa does. Her letter is such a creation.

The letter communicates to Stefan the knowledge he previously lacked. But it does more than that. This sort of knowledge is not limited to the cognitive aspect of human nature, but is deeply involved with the will and the affections as well. Accordingly, it is appropriate that the letter that communicates this knowledge has some very practical consequences as well. As I have already pointed out, the letter comes to Stefan's attention just as he is in the process of—once again—dropping an enterprise previously taken up. To the two men in Stefan's

carriage who arrive with him in the Prologue, the stop at his apartment is meant to be merely a three-hour rest on the way to the field of honor. The experience of reading the letter has such a powerful effect on him that in the Epilogue he actually completes the journey begun in the Prologue. In effect, the images that begin and end *Letter*, showing the dark carriage arriving at Stefan's apartment and departing from it, represent a single action with the elaborate flashback structure of the letter serving to connect its two halves. What they depict is the only action we ever see Stefan carrying to completion. Regrettably, but inevitably, the completion of this action will be his own death.

I sometimes ask people: Who was the author of the letter from an unknown woman? Since they (in contrast to you) have the disadvantage of being unable to see the absence of italics in my question, they never guess the answer to my trick question. Stefan Zweig? Howard Koch? Max Ophuls? The author was, of course, the unknown woman. My point is that the film presents Lisa as doing, broadly speaking, what these others do. She is an artist. That is one way of explaining the two leitmotifs I described earlier. The fact that in the flashbacks prompted by Stefan's reading of Lisa's letter there are persistent images of curtains parting and closing, and many details suggesting that various characters are in effect theatrical support staff humbly assisting a theatrical presentation in which Lisa and Stefan are the protagonists, underscores the fact that Lisa's letter is an artful reconstruction of events with a purpose of her own.[16]

Images of curtains can represent theatricality and artifice. As such, given that what the theater and art do is display false semblances of real things, they might also represent illusion.[17] However, they can also have the virtually opposite meaning of *revelation*, as they might, for instance, when they part to show something that was previously hidden. I think the role they play in *Letter* can best be characterized as revelation through artifice. Her letter constructs a version of events that definitely represents her own intensely personal point of view: the film in fact underscores how alien her point of view is from ours and, by implication, how different her account is from the one that we would give. Nevertheless, precisely because it does represent *her* point of view, it supplies Stefan with what he previously lacked: after all, what was previously unknown to him was—Lisa.

V

George Wilson, as I have suggested, has ably defended an interpretation that is sharply divergent from mine. He claims that Lisa is profoundly deluded about what sort of person Stefan is. If Wilson is right about this, it might be very difficult to defend the idea that the letter's effect on Stefan is redemptive in the particular way that I have claimed it is. If Lisa's consciousness is as limited as that, then she will have no knowledge to communicate to Stefan. Her letter would be an instrumentality by which she infects him with her ignorance.[18]

Wilson's main argument for this is that she pursues Stefan even though we can see that he is a philanderer who is not capable of settling down with one woman.[19] I could defend my own view against this argument by pointing out that the alleged false belief here is not about what sort of person Stefan is but about how he is related to her. However, I think there is a deeper issue involved here. The assumption behind Wilson's line of reasoning is that what Lisa is embarked on here is a practical sort of undertaking: that she is, in effect, trying to land a husband or a permanent lover. He notes that on at least two occasions she seems to realize that he will not settle down with her: when she is saying goodbye to him when he leaves on the train, and when she says to him, with emphasis on the first person singular, "*I* won't be the one to disappear." But he interprets these moments as evidence of "the immense oppressive weight" of her "fantasies," that they could actually blot out her conscious awareness that they do not represent reality. These moments could at least as easily be interpreted as evidence that her love is not the sort that is based on the belief that such fantasies are true in the first place. Wilson's argument seems to be based on the assumption that if she ever did fully and lucidly realize that Stefan would never be exclusively hers, she would give up her pursuit of him as pointless. But this does not cohere well with her declaration at the end of her letter, when all is lost: "I love you now as I have always loved you." This comes close to saying not exactly that she has no regrets but that the point of her pursuit of him was not to settle down with him.

This raises the interesting question: What exactly does Lisa want, anyway? This, I maintain, is not an easy question to answer. Her actions are actually difficult to understand if we insist on seeing them as aimed at the cost-effective realization of some normal human objective. As Robin Wood pointed out long ago, it is actually rather curious that she leaves Stefan's apartment during their final encounter in Act III without confronting him or revealing who she is. In fact, he has just told her that something she said the evening before at the opera keeps going through his mind (p. 128). We never learn what it was.[20] This rather startling failure of self-disclosure culminates a rather longish series of such failures that run through Act II. When, upon meeting her in front of his apartment, he offers to introduce himself, she interrupts him: "No, I know who you are," and then, in the moment when we would expect her to tell him who she is, there is simply a silence in which neither speaks (p. 74). In the restaurant, when he says, "I believe you really want to hear about me. Why?" and she does not volunteer an answer, he says, "Oh, never mind why" (pp. 78–79). When he asks her how long she has been hiding in his piano, there is a slight pause in which it might have been fitting for her to confess that she actually had listened to him practicing for many hours when she was an adolescent, but he brings it to an end by saying, "Never mind explaining" (p. 79). Obviously, there is a pattern here. Stefan's inadequate curiosity about Lisa is complemented—tragically, as it turns out—by a weakly developed will to self-display on her part.

This trait of hers, or rather absence of a trait, makes it difficult to attribute any of a wide array of conventional motives to her. In general, her actions do not seem calculated to entice him into forming a lasting relationship with her at all. We probably should not be too quick to rule out the possibility that her conduct is to some extent ineradicably mysterious. Perhaps the best and most truthful way to neutralize this mystery is to realize that, as I said earlier, Lisa is all *eros*. In ordinary life, we only see love together with various other psychological states that tend to obscure its essential features: sexual desire, vanity, the longing for security and domestic comforts, and the desire to charm and impress others. One of the things that make Lisa a great character is that she is very nearly denuded of all these other trappings. In her, we see pure love, at least according to a certain conception of love. What conception of love is this?

In an essay in which he defends the idea that love is absolutely distinct from any sort of desire, Ortega y Gasset says that "in love we feel united with the object" of our love. But this, he says, "is not merely physical union, or even closeness. Perhaps our friend (friendship must not be forgotten when love is generically considered) lives far away and we do not hear from him. Nevertheless, we are with him in a symbolic union—our soul seems to expand miraculously, to clear the distance, and no matter where he is, we feel that we are in essential communion with him."[21] We might add, though Ortega does not do so explicitly, that desire on the other hand makes us painfully conscious of the fact that we do *not* possess the object, and irks us until we do possess it, at which point the desire is extinguished. This suggests a not implausible view of the nature of love, more or less in the spirit of Ortega's comment. According to it, love has a completely different structure from desire as I have just characterized it. Love is a certain psychological state in which one places supremely high value on something or someone. To the extent that love necessarily involves having desires, they consist for the most part in the desire to contemplate the love-object, either directly or through symbols that represent it.[22] Other than that, the only desires that are necessarily involved have to do with acting toward the love-object in the way that is appropriate toward a supreme value: namely, by acting *favorably* toward it, doing things *for* it.[23] The principal symbols through which the love-object is contemplated, and no doubt the ones that Ortega has in mind when he speaks of "symbolic union," are mental images and other thoughts of the love-object. However, there are other sorts of symbols that can serve the same function. In some ways, the most powerfully satisfying symbol is a child who is the offspring of the loved one.

Lisa's behavior seems to conform to this conception of love, and this conception seems to offer explanations for some of the oddities of her behavior. In particular, it can explain why she pursues a man who was not likely to form a lasting relationship with her. On this view, although a long-term relationship is most desirable, because it is the most intense form of "symbolical union," other sorts are available: it is not a matter of marriage or nothing. In particular, once she becomes pregnant, she has a particularly satisfying sort of symbolic union in her grasp. In her valedictory statement at the end of her letter, Lisa mentions, as if they were the things that have given her life meaning, "the moments I've had with you and your child." She identifies the child, not as hers or theirs, but as his. And surely every viewer notices that the younger Stefan (Leo B. Pessin) uncannily resembles the older one, physically and otherwise. Evidently, young Stefan gave Lisa a sense of closeness to Stefan-*selbst* and for some ten years she was content with this.

Her contentment came crashing down in the encounter in front of the opera house. I think it is possible to identify precisely the reason it did. The one thing he says that makes the strongest impression on her is this: "I can't explain it, but I feel that you understand what I can't even say, *that you can help me*" (emphasis added, p. 111). At this point, there is a cut to a closeup of Lisa and we see that those last words have hit home. On the conception of love that I have schematically indicated above, the way to entice someone who loves you is not to offer or promise them anything, but to *ask* them for something. That is just what Stefan, with his usual unwitting penetration, has done.

I have been arguing that we can explain why Lisa acts as she does without assuming she is deeply deluded about what sort of person Stefan is. Having said all this, I am sure I have given some impression that I have gone too far in defending Lisa. After all, if the film represents her in an entirely positive light, would that fact not constitute a very serious objection to it? My answer is that *Letter* obviously does present Lisa's action, and her position in the world, as in some way erroneous: the interesting exegetical and philosophical issues have to do with the nature and magnitude of this error. The film presents Lisa as a character in whom love exists pure and unconstrained by any of the quotidian traits that bring it into a (perhaps delicate and unstable) consistency with the requirements of happiness and elementary decency. In this way, she is depicted as a flawed departure from the normal course of things: as, in a sense, a monster of *eros*. But in her moral deformity there is an element of greatness because the trait that in her is monstrously unconstrained is good in itself. To some extent, I think, a film has a right to take this idea for granted—the idea that love, the most intense experience of value that human beings are capable of, is intrinsically good. But *Letter* goes further than this, since it enables us to see, in the contrast between the characters of Lisa and Stefan, that love provides a basis for the persistence of attention that is needed if the various impressions we have of another person are to be integrated into an object of knowledge.[24] It is good, and its absence is bad, in a way that was previously unknown to us.[25]

LESTER H. HUNT
Department of Philosophy
University of Wisconsin, Madison
Madison, WI 53706
USA

INTERNET: lhhunt@facstaff.wisc.edu

1. George Wilson, *Narration in Light* (Johns Hopkins University Press, 1986), ch. 6. Robin Wood, "*Ewig hin der Liebe Glück*," reprinted in Virginia Wright Wexman and Karen Hollinger, *Letter from an Unknown Woman: Max Ophuls, Director* (Rutgers University Press, 1986), pp. 220–236.

2. Stanley Cavell, *Contesting Tears: The Hollywood Melodrama of the Unknown Woman* (University of Chicago Press, 1990).

3. Wilson, *Narration in Light*, p. 104. Berys Gaut more or less repeats Wilson's interpretation, saying that Lisa "is projecting her romantic fantasies onto a figure who does not in the least conform to them," in his "Identification and Emotion in Narrative Film," in *Passionate Views: Film, Cognition, and Emotion*, ed. Carl R. Plantinga and Greg M. Smith (Johns Hopkins University Press, 1999), pp. 213–216. I should mention that, though I will disagree with him on one point, my treatment of *Letter* is heavily indebted to him on others.

4. The quoted remark is from an otherwise very favorable review in *Variety*. See Wexman and Hollinger, *Letter from an Unknown Woman*, p. 215.

5. We might call this "literary paradox." Philosophical paradox, which might be defined as a set of propositions that are individually plausible but jointly contradictory, is a distinct but related idea. The paradoxes of Zeno are paradigm cases. See Nicolas Rescher, *Paradoxes* (La Salle, IL: Open Court, 2001).

6. I will identify details in the film by placing, in parentheses, the page number in the continuity script in Wexman and Hollinger. Even when the detail is visual, and not a passage of dialogue, the continuity script is a useful way to identify it precisely.

7. Another feature of the tone of *Letter*, one that we might suspect is somehow related to its paradoxicality, is its irony. It is remarkable, not merely for the pervasiveness of its irony, but for the multiplicity of the different *ways* in which it is ironic. One could write an encyclopedia article, "Irony, Varieties of" illustrated entirely by examples from this film. Had I space enough, I would argue that one function of the film's irony is the same as the one I will later attribute to some of its other meaning-bearing elements: it tends, to some extent, to align the film's point of view with that of Lisa.

8. I will have to leave for another occasion the question of whether, and to what extent, the other leitmotifs mentioned are related to this idea.

9. Wilson, *Narration in Light*, p. 115.

10. In one of the film's seemingly countless cross-references, the catastrophe at the opera takes place on Lisa's birthday, that is, on the anniversary of her physical birth.

11. The shooting script says: "Apparently, the precious objects emerging from the van hold a fascination for [Lisa]. More than house furnishings, they are the romantic props of a fairy-tale world." Wexman and Hollinger, p. 138.

12. Wilson claims that John, like the Anton Walbrook character in *La Ronde* and the Peter Ustinov character in *Lola Montes*, is a sort of stand-in for the director (*Narration in Light*, p. 125). For my part, I do not think that a mute and self-effacing character would be an appropriate representative for a director, or indeed for any sort of artist. My own view is that, if the filmmaker has a representative in the film, it is Lisa. Wilson's claim is bound up with his claims about the relation between love and knowledge in *Letter* and, as such, I will return to it later.

13. On this point, my argument is a more elaborate version of that of Wilson in *Narration in Light*, pp. 106–107.

14. For convenience, I am using "values" in an extended sense, in which a value might be a concrete particular, such as an individual human being, as well as an abstract quality.

15. Wilson, *Narration in Light*, p. 117.

16. It is interesting that two of the stagehand-like menials, the seconds who appear in the Prologue, are in effect conscripted into playing this role (that is, in the Epilogue) by the letter itself. But for the letter, Stefan would have decamped during the night, leaving them with no such role to play.

17. I think this is essentially Wilson's view of what they mean here. See *Narration in Light*, pp. 111–115.

18. This, or something very much like this, seems to be Wilson's view. He says that as a result of reading the letter, Stefan assimilates the letter's (in Wilson's view) "distinctive but somewhat dubious view of their relations" (*Narration in Light*, p. 123). I should add that Wilson maintains that the film's view of Lisa is on the whole "balanced" between the "redemptive and destructive sides of Lisa's passion" (p. 121). However, if Lisa is as ignorant as Wilson thinks she is, it is hard to see how the film's implicit claim, that her letter's effect is redemptive, could be true. If he is right, the film would seem to be, in this respect, incoherent.

19. This is the argument on which I will focus my attention. Wilson develops another line of argument, which I will comment on here very briefly. Basically, it consists in claiming that the film depicts or suggests that Lisa's consciousness of Stefan arises in epistemically inadequate ways. First, Lisa's love for Stefan is born as she listens to him playing, "without significant contact with the man himself." Second, there is very often a literal physical barrier (such as the glass panes of a window or door) between Lisa and Stefan, which Wilson interprets as representing Lisa's consciousness as being at a distance from its object and, consequently, as constituting an inadequate sort of consciousness. See *Narration in Light*, pp. 108–110. Very briefly, my response to the first point is that, rightly or wrongly, in this film art is presented as revealing the truth (or at least *a* truth) about the artist, as we see in Lisa's insightful comments on Stefan in the Act II restaurant scene. As to the second point, I would interpret these same images in a way nearly the opposite of Wilson's. They show Lisa observing Stefan from various hiding places but they do depict her as observing. Her position relative to Stefan is that of one who knows him from a position of secrecy and, thus, of noninteractivity: she is related to him as a *pure observer*.

20. Robin Wood, *"Ewig hin der Liebe Glück,"* in Wexman and Hollinger, p. 234.

21. José Ortega y Gasset, *On Love: Aspects of a Single Theme* [*Estudios Sobre el Amor*], trans. Toby Talbot (New York: World Publishing, 1957), p. 16.

22. I say "it" because, as Plato would insist, the love-object need not be a person. It can, for instance, be music or physics—or, indeed, beauty or truth.

23. Many would wish to say that one *serves* or *makes sacrifices* for the love-object. But "serving" carries with it connotations of self-abasement, and "sacrifices" suggests that things done for the love-object are detrimental to the interests of the person who does them. As such, these additions would represent stronger statements than I am making here. I have no need to commit myself here concerning the truth or falsity of these stronger statements.

24. It would be interesting to pursue the hypothesis that love, perhaps in some extended sense of the word, is actually a *necessary condition* for knowledge of others. That would, of course, be a much stronger claim than I am making here.

25. I would like to thank Claudia Card, William B. Macomber, Dan McCall, the editors of this special issue of *The Journal of Aesthetics and Art Criticism*, and participants in the University of Wisconsin Film Studies Colloquium for comments on earlier drafts of this essay.

DAN FLORY

Spike Lee and the Sympathetic Racist

Know thyself.
　　　Inscription on the Temple of Apollo at Delphi[1]

In his recent book *White*, Richard Dyer argues that racial whiteness has operated in Western film and photography as an idealized standard against which other races have been judged. Making his case inductively using instruction manuals, historical theories of race, and traditional lighting and make-up practices, as well as the dominant ideals for human beauty utilized in developing film stocks and camera equipment over the last 150 years and more, Dyer maintains that Western visual culture has presented whites as the norm for what it is to be "just human" or "just people," whereas other human beings have been presented as raced, as different from the norm.[2] This manner of depicting whiteness has invested the category itself with the power to represent the commonality of humanity. Furthermore, Dyer argues that this historical function of whiteness's normativity continues to be profoundly influential in current practices and instruction.[3]

Dyer's argument is in accord with what philosophers such as Charles W. Mills and Lewis R. Gordon have advanced in broader theoretical terms regarding the operation of whiteness as a norm against which nonwhites—and particularly blacks—have been negatively judged.[4] Like Dyer, Mills and Gordon argue that presumptions of whiteness institutionalize racial beliefs at the level of background assumptions that most would not even think to examine. Based on this claim, these philosophers reason that whiteness functions not only as a social norm, but also at the epistemological level as a form of learned ignorance that may only with considerable effort be brought forward for explicit critical inspection.[5]

Similarly, many of Spike Lee's films place into question presumptions about the normativity of whiteness. A crucial aim in his ongoing cinematic *oeuvre* has been to make the experience of racism understandable to white audience members who "cross-over" and view his films. Because seeing matters of race from a nonwhite perspective is typically a standpoint unfamiliar to white viewers, Lee has sought to make more accessible such an outlook through the construction and use of specific character types. One way he achieves this goal is by offering depictions of characters who function as what I will call "sympathetic racists": characters with whom mainstream audiences readily ally themselves but who embrace racist beliefs and commit racist acts. By self-consciously presenting white viewers with the fact that they may form positive allegiances with characters whose racist bigotry is revealed as the story unfolds, Lee provokes his viewers to consider a far more complex view of what it means to think of one's self as "white" and how that may affect one's overall sense of humanity.

Lee thus probes white audiences' investment in what might be called their "racial allegiances," a dimension of film narrative pertaining to the manner in which audiences become morally allied to characters through categories and presumptions about race.[6] Foregrounding racial allegiances allows him to depict the way in which ideas of race may affect characters' and audience members' behavior at much deeper levels cognitively, emotionally, and morally than many of them realize. By offering a critical perspective on their investment in race, Lee issues his viewers a philosophical challenge, both within the context of their narrative understanding and their lives generally. In focusing audience attention on a character toward whom they feel favorably while also revealing that character's racism, Lee constructs a film that philosophizes by developing a conception of what it means to be racist that fundamentally challenges white viewers to inspect their own presumptions about how they see themselves and others.

Lee depicts sympathetic racist characters so that viewers may initially forge positive allegiances with them in spite of those characters' anti-black beliefs and actions, which in earlier stages of the narrative seem trivial, benign, unimportant, or may even go unnoticed. He then alienates viewers from such characters by revealing the harmfulness of these typically white beliefs and actions. Through this technique, Lee contests the presumed human commonality attached to being white by providing viewers with an opportunity to see their conceptions of whiteness analytically. By introducing a critical distance between viewers and what it means to be white, Lee makes a Brechtian move with respect to race. As Douglas Kellner points out, he "dramatizes the necessity of making moral and political choices" by forcing his viewer "to come to grips" with certain crucial issues and "adopt a critical approach" to the emotions and cognitions involved.[7] The opportunity offered to white viewers who cross-over to see Lee's films is that of experiencing what they have been culturally trained to take as typical or normative—being white—and see it depicted from a different perspective, namely, that of being black in America, which in turn removes white viewers from their own experience and provides a detailed access to that of others. Exploiting this kind of anti-egoist strategy regarding fiction's capacities to give audiences access to the perspectives of others is something that philosophers such as Kendall Walton, Iris Murdoch, Martha Nussbaum, Alex Neill, and others have long recognized.[8] It is just this strategy that Lee takes advantage of in his films.

Given this characterization of Lee's goals, I would argue that we should recognize the opportunity he offers white viewers as a chance to imagine whiteness "from the outside"—see it acentrally and sympathetically, as opposed to

imagining it centrally and empathetically. Both kinds of responses are modes of imaginative engagement; sympathy, however, is generally a more distanced attitude in which we imagine *that* such-and-such were the case, whereas empathy calls for something closer to imagining from one's *own* situation.[9] By encouraging viewer response to be more sympathetic than empathetic, Lee promotes a mode of detached critical reflection that is not merely Brechtian, but philosophical, for it involves reflectively considering presuppositions of the self and humanity that are among the most fundamental in contemporary conceptions of personal identity, namely, those regarding race.[10] In this sense, Lee challenges his white viewers to know themselves along the lines of the Delphic inscription made famous by Socrates.

Lee's crucial insight here regarding his use of sympathetic racist characters is that, analogous to white viewers' generally favorable "internal" predisposition to white characters, such viewers also have trouble imagining what it is like to be African American "from the inside"—engaging black points of view empathetically—because they often do not understand black experience from a detailed or intimate perspective. It is frequently too far from their own experience of the world, too foreign to what they are able to envision as ways in which human life might proceed. Thomas Hill and Bernard Boxill have argued that this limitation in imagining other life possibilities may interfere with whites knowing the moral thing to do because they may be easily deceived by their own social advantages into thinking that such accrue to all, and thus will be unable to perceive many cases of racial injustice. Hill and Boxill note that such a cognitive insensitivity may affect even well-meaning sincere individuals who wish for nothing more than to act morally in situations where questions of racial injustice might arise, a phenomenon that Janine Jones refers to as "the impairment of empathy in goodwill whites."[11]

To counteract such an imaginative limitation in film viewing, Lee offers depictions that invite a deeper imagining with respect to blackness. Not only does he provide numerous detailed representations of African-American characters in his films, but he also offers sympathetic racist character types who provide a conception of how it might be possible for a white person to act favorably toward blacks but still be racist toward them. In this sense, Lee constructs the sympathetic racist character type as an "alloy" of morally good and bad characteristics, in the terminology developed by film theorist Murray Smith in *Engaging Characters* and elsewhere.[12] As Smith notes, the moral complexity of such characters can force us "to question certain habits of moral judgment," which is precisely what Lee achieves in many of his films.[13]

What Spike Lee offers, then, is a more acentral access (that is, detached access "from the outside") to white characters so that white viewers may look at these characters more critically. This type of access might be thought of as the first step in giving whites a sort of "double consciousness" regarding their own race. If W. E. B. Du Bois was correct in observing that African Americans possess a sense of "twoness" regarding themselves racially in American society, then the "single consciousness" of whites would make them particularly susceptible to narrative allegiances based on whiteness and resistant to seeing white characters from other perspectives.[14] The presupposition of white racial experience in much film narrative, then, contingently predisposes viewers, especially white viewers, to understanding characters from a racialized point of view. Thus, counteracting this phenomenon and creating an incipient white double consciousness might be conceived as another way to think of Spike Lee's overall aim with regard to his white viewers. As Linda Martín Alcoff has explained, such a perspective would involve a critical sense that white identity possessed a clear stake in racialized social structures and inequalities as well as some sense of responsibility for helping rectify these inequities.[15] In this sense, the technique of self-consciously depicting sympathetic racists throws into question white racial allegiances, for the self-conscious use of this character type provokes in white viewers a philosophical examination of why one might feel favorably toward such characters, in spite of their racist beliefs and actions.

Lee also encourages his viewers to reflect on how whiteness possesses specific characteristics that make white experience different from nonwhite experience, and vice versa. African-

American experience, for example, is constituted by specificities that involve a history and legacy of racialized slavery, as well as the ongoing "scientific" research project that has time and again ranked blacks at the bottom of what was claimed to be an empirically verified racial hierarchy, and that frequently served as grounds for arguing that blacks possess lesser capacities to be moral, intelligent, and law-abiding. African Americans have been subject to the burden of representation established across decades (one could also now say centuries) by stereotypes that arose out of blackface minstrelsy as well as a history of having been subject to lynching on the basis of one's skin color.[16] These features need to be kept in focus when thinking about and assessing the actions, beliefs, and emotions of black American characters in many films, as it is not unusual for blacks to have the capacity to imagine that whites who are sympathetic toward them might also harbor racist beliefs or act in racist ways. History provides many examples of African Americans having to deal with such individuals, among them Abraham Lincoln.[17] Thus it would not be difficult to transfer this cognitive capacity over to understanding film narratives. On the other hand, neither this history nor its related imaginative capacities are generally shared by whites. Lee's self-conscious use of sympathetic racist character types, then, aims to assist whites in acquiring the rudiments of these imaginative competencies.

Spike Lee is not the only filmmaker to employ the narrative technique of constructing sympathetic racist characters, but his work seems to be the *locus classicus* for such figures in the new "black film wave."[18] From *Do the Right Thing* (1989) to *Clockers* (1995) and *Summer of Sam* (1999), Lee's films have self-consciously foregrounded allegiances with sympathetic racists or similar morally complex "good-bad characters" for the inspection and contemplation of his audiences.[19] In this fashion he has sought to make white viewers more critically aware of anti-black racism and fear of difference. I should add here that I do not believe that Lee and other filmmakers necessarily devised these narrative techniques with exactly the theoretical goals I describe or by using the philosophical considerations I outline in this essay. Rather, while I assume that there is some overlap between their goals and the ones I describe, filmmakers use these techniques because they work well in depicting certain characters and narrative situations. In contrast, what I provide here is a theoretical explanation and clarification of what these techniques are, how they work cognitively, and why they achieve the effec   at they do.

Even as Spike Lee offers his white viewers an opportunity to contemplate their racial allegiances, it is important to note that one problem associated with the depiction of sympathetic racist characters is that their critical use may not always be evident to viewers. Some audience members may not detect such narrative figures as racist; others will. What I offer next is a detailed analysis that makes clear what Lee seeks to accomplish by presenting this character type as well as an explanation of the fact that some viewers are unable to apprehend it as racist.

I. WHO—AND WHAT—IS SAL?

In an otherwise astute examination of *auteur* theory, Berys Gaut argues that the character of the Italian-American pizzeria owner, Sal (Danny Aiello), in *Do the Right Thing* is not a racist figure (p. 166).[20] Aiello's performance, Gaut asserts, overcomes Lee's explicit directorial intention of revealing racist beliefs in a character who is for many viewers the film's richest, most complex, and sympathetic narrative figure.[21] Despite Lee's clearly stated aim to portray this character as a racist, Aiello allegedly trumps that aim through his rendition of Sal.[22] Gaut sees this conflict between director and actor as an "artistically fruitful disagreement" that contributes to "the film's richness and complexity" (p. 166), in spite of Sal's "complicity in a racial tragedy culminating in a horrifying murder" (p. 165). Gaut quotes film scholar Thomas Doherty to support his point, noting that, "'on the screen if not in the screenplay [Aiello's] portrayal wins the argument'" by depicting Sal's character as someone who is not racist.[23]

Other viewers, however, have regarded Sal's character differently. Film scholar Ed Guerrero argues that despite Sal's humanity and reasonableness through most of the film, when confronted with Radio Raheem (Bill Nunn) and Buggin' Out's (Giancarlo Esposito) demands at the end of a long, hot day, "Sal's good-natured paternal persona quickly cracks and out comes a screed of racist invective about 'jungle music,' accompanied by egregious racial profanities, the likes of 'black cocksucker,' 'nigger motherfucker,' and so on."[24] Guerrero's point is that by using these terms nonironically and ascriptively with respect to black characters in the narrative, Sal reveals himself as a racist. Similarly, African-American studies scholar Clyde Taylor notes that it is Sal who explicitly racializes this confrontation by insulting his adversaries' choice of melodic accompaniment with the angry exclamation: "Turn that jungle music off! We ain't in Africa!"[25] From this point on, racial epithets explode from Sal's mouth.

Unlike these critics, however, many white viewers tend not to notice or acknowledge this dimension of Sal's character. Instead, like Gaut and Doherty, these audience members often see him as a good person who does a bad thing, or a rational person defeated by an irrational world, but not as someone who is a racist.[26] This form of explanation also seems to have been actor Danny Aiello's own understanding of Sal. In St. Clair Bourne's documentary *Making "Do the Right Thing"*, Aiello remarks during an early read through of the script that "I thought [Sal is] not a racist—he's a nice guy; he sees people as equal." In a later discussion of his character, Aiello further explains: "The word ['nigger'] is distasteful to him." Finally, after acting out Sal's explosion of rage that sparks Raheem's attack and brings down the New York City Police Department's fatal intervention, Aiello summarizes: "Is he [Sal] a racist? I don't think so. But he's heard those words so fucking often, he reached down ... If it was me and I said it—I'm capable of saying those words; I'm *capable*.—And I have said them, but I'm not a racist." Aiello thus consistently believed, in developing and acting out his character during the production of the film, that Sal was not a racist, but rather a fair and equal-minded character who *in this one case* made a mistake and did something that was racist. In his anger and fatigue, he "reached down" into himself and found the most insulting words he could to throw at those who made him angry and thus ended up acting *like* a racist, even though he himself was not one. This under-standing of Sal would thus seem to be a com-mon strategy for white viewers to use in explaining the character.

Such a conflict in viewers' understanding of Sal presents an interpretational dilemma, which, I argue, the concepts of racial allegiance and the sympathetic racist help to resolve. Accordingly, the explanation for why many white viewers—and Aiello himself—resist seeing Sal as a racist might be formulated in the following way. A white audience member's understanding of a white character's actions often accrues from a firm but implicit grasp of white racial experience, which presupposes the many ways in which the long histories of world white supremacy, eco-nomic, social, and cultural advantage, and being at the top of what was supposedly a scientifically proven racial hierarchy, underlay and remain influential in white people's lives. After all, the circumstances that resulted from hundreds of years of pursuing the goals of presumed Euro-pean superiority—namely, global domination by whites in economic, cultural, social, religious, intellectual, national, governmental, and various other ways—remain structurally in place.[27] Such dimensions of white experience are part of the "co-text," what Smith refers to as the internal system of "values, beliefs, and so forth that form the backdrop to the events of the narrative," for individuals raised in white-dominated cultures regardless of their race.[28] As dimensions of white experience in particular, they operate as implicit, nonconscious presumptions and expectations that form the background for viewing narrative fiction films. For white viewers, this co-text is part of what Smith calls their "automatized" or "'referentially transparent'" belief-schemata, which here I take to form a crucially important and racially inflected ground for understanding and empathizing with white characters.[29] This system of beliefs, values, emotional responses, and so on amounts to a set of readily available, albeit largely unconscious, cultural assumptions concerning what it is to be white that have been implicitly built into much Western visual media like film.

Because white viewers are rarely called on to imagine their whiteness from the outside, they tend to have difficulty looking at it critically. This circumstance of rarely having their back-ground beliefs put to the test means that many

white viewers find it hard to question or give up their racial allegiances, even to characters like Sal. In fact, they resist *not* empathizing with him and seeing him from a nonwhite perspec-tive. Unlike nonwhite viewers, who, often out of necessity, develop a critical sense of race or double consciousness merely to function and survive in cultures like America's, most white viewers lack the cognitive tools that would allow them to recognize and question the typi-cally presumed cinematic viewpoint of white-ness. Their life experience as well as their viewing experience are such that they ordinarily have neither opportunity nor need to develop such forms of cognition. Thus, when confronted with narratives that call for them to utilize such cognitive forms or to incorporate new information concerning them, they may react in confused or myopic ways. They resist the possibility of race being an issue and overlook crucial pieces of information that would require them to revise their typical ways of thinking about race because their previous experience has prepared them cognitively neither for the possibility of changing their standard ways of thinking nor for properly incorporating such information.

Clearly, it is not that such audience members are logically incapable of doing so, but rather that given their strongly ingrained and rein-forced "initial schema" for conceptualizing race, there is little or no cognitive space for per-ceiving certain crucial details offered by Lee's narrative. Were this flaw pointed out and explained to them, no doubt many audience members would modify their viewing stance toward race and seek to properly absorb the crit-ical points advanced. From a cognitive perspec-tive, this epistemological limitation should not be particularly surprising; as E. H. Gombrich noted decades ago, sometimes when our initial belief schemata for art works "have no provi-sions for certain kinds of information…it is just too bad for the information."[30] We simply lack the requisite tools for absorbing it, although with some conceptual assistance we could make the necessary changes.

Because many whites may easily live lives oblivious to how matters of race have had and continue to have an impact on their lives, it is quite possible for them to wholeheartedly embrace the belief that race is no longer a major factor in *anyone's* existence. This de-racialized outlook is one version of the cognitive insensitivity stressed in the work of Hill, Boxill, Jones, Mills, Gordon, and others.[31] As they point out, absent from such an outlook is a sense that race could be of any major importance in human life experience. Those who believe otherwise, by contrast, appear to be paranoid, morbidly focused on the past, or otherwise psychologically impaired.

When watching films, then, many white viewers may strongly resist the invitation to reconsider their racial allegiances because, from their perspective, such a reconsideration does not make sense. It flouts a system of beliefs, values, and emotional responses presupposed by their everyday lives as well as their typical film viewing and would require a fundamental upheaval in their overall belief-schemata if those elements needed to be substantially revised or abandoned. Such an invitation asks them to consider as a problem something that they believe to have been resolved long ago. To accommodate a character like Sal and make the least disruptive changes in their system of belief—which unconsciously presupposes aspects of white advantage and power—rather than seeing Sal as a sympathetic racist character, they view him as an empathetic and morally good character. The hateful, bigoted dimensions of his racist beliefs and actions drop out; these aspects of his character are seen as not really racist. Perhaps for some viewers, these matters are explained away as an accurate reflection on "how things are" with respect to nonwhites and are therefore not thought to be racist because they are thought to be true, alluding back to explicit racial hierarchies of times gone by. More frequently, however, such viewers explain away Sal's racist actions at the end of the film as not truly representative of his character. Instead, his actions are seen as an aberration, an exception to his overall good character. Many white viewers thus empathize with Sal and do not understand him as a "good-bad" moral alloy, but simply as a morally good character who is trying to do the right thing—an "amalgam," in Smith's terminology.[32] He becomes a good person who does a bad thing, or a rational person defeated by an irrational world, as some reviewers described him, a character who is not racist but through a bad moral

choice toward the end of the narrative is unfortunately complicit in a racial tragedy that culminates in a horrifying murder.[33] Such explanations of the character fit better into their existing schemata for viewing racial matters on film as well as in life than do alternative explanations, such as that Sal is a sympathetic racist.

A major task facing viewers of *Do the Right Thing* is that of constructing Sal such that his actions, beliefs, and characteristics fit together coherently.[34] However, white racial allegiances can distort this process in such a way that Sal's racism may seem peripheral or temporary rather than central and ongoing. An ignorance of the fundamental role race plays in currently existing versions of human identity—especially white identity, as explained by the philosophers noted above—may prevent viewers from seeing racism's centrality to Sal's character. Again, the monocular nature of white racial consciousness may well prevent viewers from constructing Sal's character in a way that coherently assembles his actions, beliefs, and primary characteristics.

A careful examination of the film, however, indicates that such an approach would be to misunderstand Sal as the narrative presents him. A variety of cues provide ample support for the idea that the film directly addresses the matter of anti-black racism at the core of Sal's character and militates against the interpretation that Sal is merely the victim of a bad moral choice. In closely watching the scene depicting the confrontation between him, Raheem, and Buggin' Out, for example, audiences may detect Lee signaling to the audience that the issue of racism will be explicitly raised. As Buggin' Out and his associates stand in the doorway of Sal's, one hears on the soundtrack Raheem's boom box playing once again Public Enemy's song "Fight the Power." Specifically, the lines sung by Chuck D. blast forth, observing that "Elvis was a hero to most but he never meant shit to me … a straight-out racist sucker; it's simple and plain." The function of the music in referring to Elvis Presley, who appropriated from black culture the music, clothes, and movements that originally made him famous, is to foreshadow what will be presented as the scene unfolds—namely, that issues of race that normally remain hidden will be brought to the surface and scrutinized.[35] In other words, the music operates as a textual as well as a narrative prompt employed by Lee to encourage viewers to imagine that the sequence to follow will address anti-black racism.[36] Moreover, during the sequence itself Sal's insults to blacks are underscored by other characters repeating them indignantly and resentfully. Sal's initial racializing of the incident through the use of the terms "jungle music" and "Africa" to denigrate Raheem's choice of acoustic accompaniment is explicitly noted by Buggin' Out, who argues that such terms are irrelevant regarding what pictures should hang on the wall of Sal's Famous Pizzeria. "Why it got to be about *jungle music*? Why it got to be about *Africa*? It's about them fucking pictures!" Buggin' Out doggedly protests, refusing to let Sal get off the subject. Similarly, Sal's use of the term 'nigger' is repeated indignantly and resentfully by the group of teenagers waiting for one last slice before the pizzeria closes. Lastly, after Sal has smashed Raheem's boom box, he looks its erstwhile owner in the eye and unapologetically declares, "I just killed your fucking radio." By explicitly stating that he has destroyed the source of the "jungle music," the origin of the unwanted "African" melodic presence, as well as Raheem's pride, joy, and sense of identity, Sal underlines his own violently imposed and racially inflected dominance.

Perhaps most damning of all, however, is Sal's immediate reaction to Raheem's death. With the eyes of the entire community looking to him for some sort of appropriate response, Sal can think of nothing better to say than the tired old saw, "You do what you gotta do," as if he had just stepped out of some John Wayne movie, rather than offering any hint of an apology or regret for his complicity in the events that led to Raheem's death. Sal's response self-servingly portrays his violent destruction of Raheem's boom box as justified, as the best and most appropriate reaction to the situation, given the circumstances. His listeners in front of the pizzeria shout him down in anger and resentment at the outrageousness of such a stance. Getting Raheem to turn down his boom box did not require Sal to destroy it, then rub his triumph in with a humiliating remark. Plus, in no way does Sal's alleged justification of his actions speak to the events that ensued, specifically, Raheem's murder at the hands of the police.

As much as any other factor, Sal's breathtaking callousness at this point of the narrative in seeking to exonerate himself and unfairly justify his actions as appropriate brings on the riot that follows. His moral insensitivity is at least threefold. First, Sal lacks an understanding of the racial issues involved in his own response to the confrontation between himself, Raheem, and Buggin' Out. Second, he does not grasp the racial dimension of Raheem's death by means of the famous "choke hold" that urban police forces long argued affected African Americans more lethally than whites. Third, his overall lack of compassion over Raheem's death sparks the neighborhood's revulsion, which surprises him to such an extent that he has no further response except to exclaim, "What'd I do?" and yell for the crowd not to destroy his business. In this way the narrative shows that Sal values his property over Raheem's life. All these factors mix and combust to the point that community members lose control and riot, burning and gutting the pizzeria in an angry *riposte* to Sal's racial and moral callousness.[37]

Spike Lee foreshadows Sal's subtly racist character earlier in the narrative as well. When describing to his openly racist son Pino (John Turturro) why they cannot move their business from the African-American neighborhood of Bedford-Stuyvesant to their own Italian-American neighborhood of Bensonhurst, Sal refers to the community's residents as "these people," thereby using language that distances himself from them, that "others" them. Earlier still in the narrative, when Buggin' Out first questions the absence of African Americans on the "Wall of Fame" in Sal's restaurant ("Hey Sal, how come you got no brothers up on the Wall here?") and suggests that Sal put up pictures of Nelson Mandela, Malcolm X, or even Michael Jordan because African Americans are the mainstay of the business, Sal ridicules the black vernacular use of the term "brother," scorning it so maliciously that even his mild-mannered, passive son Vito (Richard Edson) tells him, "Take it easy, Pop." A moment later Sal threatens Buggin' Out with the same baseball bat that he eventually uses to destroy Raheem's radio. We should note that, particularly during the late 1980s in New York City, baseball bats were symbolic of white on black violence due to their use in a number of racist incidents involving whites beating blacks for being in the wrong neighborhood, being there at the wrong time, dating the wrong (that is white) girl, and so on.[38]

After Sal commands the expulsion of Buggin' Out from the pizzeria for suggesting that the Wall of Fame might display famous people of color, Sal's delivery person Mookie (Spike Lee) defends Buggin' Out's freedom of expression by declaring: "People are free to do whatever the hell they want to do." To this very typical American declaration of freedom, Sal replies, "What 'free'? What the hell are you talking about, 'free'? 'Free'? There is no 'free' here. What—I'm the boss. No freedom. I'm the boss." For Sal, the application of freedom has limited scope. Although he couches his response in the terms of a businessman setting the rules for frequenting his establishment, because of other factors—primarily, the racial one that Sal and his sons are virtually the only whites consistently in the neighborhood and his customers are almost exclusively nonwhites—it amounts to saying that in his establishment only white Americans like himself may exercise freedom of expression, not his African-American patrons. They, in contrast, must abide by his (the white man's) rules, dictates, and desires. For African Americans then, there is no freedom inside the confines of Sal's Famous Pizzeria. Sal is the boss. No freedom. As Guerrero notes, "Sal is the congenial and sometimes contentious, but always paternal, head of what amounts to a pizza plantation, a colonial outpost in native territory."[39]

Given these redundant narrative cues, I would argue that utilizing the concepts of racial allegiance and the sympathetic racist help to make better sense of the character Sal in *Do the Right Thing* than other possible interpretational strategies because such an analysis coheres more completely with what the film actually presents, even if it does not cohere with typical white presumptions regarding race. Seeing Sal as a good-bad character, an alloy who possesses both positive moral traits as well as negative ones, synthesizes his character much more consistently and comprehensively than competing possibilities. This narrative figure coheres better if one attributes to him a racist character, even if he is also sympathetic in other ways, than if one seeks to explain away his actions late in the nar-

rative as that of a morally good character who makes a bad decision that leads him to do racist and immoral things, even though he himself is not racist.

Many white viewers tend to miss or overlook the details of Sal's anti-black racism because these particulars do not easily fit into their preconceptions of where their moral allegiances should lie. They tend to more readily empathize with white characters like Sal than black characters like, say, Mookie or Raheem, who, in spite of his intimidating character and bullying ways, was nevertheless murdered by the police and therefore deserves something more than to be forgotten or valued as less important than the destruction of Sal's business, which is what many white viewers did.[40]

Some empathy for Sal, of course, must be attributed to nonracial factors. To present a nuanced sympathetic racist character for whom viewers might initially establish a solid favorable outlook, Lee makes him narratively central and treats him compassionately much of the time. This strategy carries with it a certain risk—namely, that viewers will find it difficult to judge him negatively as a racist because they know him well and have become firmly attached to his character. White viewers in particular might be inclined to overlook or excuse the depth of Sal's wrongdoing because their attachment to the character—based on both racial and nonracial elements of the narrative—is too powerful. On the other hand, it should be noted that Lee counterbalances this possibility by making the film an ensemble piece. The story focuses not just on Sal, but on the whole neighborhood, including numerous African-American characters who receive significant screen time, such as Mookie, Da Mayor (Ossie Davis), and Mother Sister (Ruby Dee). I would argue that this narrative counterbalancing aims to keep viewers from investing themselves too heavily in Sal by presenting other, nonwhite characters with whom viewers might also ally themselves. Of course, these other character allegiances may be partly or even wholly blocked by racial factors as well, but one can see that from the viewpoint of narrative construction, these figures operate to spread out audience allegiance rather than investing it in just one central character such as Sal.

From the point of view of epistemology, white viewers may resist developing a critical distance from Sal and instead find ways to explain his actions that downplay or eliminate the matter of racism as constituent of his character. Rather than questioning their own deep-seated habits of judgment and imagining whiteness from the outside, as the narrative encourages them to do, they find fault in the narrative's inconsistency with their current, racially influenced beliefs and expectations. In this sense, the pull of empathy for Sal, the pull of white racial allegiance, is too strong for many white viewers to overcome and begin reexamining their habits of moral judgment. For these viewers, it seems less disruptive cognitively and emotionally to ignore or leave aside certain uncomfortable details in the narrative than to substantially change their belief-schemata—the narrative's co-text—to accommodate those details. Rather than working to develop a rudimentary white racial double consciousness, many viewers choose to embrace their already existing white single consciousness and use it as best they can to understand the film's narrative, even if that white-privilege-influenced perspective requires them to ignore certain clearly presented details and can only poorly explain others. If Gombrich has accurately identified our typical use of "initial schemata" in understanding visual artworks, these narrative details would be precisely the ones that white viewers would tend to overlook in any case, given the cognitive background from which they work. Whites typically lack sensitivity to the importance of these features because they tend not to see race as cognitively important in the sorts of situations presented by the film. Thus *Do the Right Thing* tends to come up short when measured by means of such an interpretive stance.

This problem of cognitive insensitivity may be further clarified by means of Janine Jones's analysis of empathetic impairment in goodwill whites. Jones argues that if whites—even whites of moral goodwill and in possession of the desire not to be racist—are unable to detect the cognitive importance of race in situations where anti-black racism impinges on African Americans in day-to-day interactions with whites (such as those depicted in *Do the Right Thing*), then they will also be impaired and

perhaps even unable to analogize from their own circumstances to those of African Americans. The construction of analogy between white and black experience, which would be critical to any sort of successful empathizing here, breaks down because certain crucial elements of the former experience are seen as strongly disanalogous to the latter. White viewers may empathize incorrectly or even not at all with black characters, and therefore misunderstand the situations and outlooks of African-American characters. Empathy, Jones points out, requires being able to produce an accurate system of mapping between another person's life and some aspect of our own. Empathic understanding thus begins with an appreciation of the other person's situation.[41] If that situation is not well appreciated or understood, then empathy will go awry or fail to occur.

This failure of "mental simulation" also makes clear why many whites fail to see Sal from what is for them the acentral, African-American perspective offered by Spike Lee's film.[42] They empathize with Sal because they fail to grasp the importance of certain details that the narrative presents to them—namely, the way his actions and statements build up to a kind of subtle, mostly nonconscious racism that is a part of his character, as opposed to being attributable to a single bad decision or two. They empathize with him, even though Lee indicates time and again through narrative cues that they should ultimately want to distance and qualify their attitude toward Sal. The details of Sal's character are meant to operate cumulatively as signals to mitigate ultimate viewer empathy for him, even if the narrative to some extent courted that imaginative stance toward him earlier. Lee urges viewers to distance themselves from Sal by the film's end and look at his character critically, instead of embracing him as someone close to their hearts. Again, nonwhite viewers, who typically possess a more finely tuned racial awareness, tend to see this suggestion much more clearly, but it is by no means beyond the cognitive capacities of whites to develop this sharper racial awareness. It is just that socially and culturally, such an awareness is not encouraged in white viewers. Rather, as Dyer argues, Western visual media tend to reinforce presumptions of whiteness as the norm, even to the extent that racial whiteness functions as the assumed standpoint from which to perceive popular film narrative. The typical viewer is presumed to be white or to at least have a full working grasp of what it is to engage films from a white perspective.

A further way to characterize this problem of audience asymmetry with respect to responses involving race is by comparing it to an example analyzed at length by Jones. She builds much of her case around the divergent ways in which many whites viewed the videotapes of the Rodney King beating on the one hand, and the attack on Reginald Denny on the other. Infamously, King, an African American, was stopped in 1991 for a traffic violation by the LAPD and was severely beaten by several police officers using riot batons. Denny, a white truck driver, was pulled from his rig by several black youths who used bricks and other objects to beat him during the riots that followed more than a year later in the wake of those same police officers being found not guilty of assaulting King. Both men were hospitalized for extended periods and suffer from permanent disabilities as a result of their injuries. Both incidents were also secretly videotaped. What Jones noted was that in viewing the videotapes of these incidents, whites did not react in the same way toward both individuals, in spite of the similarity of their situations. As one white professor of law who viewed the tapes put it: "'For King I felt sympathy; for Denny, empathy.'"[43]

I would argue that the difference in response to the two cases here may be readily explained as one of racial allegiance. White viewers of the videotapes felt closer to the situation, possibility, and overall experience of Denny than to that of King, even though both tapes depicted brutal beatings of helpless individuals by multiple attackers using clubs, bricks, and other blunt instruments. Constructing an appropriate experiential analog in the case of Denny came much more easily for most white viewers due to a shared experience of whiteness, an analog not extended in the case of King. White viewers' racial commonality permitted a much more immediate response—empathy for Denny—as opposed to the more detached attitude of sympathy for King.

Like the allegiance that many white viewers felt while watching the videotape of Denny's beating, responses to Sal often seem to be based more on racial allegiance than on close attention to narrative details. Thus these audience members are more inclined to empathize with Sal than to distance themselves from his character. They ignore, miss, reject, or downplay the African-American perspective offered by Lee's film in favor of another racially inflected one already embedded in their typical responses to popular film narratives, in spite of ample evidence that this latter perspective fails to fully explain many details presented in the narrative. At the same time, this aspect of the film allows us to see how it aims to trouble the viewer into making a closer examination of background assumptions concerning film viewing, race, and personal identity.

II. CRITICAL REFLECTION AND SYMPATHETIC RACISTS

By self-consciously depicting a character who is both sympathetic and racist—and goading his viewers to think about how it might be possible for such a character to be both at the same time—Spike Lee casts a critical eye on the assumptions that underlie white racial allegiance. In this manner he hopes to move white audience members toward a more complex perspective on race. I would further argue that through this provocation to have his viewers confront and reevaluate the racial presuppositions of their film viewing, Lee summons his audience members to think philosophically about race. By means of *Do the Right Thing*'s narrative and the character type of the sympathetic racist in particular, Lee encourages many of his white viewers to reflect on and devise a new belief schema for understanding race. In ways perhaps not unlike many students in introductory philosophy courses, however, some white viewers resist this invitation because the prospect of replacing their old way of cognizing would call for them to perform too radical an epistemological revision, require too much of a change in their existing belief structures for them to feel comfortable exploring such a possibility. At some level, perhaps they realize that such a re-examination and replacement of unquestioned background presumptions would not only concern their film viewing, but also an understanding of their own identities and humanity itself, thereby touching them at their core, so to speak.

As philosophers from Frantz Fanon to Mills have argued, our senses of personal identity in Western culture are strongly raced. For whites, however, this dimension of self-understanding is largely invisible and unacknowledged. To compel whites to recognize this invisibility, then, is a daunting and difficult task. Still, it is possible, and in fact many whites have done so, in film viewing as well as in their own senses of identity. But many others have not. Facilitating this possibility, which concerns cinematic as well as existential presuppositions, has guided Lee's efforts, I would argue, to present and depict a sympathetic racist character like Sal. Through narrative characters like him, Lee encourages white viewers to look critically at their racialized sensibilities and assess what they see.

In this sense, Lee presents his viewers with a philosophical challenge: to evaluate the contents of their souls, so to speak, and gauge how those contents influence them to perceive matters of race. This critical self-questioning was one of Socrates's highest aspirations, as evidenced in the *Apology* as well as dialogues with Euthyphro, Meno, Laches, and others. It has also inspired philosophers through the ages to the present day, such as Alexander Nehamas.[44] Socrates aspired to meet, both in his own case and that of others, the old Delphic injunction used as an epigraph for this essay. More recently, Noël Carroll has argued that Orson Welles's *Citizen Kane* (1941) stages a debate meant to "afford the opportunity for the general audience to interrogate prevailing cultural views of the nature of human life by setting them forth in competition." The Welles film is "similar in purpose to many philosophical dialogues" because it seeks "to animate a debate" about human life and personal identity.[45] In the same spirit, we may justifiably recognize Spike Lee as encouraging viewers to take up that sort of philosophical task regarding race through his construction of character and narrative in *Do the Right Thing* and other films. One could say, then, that Lee not only induces his white viewers to do something Brechtian—that is, critically distance themselves from certain characters and narrative situations in order to

consider moral and political choices—but charges them with a properly philosophical task as well. By drawing them into a favorable stance toward Sal only to alienate them from his character by means of the realization that he is also fundamentally a racist, Lee has produced a film that philosophizes, a film that calls on viewers to think philosophically about questions regarding race, identity, and cinematic viewership. Through this narrative figure, Lee urges viewers to critically reflect on their *own* senses of self, humanity, and personal identity, which is a hallmark of most if not virtually all persuasive conceptions of philosophy.

In addition, Lee's film offers indications regarding the proper shape that answers to such self-questioning might take. For example, having a fuller sense of the role race has played in the formation of one's identity as well as one's overall cognitive perspective is strongly implied as a better epistemological stance to take than one that does not possess these features. For all of Sal's compassion and patience toward neighborhood members like Da Mayor or Smiley (Roger Guenveur Smith), his lack of racial self-awareness condemns him to incomprehension regarding much of what goes on around or even inside his pizzeria, and this incomprehension contributes significantly to his downfall. The film's narrative thus suggests that having a greater racial awareness—a "double consciousness" about race, particularly for whites—would serve one better than lacking such a capacity. This attempt not only to pose but to shape fundamentally the answers to questions, to provide some sort of positive, in-depth contribution to the topic being discussed, is a further hallmark of many stronger senses of what counts as being philosophical, as this positive requirement implies that the film's call for critical reflection is solidly philosophical rather than merely social, psychological, or political.[46] Some viewers may resist this invitation by means of alternative interpretative strategies but, as I have argued, the cost of that choice is failure to achieve full coherence in grasping characters and narratives like those presented in *Do the Right Thing*, to say nothing of the costs that such choices exact in one's life or from the lives of one's fellow human beings.[47]

DAN FLORY
Department of History and Philosophy
Montana State University
Bozeman, Montana 59717
USA

INTERNET: dflory@montana.edu

1. Plato, *Phaedrus* 229e–230a, in *Plato: the Collected Dialogues*, ed. Edith Hamilton and Huntington Cairns (Princeton University Press, 1963), p. 478. See also W. K. C. Guthrie, *The Greeks and Their Gods* (Boston: Beacon Press, 1955), pp. 183–184.

2. Richard Dyer, *White* (London: Routledge, 1997), pp. 1–2.

3. See Dyer, *White*, especially pp. 70–144.

4. Charles W. Mills, *The Racial Contract* (Cornell University Press, 1997), especially pp. 53–62, and Lewis R. Gordon, "Critical Reflections on Three Popular Tropes in the Study of Whiteness," in *What White Looks Like: African-American Philosophers on the Whiteness Question*, ed. George Yancy (New York: Routledge, 2004), especially pp. 175–176, 181–182.

5. See, for example, Charles W. Mills, *The Racial Contract*, especially pp. 17–19, 91–109, and Lewis R. Gordon, *Fanon and the Crisis of European Man: An Essay on Philosophy and the Human Sciences* (New York: Routledge, 1995), pp. 22–26, 38ff. See also Peg O'Connor, *Oppression and Responsibility: A Wittgensteinian Approach to Social Practices and Moral Theory* (Penn State University Press, 2002), especially pp. 1–59, 128–131.

6. The idea of a racial allegiance was suggested to me by one of my students, Calvin Selvey.

7. Douglas Kellner, "Aesthetics, Ethics, and Politics in the Films of Spike Lee," in *Spike Lee's "Do the Right Thing,"* ed. Mark A. Reid (New York: Cambridge University Press, 1997), p. 75, and Bertholt Brecht, *Brecht on Theatre: The Development of an Aesthetic*, ed. and trans. John Willett (New York: Hill and Wang, 1962), pp. 23, 101.

8. See Kendall Walton, *Mimesis as Make-Believe: On the Foundations of the Representational Arts* (Harvard University Press, 1990), p. 34; Iris Murdoch, *The Sovereignty of Good* (London: Ark Paperbacks, 1985), especially pp. 64–67; Martha Nussbaum, *Love's Knowledge: Essays on Philosophy and Literature* (New York: Oxford University Press, 1990), especially pp. 77–79; Alex Neill, "Empathy and (Film) Fiction," in *Post-Theory*, ed. David Bordwell and Noël Carroll (University of Wisconsin Press, 1996), pp. 179–180; Murray Smith, *Engaging Characters: Fiction, Emotion, and the Cinema* (Oxford: Clarendon Press, 1995), pp. 235–236.

9. For more on the distinction between central and acentral imagining, see Bernard Williams, *Problems of the Self* (Cambridge: Cambridge University Press, 1973), especially pp. 36–38; Richard Wollheim, *On Art and the Mind* (Harvard University Press, 1974), pp. 58ff, and *The Thread of Life* (Harvard University Press, 1984), pp. 73ff; Noël Carroll, *The Philosophy of Horror, or Paradoxes of the Heart* (London: Routledge, 1990), pp. 88–96; Smith, *Engaging Characters*, pp. 76ff.

10. The claim that modern personal identity is intimately linked to race has been argued for by philosophers at least since Frantz Fanon. See Frantz Fanon, *Black Skin, White Masks*, trans. Charles Lam Markmann (New York: Grove Press, 1967), pp. 109–140; Gordon, *Fanon and the Crisis of European Man*; O'Connor, *Oppression and Responsibility*; Mills, *The Racial Contract*.

11. Thomas E. Hill Jr. and Bernard Boxill, "Kant and Race," in *Race and Racism*, ed. Bernard Boxill (Oxford: Oxford University Press, 2001), pp. 469–470; Janine Jones, "The Impairment of Empathy in Goodwill Whites for African Americans," in *What White Looks Like*, pp. 65–86. Mills also notes this problem of empathic impairment; see *The Racial Contract*, p. 95.

12. Smith, *Engaging Characters*, pp. 209ff; "Gangsters, Cannibals, Aesthetes, or Apparently Perverse Allegiances," in *Passionate Views: Film, Cognition, and Emotion*, ed. Carl Plantinga and Greg M. Smith (Johns Hopkins University Press, 1999), especially pp. 223ff.

13. Smith, "Gangsters, Cannibals, Aesthetes," p. 228.

14. W. E. B. Du Bois, *The Souls of Black Folk* (New York: Signet, 1969), p. 45.

15. Linda Martín Alcoff, "What Should White People Do?" *Hypatia* 13 (1998): 24–25.

16. For more on the history and legacy of the racialized existence of blacks, see Mills, *The Racial Contract*, especially pp. 81–89, 109–120.

17. See Emmanuel C. Eze, *Achieving Our Humanity: The Idea of a Postracial Future* (New York: Routledge, 2001), p. 27, as well as some of the title cards in D. W. Griffith's *The Birth of a Nation* (1915)! Some in the abolitionist movement might be understood in this way as well; see *Against Slavery: An Abolitionist Reader*, ed. Mason Lowance (New York: Penguin, 2000).

18. Ed Guerrero, *Framing Blackness: The African American Image in Film* (Temple University Press, 1993), p. 1.

19. For essays that argue implicitly for the use of such characters in *Clockers*, *Summer of Sam*, and director Carl Franklin's *One False Move* (1992), see my "Black on White: *Film Noir* and the Epistemology of Race in Recent African American Cinema," *Journal of Social Philosophy* 31 (2000): 82–116, especially 92–94, 101–104, and "The Epistemology of Race and Black American *Film Noir*: Spike Lee's *Summer of Sam* as Lynching Parable," in *Film and Knowledge: Essays on the Integration of Images and Ideas*, ed. Kevin Stoehr (Jefferson, NC: McFarland, 2002), pp. 174–190. As Smith notes, the original source for the concept of the "good-bad" character is Martha Wolfenstein and Nathan Leites, *The Movies: A Psychological Study* (Glencoe, IL: Free Press, 1950), pp. 20ff.

20. Berys Gaut, "Film Authorship and Collaboration," in *Film Theory and Philosophy*, ed. Richard Allen and Murray Smith (Oxford: Clarendon Press, 1997), pp. 149–174. Page numbers in this paragraph refer to this essay.

21. See, for example, Vincent Canby, "Spike Lee Tackles Racism in *Do the Right Thing*," *New York Times*, June 30, 1989, sec. C16; "Spike Lee Raises the Movies' Black Voice," *New York Times*, May 28, 1989, p. 14; Joe Klein, "Spiked? Dinkins and *Do the Right Thing*," *New York Magazine*, June 26, 1989, 14–15.

22. See, for example, Spike Lee, with Lisa Jones, *Do the Right Thing: A Spike Lee Joint* (New York: Fireside, 1989), p. 45, and Marlaine Glicksman, "Spike Lee's Bed-Stuy BBQ," reprinted in *Spike Lee: Interviews*, ed. Cynthia Fuchs (University of Mississippi Press, 2002), pp. 18–19. Gaut notes that Lee also makes this point during a read

through of the script with Aiello in director St. Clair Bourne's documentary *Making "Do the Right Thing"* (1989); Gaut, "Film Authorship and Collaboration," p. 166.

23. Gaut, "Film Authorship and Collaboration," p. 166; see also Thomas Doherty, review of *Do the Right Thing, Film Quarterly* 43 (1989): 39.

24. Ed Guerrero, *Do the Right Thing* (London: BFI Publishing, 2001), p. 75.

25. Clyde Taylor, *The Mask of Art: Breaking the Aesthetic Contract—Film and Literature* (Indiana University Press, 1998), p. 269.

26. See, for example, Richard Corliss, "Hot Time in Bed-Stuy Tonight," *Time* 134 (1989): 62; Murray Kempton, "The Pizza Is Burning!" *New York Review of Books*, September 28, 1989, 37; Stanley Kauffmann, "*Do the Right Thing,*" *The New Republic* 201 (1989): 25.

27. See Mills, *The Racial Contract*, especially pp. 1–40, 91–109; Eze, *Achieving Our Humanity*.

28. Smith, *Engaging Characters*, p. 194.

29. Ibid.

30. E. H. Gombrich, *Art and Illusion: A Study in the Psychology of Pictorial Representation* (Princeton University Press, 1972), p. 73. This point is also noted in Smith, *Engaging Characters*, p. 121.

31. See Hill and Boxill, "Kant and Race," pp. 469–470; Jones, "The Impairment of Empathy in Goodwill Whites for African Americans"; Mills, *The Racial Contract*; Gordon, *Fanon and the Crisis of European Man*; O'Connor, *Oppression and Responsibility*; Arnold Farr, "Whiteness Visible: Enlightenment Racism and the Structure of Racialized Consciousness," in *What White Looks Like*, pp. 143–158.

32. Smith, *Engaging Characters*, p. 203.

33. See Corliss, "Hot Time in Bed-Stuy Tonight"; Kempton, "The Pizza Is Burning!"

34. For more on the viewer's need to construct characters in ways that make sense of them as fictional agents, see Smith, *Engaging Characters*, especially pp. 120ff.

35. See, for example, Theodore Gracyk, *Rhythm and Noise: An Aesthetics of Rock* (Duke University Press, 1996), pp. 191–192; Ray Pratt, *Rhythm and Resistance: Explorations in the Political Uses of Popular Music* (New York: Praeger, 1990), pp. 135–139; Peter Guralnick, *Last Train to Memphis: the Rise of Elvis Presley* (Boston: Little, Brown, 1994), especially pp. 3–54.

36. I borrow here the idea of a textual prompt from Smith's "Imagining from the Inside," in *Film Theory and Philosophy*, p. 417.

37. It is worth noting that even after the riot, when Mookie (Spike Lee) returns the next morning to receive his week's pay, Sal remains unapologetic and defensive about his role in Raheem's death. Although he acknowledges that Raheem is dead ("I was there, remember?"), he blames Raheem's death entirely on Buggin' Out ("He's dead because of his buddy"), rather than seeing himself as being in any way complicit.

38. Baseball bats are negatively charged symbols of anti-black racism due to incidents in the New York City neighborhoods of Bensonhurst and Howard Beach in the late 1980s. Young black men in these incidents were either beaten to death or threatened with bats in ways that led to their death. See Lee and Jones, *Do the Right Thing: A Spike Lee Joint*, pp. 32–33, 46; S. Craig Watkins, *Representing: Hip Hop Culture and the Production of Black Cinema* (University of Chicago Press, 1998), pp. 157, 270, n.43.

39. Guerrero, *Do the Right Thing*, p. 35.

40. See, for example, David Denby, "He's Gotta Have It," *New York Magazine*, June 26, 1989, 53–54; Klein, "Spiked? Dinkins and *Do the Right Thing.*"

41. Jones, "The Impairment of Empathy in Goodwill Whites for African Americans," p. 71.

42. I use the term 'mental simulation' here with some reservations because, although I think that work by Robert Gordon, Gregory Currie, and others on this concept has greatly increased our knowledge of the workings of the mind in general and empathy in particular—especially with respect to literary fiction and film—I am not yet ready to embrace the claim that when we imagine, empathize, and so on, we run our belief systems "off-line" and operate as if our brains were just like computers, as in Currie's *Image and Mind: Film, Philosophy, and Cognitive Science* (New York: Cambridge University Press, 1995), especially pp. 141–197. I find these descriptions of how human minds work like computers to be too literal to feel comfortable endorsing them. For a fuller argument detailing reservations about mental simulation, see Noël Carroll, *A Philosophy of Mass Art* (Oxford: Clarendon Press, 1998), especially pp. 342–356.

43. Cited in Jones, "The Impairment of Empathy in Goodwill Whites for African Americans," p. 75. As she notes, her analysis is based on Joe R. Feagin, Hernan Vera, and Pinar Batur, *White Racism*, 2nd ed. (New York: Routledge, 2001), pp. 117–151, especially pp. 141–142. (It should also be noted that the white professor of law quoted here, David B. Oppenheimer, was sharply critical of his own responses to these images. His position is actually consistent with the one I outline. See his "The Movement from Sympathy to Empathy, Through Fear; The Beatings of Rodney King and Reginald Denny Provoke Differing Emotions but Similar Racial Concerns," *The Recorder* June 9 (1992): 14.)

44. See Alexander Nehamas, *The Art of Living: Socratic Reflections from Plato to Foucault* (University of California Press, 1998), especially pp. 40, 106, 185–188.

45. Noël Carroll, "Interpreting *Citizen Kane,*" *Persistence of Vision* 7 (1989): 51–61, reprinted in *Interpreting the Moving Image* (New York: Cambridge University Press, 1998), p. 163.

46. For discussion of philosophy's capacities and whether film can mimic them, see Stephen Mulhall, *On Film* (New York: Routledge, 2002), especially pp. 1–10; Julian Baggini, "Alien Ways of Thinking: Mulhall's *On Film,*" *Film-Philosophy* 7 (2003), available at <http://www.film-philosophy.com/vol7-2003/n24baggini>; Mulhall, "Ways of Thinking: A Response to Andersen and Baggini," *Film-Philosophy* 7 (2003), available at <http://www.film-philosophy.com/vol7-2003/n25mulhall>.

47. An early version of this work was presented at the "Narration, Imagination, and Emotion in the Moving Image Media" conference sponsored by the Center for the Cognitive Study of the Moving Image, in Grand Rapids, Michigan, July 24, 2004. I thank audience members there, especially Lester Hunt, Amy Coplan, and Katherine Thomson-Jones, for comments and encouragement. I also thank Susan Kollin, Murray Smith, and Tom Wartenberg for reading and commenting on earlier versions of this essay.

GEORGE WILSON

Transparency and Twist in Narrative Fiction Film

I. INTRODUCTION

One of the characteristic marks of classical narrative films is that their audio/visual narration is, in a certain sense, transparent.[1] Very roughly, this means that (1) most of the shots in these movies are understood as providing the audience with "objective" or intersubjectively accessible views of the fictional characters, actions, and situations depicted in the film and that (2) where the shots or sequences are not to be construed as objective, there is a reasonably clear marking of the fact that they are, in one of several different ways, "subjective." Of course, "subjective shots and sequences" come in various modes. For instance, some shots and sequences depict the perceptual field of a particular character. Others depict a character's visual imaginings, memories, dreams, or hallucinations. Still others render in visual terms the content of something that some character is verbally reporting or describing. This short list of possibilities is obviously not exhaustive, and the individual "subjective" modes deserve lengthier discussion. Nevertheless, let us say that (1) and (2) give us, as a crude first approximation, a specification of the norm of "the transparency of narration" in classical narrative film. Although the conception that these conditions jointly express has a recognizable intuitive import, it is not easy to elaborate the conception more sharply. The concept of an objective shot or sequence in fiction films is problematic and, correlatively, so are the various concepts of subjective depiction. Moreover, the nature and functioning of the factors that contextually mark the epistemic status of a movie segment (that is, a shot or edited sequence) can be surprisingly elusive. These are among the issues I will address in this essay.

However, my investigation is not simply motivated by an untrammeled analytic impulse. I have been struck by the fact that there are a number of fairly recent mainstream, commercial films—films that present an elaborate, detailed, and more or less coherent narrative—that depend on surprising, systematic violations of narrational transparency. The narration in the films I have in mind is significantly unreliable in particular ways, and its unreliability depends precisely on the audience's confounded expectation that the norm of narrational transparency will have been in place. These movies have come to be known as "twist movies," where the "twist" in question is predominately epistemological. *The Cabinet of Dr. Caligari* (Robert Wiene, 1919) is a celebrated early example of the strategy, and there have been scattered instances throughout the history of film. But lately we have enjoyed (or deplored) a positive explosion of epistemically twisted movies.

The films I am thinking of come in at least two broad kinds. First, there are movies in which the cinematic narration, as the audience eventually comes to realize, represents the narrative action through the subjective perspective of a particular character, although, in general, that action has not been represented from the perceptual point of view of the character in question. That is, the narration stands outside the "focalizing" character, regularly presenting him or her within the frame. Still, at the same time, the narration reflects the problematic way in which the character imagines the relevant fictional history to have transpired. *Jacob's Ladder* (Adriane Lyne, 1990) is one example of this strategy, appearing early in the recent cycle. David Fincher's *Fight Club* (1999) and the framed core story of *Secret Window* (David Koepp, 2004) are

paradigmatic instances of global nontransparency, and David Cronenberg's *Spider* (2002)
constitutes an interesting variant on the strategy.
Vanilla Sky (Cameron Crowe, 2001) and, arguably, David Lynch's *Mulholland Drive* (2001)
fall within the category as well.

In a different but related category, there are
films in which it emerges that the fictional
world contains special (typically, supernatural)
beings that can be perceived only by conscious
agents with nonstandard perceptual powers and
not by means of normal human vision. In the
course of these films, it is revealed that the central character or characters are themselves
among the "humanly invisible" special beings,
although the film's viewers have been seeing
them throughout. *The Sixth Sense* (M. Night
Shyamalan, 1999) and *The Others* (Alejandro
Amenabar, 2001) are epistemological twist
movies of this second variety.

My chief example of an epistemological twist
movie will be *Fight Club*, although I will comment briefly on *The Others* as well. The films in
question are of varying complexity and merit,
and all of them, it seems to me, have defects of
conception and execution. Still, the questions
about them that interest me most concern the
matter of how their narrational strategies can be
coherently described, and this requires one to
confront problems about how certain sorts of
subjectivity are represented, and identified as
such, within the setting of the films. These movies all pose hard problems about how spectators
are to imagine or otherwise comprehend what
they are seeing as they watch the unfolding
image tracks before them. Of course, it is hardly
news that the history of the cinema includes a
multitude of movies that fail to conform to the
norm of transparency. It is a recurrent feature of
certain kinds of art films that their instances
repudiate the familiar classical norm. *Last Year
at Marienbad* (Alain Resnais, 1961), *8 ½*
(Federico Fellini, 1963), *Belle de Jour* (Luis
Buñuel, 1966), and *Persona* (Ingmar Bergman,
1966) are some obvious examples. Naturally, it
is not my goal to examine all the ambiguous
interplay of objectivity and subjectivity in film.
For starters, that topic is unmanageably too
vast. I will begin with some simple subjective
segments and build to higher levels of narrational sophistication—the narration of *Fight
Club*, for instance.

In the history of film theory, there have been
a range of worthwhile discussions of subjectivity in film. For instance, Jean Mitry addressed
the subject in an extended section of *The Psychology and Aesthetics of the Cinema*.[2] In the
1970s, Bruce Kawin published the book *Mindscreen*, an ambitious and helpful contribution to
the topic.[3] A few years later, Edward Branigan
developed an elaborate, detailed theory of cinematic subjectivity in his *Point of View in Film*,
especially in Chapters 6 and 7 of that volume.[4]
These constitute only a small selection from a
rather extensive literature. As suggestive as
these and other works are, they seem to me to
suffer from various misconceptions, confusions,
and lacunae, although I will not engage here in
an explicit critical discussion of them. On the
other hand, film theorists who write from the
perspective of analytic philosophy and cognitive psychology have not thus far investigated
subjectivity in the cinema to any considerable
extent. However, as I will try to demonstrate,
there certainly are problems in the area—some
of them exemplified by the twist movies—that
are worthy of more careful analytic attention. In
particular, certain types of subjective cinematic
representation raise tricky issues for the phenomenology of film viewing or, as I would put it,
for a general account of what it is that spectators
imagine themselves seeing in a narrative fiction
film.[5]

Some analytic philosophers of film have
maintained that film spectators imagine seeing
and are meant to imagine seeing whatever fragment of the movie's fictional world is presented
in the relevant shot or sequence. Let us call this
"the imagined seeing thesis" as it applies to fiction film. The thesis has been principally elaborated by Kendall Walton and endorsed by
Jerrold Levinson and myself.[6] In opposition,
Gregory Currie and Berys Gaut have argued
that the thesis is mistaken.[7] It is not my intention here to revisit all the specifics of these
earlier debates. However those specifics are
eventually to be resolved, I think it is fair to say
that there are further questions about the thesis
that none of the debaters has adequately investigated. These questions include the following:
First, what is the scope of the imagined seeing
thesis for film? Is the thesis supposed to apply
only to the objective or impersonal shots and
sequences in a film? Or, is the thesis supposed

to apply in some fashion to various categories of subjective shots and sequences as well? Second, if it is contended that we do imagine ourselves seeing something in a subjective segment of such-and-such a type, then how does the specific subjective character of the segment affect or qualify the content of what we imagine ourselves seeing in the scene? Finally, what difference, if any, does it make to what the viewer imagines seeing in a subjective segment when it is not immediately identified as such in its broader narrational context? For reasons that will emerge in time, answering these last two questions, for certain types of subjective segment, is a delicate matter. In the ensuing discussion, I am going to assume provisionally that the imagined seeing thesis is true in the case of objective segments, and I will go on to investigate how the thesis is likely to fare when it is extended to different kinds of subjective shots and sequences.

However, let me say something to explain and motivate, at least minimally, the assumption I am here adopting. The phrase 'to imagine seeing' has various readings and, in the present context, its employment is potentially confusing. "Jones imagined seeing his mother" may mean that he formed an inner visualization of her. Or, it might mean that Jones had a false visual impression of seeing her where that impression was crucially triggered by his imagination. Neither use is in question here. In watching a film, we regularly speak of "seeing" the fictional characters and situations depicted in the work. But what it is to see such fictional items in a movie is significantly different from what it is to see (as film viewers also do) the actors, the acting, and the configurations of *mise-en-scène* that portray those fictions. In newsreel footage of the Yalta conference, there may be a segment that shows Stalin waving, and I can say correctly that I see Stalin waving in that segment. Similarly, in a fictionalized movie reenactment of the conference, there may be a segment in which the actor playing Stalin gives a wave. In this case also, fully cognizant of the movie's artifice and fiction, I can also say that I see Stalin waving in the segment. The proposition that I principally intend to assert by my second utterance is different from the first. In the second case, I am manifestly describing some episode in my imaginative engagement with the

fictionalized film and that fact conditions what I am rightly understood to be asserting. What I assert is that, in my imaginative engagement with the film, it is fictional for me that I see Stalin waving in the segment—or something of the sort. It is in this sense that I imagine seeing Stalin wave in a segment of the docudrama.

So, in this essay, I will follow Kendall Walton in saying that viewers *imagine seeing* the fictional contents in a fiction film. However, I use the phrase to designate whatever kind of imagination-conditioned seeing is involved in seeing fictional objects and events in movies, without proposing any specific account of this delicate phenomenon. In fact, I am sympathetic to a Walton-style approach to the matter. A viewer imagines seeing a certain fictional situation in a segment S just in case, in watching S, it is make believe for the viewer, from the inside, that he or she is thereby seeing that situation in S. Without extended commentary, this characterization yields limited enlightenment at best, and alternative approaches are feasible as well. I think that I can afford to be neutral, in the following discussion, concerning the details of an acceptable plausible explication, but I have wanted to signal the special character of the use that I will employ—a use in which it figures, to some degree, as a convenient term of art.

Viewers know an indeterminate host of things about what is fictionally the case in a given movie, but they come to know different fictional film truths in very different ways. It is difficult to make sense of basic differences in the nature of their knowledge of what is fictional in a film story unless some version of the imagined seeing thesis is accepted. For instance, viewers of *The Searchers* (John Ford, 1956) know that it is fictional in the movie both that Scar's (Henry Brandon) tribe of Comanches is slaughtered by the cavalry and that later Ethan (John Wayne) disrupts a marriage ceremony. However, they know that in *The Searchers*, the cavalry slaughters the Commanches because they make a correct inference from what they see and hear in a central, rather elliptical section of the movie. On the other hand, they know that fictionally Ethan disrupts Laurie's (Vera Miles) wedding because they imagine seeing him do just that. Certainly, this is the easiest and most natural way of distinguishing between instances of perceived and inferential knowledge of what is fictional in a movie, and it is unclear what better way of distinguishing them might be drawn. Perhaps, one is inclined to protest that the viewers simply *see* Ethan disrupt the wedding—no qualification by "imagined" is required. However, in watching the very same scene, viewers also see John Wayne stride onto a Hollywood set and act out the pertinent prescriptions of the script. And yet, surely, viewers do not "see" both the behavior of the actor John Wayne and the actions of the character Ethan in the same way, although it is also not credible that "see" is lexically ambiguous across the two assertions. The difference, I am assuming, should be explained in this way: viewers actually see John Wayne and his behavior, and it is make believe for the viewers that they see Ethan and what fictionally he does, that is, the viewers *imagine* seeing those constituents of the fiction.

II. POINT-OF-VIEW SHOTS AND SUBJECTIVE INFLECTION AND SATURATION

I will begin by introducing some reflections on the concept of a "subjective" shot and about some of the important subdivisions within the category. These considerations will be pretty rough and ready, since each category to be discussed involves considerable variation and complexity, but I will say enough to argue for two points. First, subjective segments of the sorts that I will examine involve at least two different notions of "the subjective." Second, subjective segments, of these different kinds, do not pose a serious problem for "the imagined seeing thesis," if the thesis is suitably formulated. Finally, it will be crucial for us to have at least a schematic overview of a number of the main kinds of subjective shots. Later, I will distinguish, from the more familiar kinds, one special type of subjective shot—what I will call "impersonal but subjectively inflected shots." This category does not seem to be adequately delineated in the literature, and I will highlight its interest later in the discussion. I will start out by considering segments whose "subjective" character is more or less clearly indicated in their immediate context. In the last part of the essay, I will turn to some issues that are raised by

segments whose "subjective" status has not been marked immediately in this fashion—segments of nontransparent narration, in other words.

Among the shots commonly deemed to be "subjective," one naturally thinks first of veridical point-of-view (POV) shots. These are shots that represent (at least approximately) the visual perspective, anchored in an implicit visual vantage point, of a designated character at a given time. Although this is the simplest case, it is not really clear why veridical POV shots are regularly counted as "subjective." It is often said that viewers are meant to imagine that they are seeing the relevant fictional items and events "through the eyes" of the relevant character. In some sense, this is no doubt true, but the sense in question is not so easy to pin down. In my opinion, what film viewers imagine seeing in a veridical POV shot are the fictional circumstances that the character perceives, and viewers imagine that they are seeing the depicted fictional material from a visual perspective that coincides more or less with the visual perspective of the observing character in the film. Nevertheless, certain tempting misconceptions need to be avoided. As Kendall Walton and I have argued elsewhere, film viewers, in so imagining, do not imagine either that they are, at that moment, identical with the movie character or even that they occupy the implied vantage point of the character within the movie's fictional space. Rather, it is to be imagined that the visual perspective offered on the screen arises from the same vantage point as the vantage point that fictionally the character is occupying at the time of his or her viewing.[8]

So, in what sense is a veridical POV shot subjective? After all, if what viewers imagine seeing in the shot is, in the first instance, the objective circumstances in the fictional world that fall within the character's gaze, then the depicted content of the shot is not subjective. Both the film viewers and the viewing character are being supplied with intersubjective information about these observable circumstances. In this respect at least, the information that is fictionally presented in the shot is just as "objective" as the information in shots whose visual perspective is not identified with that of any character.[9] Of course, the veridical POV shot simultaneously makes it fictional that the character is seeing the circumstances before his or her eyes and seeing them from the vantage point implicit in the shot. And yet, a non-POV shot that showed the same character gazing at the same fictional circumstances (for example, in an over-the-shoulder shot of those circumstances) would generate more or less the same fictional truths about the character's seeing and what it is he or she sees. However, such a shot would not normally be deemed subjective. If we were to suppose that the visual contents of the POV shot are to be imagined as representing the private field of vision of the perceiving character, then that putative fact would yield an obvious sense in which POV shots are "subjective." Nevertheless, it is doubtful that this *is* a part of what viewers normally imagine or are meant to imagine when they watch veridical POV shots. Hence, it is correspondingly doubtful that this explanation of POV subjectivity should be endorsed.

The subjectivity of veridical POV shots may well consist in nothing more than the coincidence of vantage point between the onscreen imagery and the character's visual perspective. Or, alternatively, it may be that POV shots are thought of as subjective because the occupation of their vantage points by a fictional perceiver always raises the question, at least potentially, of whether the shots in question are fictionally veridical. By contrast, given the strong but defeasible expectation of transparency, non-POV shots are tacitly and almost automatically construed as offering film viewers intersubjectively accessible information about the objective scene in view. I will leave this question about the general nature of the subjectivity of POV shots unresolved, but I want to stress the fact that the sense in which veridical POV shots are subjective is really pretty weak.

On the other hand, there *are* POV shots and sequences in which a viewer *is* expected to imagine something about the phenomenal qualities or contents of a character's field of vision. We are all familiar with POV shots that are, as I will say, *subjectively inflected*. That is, a range of the visual properties of the shot are supposed to represent subjective enhancements and distortions of the character's field of vision at the time. For instance, when the character is drunk, dizzy, or otherwise perceptually disoriented, then special effects of focus, lighting, filtering, or camera movement may be employed to

depict the way these psychological conditions have affected the character's visual experience. Similarly, consider a POV shot in which a character is seeing items in his or her immediate environment, but the character's field of vision also includes some hallucinatory objects or events. For example, in a POV shot, some character may be represented as looking into his or her garage and hallucinating a pink aardvark on the car. Of course, partially hallucinated perceptual structure shots of this type occur in many films. Robert Altman's *Images* (1972), which is itself a kind of epistemological twist film, features many partially hallucinatory POV shots from the heroine's (Susannah York) perspective, and the psychological drama of the movie is centrally built up around them. In any case, I am stipulating that these partially hallucinated POV shots are to count as subjectively inflected as well. Since certain internal properties of a character's perceptual state are represented in such shots, they are understood to be "subjective" in a straightforward sense. Normally, the objective and subjective aspects of the image and the way the two are related are specified clearly enough in the immediate film context. Let us say that these aspects and the relations between them constitute "the epistemic structure" of the pertinent shot or sequence. That is, in standard segments of this type, it is plainly indicated by the context that the character is actually seeing a certain fictional situation before his or her eyes and that he or she is also seeing the situation from a certain visual perspective that is subjectively inflected in a certain way—the way that is depicted on the screen. Correspondingly, film viewers imagine seeing the same fictional objects and events as does the character, and they imagine seeing them from the very same inflected visual perspective.

On one extreme of the subjectively inflected mode, the subjective inflection of the visual perspective may be *total*. That is, movie spectators are to imagine that the character's visual perspective is completely determined by his or her present state of dreaming, hallucination, or inner visualization of one sort or another and to imagine themselves seeing those private visual contents. I will call such shots "subjectively saturated." In this sort of case, spectators are mandated not to imagine that they are being provided with information about whatever fictional environment lies outside the character's mind. So, is it correct to say that spectators imagine seeing *anything* in such cases of total subjective saturation? Well, should we say that people who are subject to total hallucinations are seeing something? In one sense, "yes," and in another sense, perhaps "no." "No" because they are blinded to their environment by their total hallucination. "Yes" because they "see" the things that they hallucinate. In the case of film spectatorship, if the viewed segment is contextually marked to indicate that it depicts, for example, what a character is dreaming, then spectators do imagine seeing something, but it is "seeing" in the more inclusive sense. What they imagine "seeing" is what they recognize to be the visual contents of the character's dream.

However, none of this implies that the film viewers imagine themselves dreaming that very dream. More generally, it seems to me that visually subjective shots (whether the shots are subjectively inflected or saturated) never call on spectators to imagine that they are identical with the visualizing character nor that they are actually having the fictional visualizer's visual experiences. Film spectators merely imagine that the visual perspective presented onscreen coincides in its important, salient respects with the phenomenal qualities and contents of the character's visual experience, but not that those subjective visual experiences are their own. (This generalizes a point I mentioned earlier.) However, is the imagined seeing by one person of the private visual experiences of another really coherent? It depends, I believe, on how deep we expect the coherence of what viewers imagine in such a case to be.

The following is one way we might imagine seeing the visual contents of someone else's dream. We can imagine that neuroscientists have discovered in exhaustive detail the physical basis of dreaming. Implementing their discoveries in video technology, they come to have the capacity to introduce sensitive probes into a dreamer's brain and record the dream-relevant electrochemical activity that is taking place. Suitably transforming that recorded information, they are able to project a phenomenologically accurate visual representation of the dreamer's dream imagery on a large monitor above the dreamer's head. Thus, anyone suitably placed before the monitor is able to see the contents and phenomenal qualities of the projected dream.[10] If we can imagine this scenario, then we can imagine seeing (as observers) the contents of someone else's dream, and we can imagine this without imagining that we are having the dream experiences ourselves. In a similar way, when viewers watch a dream sequence in film, they imagine themselves seeing the contents of the fictional dream, but they do not imagine themselves to be experiencing that very dream.

I am claiming that we can imagine dreams to have a kind of public visual accessibility, but I do not claim that what we imagine is philosophically or scientifically coherent in any substantial detail. Almost surely it is not. (The superficial coherence may well depend on our tendency to imagine our dreams as if they were movies in our heads.) After all, a fair amount of what we imagine to ourselves is only superficially coherent in just this way. Also, I am not supposing that when we imagine seeing someone's dream in the movies that we imagine this *by* imagining that some agency of dream engineering has projected the dreamer's experience on the movie screen in front of us. On the contrary, we simply do not imagine much of anything in particular about how the dreamer's visual perspective has been presented to our view. It is imaginatively indeterminate how this has come to be, but this indeterminacy is nothing special. In the same way, we imagine almost nothing about the means or mechanisms by which the movie's impersonal views of objective circumstances in the story have come to be fictionally visible to us.[11]

One further observation is in order. In general, it will be significantly indeterminate as to how close the detailed match of movie images and fictional private experience is supposed to be. For instance, we presumably are supposed to imagine that we share our visual perspective on the dream with the dreamer's own perspective, but the film segment may offer a slight and rather unconvincing basis for imagining this. In particular, the screen imagery will establish fairly definite fictional vantage points from which the various visual perspectives arise, but these are implicit vantage points within the constructed and often shifting spaces of the dream. As film viewers, we do not imagine that the dreamers actually occupy those vantage points.

The dreamers are fictionally located wherever it is that they are sleeping. Perhaps we imagine that they dream that they occupy (usually in a highly indeterminate fashion) those vantage points. This sometimes is so but, more often, what we imagine on this score is probably even more thoroughly indeterminate. For example, dreamers in movies frequently make an appearance within their own dreams. So, is it fictional for the viewer that the dreamers dream that they occupy two different places at the same time? Of course, we know that dreams can be like that—featuring the bizarre and even the absurd. And yet the dreamers' visible presence in the shot does not normally strike us as paradoxical or even especially odd. I suspect that, in general, the question of the dreamers' vantage points on the scenes of their dreams is supposed to be passed over in the spectator's imagination. Perspectival implausibility here is accepted as the consequence of a standard and convenient practice in showing dreams in movies. It is easy to disregard the question in movies because, in real dreams, the matter of vantage point is normally vague as well. Hence, there is no presumption in "dream sequences" that the vantage points of the film shots and of the fictional dreaming are meant to correspond in any sharply determinate way. This has the consequence that the thought that we imagine seeing the contents of the dream (or hallucination or whatever) from the subject's point of view has to be understood as having a significant looseness of fit. It follows from this fact that such shots are not POV shots in a strict and unqualified sense. At the same time, there is an important sense in which subjectively saturated shots are *not* impersonal shots either. The visual perspective of these film shots does provide us with the visual perspective defined by the character's private sensory manifolds. For this reason, I do not take the concept of a POV shot to be strictly coextensive with the concept of a shot whose visual perspective is personal.

III. IMPERSONAL SUBJECTIVELY INFLECTED SHOTS

Let us now consider an important way in which the epistemic structure of a segment may be even more complicated. All the types of subjective shot that I have described are to be contrasted with another kind of subjective shot. It is a type that is not as frequently deployed as, say, POV shots, but it is common enough in conventional narrative films. These are non-POV shots (more broadly, impersonal shots) that are subjectively inflected but do not share their vantage point with the visual perspective of any character in the film. Here is one simple and fairly well-known example: In *Murder, My Sweet* (Edward, Dmytryk, 1944), Phillip Marlowe (Dick Powell) has been knocked out and drugged. When he eventually comes to, we see him (that is, we imagine seeing him) stagger around the room. However, these shots of him are, in a certain respect, clearly subjective. In voice-over, Marlowe describes his clouded perceptual experience, and the shots with which we are presented look as though they had been filtered through smoke and spider webs. The look of the shots in this respect is obviously meant to correspond to key aspects of the way that things are looking to Marlowe in his drugged condition, but the screen image here does not purport to give us his actual visual perspective. As in an objective shot, we imagine seeing Marlowe as he wanders around the room, but, at the same time, we do not imagine that the room is filled with smoke and spider webs. The look of smoke and spider webs is imagined to represent certain phenomenal properties present in Marlowe's field of vision. In this example, we are prompted to the conclusion that these features of the image are subjective because Marlowe, in voice-over, tells us that this is what his drugged visual experience is like. So, we imagine seeing Marlowe and his actions from a visual perspective he does not and could not occupy. Moreover, it is a visual perspective that is not experienced by anyone else in the film. Still, we are keyed to suppose that the pertinent phenomenal properties included in the onscreen visual perspective reflect specific qualitative inflections with which we imagine the detective's visual perspective to be suffused. This constitutes a third kind of subjective shot, and I will call it "an impersonal, subjectively inflected shot." In this example, we imagine ourselves seeing Marlowe and his actions from an unoccupied visual perspective that is subjectively inflected in specific ways.

The concept of "impersonal but subjectively inflected shots" should be understood strictly to entail that the phenomenal qualities or contents of a character's perceptual experience are mirrored in the shot. They should be distinguished from still another type of psychologically charged impersonal shot. Mitry and Branigan both point out that there are impersonal shots that pick out objects and events that have been shown to be perceived by a character and present them in a way that illuminates the psychological significance they have for the character. For instance, the clenched fist of one character, Jones, may be shot in a closeup that expresses the looming threat that Smith feels when he notices the clenching of Jones's hand. The hypothetical shot is a closeup, but Jones is standing at a considerable distance from Smith. The shot is therefore not literally a shot from Jones's visual perspective, although, in its narrative context, it may tell us a fair amount about Jones's reactive thoughts and emotions. This would be a good example of what Mitry refers to as a "semisubjective shot." Nevertheless, since the shot does not show us anything about the *phenomenal* character of Jones's visual field, it is not a subjectively inflected impersonal shot, as I have introduced that concept. I have the impression that Mitry's category may include impersonal, subjectively inflected shots, although he never describes an instance of this narrower kind. The danger is that he effectively conflates them with other types of impersonal shots whose chief function is to *imply* something about a character's *cognitive* or *affective* states.[12]

Still, one might worry that my characterization of subjectively inflected impersonal shots verges on inconsistency. The characterization seems to ask us to suppose that film viewers imagine that they are visually presented with a subjectively inflected field of vision, but a field of vision that impossibly belongs to no one. Of course, if we assumed that the various non-POV shots in a transparent film depict, in the first instance, the perceptual experience of an invisible-camera witness, then there would be no problem here. We could readily allow that subjectively inflected images present the phenomenal contents and qualities of the field of vision of this implicit witness. However, the general identification of the camera with such an invisible spectator is, for well-canvassed reasons, quite implausible. It is equally implausible to posit that such a witness pops into fictional existence

only to accommodate the subjectivity of these impersonal shots. As I have argued before, there really is no incoherence in the concept. The visual perspective of a shot is not to be identified with the field of vision of a character, explicit or implicit in the fiction, unless the film narration specifically establishes such an identity. We imagine the shots in *Murder, My Sweet* as showing us Marlowe's action from the visual perspective a person would have if he or she were viewing the action from a certain vantage point *and* if he or she were afflicted with the type of clouded vision that Marlowe is experiencing. This visual perspective is not fictionally identical with anyone's actual field of vision. The distinction between veridical POV shots and impersonal subjectively inflected shots underscores the treacherous ambiguity of the phrase "point of view," even when that phrase is constrained to apply to matters of strict visual experience. Shots of the latter kind show us the character's perceptual point of view in one sense (they delineate the qualitative nature of his or her perception) but not in the other (they do not present the vantage point from which he or she looks).

Impersonal subjectively inflected shots and sequences range from the trivial to the rich and intricate. A segment in which a character is shown pondering some decision while the character's visualized thoughts appear as if they were projected behind him or her is subjectively inflected in a trivial way. However, subjectively inflected shots can exhibit a nuanced epistemic structure. They offer the possibility of directly showing the audience intersubjectively accessible information about a character and his or her behavior while, at the same time, presenting important facets of the character's private perceptual impressions. We can see the character and, to a significant degree, see with him or her at the same time. Such shots have the further potential of insinuating some outside comment from the filmmaker about the relations between the characters' depicted states of sentience and the actions they produce.

We can invoke some sense of the more interesting possibilities here if we remind ourselves of the famous shot from Hitchcock's *Vertigo* (1958) in which Scottie (James Stewart) kisses and embraces Judy (Kim Novak) just after she has remade herself as Madeline.[13] The couple is in Judy's hotel room and, as they kiss, the camera (or so it seems) begins to track around them.[14] In the course of the shot, the hotel setting gradually fades into blackness and is replaced by a slightly dimmed view of the stable in San Juan Bautista—the place where Scottie had kissed Madeline just before her apparent death. Still embracing Judy, he looks around him, appearing troubled and disoriented. The background view of the stable fades back to black, and the hotel room gradually reappears, bathed now in a ghostly green. This shot contains additional complications that I will ignore, but the effects of the features I have already mentioned are tricky to characterize accurately. I take it that this is a subjectively inflected shot, but the inflection is more elaborate than in the shot from *Murder, My Sweet*. Presumably, the circling "camera" vantage point is meant to depict the nature of the overwhelming emotion Scottie feels at that moment, and it is an emotion that is here being linked to the film's recurrent motif of vertigo. The background shot of the stable represents a hallucinated memory image—an image that has flooded into Scottie's consciousness, superimposing itself on his view of the hotel room. Presumably, the experience is so unexpected and so vivid that it causes the bewilderment that is registered in Scottie's face. So, what is it that film viewers imagine seeing in this extended shot? They imagine seeing Scotty's and Judy's intense embrace in the Empire Hotel, and they imagine seeing the embrace from an impersonal moving vantage point that circles around the couple. Spectators also imagine that the circling visual perspective expresses the vertiginous sensations that Scotty is experiencing at the time. When the view of the stable appears, they imagine seeing Scottie hallucinating as he holds Judy/Madeline to him *and* the content of what he is then hallucinating. What is more, the dynamics of this non-POV shot suggest a narrational comment on the narrative situation. For example, they hint at the entrapment of both characters in their private obsessions and the uncanny nature of the circumstances that these obsessions have led them to create. I say that this subjectively inflected shot is impersonal, but this application of the term should not mislead. The vantage point is impersonal—it is not occupied by anyone in the fiction—but what the shot expresses about the

characters is not emotionally impersonal. It is engaged and sympathetic, expressing the filmmaker's attitudes toward the scene.

IV. UNMARKED SUBJECTIVE INFLECTION

In the example from *Vertigo*, the structure of objective and subjective elements of the shot is elaborate, but its structure and import are reasonably clear. Viewers may differ about interpretative details, but it is apparent that we are seeing Judy and Scottie embrace in the hotel room as Scottie flashes back in memory to the earlier incident in the stable. The epistemic structures of the segments in my earlier examples are simpler and, correspondingly, the structures are even more plainly delineated in their immediate narrative contexts. So, these are shots and sequences in which the norm of narrational transparency has been locally preserved.

However, there are numerous exceptions to the practice of immediate transparency. Even in classical narrative films, there are many cases in which the epistemic structure of a segment is not specified straight away when the segment occurs. In fact, there are many instances in which there is some deliberate delay in identifying a significant aspect of the segment's epistemic structure. Indeed, in a number of these examples, the specification of structure is long postponed, sometimes for almost the whole length of the film. In these instances, the nature of the epistemic structure of particular earlier segments is eventually settled at narrative closure. Epistemological twist films are defined by the fact that global aspects of the epistemic structure of their narration are clarified, in a surprising way, only toward the end of the movie.

Hitchcock's *Stage Fright* (1950) opens with a notorious "lying" flashback. One character (Richard Todd) verbally tells another (Jane Wyman) about what happened when a murder took place and, as he narrates his story, there is a long visual sequence that seems to be a flashback to the events that he is recounting. It is only at the film's conclusion that we learn that this character has been lying and that the relevant sequence has to be reconstrued as merely a visual illustration of the content of the liar's false assertions. Of course, this segment is "subjective" in still a different sense—it is the rendering of what a character has verbally *reported*. In this instance, the report is false and, for present purposes, what is important is that the movie suppresses the fact that it is false until the story's end approaches.

In Fritz Lang's *The Woman in the Window* (1944), we discover near the conclusion that the whole story of Professor Wanley's (Edward G. Robinson) involvement with a treacherous *femme fatale* (Jane Wyman)—an involvement that leads him to murder her lover—has been a nightmare that the professor has been dreaming. Almost nothing in the style of the film's visual narration prompts us to suppose that what we are seeing is a dream. That disclosure is simply announced by showing Wanley as he finally wakes up in a chair in his club. In both these cases and others like them, the movies wind up revealing an epistemological twist, but the twist, as it is handled here, can seem arbitrary and artificial. Viewers often feel cheated by the tricks. Be this as it may, suppose that long-delayed and suppressed issues of epistemic structure are eventually settled in a given film. Should we say that the movie satisfies the norm of narrational transparency? Must epistemic structure be clear more or less continuously throughout the film? I do not think it matters much what stipulation we adopt, but the twist movies certainly violate at least the classical implementations of transparency.

Returning to *The Woman in the Window* for a moment, there is a question about what viewers, who already know about the dream twist, imagine seeing in the scenes that relate the contents of the dream. As one first watches the relevant segments, one imagines seeing, for example, the professor murder his romantic rival. However, after it has been revealed that Wanley has been dreaming all along, do viewers still imagine themselves as having seen the murder? Or, alternatively, when viewers see the movie a second time and know that Wanley dreams his adventures, then, as they rewatch the murder scene, do they still imagine seeing the professor commit the crime? Or, at this juncture, do they merely imagine seeing the contents of his dream? My own strong inclination is to say the following. Both the first time and the second time that viewers watch the scene, they do imagine seeing Professor Wanley kill his rival. The murder is, as it were, visually present on

the screen. However, on the first viewing, while implicitly accepting the assumption of transparency, viewers suppose that the murder *actually* takes place (in the overall world of the story). Seeing the same scene again, they have learned that this supposition about the status of what they have imagined seeing is false. Thus, on a second viewing, they continue to imagine seeing Wanley perform the murder, but this time they imagine, that is, they suppose, that the murder is merely something that the professor fictionally has dreamed. Hence, we need to draw a distinction between what viewers imagine seeing in a stretch of film and the imaginative suppositions that they adopt about the epistemic and ontological standing of the things and events that they imagine seeing. The "core" contents of what viewers imagine seeing remains roughly the same from viewing to viewing. It is what the film viewers imagine (suppose) about the epistemological status of what they imagine seeing that alters so sharply.

Compare this with a case in which there is a notable change of dramatic aspect for the viewer between two viewings of the same scene. Watching a closeup of Octave in *The Rules of the Game* (Jean Renoir, 1939), the viewer might, the first time through, imagine seeing Octave's (Jean Renoir) face as expressing one set of emotions, but imagine seeing, the next time around, a different mix of feeling and motivation in Octave's countenance. Here, I am inclined to say that there *has* been a change in the "core" content of what the viewer has imagined seeing from one showing to another. The very look of Octave's face, as the viewer imagines it each time, has changed. In my opinion, this contrasts with the situation of the viewer before and after the disclosure of a systematic epistemological twist.

Jacob's Ladder, *Vanilla Sky*, and *Mulholland Drive* are twisted like *The Woman in the Window*.[15] The greater part of the narration turns out to be a rendering of a character's dreams, and this is a fact that is disclosed only late in the movie. In these cases, the strategy is handled in a much more elaborate fashion than it is in Lang's film. On the other hand, *Fight Club* and *Secret Window* portray the hallucinated experiences of their main characters, although the drastic subjective inflection that predominates in the film narration is, for the most part, impersonally represented. Large sections of the cinematic narration are partially inflected by the hallucinations experienced by the chief character in each film and depicted from a vantage point the characters do not occupy.

Let me explain this claim by focusing specifically on *Fight Club*. First, here is the barest skeleton of its plot. An unnamed character played by Edward Norton—I will call him "Jack"[16]—meets an intense, charismatic young soap salesman, Tyler Durden (Brad Pitt). Jack and Tyler form a close friendship, live together in a house on Paper Street, and become founders of a series of underground fight clubs—clubs in which marginalized young men meet together and pound each other into pulp in arranged fights. Jack has a tentative, sour friendship with a woman Marla (Helena Bonham Carter), but it is Tyler and Marla who come to have an explosive sexual affair. The fight clubs evolve into Project Mayhem, a quasi-fascistic organization of urban guerrillas who aim to destroy the credit-based foundations of the contemporary economic system. Tyler is the moving force behind Project Mayhem, while Jack is apparently a more passive fellow traveler in that enterprise. What we discover, as the narrative concludes, is that Tyler is the hallucinated ideal projection of Jack's volatile and distorted psyche. Jack imagines seeing Tyler in his company and he imagines that they regularly talk and interact. Nevertheless, Tyler is a creation of Jack's imagination. We also find out, late in the movie, that Jack has sometimes adopted the Tyler persona and acted under that fantasized identity. For instance, he travels around the country promoting the fight clubs and expanding Project Mayhem. Apparently, Jack has no memory of what he does as Tyler and it is only in the scene of revelation that we are directly shown a moment in which Jack assumes the role of Tyler. However, we are repeatedly shown scenes in which Jack and Tyler appear together—conversing, fighting, engaging in horseplay, and so on. These are the scenes that most straightforwardly raise the question of the overall coherence of the film's narration. After all, Tyler really does not exist, so how do we construe his repeated appearances in the film's narration?

Take, for example, all the scenes in which we imagine seeing Jack and Tyler together in their house on Paper Street. It simply does not make sense to suppose that nothing of what we imagine seeing in this setting actually took place. Many of the events portrayed in these inflected scenes have causal consequences that turn out to be real in the ultimate fiction of the film. The chemical burn that Tyler inflicts on the back of Jack's hand is just one rather emblematic illustration of the point. What we have to imagine, when we consider the film in retrospect, is that Jack does utter most of the things we hear him say and performs most of the actions that we observe. We are also meant to imagine that, on these occasions, Jack is simultaneously hallucinating Tyler's presence, his deeds, and speeches, and that Jack is responding to these fantasized occurrences. Characteristically, the two characters are presented together in the frame and shot from an impersonal vantage point. However, in light of the culminating disclosure, we are forced to look back and reconstrue these sequences as perspectivally impersonal but subjectively inflected. They are inflected to represent in a single shot both Jack's actual behavior and the content of his concurrent delirious experience. That these segments are to be understood as inflected versions of an otherwise objective situation is implied by the following considerations: There are scenes in which Jack and Tyler are together in the kitchen, scenes that are either preceded or followed by Marla's entrance into that room. When she is there, Tyler is always absent. The scenes between Jack and Marla would seem to be patently objective, and the continuity of the space between these scenes and the adjacent sequences with Tyler indicates that Jack remains objectively present in the kitchen throughout. But when Tyler also seems to be present, Jack is actually by himself and talking to a hallucinated figure.

Near the end of the movie, as the truth begins to dawn on Jack, we are given several short shots that show Jack acting by himself in situations where earlier we had seen Jack and Tyler acting together. These later shots model for us what we are now to imagine about the real circumstances after we have discounted for the subjective inflection. In certain scenes, the fantasized relationships are even more complicated. When Tyler finally explains the psychological state of affairs to Jack, he says:

FIGURE 1. The aftermath of the first fight in a subjectively inflected view.

FIGURE 2. The aftermath of the first fight in an "objective" view.

"Sometimes you're still you—sometimes you imagine yourself watching me." At this juncture, there is a shot of Jack lecturing the members of the fight club, echoing an earlier shot in which Tyler delivered the lecture. The late shot establishes that it was Jack who had spoken these words, imagining himself as Tyler. However, in the earlier counterpart scene, we were also given brief glimpses of Jack standing in the crowd and gazing at Tyler. So, presumably, Jack both hallucinates being Tyler and being himself (qua Jack) watching Tyler perform. In any case, given the ultimate perspective of the film, we are asked to reimagine earlier critical scenes either in these kinds of terms or in minor variants thereof. The sequences with Jack and Tyler constitute the most extensive and daring uses of impersonal subjective inflection that I know. They are particularly audacious because the massive subjective inflection is left unspecified until so late in the movie.

The global narrational structure of the film is cleverly designed. Jack is the intermittent voice-over narrator of the film, and the film's narration is probably best understood as an audio/visual rendering of the narrative that he is verbally recounting.

The film narration includes many segments (most of the ones in which Tyler does not appear) that are, even with hindsight, genuinely objective. However, as we will see in a moment, it also interpolates some shorter sequences that are marked in the immediate context as subjective depictions of Jack's fantasies. So the narration, in an apparently conventional manner, moves between depiction of the objective world of the fiction and the private perceptions and fantasies of the main character. The twist, of course, is the fact that the full extent of the inflection of the narration of Jack's consciousness has been systematically obscured.

The objective presentation of the story, then, is troubled from the outset by odd, seemingly unmotivated incursions from the contents of Jack's mind. At the beginning of the movie, we are given a POV shot from Jack's perspective as he looks out the window of an office building, but his view out the window morphs seamlessly into a dizzying traveling shot that careens down through the building and into the underground parking garage below. This highly dynamic subjective shot encapsulates in a flash Jack's memory of the bomb that Project Mayhem has planted in a van that is sitting in the garage. Also, on two occasions, we see Jack's surreal daydream of wandering through an icy cavern. The first time he is accompanied by a playful penguin, the second time he discovers Marla there. Or, taking a business flight, Jack wishes in voice-over for a plane crash and hallucinates the disaster in grim detail. This hallucination immediately precedes his meeting Tyler, who is sitting next to him in the airplane. All *these* segments are subjectively saturated, but there are also short instances of subjective inflection, plainly identifiable as such. Thus, Jack sits on the toilet reading a home decoration catalog, and the movie cuts to a tracking shot that explores his fantasy of his apartment fully furnished with Ikea-like products, each item still labeled by its blurb in the catalogue. Subsequently, we see Jack, having risen from the toilet, still in his underwear, amble through the blurbed apartment and go to the refrigerator. Or, prior to the point at which Tyler has made his entrance as a definite character in the film, various "objective" shots of sundry circumstances incorporate brief, usually subliminal, images of him. It is as if the narration were already haunted by Tyler-laced eruptions from Jack's volatile subconsciousness. I do not believe that we can understand the overall film narration as a representation from the inside, as it were, of Jack's actual hallucinated memories of his history with Tyler, but, as these last examples illustrate, the narration is repeatedly ruptured by outcroppings from Jack's imagination and memory. In this fashion, the movie's narration subtly hints at the larger strategy of nontransparency that it so cunningly constructs.

The Others is a kind of epistemological twist-of-the-screw movie, but the twist it takes raises an interesting question about the characterization of film narrational transparency with which we started. For most of its duration, the film seems to tell a rather traditional type of ghost story. A young woman, Grace (Nicole Kidman), and her two children (Alakina Mann and James Bentley) live in an isolated house on the Isle of Jersey, where they are joined by a trio of creepy servants. The house appears to be haunted and the family is regularly troubled by spectral sounds and other weird disturbances. The ghosts, it seems, are invisible, although Grace's young daughter has intimations, including sketchy visual intimations, of them and their doings. In the culminating twist, it turns out that it is actually the family and the servants who are dead and that they are actually the ghosts. The source of the disturbances is a family of living human beings who are trying to move into the house, and the genuine ghosts, about whom members of the living family have their own intimations, are completely invisible to them. And yet, Grace and her children and servants have been visible to the audience throughout the movie, normally in impersonal "objective" shots. This is the basis of the narration's problematic transparency. It is natural to explain an "objective" shot or sequence as one that represents the intersubjectively accessible visual appearances of the situation it depicts, and it is natural to take "intersubjectively accessible" to refer to the powers of normal human perceivers. Accepting the narrative's implicit assumption that ghosts and ghostly behavior are not accessible to human vision, and presupposing the

transparency of this film's narration, audience members unreflectively take it for granted that Grace and her children cannot be ghosts. But the audience has just been fooled. In retrospect, what film viewers have been watching in the film is a certain course of narrative action as only the sentient dead could perceive it. The viewer's imagined seeing has been systematically linked to what fictionally "the others" might see. In most other twist movies, we are encouraged to construe certain shots and sequences as objective that in fact are inflected (partially or totally) by the subjectivity of one of the characters. In *The Others*, we construe the visual objectivity of the film narration with reference to human perception. We fail to notice that there is an alternative standard of perceptual objectivity that the film has tacitly invoked and then quite systematically exploited.

It would be interesting to inquire why cinematic assaults on the norm of narrational transparency have become so common around the turn of the century.[17] I do not know the answer, and I am not sure how such an inquiry, responsibly conducted, should proceed. No doubt a certain amount of copycatting has gone on, and perhaps some kind of postmodern skepticism about the duplicity of reality and the photographic image has drifted over Hollywood. In any event, my present aim has been to say something fairly systematic about what some of these subversions of cinematic transparency amount to. Much earlier in the essay, I raised a related but more general question about the thesis of imagined seeing as it applies to film. I asked whether the thesis can be sustained, in some form, when various types of subjective segments are examined, particular segments that are nontransparently subjective. The answer, implicit in the foregoing discussion, is "yes," although it has emerged that an adequate formulation of the general thesis will necessarily be multifaceted.

There are two broad points that I would like to emphasize. I have reaffirmed the claim that when viewers watch a POV shot that is from the visual perspective of a character C, it does not follow either that the viewers thereby imagine that they are identical with C or that they imagine themselves located at the implicit vantage point from which C is looking. In this essay, I have argued for a similar stricture concerning

POV shots that are totally subjective. If, in such a case, viewers imagine themselves seeing the visual contents of C's private visual experience, then again it does not follow either that they thereby imagine that they are identical with C or that they imagine that they are experiencing C's own visual sensations. These negative strictures and the basis for them are important. If the strictures are not observed, then the imagined seeing thesis will wrongly seem to be committed to disastrous absurdities. But really, the imagined seeing thesis, properly stated, engenders no such commitments.

Second, if viewers imagine seeing an item X perform or undergo Φ (for example, they imagine seeing Professor Wanley drive off) from a certain visual perspective P, then the content of what they imagine seeing in this way is not on its own sufficient to determine how they are to understand the epistemic structure of the shot or sequence they are watching. That is, the fact that they imagine seeing X Φ in the segment does not determine for them whether X's Φing constitutes an objective situation in the world of the fiction or whether it is merely a content of the visual experience of some character in the film. Or, somewhat more subtly, it does not determine whether certain aspects of the visual perspective P are to be imagined as intersubjectively accessible properties of the observed circumstances or as phenomenal qualities of the manner in which some character is perceiving the depicted situation. The possibilities of epistemic structure, as I have explained, can get pretty complicated. How viewers understand or imagine the epistemic structure of a given segment turns both on what they imagine seeing in the segment and what they take the wider context to prescribe about the epistemic status of the contents of their imagined seeing. Moreover, sometimes viewers imagine, when they view a segment, that its epistemic structure is such-and-such, discovering only later that what they earlier imagined about that structure was mistaken and that the segment needs to be differently construed. So, at least two types of imagining are characteristically involved in our basic comprehension of a shot, a sequence, and, sometimes, a film's cinematic narration overall. Spectators imagine seeing various items and situations as the film is shown, and they imagine

that these items and situations have one or another epistemic standing within the larger contexts of the narrative and its narration.

This point is implicit in some remarks of Walton's on the theme of subjective shots. He says: "We imagine seeing things from a certain point of view, noticing certain aspects of them, and so forth. And we *understand* [emphasis added] that what we imagine seeing is what fictionally the character sees; we *imagine* [emphasis added] that that is what the character sees. The film thus *shows* what the character's experience is like."[18] In this passage, Walton is concerned only with POV shots, but notice that, even to analyze the basics of that basic case, he invokes a contrast between "what we imagine seeing" and "what we understand about it," for example, that it constitutes the content of what a certain character is experiencing. Notice also that the understanding to which he here refers is immediately equated, in the next sentence, with a kind of suppositional imagining—the viewer understands or supposes or imagines *that* so-and-so. Walton is right to suggest that both the concept of "imagining seeing" and the concept of suppositional imagining need to be introduced if we are to be in a position to articulate properly our intuitions concerning the visual contents of a shot or sequence. The pertinent suppositional imaginings one brings to the viewing of a segment will affect what one imagines seeing in the segment, and further suppositional imaginings will influence the way one parses the epistemic and dramatic structure of what one imagines seeing. Acknowledging this point and its importance leaves one with a considerable and difficult project. How should we conceive of the interrelations between imagined seeing and suppositional imaginings in a manner that is adequate to describe the rich varieties of visual content in film shots and longer sequences? Walton's brief comments on one simple, albeit paradigmatic, type of subjective shot do not begin to cover the wealth of varieties that are in question here. It has been my ambition in this essay to sketch some of the intricacy of the broader topic of transparent and nontransparent subjective segments in movies and to elaborate some of the considerable conceptual complexity that the topic potentially subsumes.

GEORGE WILSON
School of Philosophy
University of Southern California
Los Angeles, California 90089
USA

INTERNET: gmwilson@usc.edu

1. Earlier versions of this essay were read at the 2004 meetings of the American Society for Aesthetics in Houston and at departmental colloquia at both the University of Southern California and the University of California at Riverside. The final version has benefited from each of these occasions. Among the people whose comments were especially helpful to me are William Bracken, David Davies, Berys Gaut, John Martin Fisher, Janet Levin, Jerry Levinson, Katalin Makkai, Michael Renov, Dana Polan, Murray Smith, Gideon Yaffee, Tom Wartenberg, and Gareth Wilson. However, I was most influenced by many long discussions with Karen Wilson.

2. Jean Mitry, *The Aesthetics and Psychology of the Cinema*, trans. Christopher King (Indiana University Press, 1977).

3. Bruce Kawin, *Mindscreen* (Princeton University Press, 1978).

4. Edward Branigan, *Point of View in Film* (Berlin: Mouton Publishers, 1984).

5. Here and elsewhere in the essay, I speak of the subjectivity of the visuals in a film and of what it is that viewers imagine seeing in a visual segment. But, as Michael Renov stressed to me, this is a serious oversimplification, perhaps even a significant distortion. The representation of cinematic subjectivity is often a crucial dimension of segments of the soundtrack, and related issues arise concerning what film viewers imagine hearing in the soundtrack. I stick to my oversimplified statement of the issues *only* to avoid recurrent qualifications and complexities of formulation that are likely to impede the reader's comprehension.

6. For Walton, see *Mimesis as Make Believe* (Harvard University Press, 1990), especially section 8, "Depictive Representation," and also "On Pictures and Photographs: Objections Answered," in *Film Theory and Philosophy*, ed. Richard Allen and Murray Smith (Oxford: Clarendon Press, 1997), pp. 60–75. For Levinson, see "Film Music and Narrative Agency," in *Post-Theory: Reconstructing Film Studies*, ed. David Bordwell and Noël Carroll (University of Wisconsin Press, 1996), pp. 248–282. See my "*Le Grand Imagier* Steps Out: On the Primitive Basis of Film Narration," *Philosophical Topics* 25 (1997): 295–318. This essay is partially reprinted in *Introduction to the Philosophy of*

Film, ed. Thomas Wartenberg and Angela Curran (Oxford: Blackwell Publishing, 2005), pp. 198–207.

7. For Currie, see *Image and Mind: Film, Philosophy, and Cognitive Science* (New York: Cambridge University Press, 1995), pp. 170–179. For Gaut, see "The Philosophy of the Movies: Cinematic Narration," in *The Blackwell Guide to Aesthetics*, ed. Peter Kivy (Oxford: Blackwell Publishing, 2004), pp. 230–253.

8. Walton argues this thesis in "On Pictures and Photographs," and I argue it in "*Le Grand Imagier* Steps Out."

9. Murray Smith makes this point in *Engaging Characters: Fiction, Emotion, and the Cinema* (Oxford: Clarendon Press, 1995), pp. 158–160.

10. It is not simply that this scenario is something we can imagine. It is a scenario that is actually depicted in an episode of the television series *The Prisoner*. "A, B, & C," *The Prisoner*, directed by Pat Jackson and written by Anthony Skene, ITV1 (UK), Oct. 15, 1967. I owe this reference to Steve Reber and Geoff Georgi.

11. The thought experiment and the argument based on it that I give here parallels a similar thought experiment and argument in my "*Le Grand Imagier* Steps Out," pp. 306–307.

12. Mitry, *The Aesthetics and Psychology of the Cinema*, pp. 214–219. On p. 216, Mitry gives an example from *Jezebel* (William Wyler, 1938) that is similar to but somewhat more complicated than the one I offer.

13. The aptness of this shot for my purposes was suggested by Deborah Thomas's sensitive discussion in *Reading Hollywood: Spaces and Meanings in American Film* (London: Wallflower, 2001), pp. 102–105. Our conclusions concerning the shot are somewhat different, however.

14. Despite appearances, the shot was not made with a tracking camera. See Dan Auiller, *Vertigo: The Making of a Hitchcock Classic* (New York: St. Martin's Press, 1998), p. 119. This is cited in Thomas, *Reading Hollywood*.

15. For an interpretation of *Mulholland Drive* with which I am in broad agreement, see Todd McGowan, "Lost on Mulholland Drive: Navigating David Lynch's Panegyric to Hollywood," *Cinema Journal* 43 (2004): 67–90. In particular, McGowan interprets the first two-thirds of the movie as the dream or fantasy of the character Diane (Naomi Watts) as she emerges in the last third of the movie. This line of interpretation has been suggested by many, but McGowan works it out in an especially careful way.

16. It has become standard, in the literature on *Fight Club*, to refer to this character as "Jack," for reasons that are easily enough inferred from the movie.

17. Murray Smith reminds me that transparency was also assaulted with significant regularity in Hollywood films during the 1940s.

18. Walton, "On Pictures and Photographs," p. 63.

STEPHEN MULHALL

The Impersonation of Personality: Film as Philosophy in *Mission: Impossible*

One reason I chose the *Alien* quartet as the central concern of my book *On Film* was that its unusual combination of features invited, even demanded, the simultaneous exploration of a number of different questions about the relation between cinema and philosophy.[1] At the level of content, its themes—the relation between human identity, integrity, and embodiment, as encountered in the field of our fantasies of sexual intercourse, pregnancy, and birth—evoke undismissible questions about what it is to be human. At the level of form, its nature as a series of sequels suggested that the question of what it is to make a sequel—to inherit a particular narrative world, together with whatever preceding directors have managed to make of it—would become an increasingly central preoccupation of its successive directors and would thereby naturally lead them to confront further questions about related conditions of filmmaking (the relation between actors and characters, the phenomenon of stardom, the photographic basis of projected individuals and worlds, and so on). In particular, since each film in this series had a different director, each of whom—although hired relatively early in his career—had nonetheless begun to establish a considerable body of work, the perennial question of the significance of the cinematic *auteur* seemed impossible to avoid.

One might think of each of these three sets of questions as isolating one aspect of our concept of individuality: the individuality of the directors (Ridley Scott, James Cameron, David Fincher, Jean-Pierre Jeunet), of the character (Ellen Ripley) and the actor (Sigourney Weaver), and of human individuality as such. Furthermore, the particular way these films engaged with such matters was understood by me to illuminate the individuality of cinema— as a distinctive art form and as a distinctive phenomenon of everyday human experience. And, of course, perhaps the most provocative aspect of my understanding of the films' mode of engagement found expression in my claiming it, and so them, for philosophy. I wanted to understand these films not as raw material for philosophers, and not as handy (because popular) illustrations of views and arguments properly developed by philosophers, but rather as themselves reflecting on and evaluating such views and arguments, as thinking seriously and systematically about them.[2]

In this essay, I propose further to test the coherence and plausibility of this way of understanding one of the possibilities of cinema by examining the only other sequence of movies I know of that holds out some prospect of matching the unusual combination of features that made the *Alien* quartet so suitable for my book's purposes—the two *Mission: Impossible* films. The first (released in 1996) was directed by Brian De Palma, the second (released in 2000) by John Woo; the third was due to go into production in 2005. It might seem foolhardy to embark on a reading of the two existing films in the absence of the third; nevertheless, this much can, I think, already be said.

Each film in the sequence centers on the same protagonist, Ethan Hunt (played by Tom Cruise), an experienced member of the IM force, a covert offshoot of the CIA; each is scripted by

Robert Towne; each has a different director who brings to bear an established and highly influential body of work. The structural analogies of continuity and discontinuity at the level of character, author, and director are thus evident, but so, it might be thought, are the differences. For first, concerning content, there is no obvious correlate in the *Mission: Impossible* sequence to the thematic preoccupations of the *Alien* quartet—nothing apparently concerning human identity, embodiment, and individuality of the kind so familiar to modern philosophy. And second, concerning form, the two directors so far involved have a reputation for, let us say, valuing surface sheen over human and artistic depth.

David Thomson, for example, in his *Biographical Dictionary of Film*, suggests that John Woo's early work supplies "evidence of how a culture like that of Hong Kong had become degraded, long ago, by the attempt to live up to American models," characterizes his later work in America as not so much "streamlined poetry" but rather the kind of film "that make[s] hay with the idea of a nuclear explosion," and goes on more specifically to say that *Mission: Impossible II* "is—and isn't—the new version of *Chinatown*."[3] Beyond its reminder of Robert Towne's illustrious past, the precise point of that comparison remains unclear, but it seems clearly to the detriment of the new version. However that may be, Thomson reserves his real, unambiguous venom for De Palma.

There is a self-conscious cunning in de Palma's work, ready to control everything except his own cruelty and indifference. He is the epitome of mindless style and excitement swamping taste or character...I daresay there are no "ugly" shots in de Palma's films—if you feel able to measure "beauty" merely in terms of graceful or hypnotic movement, vivid angles, lyrical color and hysterical situation. But that is the set of criteria that makes Leni Riefenstahl a "great" director...De Palma's eye is cut off from conscience and compassion. He has contempt for his characters and his audience alike, and I suspect that he despises even his own immaculate skill. Our cultural weakness admires and rewards technique and impact bereft of moral sense. If a thing works, it has validity—the means justify the lack of an end.[4]

We are not, then, surprised to find Thomson characterizing the two *Mission: Impossible*

films as "those two horrible wastes of time, expertise and writing talent."[5]

Since Thomson is not only a critic of justified renown, but one properly attuned to the basic merits of the *Alien* quartet, his particular way of speaking for the critical majority in this context deserves to be taken seriously. So, too, however, does the edge of hysteria that undeniably (to my ear at least) invades his graceful and hypnotic, vivid and lyrical denunciation. Something about the way these two directors are so quickly taken as symptomatic of a larger (originally American) cultural weakness and degradation suggests to me that their work is being made to bear the brunt of much more general anxieties about Western modernity in general, and about the possibilities of the medium of cinema itself. Is it always a manifestation of moral weakness to acknowledge the motion picture camera's capacity to detect beauty in the flowering of an explosion or the trajectory of a human body caught up in its blast? And are the ways artists in film have previously taken up the challenge to make something humanly meaningful of such possibilities of the medium the only ways that challenge can be met? What if, for some directors in contemporary circumstances, film is experienced as being in the condition of modernism—a condition in which the conventional ways of ensuring the human significance of the projected worlds of movies have, for them, lost their power?[6]

To be sure, one way of reacting to that loss of assurance would be to cut oneself loose from those conventions altogether, and thereby from the artistic enterprise they were able to support; call this the modernizing, or postmodernist, response. For such filmmakers, the history of cinema is a dismissible problem, to be transcended or simply left behind in favor of something essentially discontinuous, radically new. Another way, however, is to try to find another relation to those conventions, or another set of conventions, that can continue the basic enterprise otherwise; call this the modernist response. For such filmmakers, the history of cinema is an undismissible problem; they undertake to maintain a relation to it (however critical, however troubled or kinked), and hence to continue or inherit it. Such a response will inevitably place the question of that enterprise's continued existence, and so of its present nature in the light of its past achievements and their conditions of possibility, at the heart of its own endeavor. It will, in other words, take up within its work as its essential subject matter the question of cinematic practice—its point, its conditions of possibility, its present possibility altogether.

One might say the following: Thomson's critique of Woo's and (especially) De Palma's work identifies it as postmodernist; it is held to deploy cinematic techniques with great skill, but in ways that are essentially unrelated to cinema's artistic, moral, and human ends, as established by the great cinematic works of the past. Hence it exemplifies an essential discontinuity in the enterprise, a body of cinematic work unworthy of the name. But it is, of course, sometimes very hard to distinguish the modernizer from the modernist; for what the modernizer merely deploys (emptily, without human meaning) is what the modernist makes his or her subject, thereby aligning the content of his or her work with its form. In Thomson's terms, the end of the modernist is that of putting the means in question, which entails that the modernist may well appear to have no independent end, or no independent interest in ends. This essay will explore the possibility that, at least in the *Mission: Impossible* movies, Woo and De Palma should be identified as modernist rather than postmodernist filmmakers.

I. ALIENS IN HUMAN GUISE: THE TELEVISUAL ORIGINS OF *MISSION: IMPOSSIBLE*

In *Alien* (1979), Ridley Scott created a narrative world that would constitute the central inheritance of the directors who were to follow him. In *Mission: Impossible*, beyond the general and generic forms of indebtedness to cinema's past that he shares with Scott, the origin of De Palma's work lies outside the world of this film, and indeed outside the medium of film altogether. For, of course, before it was a film, *Mission: Impossible* was a highly popular American television series, running from 1966–1969. How might a film director take responsibility for such a source, and for such a task of transformation and renewal? Just what kind of TV series was *Mission: Impossible*?

I want to take my initial bearings here from some remarks by Stanley Cavell, published in 1971.

It at first seemed that [*Mission: Impossible*] was merely a further item among the spies-and-gadgets cycles that spun off from early science-fiction movies or serials, mated with films of intrigue. But it went beyond that. Its episodes contained no suspense at all. Because one followed the events with interest enough, this quality did not show until, accidentally reverting to an older type, a moment of suspense was thrown in (say by way of an unplanned difficulty in placing one of the gadgets, or a change of guard not anticipated in the plan of operation). This felt wrong, out of place. The explanation is that the narrative had nothing to do with human motivation; the interest lay solely in following out how the gadgets would act. They were the protagonists of this drama. Interest in them depended not merely on their eventual success, this being a foregone conclusion, but on the knowledge that the plot would arrive at that success through foregone means, absolutely beyond a hitch, so that one was freed to focus exclusively on how, not whether. Then one noticed that there were no human exchanges between the characters in the mission team, or none beyond a word or two exchanged at the beginning, and a faint close-up smile here and there as the perfect plan was taking its totally envisioned course. The fact that the format required the continuing characters to pass as foreigners and, moreover, required one of them to use perfect disguises so that he could temporarily replace a specific foreigner, itself disguised the fact that these characters were already aliens, disguised as human. This displacement permitted us something like our old conviction in spy movies.[7]

I find that the features Cavell identifies as capturing the peculiarly evanescent essence of *Mission: Impossible* to be true to my experience of it. It is striking how far his talk of the mission team as aliens in human guise might seem to reinforce the Thomson case against De Palma. For to a filmmaker supposedly capable only of realizing simulacra of human beings, essentially emptied of moral and motivational intelligibility, the prospect of directing characters whose sole business is (what Cavell, elsewhere in his footnote, calls) the impersonation of personality would seem like the perfect project, an exact match for his specific (anti)-talents. Moreover,

De Palma's film undeniably invites its audience to take an interest in the independent life of gadgets. I think here of the articulated electric screwdriver that can remove and collect screws from the farther side of an air-conditioning grille, and the spectacles with in-built video positioned on a pile of books to catch the "traitor" Golitsyn in the act; but the computer—utterly ubiquitous in the film's various plots, and essentially immune to malfunction (other than those caused by others' manipulation, or the limits of its material medium)—is perhaps the contemporary gadget that best absorbs this fantasy of technological success as an absolutely foregone conclusion. About such gadgets, and the operations of which they form a central part, our interest is certainly in the how, not the whether; and this might seem to support the Thomson claim that De Palma is all means and no end.

Why, however, should such a series have been so widely and enduringly popular? Is there some particularly powerful way in which its format discovers a potential of the televisual medium? Here, I think, we need to see the connection between Cavell's impression of the mission team as in human guise, and the nature of their business in the world. For, of course, their prime function in relating to their gadgets is not merely to dissimulate (to hide their true motives and identity) but to simulate (to become other people—both real and fictional); and a form of life that consists of endlessly discarding one role in favor of the next, in which one's calling is precisely to disguise one's identity with another, will not only attract impersonators of personality but threaten to transform real people into mere wearers of human guise.

One might say the following: This TV format consists of the unending, varied repetition of acts of theater; Jim Phelps's taped briefings assign him the role of director in a sequence of theatrical productions. And, as Stanley Cavell has argued, one defining characteristic of theater is that, in it, the actor is subordinate to the character.[8] Various people can play a given role; one does so well by working oneself into that role, accepting and training one's skill and instincts so that they match most intimately with its possibilities and necessities. Those best suited to inhabit a world of theater such as that of *Mission: Impossible* are those whose own personality interferes as little as possible with

their ability to occupy an unending series of different roles.

This point, of course, applies at the level of character and actor. The characters in *Mission: Impossible* are human ciphers because that is what their job demands; and the actors who play those characters correspondingly lack any distinctive personality, any powerful expression of individual character through the physiognomy captured by the television camera's recording of their presence—that is what *their* job demands in this case. The apparent actorly exceptions to this claim in fact simply prove its validity. The member of the cast with the most striking individual presence was Martin Landau, but his was the role that involved the donning of a face mask; and when Leonard Nimoy joined the series at a relatively late stage, he did not last for long, precisely because he brought with him not only a distinctive identity as an actor, but also an identification with a role in another TV series of apparently undying fame—the Vulcan Spock in *Star Trek* (Gene Roddeneberry, 1966–69). This alien presence was not one that our series could accommodate.

A comparison with *Star Trek* is in fact more generally instructive here, for it, too, has been subject to a displacement into the medium of film, but that displacement was unimaginable without the retention of the original actors from the TV series. Indeed, what is, to my eye, the most successful of the *Star Trek* films (the second, entitled *The Wrath of Khan* (Nicholas Meyer, 1982)) is so in large part because it makes its reliance on those actors—hence its need to acknowledge their age, and hence their aging, their mortality—the thematic center of the narrative world they inhabit, in ways ranging from its villain (Ricardo Montalban) (a character escaping from an exile created in an episode of the TV series), through its McGuffin (the Genesis device, which can create animate from inanimate matter, or the reverse), to its preoccupation with the avoidance of death (Kirk's (William Shatner) solution to the Kobayashi Maru test being to reprogram the test conditions) and its acceptance (Spock's concluding self-sacrifice).

A similar kind of resistance would attend any attempt to recast characters in any successful TV series or sitcom; just as the loss of Farrah Fawcett in *Charlie's Angels* (Ivan Goff and Ben Roberts, 1976–81) demanded the introduction of a new character for the new actor to inhabit, so the death of the actor who played the grand-father (Lennard Pearce) in *Only Fools and Horses* (John Sullivan, 1981–2003) necessitated the arrival of another elderly relative (Buster Merryfield) in the Trotter brothers' (David Jason and Nicholas Lyndhurst) world. This suggests that, in television, as in cinema but in contrast to theater, the character is subordinate to the actor. The screen actor takes a role onto himself or herself, lending his or her physical and temperamental endowment to it and accepting only what fits—the rest is nonexistent; the specific, flesh-and-blood human being is the primary object of the camera's study, since the reality of whatever is placed before it is what the camera places before us. And yet, in the film of *Mission: Impossible*, we accept a wholesale recasting of the team, even when it involves certain actors who bring with them not only a substantial body of work but also the aura of fully-fledged cinematic stardom.

Shall we say, then, that the TV series in fact works precisely counter to the possibilities of its medium—perhaps even that its enduring (if limited) power and interest for us shows the emptiness of this idea of a medium and its conditioning possibilities? I am rather inclined to suggest that if we can understand why this series needs human impersonators as both characters and actors, we will thereby come to understand how it discloses certain possibilities of the televisual medium.[9] I claimed earlier that any such explanation must acknowledge the theatrical mode of their inhabitation of their world, but the TV camera's relation to their theatricality has not yet been specified. Once again helping myself to ideas of Stanley Cavell's, I would like to say that the camera monitors these acts of theater: each episode in the series allows us to attend in that particular way to the preparation for, the enactment, and the immediate aftermath of a theatrical event.[10]

What mode of attending is captured by the concept of monitoring? Some facets of the concept are implicit in the way a security guard might attend, via his bank of monitors, to the empty corridors leading from points of entry to a building, and Cavell emphasizes how the same mode of access to reality underpins that staple and paradigm of televisual coverage, the sports event.

[A] network's cameras are…placed ahead of time. That their views are transmitted to us one at a time

for home consumption is merely an accident of economy; in principle, we could all watch a replica of the bank of monitors the producer sees…When there is a switch of the camera whose image is fed into our sole receiver, we might think of this not as a switch of comment from one camera or angle to another camera or angle, but as a switch of attention from one monitor to another monitor…The move from one image to another is motivated not, as on film, by requirements of meaning, but by requirements of opportunity and anticipation—as if the meaning is dictated by the event itself. As in monitoring the heart…say, monitoring signs of life—most of what appears is a graph of the normal, or the establishment of some reference or base line, a line, so to speak, of the uneventful, from which events stand out with perfectly anticipatable significance. If classical narrative can be pictured as the progress from the establishing of one stable situation, through an event of difference, to the reestablishing of a stable situation related to the original one, [television's] serial procedure can be thought of as the establishing of a stable condition punctuated by repeated crises or events that are not developments of the situation requiring a single resolution, but intrusions or emergencies—of humor, or adventure, or talent, or misery—each of which runs a natural course and thereupon rejoins the realm of the uneventful.[11]

The baseline of the *Mission: Impossible* serial lies in the repeated elements that make up the formula generating its instances or episodes: the taped instructions, the initial briefing, the technological preparations, the allotting of roles, and so on, on the side of the IM team; and on the other, the everyday flow of activities in the realm of foreigners into which our team will insert itself. As with a live TV broadcast of an operatic performance, the camera then prepares us for a certain eventuality—here, a theatrical event—that differs in each case from its predecessors, but naturally completes itself and returns the team to its uneventful state of generalized readiness. More specifically, the technologically-driven nature of this series' events (creating the sense that its success is foregone) is precisely responsive to the way monitoring invokes anticipatable—essentially predictable—opportunities for attention; the placing of each camera, and the meaning of a given switch from one image to another (unlike that of any particular camera placement or edit in a film), is dictated by the event itself. Hence, the peculiar power of this televisual format or formula: its way of invoking the essentially anti-televisual medium of theater in fact discovers a way of acknowledging a perceptual mode characteristic of its own medium.

II. "I AM NOC": BRIAN DE PALMA'S *MISSION: IMPOSSIBLE*

Can we understand De Palma's cinematic transfiguration of this TV format as acknowledging the aspects of it I have identified? That would presumably mean finding an essentially cinematic acknowledgement of its distinctive aesthetic achievement, and hence of the intimate distances between television, theater, and cinema.

We might begin by examining the two scenes that open the film, preceding even its title sequence (with its loving reconstruction of the TV series' driving theme music and jump-cutting, lit-fuse sequence of images from the episode to come). The first shows the IM team at work in Kiev, enacting a trademark De Palma scenario of sex and violence to acquire crucial information from a foreigner: we see Jack Harman (Emilio Estevez) monitoring events on a self-contained stage set constructed within a warehouse (or sound-stage) through his computer screen. All three media are thus invoked, but the film camera's domain encompasses that of the video monitor and the theatrical performance to which it gives access; the hierarchy of this triple nesting states an ambition to declare cinema's difference, perhaps its superiority. The first obvious difference it declares is its immediate, inherent capacity to generate suspense: the IM production involves injecting one member with a drug that simulates death, and the pace of the improvised performance is such that the time within which it can be brought to a successful curtain call, and the necessary antidote injected, is running out. Will Claire Phelps's (Emmanuelle Beart's) life be foregone?

We, the film audience, see all and can do nothing; the cinematic medium subjects us to the world it projects, including the anxieties that inform it, but also mechanically screens us from it, rendering our passivity unavoidable, hence conferring on us awareness without the capacity to act on it—Is this absolute freedom, or indelible guilt? Harman knows and declares the nature of Claire's situation and could intrude on the stage set to save his colleague, but he remains transfixed at his computer, quite as if monitoring induces a kind of paralysis, a pure reception of the monitored events that utterly fails to carry over to action. The medium of his awareness offers no automatic absolution; to continue to monitor events without acting on what one thereby perceives is something for which each perceiver is responsible. Ethan Hunt is aware of Claire's predicament, and is already on the stage set with her; but the very thing that brings him so close—his role in the play—is also what prevents him from helping her. To offer help would be to step out of character, to destroy the performance, and all that he is willing to do is to accelerate it. The show must run its course to completion before he is prepared to step outside the stage space and bring back the antidote; the actor's interests are subordinate to those of the character, hence at once to the character's audience and the character's author/ director.

The effect of this cinematic suspense is thus to illuminate the differing modes of villainy that attach to each of the three modes of attention under study. One might say that whereas the film audience is subjected to suspense, the monitor and the performer subject themselves to suspense, by choosing to suspend the humanly required course of action. What is required to resolve that suspense is Ethan Hunt's transgression of the boundary between stage set and sound stage, between the space of theater and the space of film: more specifically, he must introduce a cinematic resource into the world of theater, an antidote to its potentially lethal demands. Since in so doing, he pulls off his face mask, revealing for the first time that Ethan Hunt is Tom Cruise, and since only Ethan Hunt ever uses face masks in this film (so that each signature act of removing a mask reveals Cruise's face beneath, as if that physiognomy cannot be masked, is destined always to break through its guises), we might provisionally call this life-giving element "stardom"—that epitome of the actor's priority over character in the medium whose material basis is the photographic presentation of reality. It stands for whatever in human individuality exceeds or transcends the individual's roles—that from which those various masks are suspended. Even at this early stage, we can see from Claire's languorous attempt to brush Hunt's hand with her lips on returning to consciousness that each at once recognizes and disavows the other's role-transgressing significance.

The second pretitle scene shows us the play's author-director, seated god-like in business class among the clouds. Phelps (Jon Voight) immediately declares his status, when initially turning down his new briefing tape, presented to him as an in-flight movie, by saying that he prefers the theater: that definite article, with its implicit snobbery, further suggests that any such preference would, to the director of this film, amount to a taint of villainy—a suggestion that the remainder of the movie massively confirms. Then he views his briefing on a monitor—an updating of the iconic audiotape of the TV program that reiterates the nature of its original medium, and Phelps's implication in it and its villainy.

The content of the briefing appears to conform impeccably to the TV model, right down to its concluding promise of disavowal should the proposed mission be exposed, but the reality is very different. For whereas the TV series offered no room for skepticism about the truth and truthfulness of the briefing tapes, and hence of the authority originating them, this film will later reveal that its briefing tape is a tissue of lies: the proposed mission is the cover for a mole hunt, the "traitor" Golitsyn (Marcel Iures) is an IMF operative, and what he seeks to "steal" (the second half of the NOC list, containing the true identities of every agent operating under nonofficial cover in eastern Europe) is a fake designed to self-destruct and to bring destruction down on its possessor. Further, whereas the TV series left no room for skepticism concerning the loyalty of the IM team, in this film its leader and one of its key members are prepared to betray everything they are supposed to stand for, and the idea of this betrayal is, we later learn, being conceived behind Jim Phelps's expressionless reception of his fake briefing.

The absence of such possibilities in the world of the TV series indicates its unquestioning acceptance of certain conventions of the spy genre it inhabits, and it is intimately tied to its

capacity to create a sense of success as a foregone conclusion in every one of its operations. For no matter how fantastically reliable one's gadgets, success against an unsuspecting foreign enemy can be guaranteed only if one can exclude the possibility of an enemy within. By contrast, De Palma puts these conventions in question: the film's IM team is multinational, thus internalizing foreigners, and its IM force as a whole is ridden with internal duplicity, with every member of it capable of being other than he seems. As a result, the film's three theatrical performances are in fact each the site of three simultaneously staged, mutually conflicting dramas.

In Prague, Ethan Hunt and his colleagues try to perform one set of roles as they track a supposed traitor's activities, but they are unsuspecting participants in Jim Phelps's genuinely traitorous counterdrama, while he and they are all unsuspecting participants in their boss Kitteridge's (Henry Czerny's) mole hunt. In the film's conclusion on the Eurostar train between London and Paris, three competing dramas are again created and directed by Hunt, Phelps, and Kitteridge, with only Hunt aware of every role he plays, and Max (Vanessa Redgrave) unknowingly manipulated by all three. The second, central piece of theater—the theft of the global NOC list from the IMF mainframe in CIA headquarters—appears closer to the TV model, in that it involves an IM team, united in their desire for the list, confronting an unknowing enemy. In reality, however, two of the four team members have a different agenda from Hunt's, which he has anyway not fully revealed to his team, and that team is working against the IM force as such, that is, against itself. Hence, the third contending drama here is just the TV series' single, overarching script: the consistent rationale of the IM force, represented once again by Kitteridge, as he plots his own anti-Hunt drama in the very building Hunt is infiltrating.

In this sense, the narrative thrust of *Mission: Impossible* attacks the basic integrity of the TV series by simultaneously attacking the integrity of the IM force, its crack team, and the key members of that team. The film all but declares that this is its concern—that its subject matter is the very existence and nature of the IM force— by taking as its McGuffin the NOC list: for this entails that the "threat" that the IM team aims to neutralize is not (as in the TV series) a threat to the country it serves or any of its other interests, but rather a threat to all those in its own condition, that of operating under nonofficial cover, and hence a threat to itself; and what Hunt risks in using the global NOC list in his hunt for the real traitor is the destruction of IM operations altogether. In the film, the IM force turns on itself and very nearly tears itself to pieces; *Mission: Impossible* the movie puts in question the key condition of the TV series to which it owes its own existence, and thus puts in question its own conditions of possibility.

What induces this threat of fission? The primary act of betrayal—by Jim Phelps—is later explained by him in the following terms. After the end of the Cold War, he woke up to discover that he was "an obsolete piece of hardware not worth upgrading, with a lousy marriage and $62,000 dollars a year." In short, he recognizes that to be a member of an IM team is to be essentially subordinate to, hence to be nothing essentially more than, a piece of hardware, a human version of a gadget, and he responds to this sudden self-revelation by throwing a spanner in the machinery. The second act of disruption is Ethan Hunt's: and his is effected by the realization of his own already-divided loyalties and consequent lack of integrity. In Prague, he first disobeys his team leader's command to abort in order to maintain contact with Golitsyn and the NOC list, then he abandons his mission to go to his mentor's aid on the bridge, and then he watches as this enacted conflict between his professional role and his human ties results in the violent deaths of members of his team. This abortion of a stage play leaves real blood on the floor, the destruction of colleagues who have become family. It forces him to recognize that he is more than his professional role, that his identity is not exhausted by the conditions of his existence—conditions that the film insistently identifies with doubleness or internal splitting, hence fragmentation.

The IM world as the film represents it is one in which identity in general is necessarily open to impersonation precisely because it is validated by mechanical recognition of (parts of) the body. One's visual appearance, one's fingerprints, one's voice and retinae, even the

heat and weight of one's body—these are what declare the reality of one's existence, and the IM force can operate precisely because all such features can be made to appear present when they are not, or to appear absent when they are really present (and, one might ask, which form of words best captures cinema's screened projection of reality?). Human existence is hollowed out, reduced to the occupation of space by matter of the appropriate form and surface appearance.

Accordingly, the NOC list comes in two parts. First, there is the list of cover names, to which the contending parties all have access from the beginning. What they are all in search of is the second part, the list of true names, the real identities lying behind that of the roles they play—and that proves singularly elusive. First we encounter a fake list of true names, the bait for the mole hunt, which ultimately goes up in smoke; then, once the true list is duplicated from Langley, Hunt leaves Krieger (Jean Reno) and us uncertain which of his two disks contains it; then various attempts are made on the Eurostar to duplicate the disk with the true list—attempts that are variously jammed and disrupted by circumstance and enemy action. The implication is twofold: that once they have been dislocated by the nature of one's work in the world, it is inhumanly difficult to bring the two halves of oneself back together again, to locate the truth of oneself behind or beyond the roles one is asked to perform; and that if one ever succeeds in doing so, then the effect would be rather similar to that induced by fusing the two halves of the chewing gum that Harman supplies to Hunt—highly explosive.

When he first uses it, the fish in the Akvarium restaurant's vast storied tanks (their serried ranks shining with the blue-gray radiance of a bank of monitors) are set free from their confinement for consumption, but as Hunt outpaces the tidal wave of unleashed water, its loss of energy leaves them gasping on the pavement, deprived of the essential medium of their existence. He uses it again in the railway tunnel under the channel—once again in a no-man's land, this time between one country and another, perhaps even between one (Anglo-American) cultural alignment and another (Europe). He saves himself, and kills the remaining traitors in his IM team, by destroying the helicopter by means of which they had hoped to escape from the train. Should we, then, say that—unlike the fish—this film has allowed Hunt to escape from the self-emptying theatrical conditions of existence specified for IM operatives in the TV series, and hence that the medium of cinema is inherently more able to acknowledge the humanity of its subjects than that of television?

This climactic scene is certainly one of liberation, and its acceptance depends on cinema's capacity to make the fantastic real, for, of course, in accepting it, we accept the literal impossibility of a helicopter attached to a train being able not only to survive being drawn into a tunnel, but also to maneuver with delicate malevolence within it. But then we have to say that De Palma here identifies the medium of cinema as such with the business of the IM team—that of making the impossible a reality. In so doing, he locates a taint in the powers of his medium—a risk that its magic conjures up a mere simulacrum of the real world, hollowing out its constraints and conditions, and thereby tainting the heroism that depends on our graceful and courageous bearing of reality's burdens for goodness' sake with the moral weightlessness of such fantasies. I take De Palma's decision, at the end of this scene, to place his camera so that it looks along a rotor blade of the destroyed helicopter whose tip almost slices through Hunt's exposed neck, to declare this risk, for it identifies the camera with lethal decapitation, with the reduction of a human being to a head severed from its body, and thereby identifies Tom Cruise's fate to stardom with his reduction to a handsome, smiling face.

A similar ambiguity emerges in the conversation between Jim Phelps and Ethan Hunt in Liverpool Street station as Ethan lives out the realization of his self-flagellating dream in Prague—the resurrection of the father he failed. Jim attempts to persuade Ethan that Kitteridge is the real traitor, but Ethan—having just noticed the incriminating Drake Hotel stamp in Job's Bible—is in the process of realizing that Jim himself has betrayed them all. Hence, as his words appear to take up Jim's suggestion, De Palma shows us a series of flashbacks covering the events in Prague—or rather he shows us Hunt's interior discovery of the truth of those events, with every uttered word in Ethan's dis-

course that Jim takes to refer to Kitteridge being shown to refer in reality to Jim himself.

Once again, two conflicting plots contend with one another, this time at the level of conflicting assignments of reference to a set of pronouns; once again, the apparent meaning of a set of utterances is subverted by its covert sense. Here, however, the discrepancy is between what is said and what is seen, or imagined, by a single individual; we see Hunt once more playing a role, this time to his role-playing mentor—another mode of his interior split or doubleness. On this occasion, however, that splitting is seen to make possible his eventual liberation from the deceptions of others, for it declares the moment at which he understands what has really been going on throughout the film, and hence the moment at which he can create a drama that incorporates and controls the dramas in which others wish to cast him, and thereby control him. In conveying this so economically and exhilaratingly to us, De Palma employs a key condition of talking motion pictures—their capacity to synchronize sound and vision, and hence their capacity to desynchronize them. Is he thereby declaring that this aspect of his medium is inherently liberating?

Not exactly. For we must recall that Jim's and Ethan's talk is of the past, and De Palma is here using film's marrying of sound and vision in order simultaneously to present us with that talk, and with its subject matter—that is, with the past reality to which it refers, and to the stream of consciousness to which it gives (misleading) expression. The camera thereby claims the power to penetrate the interiority of its human subject—to declare the existence and nature of the inner life lying beyond that character's inherently deceptive words, deeds, and appearance, and hence to confirm his humanity. But in so doing, it simultaneously declares its own unreliability: for the past reality its images now show is not what it declared when we first viewed it—rather, every shot of that original sequence was framed so as to deceive us, as the events depicted were designed to deceive Hunt. The camera did not present fantasy as reality: it rather framed or cropped its presentation of what really happened in such a way as to allow us to misinterpret it—just as Jim Phelps manipulated the video images relayed to Ethan from his wrist camera to imply that he had been shot by another person on the bridge. No particular acts of framing are needed to achieve such duplicity: for if the camera can declare the inner life of its subjects, even when that fails to match its expression in their words and deeds, it can also fail to do so. As in the second pretitle sequence of Phelps's initial briefing by Kitteridge, it can simply record everything there is to record of what they say and do, and invite, or at least allow, us to take that at face value.

Such ambiguities suggest that it is De Palma's concern to suggest that the powers of cinema are neither inherently villainous nor inherently truthful; rather, they can be turned to good or to villainy. They can either consort with those forces in our culture that reduce reality to appearance and disavow substance and meaning in favor of an endless play of interlocking images and traces, or they can disavow such reductiveness. It is my concluding contention that De Palma decisively declares his particular hand, the turn to which he wishes to subject his audience, in the second of his three theatrical set pieces, the central sequence that everyone who has seen this film will remember.

Here, the context is an epitome of the IM world's reduction of identity to fragmentary traces of a human body: the sterile space containing the IM mainframe's console verifies human presence by digital code and double electronic key card, voice print, and retinal scan, and guards against human intrusion by evaluating the evidence of sound, temperature, and pressure. In this space, to be is to be matter in motion. Hence, the condition for Hunt's recovery of the NOC list, and so of himself (insofar as he claims to Max "I am NOC—was; now I'm disavowed") is that he achieve cool, soundless weightlessness—an immaterial presence. Since the space in its alarmed state is composed of white panels outlined in black, which the triggering of the alarm turns red, Cruise must also ensure that his world remains colorless. In sum, he must attain silence and (as it were) a merely two-dimensional salience, the sheer black-and-white outline—the bare cinematic minimum, as well as the original form of cinema's projection—of personhood.

De Palma presents Hunt's presence in this purely cinematic world as dependent on a literalization of suspense; he achieves his goal by utilizing a flexible trapeze-like harness that displaces his weight onto Krieger in the overhead airshaft. He shows that this presentation achieves the immediate translation of literal suspense into psychological suspense—the mechanical into the human. We hang on Hunt's fate because we see even this pared-down visual schema as a human presence, even this black-and-white short with its uncanny canonical combination of slapstick and grace is capable of subjecting us to exhilarating anxiety about another's well-being. No matter how systematically De Palma deprives Hunt of any complex interior and exterior life, no matter how intensively he strips away anything other than the logic of the cinematic type of the undercover spy, and then makes that logic the defining subject matter of the character and the film, thus luring the viewer into the closed circuit of a movie's obsession with itself, it remains possible to call on our capacities for identifying with this screened projection of his embodied mind, and hence for identifying his presence as (some transfiguration of) the human presence as that is inflected for and by the camera in the physiognomy of Tom Cruise.

There is, then, nothing mechanical or assured about cinematic reductions or hollowings-out of human meaning from its projected worlds; when we encounter such wildernesses of sense, the responsibility always lies not with the medium but with the work of specific human beings within it. Any movie that can be understood to convince us of this surely earns the right to be taken seriously as reflecting on, not merely reflecting, such reductiveness, within and without the world of cinema.

III. "THE BURDEN OF SEX": JOHN WOO'S
MISSION: IMPOSSIBLE II

John Woo's sequel systematically denies any indebtedness to the TV series with which *Mission: Impossible* is in such intense dialogue; no specific detail of that televisual world is reproduced in *Mission: Impossible II* that is not given its own independent (and often altered) significance in De Palma's cinematic world. It is as if, for Woo, the televisual origins of the IM universe are of precisely no interest to him; that debt is one that De Palma has entirely or at least decisively discharged. On the other hand, Woo's film does systematically declare its indebtedness to De Palma's film, as if insisting that the IM universe is for him a purely cinematic phenomenon, and in ways that go beyond its continued focus on Hunt, his IM force, and the sole member of the disavowed team who survived the vicissitudes of that film. These declarations include reiterations of detail (such as the re-appearance of a carpet of shattered glass across which Hunt's beloved colleague walks to confront him) and efficient transfigurations of technology (such as the use of digital cameras and viewers, and the opening conflation of video briefing with remote-viewing spectacles). They also include declarations of an intimate understanding—such as his pivotal variation on the De Palma signature theme of conflating literal with dramatic suspense in Hunt's infiltration of the BioCyte HQ, and his decision to divide his McGuffin into two parts, distinguished by the same pair of colors that distinguished the components of De Palma's explosive chewing gum.

Nevertheless, Woo does choose to incur another essentially cinematic debt by aligning his basic plot with that of Alfred Hitchcock's *Notorious*, made in 1946, starring Cary Grant and Ingrid Bergman. Perhaps it would be more accurate to say that this fact constitutes his further acknowledgement of De Palma, whose work has been understood (for better and for worse) from the outset to be the persistent expression of a sense of indebtedness to Hitchcock, and in particular to Hitchcock's ability to construct stories of crime, voyeurism, murder, and psychosis that can be understood as studies of the resources and condition of cinema. As I have just argued, the only way to appreciate the real richness of *Mission: Impossible* is to understand its presentation of the world of spying in exactly such terms.

One might well question the wisdom of any director who invites us so explicitly to compare his work with a masterpiece by one of cinema's acknowledged masters. But Woo, I think, means this Hitchcockian invocation to permit him to achieve a more specific, and more critical, relation to De Palma's version of the IM world, and of its protagonist, Ethan Hunt. For by drawing on the basic plot structure of *Notorious*, in which the daughter of a Nazi (Alicia/

Bergman) works with an American agent (Devlin/Grant) to subvert a group of Nazi sympathizers by marrying their leader (Alex Sebastian/Claude Rains), Woo ensures that a relationship with a woman is central to his version of Hunt's world, and implies that the equivalent relationship in De Palma's world was at the very least insufficiently substantial or well realized—hence, that, in this respect, De Palma fails to live up to his master.

Such a criticism is hard to gainsay. As I mentioned earlier, Claire Phelps is from the outset identified as a forbidden but responsive love-object for Hunt in *Mission: Impossible*—forbidden first as the wife of his father figure, then as that father's possible co-conspirator, then as his victim. But Emmanuelle Beart has very little to work with in breathing life into this intermediary between male rivals, and Ethan's confirmation of her (conflicted) treachery seems decisively to negate her attractions for him: "Of course, I'm very sorry to hear you say that, Claire" is the best he can do when—disguised as Jim—he listens to her risk bargaining with an unloving husband for his own life. Of the various indications De Palma offers of the ways Hunt's humanity exceeds his role, his invocation of male and female companionship growing out of the world of work carries far more plausibility than his invocation of romance.

Woo's sense of this absence, or inadequacy, leads him to embody the issue in the mythic identity he assigns his McGuffin. For the two complementary elements of Dr. Nekhorvich's (Rade Sherbedgia's) experiment in molecular biology are called Bellerophon and Chimera; the disease is thus named after a monster who plagued the ancient world, which the film characterizes as possessed of "the head of a lion and the tail of a serpent," and the cure named after the prince who killed it. In fact, however, the real Chimera of legend also possessed the body of a goat; one might think of the film's silence on this matter as inviting us to see in it a certain disavowal of what links head and tail—a disavowal that matches Hunt's silence on the internal relation between himself (with his lion's mane of hair contrasting so starkly with his martial, clipped cut in the first film) and his dark other, Sean Ambrose (Dougray Scott)—the serpent in the IM bosom. For if a lion mythically signifies courage, and a serpent cunning, then a goat can only signify what Ambrose at one point calls "the burden of sex." And the key point of contact between *Notorious* and *Mission: Impossible II* is that Nyah Nordhof-Hall (Thandie Newton) is the key point of contact between Ambrose and Hunt.

In other words, beyond the way in which the idea of the chimerical alludes to De Palma's theme of identity in general (and Hunt's identity in particular) as an endlessly elusive fantasy or mirage of the overheated imagination, Woo means his invocation of the Chimera to inflect De Palma's related theme of the internal division between role and actor in spies, in the direction of a division within the actor as spy. Hunt is not simply Bellerophon to Ambrose's Chimera, a hero in need of a villain, he is also the Chimera's lion-head, needing to find a way of acknowledging his identity as a sexual being without simply denying its serpentine side. At which point, it is implied, the Chimera would no longer be a monstrous assortment of body parts, but rather a properly integrated, fully embodied human being—Chimera would really become chimerical (merely imaginary) by becoming Bellerophon. *Mission: Impossible II* tracks this attempted transformation.

The film underlines the intimacy of the antagonism between Hunt and Ambrose by ensuring that what we think of as our first sight of Hunt (in the doomed airliner) is in fact of Ambrose wearing a Hunt face mask—a doubling to which he has resorted twice before, at the instigation of the IM force. In fact, in a significant inversion of De Palma's practice, according to which only Ethan Hunt wore masks, and hence every mask was a cover for Cruise's stardom, almost every mask used in Woo's film is of Hunt/Cruise's face, and each time it is worn either by Ambrose or his second-in-command, Hugh Stamper (Richard Roxburgh). Tom Cruise's first task in this film is thus to play another character disguised as his own character. By thus calling on his leading man to pretend to be who he really is, and thereby suggesting that his screened reality is a pretence, Woo invites Cruise (and us) to contemplate a darker side of Cruise's stardom—a mysterious taint of violence and deceit lying behind the undeniable charm of his physiognomy and temperament. It is exactly this dual aspect of Cary Grant's screen persona that Hitchcock brings out in his role as Devlin in *Notorious*.

In *Notorious*, Grant's demonic side is externalized in the character of Alex Sebastian, the Nazi whom Alicia marries and spies on; and part of Devlin's torment over Alicia, part of what makes him torment her over her willingness to play the role for which he recruited her despite their having fallen in love, is the anxiety that she is not only a fully sexual being with a long history of male "playmates," but also that she is genuinely attracted to this particular man, with whom she shares a nonsexual past through her father, and whose essentially duplicitous role in the world (combined with an obsessive sexual jealousy) so closely matches Devlin's own.

Hunt's, Nyah's, and Ambrose's relationship in *Mission: Impossible II* offers a variation on this triangular theme that suggests a certain understanding of its original. After the destabilizing discovery that his professional seduction of Nyah has opened him to a more personal relationship with her (a discovery whose mood is expressed in the film's background shift from flamenco to flames—from ritualized social intercourse to the self-denying ecstasies of religion), Hunt is informed that Nyah has already made and broken a sexual relationship with Ambrose, one that his job will require that he arrange for her to renew. And even when, faced with her disgust at the thought that he could now ask her to do this, he makes it as clear to her as he can that he wants her to refuse ("Would it make you feel better if I didn't want you to do this?" "Much." "Then feel better!"), she decides that she will accept it nevertheless. Here is Woo's most significant variation on the *Notorious* model, for in the analogous scene at the heart of that film, Alicia is moved to take the job precisely because Devlin refuses to affirm to her what he has forcefully declared to his boss—that he does not want her to do it.

Why this variation? We might imagine Ethan's response to the mystery of Nyah's choice finding expression in the following questions. Has she done this because she feels that the task is more important than our relationship? That would be bad, but understandable, given Ambrose's track record and present intentions, and no more than I, her recruiter, deserve. Or is it because, having spent the night with me, she prefers Ambrose? She as good as denied it last night; but she also began last night by asking, "Who wants to be decent?" and ended it by remarking on our having gone beyond any manual or rules ("They have a book for this?"), and my boss has just remarked that, being a woman, Nyah has "all the training she needs to go to bed with a man and lie to him." Her deciding for that reason would be far worse—and understandable only if what I had been able to give her during that night had lacked something, something without which she was not (sexually) satisfied.

What kind of relationship had she and Ambrose shared? Hunt has already told us that he understands Ambrose to be the kind of spy who thinks "he hasn't done the job unless he's leaving hats on the ground," someone he later describes as needing to "get his gun off." The sense of violent menace around Nyah's arrival in Ambrose's Australian residence is palpable. When her presence is questioned by Stamper—whose latently homosexual relationship with Ambrose is Woo's displacement of Alex Sebastian's relationship with his mother in *Notorious*—Ambrose slices off the tip of one of his fingers, forcibly held erect, with a cigar-trimmer; and when Hunt makes contact with Nyah at the race course after her first nights back with Ambrose, she responds to his criticism of her failing to follow instructions by saying: "What are you going to do—spank me?" I take these to be grounds enough for Hunt, certainly disconcerted by falling in love, and perhaps disconcerted by, let us say, the forcefulness of the sexual response he has elicited from his lover, to suspect that Ambrose's blend of sex and violence might be a more attractive version of whatever he has to offer.

In the terms of Woo's mythology, Hunt's discomfort reflects an unwillingness to acknowledge that human sexual identity—hence, both his own and Nyah's—has a serpentine as well as a leonine aspect. It finds expression in his disavowal of his promise at the racetrack to extract Nyah immediately from Ambrose's residence. Instead, he concentrates on staging a piece of theater for the CEO of BioCyte in order to discover the location of the remaining samples of Chimera. This is one of two points in the film in which Hunt is seen wearing a mask; here, it indicates that he is covering up or denying something of himself. For Ambrose uses the time to deceive Nyah by disguising himself as Hunt, and requiring her to stay at his residence; he incarnates the potentially fatal consequences of Hunt's refusal to sacrifice his job for his love.

The task of overcoming Hunt's anxieties falls, then, to Nyah herself. She walks into the middle of the stalemated conflict between Ambrose and Hunt, retrieves the injection gun containing the sole remaining sample of Chimera, and fires its contents into her own bloodstream. Once again, Woo varies a theme from *Notorious*: for the protracted suspense of that film's final half-hour turns on whether or not Devlin will be able to rescue Alicia from her husband's (and mother-in-law's) conspiracy to poison her. But Nyah is not the unknowing, passive victim of another's actions; she takes action, declares that her own violence can find expression in ways not lethal to others, and stakes her own existence in a way that at once deprives Ambrose of what he wants and transforms her own body into the unified focus of Hunt's professional and personal goals (to save her is to frustrate Ambrose and to eliminate Chimera). Her plan thus embodies courage, cunning, and sexuality; it declares that she is capable of transforming Chimera into Bellerophon in her own person, and if Hunt can properly acknowledge her achievement, he might match it.

The conclusion of the film manifests his willingness and ability to do so. Its first phase—in which he dupes Ambrose into killing Stamper and steals his samples of Bellerophon and Chimera—culminates in the second point at which Hunt tears off a face mask, thereby revealing himself to be impersonator rather than impersonated, a man rather than a series of masks, and revealing Tom Cruise as a star capable of acknowledging the obscure darkness behind his handsome smile. Its final phase—the climactic joust between Hunt and Ambrose on motorbikes, culminating in unarmed combat on the beach—recalls that of De Palma's original movie, with its reiteration of the camera's identification with a blade poised over Cruise's features, and its final conjuring of the necessary gun for Ambrose's execution from the wind-scoured sand itself, quite as if declaring nature's siding with those who would thwart a global plague, as well as the camera's ability to realize our fantasies of good triumphing over the evil that is good's necessary other. Its epilogue shows us that, in their achievement of genuine humanity, Ethan's and Nyah's joint wish is to lose themselves in the crowds thronging Sydney's parks and harbor, to rejoin the everyday rhythms of life beyond the reach of those who would track them down and force them into roles that would make them into monstrous parodies of human existence. For when Chimera is made truly chimerical, the hero Bellerophon becomes nothing more, and nothing less, than a human being.

STEPHEN MULHALL
New College, University of Oxford
Oxford OX1 3BN
UK

INTERNET: Stephen.mulhall@new.oxford.ac.uk

1. Stephen Mulhall, *On Film* (London: Routledge, 2002).

2. For a more direct and elaborated defense of my attempts to claim such films for philosophy, see my "Ways of Thinking: Reply to Anderson and Baggini," reprinted (together with the papers to which it responds) in Special Interest Edition on Philosophy and Science Fiction, *Film and Philosophy* 9 (2005): 24–29.

3. David Thomson, *Biographical Dictionary of Film*, 4th ed. (London: Little, Brown, 2003), p. 946.

4. Thomson, *Biographical Dictionary of Film*, pp. 225–226.

5. Thomson, *Biographical Dictionary of Film*, p. 192.

6. For more on this idea of modernism, see the Introduction to my *Inheritance and Originality* (Oxford University Press, 2001).

7. Stanley Cavell, *The World Viewed*, enlarged ed. (Harvard University Press, 1979), n. 33.

8. See especially "The Avoidance of Love," in Cavell's *Must We Mean What We Say?* (Cambridge University Press, 1969), and ch. 4 of *The World Viewed*—analyses I cite and expand on at various points in *On Film*.

9. This might be the point at which to acknowledge that the emphases of my essay, following Cavell, on the relation between aesthetic achievement in a medium and exploitation of that medium's possibilities, and between that medium's possibilities and its material basis, are ones that have been forcefully criticized—for example, by Noël Carroll in his *Theorizing the Moving Image* (Cambridge University Press, 1996). But I find that Carroll's criticisms of medium-specificity arguments simply fail to engage with Cavell's way of invoking the specificity of various artistic media. For example, Carroll objects to the idea that a prior identification of the essence of an artistic medium can determine its proper, or best, line of artistic development; but Cavell not only does not advance such an idea, he flatly contradicts it by arguing that a possibility of the medium can be discovered as such only through an artistic achievement in that medium whose significance is to be understood as exploiting that possibility, and thereby acknowledging some aspect of its material basis. Again, Carroll objects to Cavell's way of characterizing the relation between photographs and reality, but he conflates Cavell's position with that of Bazin. For example, he treats as broadly equivalent Bazin's claim that "the photographic image is the object itself" and Cavell's claim that "a photograph...presents us, we want to say, with things themselves" (see *Theorizing the Moving Image*, p. 37). The latter formulation makes no identity claim, invokes the concept of presentation rather than representation or reproduction, and is explicitly framed as an expression of what we are inclined to say—that is, as raw material for philosophy rather than its product. It would take another essay to properly elaborate these claims; these remarks are meant only to indicate ways of showing that and how criticisms such as Carroll's offer far less of an obstacle to Cavell's procedures than might seem to be the case.

10. Ideas expressed in Stanley Cavell, "The Fact of Television," in *Themes Out of School* (San Francisco: North Point Press, 1984).

11. Cavell, "The Fact of Television," pp. 257–258.

DANIEL SHAW

On Being Philosophical and *Being John Malkovich*

One of the most puzzling and intriguing questions to emerge in the philosophical conversation about film is precisely what it means to say that a film can *be* philosophical. Alternatively, the question has been framed as follows: Can a film actually *do* philosophy, in some important sense of that term? As is often the case in such matters, adequately framing the question is the hardest part of the task.

The following essay provides a summary of various ways films have been described as being philosophical (or as doing philosophy) by surveying articles that have appeared in the print journal *Film and Philosophy* since its inception over a decade ago. I will then propose that "being philosophical" admits of degrees, while offering an original reading of *Being John Malkovich* (Spike Jonze, 1999) as a paradigmatic exemplar of what it is for a film to be capable of *doing* philosophy.

I

One of the many unfortunate consequences of the high art-low art divide is that while works of literature have long been considered capable of being philosophical, for most of the twentieth century the cinema was seldom seen as aspiring to such lofty goals, except for the art films directed by the likes of Ingmar Bergman or Jean-Luc Godard. Philosophers first started writing about such films in the 1960s, no doubt because of the intellectual respectability of their existential and/or political content. But, as Thomas Wartenberg observed in a recent edition of *Film and Philosophy*: "Not only has the art film been eclipsed as an *avant garde* film practice, but contemporary philosophic work on film has moved beyond it as well."[1]

Philosophers are becoming increasingly more comfortable talking about popular Hollywood films. For example, an intriguing notion of what makes a film worthy of philosophical attention was proposed in the premiere edition of *Film and Philosophy* (1994) by Stephen Mulhall, whose recent book on the *Alien* quadrilogy plays such a central role in contemporary debates on the subject.[2] He offered a reading of *Blade Runner* (Ridley Scott, 1982) that saw it as "explicitly concerned with what it is to be a human being," and as self-consciously philosophical.[3] However, the subgenre of science fiction that deals with robots and cyborgs characteristically raises such questions.

The typical philosophical article on film pairs some philosopher's theory with one (or more) of the author's favorite films to demonstrate how the theory can enhance our understanding and appreciation of the films. Such pairings strike us as more or less convincing, as the parallels drawn seem more or less natural (or strained). Often, a film seems shoehorned into a model that does not really fit, especially when profound depth readings are proposed for pieces of mass entertainment that cannot sustain them. Here, the implicit assumption seems to be that if a film can be shown to instantiate a philosophical theory or principle, then the film can be considered philosophical.

At another level of sophistication, and less often, certain directors have made films with a particular philosophy *explicitly* in mind, and philosophers of film evaluate whether the film in question is an adequate or inadequate embodiment of that philosophy. Fyodor Dostoevsky has long been praised for being a truly philosophical writer, for example, in his rhetorically brilliant portrayals of the catastrophic consequences of nihilism in *The Possessed*, or of atheism in *The Brothers Karamazov*. Similarly, in Volume 1 of *Film and Philosophy*, Sander Lee identifies "Sartrean Themes in Woody Allen's *Husbands and Wives*" and praises Allen for his ability to embody them so fully.[4] Lee convincingly demonstrates how Allen intentionally exemplified Jean-Paul Sartre's pessimistic views on love. Allen's undergraduate degree in philosophy, professed love for Sartre, and recurrent allusions to Sartrean themes makes this application of theory to film far more convincing than if the director and/or screenwriter were likely to be unfamiliar with the philosopher in question.

For Lee, *Husbands and Wives* (Woody Allen, 1992) is a truly philosophical picture because Allen chose Sartrean themes that he grasped clearly and took personally and expressed them successfully in a cinematic context. Similar praise is offered in several of the articles on Allen that were included in the special edition of *Film and Philosophy* (2000) that was guest edited by Lee. From this perspective, Allen's films can be described as philosophical because they are explicitly informed by philosophical concepts and theories.

So far, then, we have three answers to the question of what makes a film philosophical: (1) a film is philosophical if it furthers our inquiries into philosophical questions and concerns; (2) a film is philosophical if our understanding of it can be deepened (and/or our appreciation of it can be enhanced) by applying preexistent philosophical theories to it; and (3) a film is philosophical if it self-consciously mirrors a philosophical theory. The second and third senses in which a film can be philosophical have been belittled recently by a proponent of the first. Stephen Mulhall argues in *On Film* that neither (2) nor (3) are adequate to earn a film the honorific designation of *doing* philosophy. On this view, for example, the mere fact that Roland Barthes can offer us an enlightening semiological analysis of fashion does not make fashion philosophical, nor does Woody Allen's skillful depiction of Sartrean themes in *Husbands and Wives* constitute *doing* philosophy.

Mulhall is at great pains to specify *his* paradigmatic account of film as philosophy so that he can contend that films should *not* be seen as grist for one's philosophical interpretive mill.

He is equally disdainful of directors who seek merely to illustrate philosophical positions (they fail to be true philosophers). Although I agree with Mulhall that films *can* be philosophical in his (overly demanding) sense of the term, I think he has construed what is essentially a matter of degree as a black-and-white situation.

Alternatively, I would like to propose the following hierarchy: (1) a film is (minimally) philosophical if it can fruitfully (and plausibly) be interpreted from a philosophical perspective that can enhance our understanding and appreciation of it; (2) a film is *more* philosophical if it is an explicit (and successful) attempt by a director to illustrate a philosophical theory or concept; and finally (3) the *most* profoundly philosophical films are those that further the conversation of mankind (to use Richard Rorty's apt phrase) about the topic in question, that is, those that are capable of making a real contribution to ongoing philosophical inquiries into that issue. Films can ask genuinely philosophical questions, as well as offer new ways of viewing (and sometimes new answers to) such questions. When they do, they can rightly be praised for *doing* philosophy. One of the most philosophically interesting films to find a substantial audience in recent years is *Being John Malkovich*, which, as my paradigm of how films can *be* philosophical, can help us understand this difficult concept. Before turning to my reading of that work, we need to examine some further examples of how films have been said to be "truly philosophical."

II

Various writers have remarked that this or that particular film asked genuinely philosophical questions. Noël Carroll, in *Interpreting the Moving Image*, comes up with a novel solution to the ambiguity about the essence of the human personality that emerges from *Citizen Kane* (Orson Welles, 1941). According to Carroll, rather than urging a particular theory, Welles intended to *raise* the question, not solve it; to *problematize* personal identity rather than define it.[5] It is for this reason, Carroll seems to suggest, that *Kane* is one of the most profound movies ever made in Hollywood. In the same vein, Jerold J. Abrams, in an article for Volume

7 of *Film and Philosophy*, contends that *Rear Window* (Alfred Hitchcock, 1954) is a sublime film, in part because it "calls into question the relation between the spectator and the object."[6]

In Volume 8 of the same publication, Herbert Granger argues that *Le Feu Follet* (Louis Malle, 1963) is truly philosophical because its main character is embroiled in a genuine existential crisis that could go either way (despite the fact that Alain (Maurice Ronet) ends up killing himself, it is clear that he could have done otherwise had he concluded that his life *was* worth living). Granger makes the following observation, which is reminiscent of Mulhall's view: "If a film is used to illustrate philosophical positions, or voice philosophical arguments...[like the recent, disastrous *The Matrix Reloaded*], it merely serves to reflect the views of the director, and not those of his characters."[7] Apparently, for Granger, one of the best ways for a film to be philosophical is to have its characters engaged in an existential crisis or genuine philosophical inquiry, the results of which do not come off as predetermined by some prior theory.

Mulhall shares Granger's antipathy for interpretations that use films as fodder for theory, and for directors that merely seek to exemplify some theory or other. Woody Allen is doing precisely that in *Husbands and Wives*. Much like Sartre's own plays,[8] the film exemplifies Sartre's theory of love, but does not elaborate on or develop it beyond the philosopher's original conceptions.[9] Although I would argue that Allen's film *is* philosophical, in that it accurately depicts Sartre's challenging notions at work in convincing existential situations (no small accomplishment), it is not *doing* philosophy, that is, it does not ask deeper questions or propose new concepts or perspectives that Sartre had not himself formulated previously.

In his response to critical reviews of *On Film* first posted on the Film-Philosophy website, and reprinted in a special edition of *Film and Philosophy* (2005) on science fiction, Mulhall acknowledges that one of the goals of publishing his book was to convince us to "think of at least some films as philosophy in action, and hence of film *as philosophizing* rather than as raw material or ornamentation for a philosopher's work."[10] He argues that entries in the *Alien* series can usefully be seen as philosophiz-

ing, because they raise questions about what it means to be human, to have a body, and to be gendered. Furthermore, he contends that the filmmakers self-consciously address questions about the nature of the cinematic medium, the aesthetic phenomenon of the sequel, and overlapping genre notions.

I do not share Mulhall's apparent disdain for the *other* ways a film can be interesting philosophically, but I do agree with him that, on extremely rare occasions, a film can be said to be *doing* philosophy in the sense he prefers, that is, by actually making a positive contribution to the philosophical dialogue on the issue. As Mulhall persuasively argues in the response to his critics cited above, doing philosophy does not require films to offer new *reasons* (in the sense of deductive *arguments*) for philosophical positions. Dostoevsky furthered our understanding of the meaning of the death of God and the threat of nihilism in the late nineteenth century without offering many new arguments in rational theology (Ivan Karamazov's compelling version of the problem of evil is perhaps the only exception). Friedrich Nietzsche is recognized as a profound philosopher (indeed, as one of the most influential philosophers in the last hundred years) despite the relative paucity of traditional arguments in his work. What they both offered us were opposing *gestalten*, that is, ways of viewing the world, rather than deductively sound arguments that could command universal assent.[11]

To clarify what I mean by a film *doing* philosophy, in the best sense of the term, consider the following interpretation of *Being John Malkovich*, which explains why I believe it is one of the most intriguingly philosophical films to have been made in recent years.

FIGURE 1. Is he Malkovich or Dr. Lester?

III

Being John Malkovich is unarguably one of the most inventive films of the last decade and as such it defies easy summary. Hence, I will not attempt to offer one here, choosing instead to focus on several crucial philosophical concepts that the film mobilizes. The viewer must first accept the fabulous premise that makes possible the transformation to which the title refers: a magical (and totally unexplained) portal exists that allows one to *be* the noted actor John Malkovich for a quarter of an hour (granting such participants their own fifteen minutes of fame!). When one enters the portal, he or she has temporary access to John's sensory stream, seeing the world through what appears to be a set of goggles. For that brief period of time, the lucky individual gets to experience the world through Malkovich's senses, overhearing his utterances from within (so to speak), enjoying his pleasures, and undergoing his pains. Then the subjects are physically ejected out into a ditch adjacent to the New Jersey turnpike. Can these individuals accurately be described as having enjoyed *being* John Malkovich? And, if so, in what sense of the term?

Two of the pivotal characters in the story, Dr. Lester (Orson Bean), who apparently "owns" the portal, and Craig Schwartz (John Cusack), who mines it for his own personal gain, can do much more. They can remain in the "Malkovich vessel" permanently and manipulate the poor man's body to do their wishes. Lester has used the portal before to somehow transfer his consciousness out of his previous bodies (as they wore out) into more youthful vessels, hence achieving a kind of serial immortality. Malkovich is destined (for whatever reason) to be his next incarnation. Such miraculous transformations can occur only before midnight on the day when the vessel is ripe, the forty-fourth birthday of its original inhabitant. If the appropriate moment is missed, individuals seeking metamorphosis will end up in a "larval vessel" (a newborn infant), and lose themselves therein. Submerged in such a vessel, the unlucky individual will be assimilated and, to all intents and purposes, cease to be.

Being John Malkovich has already attracted the attention of several philosophers. Mary Litch, in her instructive undergraduate textbook *Philosophy Through Film*, uses the film, along with *Memento* (Christopher Nolan, 2000), as illustrative of various theories of personal identity and/or as challenges thereto.[12] Rehearsing the fundamentals of same-soul theories, and both physical and psychological continuity theories, Litch applies each in their turn to *Malkovich*. Same-soul theories, embracing the spiritual substance of Cartesian dualism, identify individuals by the presence of a spiritual consciousness unique to them alone. Physical continuity theories ground personal identity in material substance, which seems much simpler and more plausible; what makes us the same identifiable person on this view is our continuing physical presence over time (like Descartes's ball of wax). Besides the unfortunate drawback that physicalism seems to imply determinism, however, this hypothesis cannot answer the question of what it is to *be* John Malkovich, even if updated to include our DNA; Malkovich's body presumably retains the same DNA no matter how many personalities occupy (or even command) his "vessel." Yet he is a very different person by the end of the film. Besides, identical twins have the same DNA but different personal identities (except in *Dead Ringers* (David Cronenberg, 1988)).

Long before Gilbert Ryle lampooned Descartes's view as "The Ghost in the Machine," the "same-soul" theory of personal identity had already taken its critical licks.[13] Because souls are, in Litch's words, "enigmatic beasts" (unobservable entities whose very existence is unprovable), they do not allow us to do one of the major tasks for which such criteria are proposed: reidentify particular individuals over time. When Craig takes over Malkovich's body and makes it do his bidding, was he a new ghost in Malkovich's machine? Were both present simultaneously?

Perhaps for pedagogical purposes, Litch then proceeds to oversimplify things by claiming that the psychological continuity theory (which defines personal identity in terms of the privacy of memory, as well as long-standing dispositions and continuing personality characteristics) "meshes well" with the film, accounting for all the major puzzles that it raises. While it *is* true that certain aspects are adequately explained by this approach (Malkovich looks and sounds a lot like Craig soon after the puppeteer takes over, and like Dr. Lester after seven years of being inhabited by him and his geriatric friends), a great many questions are left unanswered.

The mechanics of the process, including how the portal originated, how Dr. Lester obtained ownership of it, how it accomplishes its miraculous feat, and how particular individuals are chosen as vessels ripe for occupation, can remain unexplained. This, after all, is comic fantasy, not science fiction. Several philosophic questions seem to beg for our attention, however. Near the end of the film, we are shown a Malkovich who has been occupied by Dr. Lester for seven years. Lester/Malkovich has married his old secretary (Mary Kay Place) and sounds a whole lot like his original self. If he continues on with his previous mode of operation, he will occupy Malkovich until the body of the former actor breathes its last. If anyone other than the original can truly stake his claim to being John Malkovich, it is Lester.

So what has happened to the "real" John Malkovich? If Lester exits the body only when it breathes its last, can the original Malkovich still be said to exist after all those years of such total submersion? If so, where has he (the original) gone? If he never regains control over his body, can we say that he remains John Malkovich? What about all the other personalities that have transmigrated into Malkovich's body? They seem to be as lost as he is; they (and he) are, at best, goggled observers of Lester's ongoing life.

After exiting Malkovich and giving him up to Dr. Lester and his geriatric crew, Craig resolves to reenter the portal and wrest control of the Malkovich vessel. Doing so *after* midnight, he instead enters into Emily (the newborn love child of his wife Lotte (Cameron Diaz) and business partner Maxine (Catherine Keener), who is destined to become Lester's next target). In the finale, as the seven-year-old is shown gazing adoringly at her two mothers, we get a reverse shot from Craig's goggled perspective, ineffectually whimpering his undying love for Maxine and wishing in vain that Emily would turn her head away from her beloved parents. Having migrated into a larval vessel, he is destined to be a powerless observer for the rest of his life.

When I first saw this film, I was convinced that Jonze, and writer Charlie Kaufman, were

thinking of personal identity as defined by the will as agent acting on the body as instrument. The crucial point for me was when Craig took control, transforming himself from just another passive observer of Malkovich's actions into the internal puppeteer that pulled the strings. Then, when Dr. Lester takes over even more completely than Craig ever could, I thought the answer to the puzzle was clear: the key to being John Malkovich was to be the will behind the actions of the Malkovich vessel. It would actually be a kind of existential theory of personal identity: we are what we do, and the real identity of Malkovich is defined by what he does, and by the reasons and values that explain why he chooses to do what he does.

Armed with my new explanatory hypothesis (which I still believe has substantial philosophic and textual merit), I looked up interviews with Kaufman to confirm my theory. Here is what he had to say.

Well, you are inside someone else's skin, but Craig doesn't have the experience of being Malkovich, he has the experience of using Malkovich. He uses him to be with Maxine, and then he uses Malkovich's notoriety to get his own career going. *So it's "Using John Malkovich."* Yeah, I'd say it's "Using John Malkovich." [laughs][14]

He made this point after having already observed that the only time anyone ever gets a glimpse of the *real* Malkovich is when (hilariously) Lotte chases Maxine with a gun through his unconscious mind. Kaufman's remarks tend to support the psychological continuity theory: what makes John Malkovich who he is are his memories, thoughts, desires, and so forth, to which he alone has access.

The implications of that theory seem to be clear. As Mary Litch saw, Craig continues to exist, even after he enters the passageway. The original Malkovich ceases to exist (or, at a minimum, is suppressed), once Craig gets control over the body. Hence, no one had truly succeeded in *being* John Malkovich, since no one (save for the brief exception noted above) had gained access to his thoughts and/or memories. Following the lead of Thomas Nagel (in his acclaimed article "What is it Like to Be a Bat?"), I suggest that what it is like to be John Malkovich would have to include accessing his consciousness.[15] Once others show themselves capable of taking over Malkovich's body, our concerns shift from what it is like to *be* John Malkovich to who this strangely amalgamated creature truly is in the end.

Notice how the criteria for who John Malkovich *is* in the later sections of the film seem to turn on whose will commands the body over which the protagonists are wrestling. Yet the psychological continuity theory cannot account for who takes control of that body at various points in the film. How does Craig succeed in reducing Malkovich to the status of a marionette, when all the other subjects could only stay for fifteen minutes and only watch and listen? Craig's history as a puppeteer is alluded to as the basis for his skill, but why would this be relevant? For that matter, how does Dr. Lester manage to take over each successive vessel, ensuring his immortality? What is clear, it seems to me, is that, after seven years of passively observing someone else's life, both Craig Schwartz and the original John Malkovich have, to all intents and purposes (an apt phrase), ceased to exist.

The choice of John Malkovich was not an accidental one on the part of the writer and director. Malkovich is an enigmatic chameleon, both in his professional and in his personal life. As Kaufman described the eponymous actor in the above-referenced interview, "there's something odd and completely unknowable about him. You never really know what's going on behind his eyes, so it becomes fascinating, and I think that works for this story." Malkovich seldom portrays strong-willed characters, except when playing the occasional villain (for example his pitiless depiction of the scheming Gilbert Osmond in Jane Campion's *Portrait of a Lady* (1996)). In the present film, he does not put up much of a fight before he is overwhelmed by his occupiers. After seven years of being submerged under Dr. Lester and his cronies, one has to wonder if his psyche even continues to exist. What about Lester's previous incarnation? We never see or hear another consciousness peer out from behind Lester's countenance.

True, seven years after merging with Emily, Craig still exists. He still has longing thoughts about Maxine, but he can have no further effects on either Emily's body or on the external world. One doubts that Emily herself is even aware of this other consciousness submerged

within her. If the personal identity of an individual is defined as the will that governs the actions of a particular body, Craig has disappeared, never to be seen again. Similarly, Malkovich ceases to exist when Lester takes permanent control. Despite a continued friendship with Charlie Sheen, Malkovich's personality seems totally lost to Lester's, to the point of his having adopted the latter's speech patterns and romantic tastes. It makes no sense to talk about the original Malkovich's psychological dispositions, since he has no way to operationalize them. We are never given any further access to his thoughts.

All this reminded me of the theory of the individual as comprised of a hierarchy of dominant and submissive drives, which was proposed by Nietzsche in *Beyond Good and Evil*. There, Nietzsche describes the individual as a bundle of power drives, all vying for dominance. The one that wins is the one that leads to action. We *are* our actions, and the ability to become who we are turns on our strength of will, especially in facing the crucial challenge of upholding a particular hierarchy of such drives over time: "The Essential thing 'in heaven and upon earth' seems…to be a protracted *obedience* in *one* direction: from out of that there…has always emerged something for the sake of which it is worthwhile to live on earth."[16] Becoming who we are hence requires resolute service to a self-made set of priorities, a daunting prospect when we realize that there are no grounds for our choices other than the strength of our individual wills.

In *Friedrich Nietzsche and the Politics of Transformation*, Tracy Strong comes up with as clear a characterization of what Nietzsche means by "Will" as any in the secondary literature: "Nietzsche is saying that if one looks at people, in fact at organisms and matter in general, their most basic characteristic is the attempt to incorporate into themselves and define all that they meet."[17] In the struggle for domination, Craig temporarily triumphs, but Dr. Lester is the ultimate victor. It is *his* will that governs the Malkovich vessel in the long run. And, in Nietzsche's words: "'Unfree will' is a mythology: in real life it is only a question of *strong* and *weak* wills."[18] Malkovich himself was weak willed in the extreme, having trouble deciding about bath towels and allowing himself to be manipulated by Maxine into having dinner with a total stranger. If nobody succeeded in truly being John Malkovich, it might also be said that, by the end of the film, John Malkovich has *effectively* (in the literal sense of the term) ceased to be. Just as poor Craig is assimilated by Emily, so, too, Malkovich's consciousness has been rendered impotent and epiphenomenal.

Nietzsche's theory of the "Will to Power," then, best answers the pivotal question of who John Malkovich *is* at the end of the film seven years after Lester has moved in. Though he contains numerous other consciousnesses (all of Lester's friends, and his own original one, all presumably with goggled views of the proceedings), the Malkovich vessel is now firmly controlled by Lester (who was, in turn, the first reincarnation of the Captain who built the office building and the quirky 7½ th floor that houses the portal). Lester's will commands the body like the pilot of a ship, and John Malkovich ends up being more like Lester than anyone else.

Admittedly, neither Nietzsche, nor the makers of *Being John Malkovich*, offer us much help in accounting for which drive or which personality becomes dominant in the struggle to act. Yet both the philosopher and the filmmakers lead us along some novel paths in thinking about the enigma of personal identity. Their work serves to complicate traditional dualistic conceptions of body and spirit, challenging our simpler and more comforting notions of who and what we are, as well as undermining accepted philosophical definitions of personal identity. The film begs to be read in light of a Nietzschean, existentialist theory of personal identity, which sees the self as defined by its actions and the projects and values to which we dedicate ourselves. Jonze and Kaufman were indeed *doing* philosophy, in the sense that Mulhall privileges exclusively and that I have argued is the paradigm of film at its most philosophical. By this I mean that, after several viewings of *Being John Malkovich*, my understanding of the problem of personal identity was deepened and enhanced because the filmmakers mapped out existentialist pathways of thought, ones that seem to be fascinating Hollywood more and more recently.[19]

Kaufman's screenplay suggests an interesting bridge between body and consciousness in its treatment of the relationship between Maxine and Lotte. Maxine pursues Malkovich and finds that she is most excited by having sex with his body when it is occupied by Lotte's consciousness. Before she switches her allegiance to Craig (when he proves himself capable of manipulating Malkovich's body), she gets pregnant from an early morning liaison with Malkovich/Lotte. In declaring her love, Maxine passionately suggests that the baby she carries *is Lotte's*, and that is why she decided to keep it! Indeed, the daughter who results from their amalgamated union looks rather like a cross between the two women, without a trace of Malkovich's oddly distinctive features, lending some credence to Maxine's rather implausible notion (given its implication that a transformation had occurred at the level of DNA).

What I have been arguing, then, is that Spike Jonze and Charlie Kaufman were (among other things) doing philosophy in *Being John Malkovich*. They were raising new questions *about* and exploring various theories *of* personal identity. Having no preconceived notion of representing some one theory or other as *the* answer that their work was intended to illustrate, they opened the way to intriguing new possibilities. As Kaufman described his creative process in the interview cited above:

If I put disparate things together, then I have to figure out what to do with them, so it puts me in a position of challenging myself and having to surprise myself. I'd like to clarify something. I've discussed my writing process before as working without a map, and people seem to misunderstand what I meant. I do explore without a plan, but that isn't what ends up on the screen, although it's completely a result of that process.

This eloquently captures the ideal of artistic creation championed by Robin George Collingwood, but it also characterizes an inquiring philosophical attitude.[20] Perhaps a theory of personal identity based on a more adequate account of the nature of the human will can yet be formulated, offering the "genuine physiopsychology" that Nietzsche called for but only gestured at in *Beyond Good and Evil*.

DANIEL SHAW
Department of Communications and Philosophy
Lock Haven University of Pennsylvania
Lock Haven, Pennsylvania 17745
USA

INTERNET: dshaw@lhup.edu

1. Thomas Wartenberg, "Looking Backward: Philosophy and Film Reconsidered," *Film and Philosophy* 8 (2004): 140.

2. Stephen Mulhall, *On Film* (New York/London: Routledge, 2002), especially the introduction.

3. Stephen Mulhall, "Picturing the Human (Body and Soul): A Reading of *Blade Runner*," *Film and Philosophy* 1 (1994): 87.

4. Mulhall, "Picturing the Human (Body and Soul)," pp. 40–51.

5. Noël Carroll, *Interpreting the Moving Image* (Cambridge: Cambridge University Press, 1998), pp. 153–165.

6. Jerold J. Abrams, "Cinema and the Aesthetics of the Dynamical Sublime," *Film and Philosophy* 7 (2003): 70.

7. Herbert Granger, "Cinematic Philosophy in *Le Feu Follet*: The Search for the Meaningful Life," *Film and Philosophy* 8 (2004): 75–76.

8. And unlike *Nausea*, where Sartre often seems to be exploring new philosophical avenues, which were only to be mapped out explicitly in subsequent theoretical treatises such as *Being and Nothingness*. For another discussion of Sartre's ideas in relation to film, see András Bálint Kovács, "Sartre, the Philosophy of Nothingness, and the Modern Melodrama," *The Journal of Aesthetics and Art Criticism* 64 (2006): 135–145.

9. In that regard, *Crimes and Misdemeanors* (Woody Allen, 1989) goes beyond its source in Dostoevsky, and is hence more philosophic than *Husbands and Wives*. Raskolnikov could not avoid being paralyzed with guilt. Judah in *Crimes* seems capable of going on with his life without confessing his crime to the powers that be. Dostoevsky intended *Crime and Punishment* as a tale of spiritual redemption; Allen's intentions are less clear, and more intriguing.

10. Stephen Mulhall, "Ways of Thinking: A Response to Andersen and Baggini," reprinted in Special Interest Edition on Science Fiction and Philosophy, *Film and Philosophy* 9 (2005): 24–29.

11. Mulhall invokes both Martin Heidegger and Stanley Cavell in order to clarify the sense in which he thinks films can philosophize, by (paraphrasing Heidegger) "opening new paths for thought" and (quoting Cavell) suggesting "directions to answers." Mulhall, "Ways of Thinking," p. 28. The latter characterization is excerpted from Cavell's essay, "The Thought of Movies," in *Themes Out of School* (San Francisco: North Point Press, 1984), p. 9.

12. Mary Litch, *Philosophy Through Film* (New York/London: Routledge, 2004), pp. 67–86.

13. Gilbert Ryle, *The Concept of Mind* (University of Chicago Press, 1949, reprinted 1984), pp. 11–24.

14. Interview for the *Being Charlie Kaufman* website, originally posted in 2000, available at <http://www.beingcharliekaufman.com/index.htm?movies/malkovich.htm&2>.

15. Thomas Nagel, "What is it Like to Be a Bat?" *Philosophical Review* 84 (1974): 435–450.

16. Friedrich Nietzsche, *Beyond Good and Evil*, trans. R. J. Hollingdale (London: Penguin Books, 1973), § 188.

17. Tracy Strong, *Friedrich Nietzsche and the Politics of Transformation* (University of California Press, 1975), p. 234.

18. Nietzsche, *Beyond Good and Evil*, § 21.

19. See, for example, *I ♥ Huckabees* (David O. Russell, 2004), *Closer* (Mike Nichols, 2004), and *Eternal Sunshine of the Spotless Mind* (Michel Gondry, 2004), for which Kaufman was recently honored with the Academy Award for Best Original Screenplay.

20. R. G. Collingwood, *The Principles of Art* (Oxford: Oxford University Press, 1958), pp. 111–119.

CHRISTOPHER GRAU

Eternal Sunshine of the Spotless Mind and the Morality of Memory

The film *Eternal Sunshine of the Spotless Mind* (Michel Gondry, 2004) is one of those movies that people tend to either love or hate.[1] Critics generally raved about it, but if you look on websites that allow people to post their own reviews, you find a fair number of "one-star" ratings and complaints that the film was confusing, pretentious, or just plain boring. On the other hand, those who like the film tend to really like it, giving it five stars and admitting to having seen the film multiple times in the theater. Why do the fans of this film seem so, well, *fanatic* in their devotion? Although I think much of their appreciation has its base in the sensitive and creative direction of Michel Gondry, the clever script from Charlie Kaufman, the beautifully melancholy score by Jon Brion, and the impressive performances by all the actors involved, I also think it is not crazy to suggest that the *philosophy* of the film helped it to achieve the cult-like status it now enjoys.[2]

What, exactly, do I mean by saying that this film has a philosophy? Well, I don't *just* mean that it explores philosophical ideas. It does this very effectively, but it also offers something more: in the course of exploring these ideas, it implicitly offers a philosophical *position*. That is, it does not just raise certain deep questions, it suggests answers to those questions. Since it is a movie and not a journal article, the position that is gestured at does not come to us by way of an explicit argument, but it is one that I think can be unpacked and defended. Accordingly, here I will be attempting to make explicit the philosophical perspective that I take to be implicit in this original and moving film.[3]

I. FORGET ME NOT

Eternal Sunshine of the Spotless Mind (*Eternal Sunshine*) is a story about a group of people who have access to a peculiar and powerful technology. Thanks to the work of one Dr. Mierzwiak (Tom Wilkinson) and his company Lacuna, Inc., several characters are able to undergo a process by which they have the memories of other people erased from their minds in order to lessen the suffering that these painful memories can cause. After watching the film, it is hard not to dwell on the possibility offered to the characters of Joel (Jim Carrey), Clementine (Kate Winslet), and Mary (Kirsten Dunst). If *you* could choose to erase someone from your life, would you? Even if you personally would not choose to undergo such a procedure, do you think someone else should have that sort of choice open to him or her? If the memories of a particular incident or relationship are truly causing someone tremendous pain, *shouldn't* they have the option of removing those memories, provided that it can be done safely and effectively?

The film is wonderfully nuanced and subtle, and thus not surprisingly it doesn't offer us easy or obvious answers to these sorts of questions. Nonetheless, the general sense one gets from the film is that the memory-removal technology exhibited in the movie does not, in fact, allow for the "eternal sunshine" referenced in the title. Indeed, it is hard to imagine someone leaving the theater thinking that pursuing such a technology would be a good thing.[4] Why not? Well, the film shows us some rather unfortunate

FIGURE 1. Joel (Jim Carrey) undergoes a preliminary brain scan in order to create a "memory map" that will be used to erase his memories of Clementine (Kate Winslet).

consequences that result from the use of the technology: Mary, Joel, and Clementine, as well as others connected to them, all experience pain and heartbreak as a result of the supposedly secret procedure going awry through various leaks. However, what is more important for my purposes is the fact that the film seems to suggest that the memory-removal technology is problematic *even if the glitches and leaks could be worked out*. There is a sense of tragedy in Joel's realization (while in the middle of the procedure) that he does not want to lose his memories of Clem, and the sadness the viewers feel with him is *not* lifted by the thought that he will eventually be ignorant of the loss. On the contrary, awareness of the future ignorance seems to *compound* the sadness: that he will soon be clueless is no cause for celebration. The harm done by this procedure does not seem to be fully accountable in terms of the harm the characters consciously *feel*. In going through the philosophical issues that are raised by the film, I hope to offer an account of why the sense of tragic loss suggested by the film resonates with viewers, and why the implicit philosophical position assumed by the film is a respectable and defensible one, even if it can at first appear to be quite puzzling and controversial.[5]

II. UTILITARIANISM

In some ways the most obvious and sensible response that could be made to the question "Is the use of such memory removal technology a good thing?" is what philosophers would call a traditional utilitarian response. Traditional or classical utilitarians (such as Jeremy Bentham, John Stuart Mill, or Henry Sidgwick) thought that the right action is the one that brings about the most happiness overall, where happiness is understood in terms of pleasure and the avoidance of pain. When deciding on what to do, the utilitarian does his or her best to calculate the possible consequences of the choices that lay before him or her. The morally right act is the one that (among the possible actions open to the person) will result in the most happiness and the least suffering, and so the utilitarian will always strive to choose those actions that are most likely to increase overall happiness and minimize overall suffering. Accordingly, if a memory-removal procedure can function in such a way that it brings about more happiness than would otherwise be possible, the use of such a procedure is not only justified, but in fact *morally required* on utilitarian grounds.

Now it should be pointed out that there is a big "if" in the claim above—it is *not at all clear* whether this sort of procedure *could* be implemented in such a way that it would increase happiness overall. In *Eternal Sunshine* the procedure seems far from foolproof. Indeed, we see fools implementing it (a stoned Stan (Mark Ruffalo) and his dimwitted sidekick Patrick (Elijah Wood)) and they do a thoroughly mediocre job.[6] We also see that the acquaintances of Clementine fail to keep her procedure a secret and in the process cause Joel no small amount of misery. In addition, the memory-removal procedure that Mary undergoes seems to increase rather than minimize the pain and suffering for everyone affected by her affair with Mierzwiak. These and other considerations would lead many people to conclude that the procedure *as displayed in the film* does *not* tend to maximize happiness overall.

The question remains, however, whether such a process *could* be streamlined so as to reliably minimize the suffering of those undergoing the procedure while not causing significant harm to anyone else. Putting aside the glitches and complications present in the film, it is natural to wonder: If memory removal was reliable, efficient, safe, and effective, are there still reasons to reject it?

One might plausibly argue that painful memories stay with us for good reason: they allow us to learn valuable lessons from the past and thus be better prepared for the future. This is no doubt often the case, and in a situation in which it appears that the removal of memory would limit the person in this way (by denying him or her useful information), such a procedure would probably not be for the best (and thus not "maximize utility"). However, there are cases in which painful memories seem to do much more harm than good, and where any lessons that could be derived from the memories could presumably be learned via other routes. In *those* kinds of cases, it seems that the misery avoided by memory removal would more than counterbalance any possible benefits that would normally arise from retaining the memories. It seems, then, that the utilitarian response to whether such a procedure is justified should be a cautious and conditional "yes": *if* suffering can be minimized in a particular case, then such a procedure is appropriate in that case. In circumstances in which the use of memory removal would increase overall happiness, the use of such a procedure is, on utilitarian grounds, a morally good thing. Moreover, as I suggested earlier, utilitarianism would seem to *require* the use of such a procedure if it was the most efficient means of maximizing utility.[7] For the utilitarian, the goodness or badness of memory removal hinges solely on the consequences, and if we can ensure that those consequences are beneficial overall, such technology would be something to welcome rather than reject.

III. THE EXPERIENCE MACHINE SHIFTS INTO REVERSE

Many people will feel that the approach we have been considering, though intuitive in many ways, is somehow too crude. The worry is that *even if* the procedure can reliably maximize happiness overall (and minimize suffering) there is *still* something wrong with it. Memory removal seems problematic in a way that cannot fully be made out within the utilitarian framework—a loss has occurred even though we cannot explicate the loss in terms of lost *utility* or happiness.

We can get at one reason why the procedure in *Eternal Sunshine* seems so troubling by considering a classic example that is often used to raise doubts about the hedonistic assumptions that lie behind traditional utilitarianism. In his 1971 book *Anarchy, State, and Utopia*, Robert

Nozick introduced a thought experiment that has become a staple of introductory philosophy classes everywhere. It is known as "the experience machine."

Suppose there were an experience machine that would give you any experience you desired. Super-duper neuropsychologists could stimulate your brain so that you would think and feel you were writing a great novel, or making a friend, or reading an interesting book. All the time you would be floating in a tank, with electrodes attached to your brain. Should you plug into this machine for life, preprogramming your life's desires?…Of course, while in the tank you won't know that you're there; you'll think it's all actually happening. Others can also plug in to have the experiences they want, so there's no need to stay unplugged to serve them. (Ignore problems such as who will service the machines if everyone plugs in.) Would you plug in? What else can matter to us, other than how our lives feel from the inside?[8]

Nozick goes on to argue that other things do matter to us: for instance, that we actually *do* certain things, as opposed to simply have the experience of doing them. Also, he points out that we value being (and becoming) certain kinds of people. I do not just want to have the experience of being a decent person, I want to actually *be* a decent person. Finally, Nozick argues that we value contact with reality in itself, independent of any benefits such contact may bring through pleasant experience: we want to know we are experiencing the real thing. In sum, Nozick thinks that it matters to most of us, often in a rather deep way, that we be the authors of our lives and that our lives involve interacting with the world, and he thinks that the fact that most people would not choose to enter into such an experience machine demonstrates that they do value these other things. As he puts it: "We learn that something matters to us in addition to experience by imagining an experience machine and then realizing that we would not use it."[9]

One way to think about the procedure presented in *Eternal Sunshine* is to consider it a kind of *reverse* experience machine: rather than *give* you the experience of your choice, it allows you to *take away* experiences that you have retained in your memory. Similar philosophical issues arise, as the worry is that in both cases we are achieving pleasure (or the avoidance of pain) at the cost of truth. Elsewhere, I have discussed Nozick's thought experiment in the context of the character Cypher's (Joe Pantoliano) choice in the film *The Matrix* (The Wachowski Brothers, 1999).[10] There, I argued that our natural aversion to sacrificing knowledge of the truth for happiness can be understood as the expression of some of our most basic values, and that these values are perfectly legitimate and need not be threatened by a hedonistic outlook that claims that only pleasurable conscious experience can ultimately have value in itself.

Not surprisingly, I think something similar can be said about the memory-removal procedure offered in *Eternal Sunshine*. Even if the use of such a procedure would maximize happiness, it is understandable and justifiable for someone to refuse such a procedure on the grounds that they do not want to "live a lie." To think otherwise is to forget that many of us value the truth in a way that cannot simply be explained in terms of the pleasure that knowledge of the truth often brings or makes possible. Our reluctance to endorse (or undergo) a memory-removal procedure is one expression of this basic value we place on the truth for its own sake.

Toward the end of *Eternal Sunshine*, Mary finds out that she has undergone the memory-removal procedure and decides that what Mierzwiak has done is horribly wrong. This realization prompts her to return the medical files of all his previous patients, telling them that she has done this to "correct" the situation. In the shooting script for the film there is an additional bit of dialogue that further suggests that her actions are motivated by considerations similar to the sort we have been considering.

MARY: Patrick Henry said, "For my part, whatever anguish of spirit it may cost, I am willing to know the whole truth: to know the worst, and to provide for it." I found that quote last night. Patrick Henry was a great patriot, Howard.[11]

Unfortunately, those not inclined to share this intuition with Mary, Patrick Henry, or Nozick (that truth has value that is independent of the good consequences knowledge of the truth can bring) are likely to complain that this position stands in desperate need of justification. *Why* is the truth valuable in itself? Why should we think it good to know the truth in situations in which it brings only misery? The natural response (we just *do* value the truth in this fundamental and basic way) is not likely to sway the person who thinks a memory-removal procedure is unproblematic. Although everyone agrees that justifications have to come to an end somewhere, rarely do philosophers agree just *where* a proper ending resides. The common response to Ludwig Wittgenstein's famous claim "my spade is turned" (that is, I have hit bedrock—I have exhausted justifications) is to tell him to pick up the damn spade and keep digging![12] I am not sure that much can be said to resolve this sort of dispute, but one point that can be made is to remind the opponent that he or she, too, hits bedrock eventually, that is, a point at which he or she can no longer provide a justification for his or her own valuation. To the question, "and what justifies the value you place on pleasant conscious experience?" it seems little can be said. This sort of concern appears to be somehow self-justifying or beyond justification. If this is right, it is unclear why we should not allow that other concerns might well be similarly foundational or beyond justification.

A further justification for valuing the truth may not be possible; however, it *is* possible to say a bit more by way of explanation regarding why many people hold this value. Colin McGinn has described the threat of general epistemological skepticism as tantamount to an individual discovering he or she is in a kind of "metaphysical solitary confinement." If we do not know what we think we know, then we are in effect cut off from the world. If the skeptic is right, it turns out that our mind does not have the kind of interaction and relationship with reality that we ordinarily take it to have, and this possibility is understandably disturbing to us. As McGinn puts it, we want our mind to be a window onto the world, not a prison.[13]

Merely losing a portion of one's memory is certainly not equivalent to the sort of radical ignorance that epistemological skeptics entertain, but it does involve a related variety of detachment from the world. Having undergone a memory-removal procedure, the individual has consented to, if not a metaphysical prison, then at least a pair of metaphysical blinkers and, worse yet, he or she has consented to make himself or herself ignorant of that very choice. The individual chooses to cut himself or herself off from the world—his or her mind represents the world less accurately than it did before and, accordingly, he or she is slightly closer to the isolation and solipsism that make skepticism threatening.[14] We have a very natural desire *not* to be cut off from the world in this way, and thus it is not surprising that the removal of memories disturbs us in a manner that cannot simply be cashed out in terms of future unhappiness. The fact that in *Eternal Sunshine* the memory removal involves isolating a person from someone who was previously very close makes the use of the procedure all the more disturbing: it is not just a metaphysical relationship that has been severed, but a personal and emotional one.

IV. WHAT YOU DON'T KNOW *CAN* HURT YOU

Granting that voluntary removal of one's memories seems to clash with the value that many people place on knowing the truth about themselves and the world, a further related question arises: Does the sort of memory loss exemplified in *Eternal Sunshine* involve an actual *harm* or *misfortune* to the person who undergoes the procedure? It is quite natural for people to think initially that such a procedure *cannot* be said to harm the person if it produces no unpleasant effects for the person. (How can I be harmed if I do not consciously experience the harm?) Although this seems straightforward enough, on reflection we can see that it is far from obvious that this simple notion of harm will suffice. Consider Thomas Nagel's comments on the view that harm must necessarily be experienced.

It means that even if a man is betrayed by his friends, ridiculed behind his back, and despised by people who treat him politely to his face, none of it can be counted as a misfortune for him so long as he does not suffer as a result. It means that a man is not injured if his wishes are ignored by the executor of his will, or if, after his death, the belief becomes current that all the literary works on which his fame rests were really written by his brother, who died in Mexico at the age of 28.[15]

Nagel reminds us that many situations that we would naturally want to characterize as involving harms would have to be redescribed if we want to embrace the narrow view that harms must be experienced. Elaborating on Nagel's insights, Steven Luper helpfully distinguishes between what he calls "harms that wound" versus "harm that deprive."[16] We can understand the harms that Nagel speaks of as harms that may not wound but do deprive the person of some good, and both Luper and Nagel suggest that a sensible account of harm should be able to incorporate these latter types of misfortune.[17]

If this approach is correct, then it would seem that the deprivation of the truth that Joel, Clementine, and Mary undergo in *Eternal Sunshine* could rightly be seen as a form of harm or misfortune.[18] The fact that it is something they bring on themselves does not change this, for we allow that people often (knowingly and unknowingly) harm themselves in other ways. (The film in fact implicitly supports this notion through characterizing Clementine as self-destructive, Mary as easily manipulated, and Joel as a depressive—just the types of people who could and would harm themselves.) The harm here is not as dramatic or obvious as some other forms of self-abuse, but it is nevertheless genuine: they have sacrificed a part of their minds and in the process blinded themselves to a part of the world.

V. IMMANUEL KANT ON DUTIES TO ONESELF

So far I have suggested that memory removal is morally problematic because it involves a clash between fundamental values: our concern with knowing the truth comes into tension with our desire for happiness. Undergoing such a procedure inevitably involves sacrificing the concern for truth and, accordingly, we are inclined to see the person who has undergone such a procedure as having been harmed through *deprivation* of the truth. Is there more to say regarding the sort of harm that one undergoes here? I think there is, and I think we can get at a deeper appreciation of the harm to self that memory removal involves through a consideration of some ideas from Immanuel Kant.

Kant famously proclaimed that persons are unique: everything else in the world is a thing and thus has a price, but persons alone deserve a kind of treatment that involves recognizing their value as *beyond* price. Persons, because of their capacity for freedom and rational agency, have a dignity that is incommensurable and priceless. Accordingly, persons deserve *respect*. Kant thought that we needed to be consistent in our thinking on these matters, and that means we have to acknowledge that you have a duty to treat *yourself* with respect and never to use yourself solely as a means to an end. Accordingly, he argued that morality prohibits both suicide and many forms of self-mutilation. In the *Groundwork*, he succinctly lays out his reasons for this view.

First, as regards the concept of necessary duty to oneself, the man who contemplates suicide will ask himself whether his action can be consistent with the idea of humanity as an end in itself. If he destroys himself in order to escape from a difficult situation, he is making use of his person merely as a means so as to maintain a tolerable condition till the end of life. Man, however, is not a thing, and hence is not something to be used merely as a means; he must in all his actions always be regarded as an end in himself. Therefore, I cannot dispose of man in my own person by mutilating, damaging, or killing him. (It belongs to ethics proper to define this principle more precisely, so as to avoid all misunderstanding, e.g., as to the amputation of the limbs in order to preserve myself, as to exposing my life to danger with a view to preserve it, etc. This question is therefore omitted here.)[19]

Many have mocked Kant's remarks, wondering if his prohibition should include such horrific acts as ear piercing or haircuts. Acknowledging that we may want to make allowances for the permissibility of suicide and bodily mutilation under certain circumstances, we can still agree with the spirit of Kant's claims here: there is something disturbing about the idea of self-manipulation that parallels the disturbing aspects of manipulating others, and consistency suggests that we should recognize that cases of treating oneself solely as a means are morally problematic for the same reasons that objectifying others is wrong. Just as it is wrong to use others for advantage (even their own advantage) in ways that do not recognize their humanity, it is wrong to objectify oneself

simply for the sake of some supposed advantage. As Kant says elsewhere: "Self-regarding duties, however, are independent of all advantage, and pertain only to the worth of being human."[20]

It is a natural extension of Kant's view to criticize the process we see in *Eternal Sunshine* on the grounds that it involves a type of morally problematic self-objectification. Part of what is so disturbing about the memory-removal procedure is that it is in fact a form of self-mutilation: in order to "maintain a tolerable condition" one uses oneself as a mere means and thus manipulates oneself as though one were an object rather than a person deserving of respect. Indeed, the kind of manipulation involved here is more obviously problematic than the sort of bodily mutilation Kant mentions. After all, what is mutilated in this case is not merely one's body but one's *mind*, and thus the violation of one's rational nature is frightfully direct. Memory removal bears closer similarities to the sort of mind manipulation that Kant had in mind when he rejected the idea of rehabilitating prisoners. James Rachels, summarizing Kant's view, explains the rationale behind Kant's opposition to rehabilitation.

[T]he aim of "rehabilitation," although it sounds noble enough, is actually no more than the attempt to mold people into what we think they ought to be. As such, it is a violation of their rights as autonomous beings to decide for themselves what sort of people they will be. We do have the right to respond to their wickedness by "paying them back" for it, but we do not have the right to violate their integrity by trying to manipulate their personalities.[21]

Kant's view is obviously controversial, but it is easy enough to understand his concern, at least when considering certain types of rehabilitation. Take the film *A Clockwork Orange* (Stanley Kubrick, 1971): in it, a young thug named Alex (Malcolm McDowell) is captured and undergoes "aversion therapy" that makes him unable to commit violent acts but does nothing to remove his immoral desires or convince him of the wrongness of what he has done. He becomes mechanical, like clockwork, rather than a free, rational agent. It is precisely the sense that Alex has been unjustly manipulated that causes us to have sympathy for an otherwise vile person. Even if he is a criminal who has committed countless immoral acts, that does not give society the right to treat him as though he is merely a broken mechanism rather than a person. Manipulating someone's mind is a particularly robust and offensive way to fail to grant him or her the respect that all people deserve.[22]

One might think the parallel between manipulative rehabilitation and self-induced memory removal fails because the case of memory removal involves a person voluntarily consenting to the manipulation while the criminal does not (presumably) consent to the rehabilitation. This brings up some rather thorny issues regarding the role of consent vis-à-vis Kantian ethics. I am inclined to think that Kant's account has to involve more than simply consent in order for an act to show proper respect, but for our purposes here we can leave this debate aside, for it seems quite likely that the person *post memory removal* is likely *not* to consent to the procedure that has been performed on him or her even if he or she did consent *prior to removal*. (Mary exhibits this pattern rather clearly in *Eternal Sunshine*.) The postprocedure person falls quite squarely into the class of persons who have had their integrity and personhood violated through the kind of manipulation that Kant criticized.

The way the memory-removal procedure creates a later self that may not approve of the earlier self's choices brings to mind another parallel, one that the film highlights in a particularly vivid fashion. The sadness we feel for both Clementine and Joel parallels the sort of sadness felt for people who, out of misery and desperation, start down a path of self-obliteration through drugs or alcohol. It is no coincidence that Clementine is characterized as an alcoholic, nor that Joel often appears so depressed as to be borderline suicidal. Their choice to utilize the memory-removal technology is presented as being of a piece with their other self-destructive tendencies. Kant would presumably agree that these behaviors all involve a morally problematic form of self-destruction. Discussing alcohol (and suicide), he remarks:

For example, if I have drunk too much today, I am incapable of making use of my freedom and my powers; or if I do away with myself, I likewise deprive myself of the ability to use [my powers]. So this conflicts with the greatest use of freedom, that it abolishes itself, and all use of it, as the highest *prin-cipium* of life. Only under certain conditions can freedom be consistent with itself; otherwise it comes into collision with itself.[23]

The removal of memories can be plausibly seen as a limitation on one's freedom, just as Kant suggests both drunkenness and suicide limit freedom. (The cliché "knowledge is power" rings true here: the self-imposed ignorance brought on through memory removal limits your power and your freedom through limiting your options.) As with the other cases that Kant discusses, utilizing one's freedom in order to remove one's memories involves a kind of contradiction: you attempt to *use* your freedom in order to *limit* your freedom. On Kant's approach, we have no right to do this to ourselves, regardless of the convenience or advantage of such a procedure.

I do not want to suggest that Kant's positions on suicide, self-mutilation, or rehabilitation are clearly correct or uncontroversial—they are not, and many smart and able philosophers have criticized them. What I do want to claim is that his overall position and the way it manifests itself in these particular cases is both insightful and worthy of consideration, and that the insights Kant offers us apply rather nicely to the topic at hand, that is, the ethics of memory removal. Kant offers a rationale for why harming oneself in certain ways is particularly disturbing and morally problematic. In cases of suicide, self-abuse, and (I have argued) memory removal, we see agents treating themselves solely as a means to an end rather than as ends in themselves. There is a failure of self-respect, and this imparts the tragic sense that someone has, out of desperation, failed to recognize his or her own worth. This harmonizes well with the mood of *Eternal Sunshine*, as the film offers up exactly this sort of tragic situation in which individuals are blind to their own worth: the three people who we see using the memory-removal procedure are all characterized as self-destructive to varying degrees, with Clem's alcoholism, Joel's depression, and Mary's insecurity and weakness of will making it all too plausible that they would also engage in the sort of harm to self that memory removal involves. The film suggests that what they have done is both sad and wrong; Kant's moral theory helps make this suggestion comprehensible.

Watching the film, we do not simply feel bad for Joel and Clementine because we suspect they have harmed themselves in removing their memories; we also naturally think that this procedure involves harming those who are erased as well.[24] Consider in particular the feelings of sympathy that arise for Joel based on Clem's actions. Aside from worrying that he will harm himself in choosing memory removal, viewers of the film cannot help but think that Joel has already been harmed by Clementine through *her* trip to Lacuna. He certainly takes her decision to remove memories of him as something of an insult, and we are inclined to agree.

There is a rather straightforward way of understanding the nature of this harm, for we see Joel's confusion, sadness, and anger on the screen as he learns about what Clementine has done. He is made miserable by the news, and the thought of removing this newfound misery seems to be at least part of the basis for his decision to undergo the procedure himself. We saw earlier, though, that there are other classes of harm that are trickier to make sense of: harms that befall a person even though that person does not experience the harms. I suggested that Joel, Clementine, and Mary can be seen as harming themselves in this way by undergoing the memory-removal procedure; they harm themselves through deprivation of the truth regarding their previous relationships. I think we can (and should) go one step further, however, and say that Clementine has not just harmed herself but also harmed *Joel* in a way he cannot experience.[25] Just as in the case of unexperienced harm to self, this claim is initially puzzling. It is clear enough that Clem has harmed Joel in a very palpable way *once* he discovers that she has had him erased, but it is a significantly harder question whether he can be said to be harmed even if he does not discover what she has done.

We can better contemplate this possibility by considering a scenario slightly different from the one we saw in the film: imagine that Clementine erased Joel, but Joel *never* came to discover the erasure. (Perhaps he left to live in another country before she underwent the procedure and he lost all contact with mutual friends, family, and so forth.) Would it be right to say that Clementine harmed Joel in her actions? Opinions are likely to be divided here, as we saw earlier that there are those (such as many utilitarians) who find the idea of an unexperienced harm nonsensical. Yet there are also folks like Nagel, who plausibly suggest that dismissing unexperienced harms may involve a larger sacrifice to our ordinary intuitions and commonsense than is initially obvious. If we can legitimately say that betraying someone behind their back involves harming them even if they never discover the harm, it would seem we should similarly be able to say that Clementine's actions harm Joel even if he never finds out.

Granting that *some* harms are not necessarily experienced, what is the nature of the non-experiential harm perpetrated by Clementine?[26] She has not exactly *betrayed* Joel, has she? After all, one might think that choosing to remove the memories of someone else is not significantly different from throwing out their old letters or deleting all their emails.[27] Is it not her right to remove mementos or even memories if she chooses? Perhaps, but here we may be riding roughshod over morally relevant differences between the case of an ex-lover burning letters and Clementine wiping all trace of Joel from her mind. There is certainly a difference *in degree* between the two cases, and that might be enough to make a moral difference, but there is also something more: entirely wiping out the memory of someone seems to manifest a failure of respect that is distinct *in kind* from merely discarding keepsakes.

On reflection, this sort of case appears to be less like the tossing of old letters and more like a genuine betrayal. Just as we might think that someone who has misrepresented the memory of someone else through slander has done him or her a disservice, we can similarly say that one who has removed *all* memory of someone has also done a disservice to the person who has been erased.[28] Though the idea may initially sound bizarre, it follows that we may have a moral obligation to remember those we have had close relationships with. Note that I did not say we have a moral obligation to have *fond* memories, or to *like* the person, for that would clearly be a ludicrous demand. Rather, I am suggesting that we are morally obliged to not distort history through distorting our own historical record.

Consider a drug that would revise one's memories such that all the memories of one's ex-spouse become both false and unflattering. Many would rightly regard the taker of such a drug as having done something that is not only imprudent but also immoral. Although *removing* memories is not the same as *distorting* them, the removal of *all* the memories of a person does amount to a form of distortion: your mind comes to have a falsified and thus distorted perspective on one aspect of the world. Through a voluntary "lie by omission," the narrative of your life has been, in part, fictionalized.

I said earlier that memory removal is disturbing because it amounts to putting on "metaphysical blinkers" that partially sever the connection between one's mind and the world—the mind no longer reflects the world as accurately as it did. There is symmetry in our values here: just as we want our mind to accurately represent the world, we also want the world to accurately represent *us*.[29] If I delete all my memories of a person, I ensure that a part of the world no longer represents that person at all, and it is hard not to think that I have thus engaged in a morally problematic form of misrepresentation. If that person were to find out what I have done, he or she would have the right to be offended. Even if they do not find out, it is plausible to think that they have nonetheless been harmed by my actions. Though the degree of wrongdoing may vary in accordance with my motives (as in the case of slander or other forms of misrepresentation), even memory removal done with the best of reasons can amount to a misfortune for the person erased because it involves this willful failure to represent the person accurately.

I suspect some skepticism remains in many readers for, despite the considerations above, a duty to *remember* can seem like a very odd thing for morality to demand.[30] If we can free ourselves from an overly narrow conception of morality as nothing more than a collection of abstract rules that regulate behavior towards others, I think we can see that what I am suggesting is not really that strange. The philosopher and novelist Iris Murdoch can provide aid here: she eloquently argued that at the core of morality is a responsibility to do our best to *get things right*, and this means not *just* to act rightly but to perceive the world and other

people accurately—to "really look" and see things as they actually are.

The authority of morals is the authority of truth, that is of reality. We can see the length, the extension, of these concepts as patient attention transforms accuracy without interval into just discernment.... Should an unhappy marriage be continued for the sake of the children? Should I leave my family in order to do political work? Should I neglect them in order to practice my art? The love which brings the right answer is an exercise of justice and realism and really *looking*. The difficulty is to keep the attention fixed upon the real situation and to prevent it from returning surreptitiously to the self with consolations of self-pity, resentment, fantasy, and despair....It is a *task* to come to see the world as it is.[31]

If this characterization of "the authority of morals" is correct, then I think it is quite reasonable to conclude that we ought to do our best not just to *look*, but also to *not forget* what we have seen. Choosing to obliterate all trace of someone else is the very opposite of the sort of focused attention that Murdoch describes as necessary for both love and justice.[32] Maintaining the ability to *look back* is just one part of our larger responsibility to look at the world with the clarity that morality requires.[33] *Eternal Sunshine* presents us with several characters who have, for various reasons, chosen to evade that responsibility, and the film effectively cautions us against such escapism.

VII. MARY'S THEFT

Eternal Sunshine, unlike some science-fiction films, is not in love with the new technology it showcases.[34] Quite the reverse: the memory-removal procedure is presented as a tempting but misguided and dangerous tool. I have attempted to make sense of and defend the pessimistic tone of the film toward this sort of procedure. I have argued that undergoing memory removal can amount to harming both yourself and the person you have erased. You harm yourself through depriving yourself of the truth about your life and the world. You harm the other person through a kind of *mis*representation that is inevitable when you remove *all* representation of that person. My hope is that a

FIGURE 2. Mary (Kirsten Dunst) leaving Lacuna, Inc. with patients' records in order to return them to those who have had memories erased.

consideration of the philosophical issues involved has helped us to better understand and justify the film's technological pessimism and its sense of tragic loss.

Our consideration of the philosophical issues raised by *Eternal Sunshine* has put us in a better position to defend the actions of Mary at the end of the film. I mentioned earlier that she ultimately decides to steal the medical records of Mierzwiak's patients and return them. From a strictly utilitarian perspective it might seem obvious that Mary is doing something morally wrong in returning those files, mementos, and audiotapes. Surely she will be causing many of the previous patients pain and perhaps even intense, prolonged suffering. Why, then, does she think she is "in the right," and why does the audience tend to sympathize with her actions? I have been suggesting in this essay that there are a variety of ways in which we can think of the memory-removal procedure as causing significant harm through deprivation. Mary is attempting to undo that harm, and even if her attempt brings with it some "harms that wound," we (and she) are inclined to think the suffering might well be worth it. Although we do not get to see the full results of her actions, the film suggests that her goal is a worthy one, and the philosophers we have considered have helped us acquire a fuller understanding of why her actions may be justified *despite* the pain they will bring.[35]

VIII. CONCLUSION

I have tried to explain how the philosophical resources provided by Nozick, Nagel, Kant, Murdoch, and others put us in a position to better understand why the scenario of *Eternal Sunshine* is disturbing and morally problematic in a way that cannot be fully accommodated by traditional utilitarian thinking alone. Nozick's and Nagel's insights suggest that we can legitimately claim that memory removal involves a conflict of values, one that results in harm to the individual that goes beyond the sorts of harms measurable in terms of utility. In addition, Kant has given us reason to worry that voluntary memory removal displays a lack of self-respect that is harmful and perhaps immoral. Finally, Murdoch's moving vision of morality as requiring accurate perception allows us to make sense of the idea that memory removal can involve not just harm to self, but also harm to others.

These considerations help us better understand our response to the film: watching *Eternal Sunshine* it is quite natural to feel uneasy regarding the decisions Joel, Clementine, and Mary make to utilize memory removal. It may initially seem puzzling that we are led to feel conflicted regarding the voluntary decisions characters have made in order to pursue happiness. (No one forces them, and they are choosing memory removal in order to feel better, so why should we feel ambivalence?) However, understanding the nature of their sacrifice, and the manner in which it involves a kind of harm to others as well as exploitation of the self, allows us to make better sense of our emotional response to the film. We can now see why the depth of sadness evoked by the film is not exhausted by a consideration of the bad consequences and suffering we witness—the misfortune the characters bring on themselves and others is not always in the form of misery, but it is misfortune just the same.

Filmmakers and novelists are often more successful than philosophers at exploring the nuances and complexity of our beliefs, desires, and values. However, philosophy has a role in helping us in the quest to make sense of and interpret this complexity. *Eternal Sunshine* is, among other things, a valuable philosophical resource because it vividly illustrates the poverty of the classical utilitarian perspective through making us aware that moral reality is significantly more complex than such utilitarian theory can allow. In particular, the film shows us that the harm caused by voluntary memory removal cannot be satisfactorily understood solely in terms of harms that are consciously experienced. Philosophical argumentation is required to make explicit these implicit lessons of the film, and it has been my goal here to utilize philosophical resources to do just that so as to better understand both this remarkable film and the philosophical issues it so eloquently raises.

IX. POSTSCRIPT: THE PRESIDENT'S COUNCIL REPORT ON BIOTECHNOLOGY

I have been discussing memory removal in the context of the film *Eternal Sunshine of the Spotless Mind*. There, a procedure is utilized to wipe out all memories of a previous relationship. I suggested that the film gives us reason to think that such a procedure is troubling, and I tried to unpack this thought through relying on the insights of various philosophers. My goal in the above essay was primarily to argue that memory removal can be morally problematic in a way that goes beyond its potential for bringing about bad experiences. It does *not* follow from this that memory removal may not, in some cases, be justified. What does follow is that even if it is justified, that does not necessarily make it an unequivocally good thing—it may instead be merely the lesser of two evils.

My qualification here is not simply for the sake of academic accuracy, for the issues raised by *Eternal Sunshine* are not as farfetched or futuristic as some might think. As *The New York Times* has reported, memory-diminishing drugs have been given to those with posttraumatic stress disorder in an attempt to lessen the horrible symptoms that can follow the witnessing of traumatic events.[36] The drugs in question do not exactly erase problematic memories, but they do diminish them through blunting the emotions connected to specific memories. The President's Council on Bioethics finds the research disturbing enough to devote a chapter on it in a recent report, and it cautions against the use of such drugs.[37] I want to briefly consider their arguments and compare them with the concerns I have raised regarding the memory removal exhibited in *Eternal Sunshine*.

The report raises many sensible worries about the safety and effectiveness of such drugs,

but the heart of its philosophical argument against memory removal seems to be threefold. First, it claims that the happiness we seek from memory removal would be a shallow simulacrum of genuine happiness.

Yet it is far from clear that feelings of contentment severed from action in the world or relationships with other people could make us truly happy. Would a happiness that did not flow from what we do and say, usually in association with others, be more than a simulacrum of that happiness for which our souls fit us? (p. 208)

Second, the Council suggests that pursuing such technology shows a failure to properly recognize our limitations.

[B]y disconnecting our mood and memory from what we do and experience, the new drugs could jeopardize the fitness and truthfulness of how we live and what we feel, as well as our ability to confront responsibly and with dignity the imperfections and limits of our lives and those of others. Instead of recognizing distress, anxiety, and sorrow as appropriate reflections of the fragility of the human life and inseparable from the setbacks and heartbreaks that accompany the pursuit of happiness and the love of fellow mortals, we are invited to treat them as diseases to be cured, perhaps one day eradicated. (p. 213)

Does not the experience of hard truths—of the unchosen, the inexplicable, the tragic, remind us that we can never be fully at home in the world, especially if we are to take serious the reality of human evil? (p. 229)

Finally, the Council worries that memory removal involves a harmful tampering of one's personal identity.

But if enfeebled memory can cripple identity, selectively altered memory can distort it. Changing the content of our memories or altering their emotional tonalities...could subtly reshape who we are, at least to ourselves. With altered memories we might feel better about ourselves, but it is not clear that the better-feeling "we" remains the same as before. (p. 212)

[A]n unchecked power to erase memories, brighten moods, and alter our emotional dispositions could imperil our capacity to form a strong and coherent personal identity. (p. 212)

[W]e might be often be tempted to sacrifice the accuracy of our memories for the sake of easing our pain or expanding our control over our psychic lives. But doing so means, ultimately, severing ourselves from reality and leaving our own identity behind. (p. 234)

These and other considerations lead the Council to issue a strong warning against such biotechnology.

Memory and mood-altering drugs pose a fundamental danger to our pursuit of happiness. In the process of satisfying our genuine desires for peace of mind, a cheerful outlook, unclouded self-esteem, and intense pleasure, they may impair our capacity to satisfy the desires that by nature make us happiest. (p. 269)

Regarding the Council's claim that memory removal might alter the patient's personal identity, the relevant issues seem to be not whether one's identity might be altered, but *how* it is altered, and whether the change is for the best. There is something morally problematic about the idea of manipulating one's mind, as our consideration of Kant's position showed, but the problem is surely not *just* that one's identity has changed. After all, there are all sorts of behaviors we can engage in that will, in some sense, alter our identity.[38] That a procedure alters the self cannot, by itself, be a reason for rejecting it.

Regarding the claim that pursuing such technology involves a denial of our limitations as humans, the Council seems to be putting forward a contentious theistic account of human nature as inherently limited. (The Chair of the Council, Leon Kass, is notorious for his conservative, theistically-based positions, including his initial rejection of in-vitro fertilization.) Although I am rather skeptical of folks like the "transhumanists" who giddily embrace the view that technology will soon allow for a seemingly unlimited increase in our abilities,[39] I also find it disturbing to encounter a government council speaking of the natural "limits" of humanity and advising against even the attempt to "feel at home in the world." A rejection of a particular technology should be based on the actual dangers it poses, not on the mere fact that it is new and appears capable of reducing our limitations in ways that would once have been thought of as "unnatural."

Regarding the claim that such drugs might tempt us to accept a shallow or fake happiness instead of the real article, I am sympathetic to the Council's point but wary of their rather narrow conception of "genuine happiness." They seem in the end to suggest that genuine happiness involves not feeling good but instead simply being a good citizen.

Perhaps a remedy for our psychic troubles lies in the rediscovery of obligations and purposes outside the self—a turn outward rather than inward, a turn from the healthy mind to the good society. And perhaps the most promising route to real happiness is to live a fully engaged life, as teachers and parents, soldiers and statesmen, doctors and volunteers. (p. 267)

No doubt engagement with the community and the society at large is often conducive to a substantial and lasting sense of happiness; however, it seems quite wrong to suggest that true happiness is available *only* through such engagement, or that such engagement will necessarily bring contentment. Indeed, this suggestion is pernicious if it implies that *unless* such engagement brings happiness it is not worth pursuing.

Rather than dismiss the idea that happiness may be available through memory removal or mood-altering drugs, I think it may be more fruitful to instead point out that happiness is not all that we care about in life. As Nozick's thought experiment shows, living a happy life is not the only thing that matters—living a *meaningful* life also has priority for most people. By "meaningful life" I mean one in which a person is able to realize his or her deepest values.[40] Since many of us value more than simply happiness, the meaningful life is not simply the happy one. Memory removal (or memory deadening through drugs) may inhibit our capacity for meaningful lives, and caution is in order when it comes to pursuing such technology. In certain situations, however, medications or technologies that blunt memories may instead allow for a happiness and meaningfulness that is not otherwise available. As Robin Henig points out in *The New York Times*:

Without witnessing the torment of unremitting post-traumatic stress disorder, it is easy to exaggerate the benefits of holding on to bitter memories. But a person crippled by memories is a diminished person; there is nothing ennobling about it. If we as a society decide it's better to keep people locked in their anguish because of some idealized view of what it means to be human, we might be revealing ourselves to be a society with a twisted notion of what being human really means.[41]

As I argued earlier, memory removal involves a sacrifice because of the conflict between the value we place on veracity and the value we place on contentment. Such a sacrifice involves a significant loss, but in certain circumstances this loss may be outweighed by the gain made in contentment, freedom, and psychic health. Our duty to remember can be trumped by the horribly debilitating effects of severe trauma and, in such cases, it would be quite cruel to deny relief to the person who is suffering.[42]

CHRISTOPHER GRAU
Department of Philosophy
Florida International University
Biscayne Bay Campus
North Miami, Florida 33181
USA

INTERNET: grauc@fiu.edu

1. I benefited from the discussions of an audience at the University of North Florida, as well as the participants of the 2005 Pacific Division Meeting of the American Philosophical Association session hosted by the Society for the Philosophical Study of Contemporary Visual Art. In addition, I owe special thanks to Susan Wolf, Tim Mawson, Murray Smith, Tom Wartenberg, Dan Callcut, Sean Greenberg, Carlene Bauer, Chris Caruso, Susan Watson, Sean Allen-Hermanson, Paul Draper, and Josh Oreck for comments on earlier drafts of this essay.

2. It might seem obvious that any philosophical themes in the film should be credited to the screenwriter, but in this case it is not clear who gets the credit (or blame). The screenplay was written by Charlie Kaufman, but based on a scenario by Michel Gondry that is, in turn, based on an idea by the French conceptual artist Pierre Bismuth. Also, Kaufman's original script is significantly different, with a bleaker and more cynical ending. Presumably, either Gondry or others pushed for the film to have a more nuanced, romantic, and (cautiously) upbeat conclusion.

3. I will not be exploring the particular aesthetic and film-theoretic issues raised by *Eternal Sunshine*, but that certainly is not because I do not think they are worth exploring—there is much that could be said about this notable film. For example, others have pointed out that *Eternal Sunshine* seems to fit rather nicely within the genre of film that

Stanley Cavell has made famous with the label "Comedies of Remarriage." See Cavell's *Pursuits of Happiness: The Hollywood Comedy of Remarriage* (Harvard University Press, 1981). Such films involve a separated couple ultimately getting back together through rediscovering why they fell in love in the first place. *Eternal Sunshine* follows that pattern, but with the novel twist of memory removal facilitating the "reunion."

4. There is an interesting exception here: the technology as it functions in the film (flaws and all) actually allows a couple to reunite in a way that may not have been possible otherwise. It is not clear whether this reunion is a *good* thing (though many viewers, myself included, take it to be). Even if a glitchy and incomplete memory removal brings about a happy result in this particular case, however, this does not warrant an acceptance of the technology in general.

5. In "Philosophy Screened: Experiencing *The Matrix*," *Midwest Studies in Philosophy* 26 (2003): 139–152, Thomas Wartenberg has usefully pointed out that the idea that film, a visual medium, *can* illustrate a philosophical claim is itself worth questioning. Although I think this is indeed a general issue worth pursuing, it seems to me the best way to do this is to consider whether a particular film can in fact succeed in such illustration. This is part of what I am undertaking here. (When discussing *The Matrix*, Wartenberg ultimately acknowledges that film can occasionally embody philosophical argumentation as a form of "thought experiment." Though I do not dwell on this issue in this essay, I think that a similar claim could be made regarding *Eternal Sunshine*. Wartenberg's comment that "the film actually provides its viewers with a visual experience that is analogous to [the protagonist's]" seems equally applicable here (p. 149). As with *The Matrix*, *Eternal Sunshine* begins by forcing the viewer to enter an epistemic position similar to that of the main character, and in the process "screens" a thought experiment that can provide philosophical insight.)

6. One of the more insightful aspects of the film involves its presentation of how the memory-removal technology is actually implemented. Unlike most "sci-fi" films, which offer naïve pictures of technological innovation being pursued and employed by only the best and brightest (for example, brainiacs in lab coats), we here see a much more realistic portrayal of how this technology (if widely marketed) is likely to be used: ordinary twenty-something slackers perform the procedure with the same degree of respect and competence that they would bring to developing film at a one-hour photo lab. (Having worked at a one-hour photo lab as an ordinary slacker I can speak with some authority here. The manner in which Patrick unethically keeps Clementine's mementos for his own purposes is similar to the way in which some of my fellow employees would make copies of photos they liked for their own use.) It is an interesting question why most futuristic films fail to contain this sort of realism regarding the manner in which technology is likely to be employed, though I will not further pursue that issue here.

7. It should be noted that one of the many difficulties with utilitarianism is that in situations such as the one we are considering, utilitarian theory would seem to require even the *involuntary* use of such technology if it would be likely to maximize utility.

8. Robert Nozick, *Anarchy, State and Utopia* (New York: Basic Books, 1974), p. 43.

9. Nozick, *Anarchy, State and Utopia*, p. 44.

10. Christopher Grau, "Bad Dreams, Evil Demons, and the Experience Machine: Philosophy and *The Matrix*," in *Philosophers Explore the Matrix*, ed. Christopher Grau (New York: Oxford University Press, 2005). My summary of Nozick's thought experiment here draws on my formulation in that essay.

11. Charlie Kaufman, *Eternal Sunshine of the Spotless Mind (The Shooting Script)* (New York: Newmarket Press, 2004), p. 111.

12. Ludwig Wittgenstein, *Philosophical Investigations* (London: Macmillan Publishers, 1958), § 217.

13. Colin McGinn, *Eternal Questions, Timeless Approaches* (New York: Barnes & Noble Audio, 2004). McGinn further explores this theme in "Being and Knowingness" (unpublished manuscript, 2005).

14. There is another less direct way in which this procedure brings on the threat of metaphysical isolation: if such a procedure were actually possible, the ordinarily farfetched skeptical worries that we may be radically wrong about our past become much less farfetched and much more worrisome. No one could be sure that they had not in fact had large portions of their lives erased at some earlier point. (This might be grounds for doubting that a utilitarian defense of such technology could ever be feasible, for it is hard to see how this sort of worry could be eliminated if the existence of the procedure became widely known.) The worry here is related to the skeptical worries regarding *artificial* memories that are raised by such films as *Blade Runner* (Ridley Scott, 1982) and *Total Recall* (Paul Verhoeven, 1990).

15. Thomas Nagel, "Death," in *The Metaphysics of Death*, ed. John Fischer (Stanford University Press, 1993), p. 64.

16. Steven Luper, "Death," in the *Stanford Encyclopedia of Philosophy*, available at <http://www.plato.stanford.edu/entries/death>.

17. Nagel's primary concern is to make sense of the idea that *death* harms the one who dies. Acknowledging death as a deprivation brings with it additional metaphysical difficulties (e.g., *when* is one deprived?) that do not confront the case of memory removal.

18. There is another way in which we can see this technology as involving harm to oneself: on some philosophical accounts of the self (such as John Locke's), personal identity consists in the continuity of and connections between memories. Put bluntly, on this sort of account you just *are* your memories. Such approaches to identity bring with them the consequence that a loss of memories is quite literally a loss of the self. Memory removal becomes "self-destructive" as a matter of definition! (I do not find such a criterion for personal identity particularly persuasive, so I do not dwell on this issue here.)

19. Immanuel Kant, "Grounding for the Metaphysics of Morals," in *Ethical Philosophy*, trans. James W. Ellington (Indianapolis: Hackett Publishing, 1983), pp. 36–37, § 429.

20. Immanuel Kant, *Lectures on Ethics*, ed. Peter Heath and J. B. Schneewind, trans. Peter Heath (Cambridge University Press, 1997), p. 125.

21. James Rachels, *The Elements of Moral Philosophy* (Boston: McGraw-Hill, 2003), p. 136.

22. It is a further question whether Kant is right to classify *all* forms of rehabilitation as manipulation. It seems that Kant should have distinguished between those methods that involve trying to *reason* with the agent from those that use nonrational means and coercion to induce change.

23. Kant, *Lectures on Ethics*, p. 127.

24. Mary's case is significantly different, of course, as she has Mierzwiak's consent and encouragement.

25. The thought that she could harm Joel through erasing him may have been her primary motivation for undergoing the procedure. She proudly admits at one point that "I'm a vindictive little bitch truth be told." However, their mutual friend Carrie tells Joel: "What can I say Joel...She's impulsive...She decided to erase you almost as a lark," so the degree of intended malice in the act is not entirely clear.

26. I do not here explore a specifically Kantian account of the harm done to others, but perhaps such an account could be defended. It is not clear that a maxim involving the desire to erase memories of someone could be universalized, and it also seems plausible to suggest that choosing to erase the memories of someone embodies a failure of respect for the person erased. Ken Rogerson has suggested (in conversation) that utilizing memory removal may violate Kant's absolute prohibition on lying, for in erasing all trace of someone you *intentionally* place yourself in a position in which, if asked, you are bound to say false things about your own history and the person you have erased. There is also the obvious possibility that memory removal will cause one to disregard a Kantian prohibition on breaking promises: if you cannot remember your promises, you cannot possibly be sure you will keep them.

27. In a recent *New York Times* article, Anna Bahney points out that thanks to the dominance of email and digital photography, these days the mementos of a love gone sour can be "expunged with brutal efficiency" ("Zapping Old Flames Into Digital Ash," April 4, 2004).

28. I am here focusing on the harm done to the person you have erased, but given the way the memory removal functions in the film, other questions come up regarding your duties to those who are constrained by your actions. Is it moral of you to request that all mutual friends refrain from mentioning the procedure you have undergone? Asking them to act as though your relationship never occurred could, in certain circumstances, amount to imposing a very significant burden.

29. If we feel that part of our nature is reprehensible, however, we may embrace the opportunity to hide this fact. (Thus Mierzwiak feels no need for Mary's mind to accurately reflect his full nature.)

30. In his book *The Ethics of Memory* (Harvard University Press, 2002), Avishai Margalit argues that we have an *ethical* rather than a *moral* obligation to remember others. He aligns ethics with what Bernard Williams has called "thick relations" with those we care about, while morality is relegated to "thin relations" with those we are less connected to. He thinks the realm of ethics is optional in a way morality is not, for he concludes that our obligation to remember is conditional on our desire to be involved in caring relations with others. Although I think there is something insightful in the distinction between ethics and morality (as well as between thick and thin), I am not as confident as he is that the line between the two can be clearly drawn, or that one is optional in a way that the other is not. Accordingly, I do not hesitate to speak of special moral obligations to those we care about. (My arguments for *why* we have an obligation are rather distinct from

Margalit's, though I do think much of what he says about the relationship between care and memory is compatible with my account. In particular, I suspect Iris Murdoch's emphasis on focused attention could be reformulated in terms of "care" as he uses that term.)

31. Iris Murdoch, *The Sovereignty of the Good* (London: Routledge & Kegan Paul, 1985), pp. 90–91.

32. It is rather ironic that Kate Winslet has played both Iris Murdoch (in the film *Iris* (Richard Eyre, 2001)) and Clementine, a character who exhibits the reluctance to "really look" that Murdoch criticized. (It is also sadly ironic that Iris Murdoch herself came to suffer from Alzheimer's, and thus gradually lost just the sort of perceptual acuteness she felt was so important for love and justice.)

33. My utilization here of Murdoch the moral particularist alongside Kant the universalist may strike some readers as bizarre. It certainly would be bizarre (and perhaps incoherent) if I were urging that we accept Kant's entire moral theory. However, I think we can benefit from Kant's insights regarding the problematic nature of self-mutilation without committing ourselves to his overall conception of morality, just as we can benefit from Murdoch's insights regarding focused attention and the connection between love and justice without accepting all that she says on the topic of morals.

34. In an insightful article, Andrew Light has argued that the film *The Conversation* (Francis Ford Coppola, 1974) can be seen as supporting what Light calls a "substantive" thesis regarding technology. See "Enemies of the State," in *Reel Arguments: Film, Philosophy, and Social Criticism* (Boulder, CO: Westview Press, 2003). This thesis (originating in the works of Martin Heidegger, Michel Foucault, and others) involves the view that technology is not "value free" or morally neutral, but has an inherently ethical dimension. In particular, Light suggests that the surveillance technology employed in *The Conversation* is presented as corrupting its users. Light explains this corruption in terms of the alienation that is inevitably imposed by the technology: by its very nature the surveillance technology tends to objectify the person being surveyed. I think something similar could be said in favor of a "substantive" interpretation of *Eternal Sunshine*. The film presents the actual employment of the memory-removal technology as inevitably involving the depersonalization and manipulation of the patient. This in turn seems to lead to other moral infractions great and small: Patrick steals both underwear and Joel's girlfriend, Stan utterly fails to show respect for Joel as a patient, Mierzwiak uses the technology to evade responsibility for his affair with Mary, and so forth. Just as *The Conversation* suggests that surveillance technology corrupts the character of those utilizing it, *Eternal Sunshine* seems to suggest that memory removal technology is also far from morally neutral and brings with it a problematic attitude of objec-

tification that infects those charged with controlling the technology.

35. I say "may be justified" here because it is possible that the return of the files will indeed cause *so much* suffering that it will counterbalance the good accomplished through undoing the harm of deprivation caused by memory removal. There are also questions of patient consent that may be morally relevant. I do not want to deny these possibilities and complications—I just want to suggest that the fact that we seriously consider the judgment that Mary's actions are justifiable shows us that both harms that wound and harms that deprive need to be recognized here. Without the recognition that there has been harm through deprivation, Mary's actions become *obviously* unjustifiable, yet when we watch the film we do not find her to be so obviously in the wrong.

36. Robin Marantz Henig, "The Quest to Forget: Drugs to Prevent Painful Memories," *The New York Times* April 4, 2004.

37. This report, *Beyond Therapy: Biotechnology and the Pursuit of Happiness*, is available at <http://www.bioethics.gov/reports/beyondtherapy>. Future references will be to page numbers only.

38. Indeed, it is hard to think of activities that do not, *in some sense*, change who we are. The incredible popularity of "self-help" books is a testament to the degree to which we not only permit, but seek out, opportunities to alter the self.

39. Resources regarding transhumanism can be found on the web at <http://www.transhumanism.org>. Nick Bostrom is perhaps the best known transhumanist who is also an academic philosopher.

40. It would take us too far afield for me to go into much more depth here, but it should be pointed out that my characterization of meaningfulness is meant to be neutral between "subjective" and "objective" accounts of meaningfulness and value. Although I am sympathetic to objective accounts, for my purposes here the subjective account can suffice. For an insightful discussion of why subjective accounts of meaningfulness are problematic, see Susan Wolf's essay "The True, the Good, and the Lovable," in *Contours of Agency: Essays on Themes from Harry Frankfurt*, eds. Sarah Buss and Lee Overton (MIT Press, 2002).

41. Henig, "The Quest to Forget."

42. Note also that some of the objections I raised to the memory-removal technology that appears in *Eternal Sunshine* may not apply to cases involving posttraumatic stress disorder and memory-blunting drugs. There may be no significant harm inflicted on others through the use of such drugs. Also, to the extent that the drugs blunt emotional tonalities rather than the factual content of memories, the proper use of such drugs may not threaten the value we place on knowing the truth.

ANDRÁS BÁLINT KOVÁCS

Sartre, the Philosophy of Nothingness, and the Modern Melodrama

Jean-Paul Sartre was probably the most influential living Western philosopher in the 1950s and early 1960s, and there is little doubt that his works had, at a certain time, a major impact on contemporary art, especially drama, literature, and film.[1] Many factors explain the influence of his works on European art. He was a writer and publicized many of his views in dramas and novels, propagating a sort of philosophical writing. He formulated existentialist philosophy on the level of everyday personal psychology—easy to translate into dramatic situations. He also made the case for a direct linkage between philosophy, art, and politics by advocating for an "engaged" literature. And finally, his philosopher persona also explains his influence. He was the most prominent instance and the model in person of what can be called the "French intellectual": a philosopher, a writer, a journalist, and a politician at the same time. He was a kind of spiritual leader, and even President De Gaulle addressed him as *Mon cher maître* [My dear master].[2]

In the essay that follows, I will explore the following question: What in Sartre's major work of phenomenological existentialism, published in 1943 and entitled *Being and Nothingness*, could be productive in modern cinema? I will briefly analyze his concept of Nothingness to show that Sartre makes a direct relationship between the concept of Nothingness and modern man's fundamental existential experiences of loneliness and disappearance, which

makes this concept susceptible to concrete artistic representation. Nothingness in Sartrean philosophy becomes an essential and invisible ingredient in the phenomenological experience of everyday life. It is an invisible but apprehensible dimension that hides behind physical reality. Cinema is a medium particularly well suited to represent the tension between the two. No other medium can represent the physical surface of reality as meticulously as cinema and no other medium can express the potential emptiness behind that surface as strongly as cinema. I will introduce the category or genre of "intellectual melodrama" or "modern melodrama" in which, I argue, the philosophy of Nothingness was the most productive in the 1960s. It is in this type of film that the concept of Nothingness finds a narrative place in a genre scheme as an overwhelming power in front of which the protagonist is helpless. In the modern melodrama, Nothingness becomes the negative power that displaces lost humanistic values.

The modern philosophical concept of Nothingness appears in German romantic philosophy with G. W. F. Hegel, Søren Kierkegaard, and Friedrich Nietzsche. An important aspect of this concept is that it is not simply conceived as something entirely alien to what exists, but is indivisibly linked to it. Nietzsche was the most radical interpreter of this notion as he made it an independent power that opposes the banality of life, and the acceptance of which is the precondition of the individual's power. Thus Nietzsche used Nothingness as a tool for fighting metaphysics. This tool, however, turned out to be inappropriate for that purpose. The assurance of the autonomy of the individual in the romantic conception is to make the individual a "divine entity," in the sense that the individual is not fatally subdued to any greater power alien to his or her own nature: the individual chooses, decides, challenges, opposes, and revolts against superhuman powers. However, the freedom of the romantic individual is limited by the fact that the source of his or her own divinity is precisely the superhuman nature of the greater power he or she opposes. Nietzsche understands the limits of the romantic conception and refuses the divine individual's dependence on the greater power. He says: "I was given a new pride by my own 'self,' and that is what I teach: do not hide your head in the sand of heavenly things any longer. But carry around freely this earthly head, which gives sense to the Earth."[3] The idea that the subject-object opposition can be avoided by the introduction of singularity as defining human individuality appears at the dawn of modernism in Nietzsche's philosophy. Nietzsche wants to anchor this "new pride" exclusively in the singularity of life, without a metaphysical background. Hence, the individual subject becomes the ultimate power, independent from any metaphysical support. Interestingly enough, however, the singularity of the individual declared as the ultimate power of life cannot stand by itself. It becomes a power of opposition, an object of choice. It is as if subjective singularity were not able to fill out the space left empty by the ostracized superhuman powers, as if there remained some vacuum around the divine individual, in which vacuum another hitherto unknown superhuman power started to grow up: *Nothingness*. Understood in this context, Nothingness becomes the shade of vanished metaphysical powers.[4] In spite of all attempts to the contrary, this notion born in the romantic philosophy of the nineteenth century maintained the metaphysical subject-object dualism up until the emergence of postmodern philosophy. With Martin Heidegger and finally with Sartre, Nothingness becomes the central concept of existentialist philosophy and, especially in Sartrean existentialism, it helps to conserve subject-object

dualism and thereby generates a new metaphysical myth.[5] It is that myth that I think makes the philosophical notion of Nothingness a subject matter that is best represented in modern film.

Sartre is the philosopher who attributes concrete content to the abstract notion of Nothingness. He pulls this concept out of pure negativity, and differentiates it from the simple emptiness of nonbeing. His conceptual operation is this: he makes Nothingness the key concept of human relations and of the relationship of man to the world. He interprets Nothingness as a product of human intentions and, at the same time, as the essence of being. Nothingness for Sartre is not another world, nor is it beyond our world. He translates the concept into a series of everyday situations where man is alone, disappointed by his beliefs and expectations, desperately looking for something solid in a situation where his own identity is called into question. Sartre places Nothingness right into the world, "into the heart of being, like a worm."[6] Nothingness does not follow after being, as it does for Hegel, nor is it beyond the world, as it is for Heidegger. Nothingness, Sartre argues, not only exists, but it exists within being, together with it and at the same time. Nothingness is not a general logical or ontological dimension; it is rather the foundation of human being.

"It is the human being who gives birth to Nothingness," Sartre writes (p. 65). Nothingness is created when a human wish or expectation is frustrated. Nothingness is not general nonbeing, it is rather the nonbeing of something, or of something that should be. In other words, Nothingness is the form of human expectation, of human frustration, or of human memory.[7] Hence, Nothingness is not simply a negative category as the notion may suggest. All expectations, all disappointments, all memories are related to concrete contents. If my purse is empty, says Sartre, it is not empty in general, but money of an expected order of magnitude or perhaps of a certain exact amount is missing. When a classroom is empty, students are missing not racing horses. When I enter a café looking for Peter but I find only John, then Peter's absence is directly mediated by John's presence. This means that Nothingness is directly represented by Being.

Nothingness is a positive category in yet another sense. Between what is and what could be there is a gap, an empty space, where man is free to choose. Nothingness is an empty moment in the world, where man is liberated from his past and has to choose. In this sense, Nothingness is the definition of freedom; it is what cancels the past in the face of the future: "In freedom man invalidates past and creates his own Nothingness.... Nothingness is freedom intercalated between past and future" (p. 76). Free choice is based on Nothingness because it obliges man to choose and it does not inform the choice. Nothingness is this empty space where the constraints of the past and the future do not affect our choice, and that is freedom. Because it is not motivated by the past and the future, this freedom is unpredictable. If choice is indeterminate, it is incalculable for others as well as for ourselves. Incalculability for us is the source of our angst, and incalculability for others represents a danger. Freedom based on Nothingness is thus the main power and the main source of danger regarding human relations. The Other is the dangerous power of Nothingness: "[Nothingness] is my being written into and rewritten by the freedom of the Other. As if there existed another dimension of my being from which I were separated by a radical Nothingness: and this Nothingness is the freedom of the Other" (p. 320). Nothingness, as presented by something that is *missing*, is the term through which man is related to the world and to others. This is how the Sartrean concept of Nothingness becomes the expression of the modern experience of human existence: lonely man, freed from his past, forced to choose and to look for his own self, endangered by the freedom of others, and constantly having to face the lack of metaphysical values or guarantees.

The "modern authentic individual" is someone who accepts Nothingness as the fundament of his or her freedom and gives up the search for traditional metaphysical values. The hostility of modernism toward mass culture stems from the fact that modernism regards mass culture as an evasion from facing the heart of being: Nothingness. Mass culture treats the traditional forces of the sublime (God, Nature, Love, History, Destiny) as continuing to work in the modern world. For postwar modernism, on the contrary, the only sublime power that can be represented as working in the modern world is Nothingness. The modern individual cannot face God as a free individual, only as a member of a nation or a congregation, as a nonindependent individual. If the modern individual is to be free, it is possible only by facing Nothingness.[8] According to the romantic conception, the individual is someone who is capable of inner freedom, and of choosing death instead of the insignificance of life. The modern individual, on the other hand, is someone whose freedom is manifested by his or her ability to accept the insignificance, the nothingness of life. Nothingness for modernism is not the contrary of life, like death in the romantic sense. Nothingness is death *within* life—life itself, that is. For romanticism, the individual is someone who can be independent from the surrounding world. For modernism, the individual is someone who can look through the insignificance of life and can free himself or herself of the angst caused by the nothingness of the world and accept his or her own life in the midst of this Nothingness.

We find a nice illustration of the difference between the romantic and the modern attitude to Nothingness in two early films by Jean-Luc Godard, *A bout de souffle* [*Breathless*] (1959) and *Pierrot le fou* (1965). In the earlier film, at one point Patricia (Jean Seberg) asks Michel (Jean-Paul Belmondo) what he would choose if he had a choice between grief and Nothingness. Michel's answer is Nothingness; Patricia's choice is grief. The real significance of this conversation becomes clear at the end of the film when Patricia finally gives Michel up to the police, then begs him to escape. The fact that she acts in this way is a direct consequence of her choice. She refuses to accept the idea of Nothingness represented by Michel's life, but she feels sorry for him, which appears to her as an insoluble paradox. That drives her to the melodramatic act of begging him to escape. Michel, on the other hand, chooses Nothingness, so that he refuses to run away anymore. Patricia can accept Michel only as a romantic hero, and that is what she makes of him when she betrays him. Michel's death is a romantic death from Patricia's point of view because this way he does not die for Nothingness, he dies for love, which Patricia can accept, and that provides her with her choice: grief. That is why Patricia does not understand Michel's last words—*Tu es dégueulasse!* [You are disgusting!]—and why she repeats Michel's gesture of rubbing his mouth with his thumb. Through this emulation she casts Michel as her mythical romantic hero who was ready to die for her. From Michel's point of view, however, this was not a romantic death at all. Not only did he not want to die for her, he did not want to die at all; he just wanted to give himself up to the police (who shot him nevertheless because he reached for the gun on the pavement). He did not escape because he wanted to be a hero, but because nothing made sense for him anymore once he was betrayed by Patricia. All he says is, "I am tired." He was killed by chance, but Patricia can make sense of this only by looking for grief and melodrama.

We find a similar ambivalence in *Pierrot le fou*. Only here the ambivalence resides within the same person. Having fled the banality of his everyday life, Ferdinand (Belmondo again) realizes that there is no way of finding what he is looking for. His love betrays him, and very much in the same way as Michel, he comes to the conclusion that if no authentic love is any longer possible, life does not make sense anymore. But unlike Michel, he decides to commit a "romantic" suicide. He paints his face in blue and wraps his head with dynamite bars. However, at the last moment, as he lights the fuse, he mutters: "After all, I am an idiot!" and desperately attempts to put out the fuse. But it is too late. Ferdinand realizes that after having devalued life, his death is worth nothing either. There is no other choice: he has to accept Nothingness, and he must continue to live.

There are direct and indirect ways of representing the power of loss as the general concept of Nothingness. For example, in Ingmar Bergman's modernist works there is a variety of ways through which the lack or loss of values is made manifest. His work *Fängelse* (1949) has a name—"hell on Earth"—which is a particularly clear formulation of the Sartrean concept (Nothingness in the midst of Being). In later films Bergman utilizes a more "romantic" conception as he replaces the "power of loss" with "death" (*Det Sjunde inseglet* [*The Seventh Seal*] (1956), *Smultronstället* [*Wild Strawberries*] (1957)) or with the "absence of God" (*Såsom i en spegel* [*Through a Glass Door Darkly*] (1961), *Nattvardsgästerna* [*Winter Light*] (1962), *Tystnaden* [*The Silence*] (1963)). But in *Persona* (1966), he clearly and directly gives it the name

of Nothingness: it is the only word Elisabeth (Liv Ullmann), the protagonist, can utter after a long period of silence at the end of the film. In Michelangelo Antonioni's career, from *Cronaca di un amore* (1950) to *Blow Up* (1966), one can trace a more linear evolution toward a clear formulation of the concept of Nothingness. Human absence and disappearance becomes increasingly abstract, especially in *L'eclisse* [*The Eclipse*] (1962) and *Il deserto rosso* [*The Red Desert*] (1964), while in *Blow Up*, Nothingness is a direct motive used as the central symbol of the film. There is also a third film from the same year, 1966, Andrei Tarkovsky's *Andrei Rublev*, in which the direct formulation of the concept of Nothingness proves that at the peak of postwar modernism a major trend of modern cinema is constructed around it.

In the next section I explore how the Sartrean concept of Nothingness becomes a central issue in the genre of the modern melodrama, and in the final section I examine in more detail the role of Nothingness in one of the key examples of this genre, Antonioni's *L'eclisse*.

I. MELODRAMA AND MODERNISM

Melodrama is commonly identified with stories provoking an intense emotional response. This emotional intensity is a consequence of a special narrative scheme. Melodrama is a dramatic form in which the conflict explodes between incommensurable forces, where a lonely human faces powers of nature or society in front of which he or she is helpless and condemned to lose right from the outset or wins only by miracle. This power can be physical (for example, fatal illness, an accident), social (for example, a war, poverty, social difference), or psychological (for example, strong love, murderous hatred, fatal addiction, moral corruption).

Melodrama as a genre appeared at the end of the eighteenth century and was the name of a dramatic genre with musical accompaniment staging pathetic scenes and involving some kind of unpredictable, fatal turn. In early melodramas, this emotional atmosphere had the function of prefiguring the unexpected, fatal turn evoked by the invincible exterior power. Melodrama has always had something to do with the lack, or insufficiency, of words and verbal expressions, which is why broad gestures and highly expressive music have had a central role in it. Moreover, melodrama has always been about the suffering of an innocent victim, even when the cause of the suffering is the victim himself or herself, as in the case of self-sacrifice. This is why a happy ending in a melodrama always comes unexpectedly, by chance or by miracle.

Melodrama is basically fatalistic. In contrast to what melodrama's high emotionality would suggest, melodramatic narrative can be fitted not only to stories representing emotional conflicts; the fatalist character of melodrama is well suited for all kinds of social, political, and historical narratives. Moreover, naturalist novels, drama, and cinema support melodramatic structure all the more since they also stage great powers of nature, society, and human instincts. The conflict in naturalist narrative is carried by the clash between the objective and unsurpassable laws of society or human nature and a helpless individual, and this type of conflict can be well adapted to the melodramatic form. Yet, naturalist *style* very rarely yields to the emotional saturation characteristic of melodrama because naturalism focuses on what it regards as objective laws, rather than on the individual's perspective. It is the individualism of melodrama that is the source of its pathetic, highly emotional character. It is only from the perspective of naturalist objective fatalism that melodramatic emotionality may appear as "excess." In reality, it is constitutive of melodrama's individualist approach. This is the key for us in understanding the relationship between melodrama and modernism.

Cognitive film theorist Torben Grodal proposes a useful approach to melodrama that will help us understand how melodrama can be operational in the modernist context. Grodal highlights two aspects of the melodramatic attitude: *passive response* and *subjectivity*. Melodrama stages an insoluble conflict between the lonely human and the overwhelming objective power from the point of view of a *passive* perception of the world. While in naturalism both the world and the victim-subject remain exterior and objective, in melodrama the repressive power of the objective world is represented as a *subjective perception*, it is "experienced as a mental event." He states:

[I]f we are transformed into a passive object for the objective laws, the hypothetical-enactive identification is weakened or blocked, and the experience loses its character of being rational and exterior-objective, and, by negative inference, is experienced as a mental event. In the great melodramatic moments in *Gone with the Wind*, the agents lose their full ability to act in the world, which is therefore only experienced as sensation, as input, and so remains a mental phenomenon.[9]

Grodal proposes that this passive, subjective experience is the source of the emotional saturation of the melodrama. In simple terms—the lonely subject is not only helpless in front of the oppressive power, but his or her helplessness is staged as a passive process, a mental perception, or an emotional state. Because the difference in the acting potential between the agent and the environment is so stark, the melodramatic hero at important moments becomes inactive, apprehends his or her powerlessness, and reacts emotionally to this realization. As fate cannot be shifted, the melodramatic hero overcomes the helpless situation by an "excessive" emotional response. High emotional amplitude is therefore not an exaggeration of melodrama; it belongs to the genre's inherent representational system—*understanding fate and helplessness through melodrama is to understand it through pure passive emotional experience.*

It is the active-passive "shifter" introduced by Grodal that is enlightening for us. For what is essential from our point of view is that passive mental experience can be intellectual as well as emotional. A purely intellectual processing of a fatal situation of helplessness may provoke the same passive subjective experience. Passive experience before a greater power may be transformed into cognitive states other than highly emotional ones, and the melodramatic narrative structure may remain operational. (Here, we must make clear that we are speaking of emotions *represented* in melodrama and not of those provoked by it in the viewer. Classical melodrama provokes emotional responses in the viewer by representing such states. Modern melodrama, as we will soon see, provokes emotional states in the viewer by radically withdrawing representation of emotions, which is why the emotion elicited by modern melodrama is always some kind of anxiety.)

The emphasis on passive subjective experience lying in the heart of melodramatic form explains the continuity between the Italian "white telephone" melodrama of the 1930s and Antonioni's high modernism. It makes clear how Italian neorealism, as a fundamentally naturalist narrative universe, could emerge on the basis of the melodramatic narrative conventions of Italian cinema of the 1940s, and also how the same melodramatic structure could survive in the introverted and increasingly "subjectivized" character of modern narrative cinema. *Naturalist* melodrama is born when the helpless agent in front of exterior powers is not individualized anymore through his or her mental or emotional states, and is represented as an *active* part of the same environment of which he or she is a helpless victim. A typical example of naturalist cinema using a melodramatic structure is Vittorio De Sica's neorealist *Ladri di biciclette* [*Bicycle Thieves*] (1948). Antonio (Lamberto Maggiorani) is not individualized through his psychological character or through his emotions, but instead through his belonging to a certain environment of which he is an active part (trying to find his bicycle). Nevertheless, active as he is, he remains a lost victim right from the start. The social order is stronger than he is. *Classical* melodrama reemerges out of naturalism when the victim of exterior powers is individualized through his or her passive emotional response to his or her helpless social situation. A typical example of the postneorealist classical melodrama is Federico Fellini's *La strada* (1954), where the story of Gelsomina (Giulietta Masina), which starts as a social struggle for life, finishes as a story of emotional and spiritual redemption. And, finally, we can speak of *modern* melodrama when the hero in the melodramatic structure of naturalism is reindividualized either by his or her subjective but *not purely emotional* representations of his or her situation, or by complementing pure emotional responses with other mental representations, such as dream, memory, or imagination. In other words, in modern cinema, as far as it uses the melodramatic structure, the "mental event" of representing one's helpless situation is shifted from a (conscious or unconscious) emotional dimension to another kind of (conscious or unconscious) mental dimension. A typical example is Antonioni's *La notte* (1960), where the characters' passivity throughout the story is due to a subjective state of uncertainty or ignorance over the reasons for their marital crisis.

We can talk about the modern intellectual melodrama when the protagonist finds himself or herself in front of an existential situation that he or she cannot understand, and this lack of understanding provokes passivity, suffering, and anxiety. Not understanding or not knowing is inherent to classical melodrama also. As Laura Mulvey notes, "characters caught in the world of melodrama are not allowed transcendent awareness or knowledge. ... they do not fully grasp the forces they are up against or their own instinctive behavior."[10] The partly unconscious state of the characters is the logical consequence of the fatalism of melodrama. But in classical melodrama, not understanding is not the main reason of suffering. On the contrary, if the heroes of a classical melodrama do not understand their situation, they still suffer. In a classical melodrama it is enough for the heroes to understand that the power they are up against is much bigger than they are. All they know is that they are helpless, and that is what provokes high emotions. In the classic Douglas Sirk melodrama *All that Heaven Allows* (1954), the female protagonist renounces her love because she feels weaker than the social conventions that drive everyone in her social class, including her two children, to disapprove of her marriage with a working-class man. She fully understands her situation, and that is what makes her break up her relationship with the man she loves. All she can feel is a total helplessness before the conventions of her social class.

By contrast, in modern melodrama, characters do not even know that their situation is critical. They can feel their inability to act, but they do not know why. The primary experience that is at stake in modern melodrama is *understanding helplessness*. That is why modern intellectual melodrama most often provokes anxiety in the viewer. What the audience of a classical melodrama understands and feels right from the beginning—that is, sympathy for the possibly and partly unaware characters—the audience of the intellectual melodrama comes to understand only at the very end. The reaction of the modern melodramatic protagonist to the provocation of the environment can be best characterized as a *mental search*. Modern melodrama is a type of melodrama where the protagonist's reaction amounts to searching for a way of intellectually *understanding* the environment, which understanding precedes or replaces physical reaction. The main cause of the protagonist's emotional distress in modern melodramas is not a concrete natural, social, or emotional catastrophe. No matter what concrete event triggers narrative action, this concrete event is but a superficial manifestation of a deeper and more general crisis, to which no immediate physical reaction is possible. The only adequate immediate reaction is a passive intellectual response of searching for a comprehension of the "general crisis," which comprehension prepares for a choice that can lead to a physical reaction. *La strada* is a classical melodrama because the protagonists always have immediate, direct, and purely emotional responses to their situation until they succumb to it. They understand their situation quite well, and they know what their problem is with it. Zampanò (Anthony Quinn) is too rough for Gelsomina, and she is too foolish for him. By contrast, Fellini's *8¹/₂* (1963), *La dolce vita* (1960), and all Antonioni's films of this period (1957–1965) are modern melodramas becasue the protagonists of these films, as helpless victims of their situations, are first of all busy trying to find out *what* the situation is of which they are the victim. In *Il grido* [*The Cry*] (1957), Aldo (Steve Cochran), left by his wife, wanders around with his little daughter to find comfort and to get rid of his emotional distress. He is, in essence, looking for his lost self. When, after a year, he returns home and sees his ex-lover with the baby of her new husband, he loses all his strength and falls from a tower of the factory where he used to work. In *L'avventura* (1959), Sandro (Gabriele Ferzetti) and Claudia (Monica Vitti) are looking for their friend Anna (Lea Massari), who has mysteriously disappeared. They try to understand their relationship to one another, to their friend, and to the world in order to grasp their situation. All they understand at the end is that their emotional emptiness is as profound as the lack created by Anna's disappearance. In *La notte*, shocked by the agony of their close friend, Giovanni (Marcello Mastroianni) and Lidia (Jeanne Moreau) try to find relief from their depression all day long until the next morning when they understand that their marriage is hopeless. In *L'eclisse*, Vittoria (Monica Vitti) breaks her relationship with Riccardo (Francisco Rabal) at the beginning of the story and hangs around aimlessly in the city trying out another relationship with an attractive but

intellectually empty broker, until it turns out that neither of them has taken this relationship seriously. Neither Vittoria nor Piero (Alain Delon) comes to the fixed rendezvous. In *Il deserto rosso*, which is the least narrative of all of Antonioni's films of this period, Giuliana (Vitti once more), the emotionally unstable protagonist, tries to find a way to survive, with her little son, the emotional desert of her own life as well as the industrial poisoning of the environment. None of these protagonists really understand what is happening to them. All of them are lost in one way or another. All they understand is that they are in an uncomfortable or even critical situation and cannot continue to live their accustomed way. Their crises, however, are not articulated sufficiently enough even to allow them to find a well-defined problem to resolve.[11] These characters are facing nothing less than *the entire world* around them, or the entirety of their own personality.

The reason why in modern melodrama the characters do not comprehend their desperate situations is to be found in the special form in which the "bigger power" appears in these films. One can speak of melodrama only if the environment represents a force incommensurable with the protagonist's powers. The incommensurable power in modern melodramatic films has a particularity that differentiates it from any other type of melodrama. The "bigger power" in modern melodrama is represented by something that is stronger than the protagonist not by virtue of its presence but by virtue of its *absence*. What is missing, however, is, in most cases, impossible to articulate clearly. One can name it only via the general terms denoting positive human values: love, tenderness, emotion, security, human communication, or God. The power that the protagonists of modern melodramas have to face is an existential *lack* of these *positive values*, and it is this lack that takes on the form of something invincibly strong. In the terms of existentialist philosophy set out in the first section of this essay, this invincible power is, precisely, Nothingness.

II. A MODERN MELODRAMA: ANTONIONI'S *L'ECLISSE*

Among Antonioni's "great period" films, *L'eclisse* is the most radical example of what can be called modern intellectual melodrama.

Moreover, it exemplifies most clearly all that I have claimed about the role of the concept of Nothingness in modern melodrama. Already the title evokes the disappearance of light and warmth: the central recurrent plot element of the story is human disappearance.

The story divides into three loosely connected parts. After a night-long argument, Vittoria breaks up with her fiancé, Riccardo. When we meet them, they are already at the end of their relationship and through the most difficult part of their conversation. "We have said everything we had to say," says Vittoria. Riccardo is still not ready to let her go, but he cannot make her change her mind. When he asks her why she wants to quit, all she replies is: "I don't know." She gives him the same answer to the question of when did she cease to love him. All through the film, that is the only thing she can say when she is asked about what she wants. The following part of the story takes place on and around the stock market where she goes to find her mother (Lilla Brignone). Vittoria tries to tell her about the breakup with Riccardo, but her mother is too busy with her stocks to listen. She meets a young, attractive, and dynamic broker, Piero, with whom she starts a new relationship later in the story. But in this second part, Antonioni concentrates on the events taking place in the stock exchange, including the dramatic market crash that pushes a lot of people, including Vittoria's mother, into bankruptcy. The stock market story is interrupted by a scene where Vittoria visits a neighbor who has returned from Kenya. The third part of the film tells the story of Vittoria's and Piero's finally aborted relationship. Both of them seem ready to start a relationship, but at the last moment, Vittoria always withdraws. She repeats, again, that she does not know why. She has the desire but she cannot find the emotional energy necessary to fulfill her desire. All through the story Vittoria is undecided and uncertain. Piero is a simpler case: all he is looking for is sexual contact. Emotional or intellectual contact does not matter for him. In the final scene, their relationship ends, but it does not break up; it just vanishes into emptiness.

The proportions of the three parts of the film alone are very telling. The first part lasts around fourteen minutes, the second part lasts twice as long (around thirty minutes), and the third part lasts about three times as long (forty-five minutes) as the first part. The shortest is the one where clear emotions, experienced and remembered, are represented. The second part, in which no emotions at all are represented, is longer. This provides the background for the third part, the longest one, where the story is told about a search for new emotions, and about the failure of this search.

The plot is built on a series of disappearances. At the beginning, the romance between Vittoria and Riccardo is finished, and Riccardo disappears from the rest of the film. Then, in the first stock market scene, the market stops for a minute to commemorate the death of a colleague. In the second stock market scene, many people lose large fortunes in one day. Piero's car is stolen. Then Piero disappears for the first time: Vittoria says goodbye to him and starts walking away, but when she suddenly stops and turns back after a couple of seconds, she sees that Piero is not there anymore. The end of the story comes with the mere and final disappearance of the characters: neither Piero nor Vittoria show up for their rendezvous. In the very last shot of the film, the light of the sun goes out.

The withdrawal of human emotions and human contacts is so radical in this story that performing represented a major problem for the actors. Antonioni reduces values in human contacts almost to the zero level, and this made it very difficult for the film's performers to find the appropriate gestures. This is what Monica Vitti, who plays the main character of the film, says about her part: "This was the most difficult role I have ever played, because I have never seen a girl like this. A girl who says: 'It is not important to know each other to love each other, and probably it is not important to love at all.' I don't know what the look, the voice, the walk of such a woman is like."[12] However, for Antonioni to represent such characters did not mean that he considered this psychological state as an indifferent, natural state of things. He did not only depict the world of lonely and emotionally empty people; he wanted to represent the emotional *drama* of emotional emptiness. He contrasts his attitude to Alain Resnais's approach: "*The Eclipse* has been compared to *L'année dernière à Marienbad* [*Last Year at Marienbad*] (1961), but this is false. I think that Resnais in *Marienbad* is satisfied quite well with simply reducing the characters to a state of objecthood. For me this is a drama. I mean the actual emptiness of the individual. Honesty and beauty tend to disappear."[13] Antonioni has a deeply critical attitude toward the world he represents, and his main artistic purpose is to show the *dramatic* character of a situation that fundamentally *lacks* humanistic values. This lack makes the characters suffer. For Antonioni, the lack is the ultimate reason for unhappiness. There is no reason in the world and no guilt or error in the characters. It is an ultimate existential condition. Therefore, the dramatic clash is not between clear values, but between the desire for values and the lack of them. Antonioni creates the *drama of vanishing*: the characters' vanished ability to love is the source of their sufferings. It prevents them from fulfilling their deepest desires. They are the only obstacles in the way of their own happiness. The characters suffer because they remember what they are lacking, but they cannot stop it disappearing. "I wish I didn't love you at all or that I loved you much more," Vittoria says to Piero. She is a captive and the victim of her own emotional "disability," and of her contradictory emotions, and this is the main source of the melodrama. As Jenö Király puts it: "In the melodrama … emotions are self-contradictory. Its disabled heroes are the enemies of themselves as well as of each other. … In melodrama lovers are opposed to each other."[14] They try to love but they are unable to.

That is why the characters' play in the film is not inexpressive. It is not that they are dispassionate "objects," or "models," along the lines of Alain Resnais's human figures in *L'année dernière à Marienbad*. Instead, what they express is the last remnant of an emotion in the state of dissolution. Two examples in the film may illustrate this. The breaking-up scene is full of emotional tension, although we are already at the conclusion of a night-long conversation before the final sentence is declared. Very few words are said; Vittoria's face and gestures suggest that she is already beyond emotions, her decision is made, and all she wants is to get out of this situation. Riccardo has already understood that Vittoria wants their relationship to end, but he still cannot accept it emotionally. The tension is wavering between them as both wait for something to happen:

Riccardo waits for Vittoria to change her mind; Vittoria tries to gather her force to leave. This wavering ends up in the loss of all dramatic tension. Several times during the scene, either Riccardo or Vittoria are shown to be preparing to say or to do something, emphasized by closer shots, but then they remain silent, withdraw, or look away. Dramatic tension is raised, but then dissolved immediately. The last thing Riccardo says in this part repeats this pattern and at the same time closes, once and for all, the process of emotional "dissolution." He walks with Vittoria back to her home, tries once again to pretend that everything is all right between them, and when he sees that this is futile, he says goodbye politely, with no emotions: "I'll see you again. No, I won't see you again. We'll call each other. No, there will be no calling. So long." He shakes Vittoria's hand. He is calm already, he has no more hopes; he has arrived at the same indifferent state as Vittoria.

At the end of the film, this pattern of emotional dissolution is repeated. Only here, Antonioni starts at an earlier phase and makes the process much quicker and simpler. Thereby, for a moment he provides us with the illusion of a fulfilled love, which only lasts for some seconds. The disappearance of the emotion lasts a couple of minutes and is without any conflict. After making love in Piero's office, Piero and Vittoria kiss and hug. Suddenly, they look at each other as real lovers. For the first time they speak accordingly, too.

Piero: Shall we meet tomorrow? Let's meet tomorrow.
  And the day after tomorrow.
Vittoria: And the next day and the day after that.
  Piero: And the day after that.
Vittoria: And tonight.
  Piero: Yes, at eight p.m. The usual place.

This sudden enthusiasm has come as something of a surprise, for in the preceding scenes, where Piero and Vittoria were lying side by side on the couch, they are shown giggling and playing, more like children than sentimental lovers. Now, we might think that what was missing from the whole story up to this point has finally happened. Real love has been born. It has, in fact, but it lives only for a couple of seconds. As Vittoria leaves the office, we watch her going down the stairs very slowly, almost painfully,

FIGURE 1. The last encounter: The surge and disappearance of emotions. (1)

(2)

(3)

(4)

(5)

fallen back to the same distress and uncertainty that has characterized her all through the story. Her face expresses sadness and helplessness. When she is out on the street we know already that her love has gone as suddenly and as quickly as it came. Then there is a cutback to Piero where we see him pacing around in his office with the same helplessness on his face,

putting back the telephone receiver it its place, but letting it ring. In the final montage sequence of the film we see the meeting place at different times of the day, but neither of them is present, and we know that they will never return.

The dynamics of disappearance makes "emptiness," "lack," or "nothingness" the ultimate explanatory category for Vittoria's situation. "Emptiness" is an existential situation that is within her, one that functions as a disability or as a "disease" of which she is not the cause, and against which she cannot fight. She does not suffer because she is bad or guilty. There is no moral reason for her suffering. That is why Vittoria cannot say anything about her emotions. "All you can say is: I don't know," Piero tells her. Vittoria is simply emptied of her emotions, and this emptiness is without any objective or subjective background. Everybody is like this in the film, to a greater or lesser degree: Riccardo does not fight much and ultimately accepts their separation quite easily. Vittoria's mother is concerned only by her stocks; she deplores her daughter's breakup only because Riccardo cannot now help her out financially. Piero is interested only in money, his car, and sex. That is how *lack*, or *emptiness*, becomes an ultimate power, incomparably stronger than the power of the characters' desire for love. This is how Nothingness becomes a sensible and active part of their situation. What distinguishes Vittoria among the other characters is that she is the one who appears to comprehend, at least in part, her situation. Among Antonioni's films, *L'eclisse* is the most direct representation of the oppressive situation of emotional emptiness that makes helpless and suffering victims of its characters. In *L'avventura* and *La notte*, such a situation appears as the conclusion of the story, while in *L'eclisse.* it is the starting point, and the story is about the accumulation and solidification of the anxiety caused by this scenario of Nothingness.

ANDRÁS BÁLINT KOVÁCS
Department of Film
ELTE University
Budapest
Hungary

INTERNET: kovacsab@emc.elte.hu

1. This essay will appear as a chapter in the author's forthcoming book, *Modern European Art Cinema* (Chicago University Press).

2. In a letter of Charles de Gaulle to Sartre on April 19, 1967. *Situations VIII* (Paris: Gallimard, 1972), p. 43.

3. Friedrich Nietzsche, *Also Sprach Zarathustra* (Budapest 3: Grill Károly Könyvkiadója, 1908), p. 38. All translations are my own except where noted.

4. It was Bergson who noted first that the romantic concept of Nothingness was essentially of a metaphysical character: "For the source of the contempt of metaphysics regarding reality in duration is that metaphysics arrives at being through 'nothing,' because being in duration does not seem for metaphysics strong enough to overcome non-being and to assert itself." Bergson, *L'évolution créatrice* (Budapest: Magyar Tudományos Akadémia, 1930), p. 252. That is why he considered it very important to deprive the concept of Nothingness of any kind of relevance, and to prove that Nothingness is only a subjective appearance. Considering the philosophy of the first half of the twentieth century, at least until the 1960s, we can say that he was not too successful in respect to this goal.

5. I use the word 'myth' here to emphasize the narrative character of the idea of Nothingness, which is a result of the disappearance of higher values. It is metaphysical, as it conserves metaphysical values in a negative form, and thus becomes itself a sort of existence that is "beyond" us or the world.

6. Jean-Paul Sartre, *L'être et le néant* (Paris: Gallimard, 1957), p. 57. Page numbers in the next two paragraphs refer to this volume.

7. At this point we cannot disregard the Bergsonian foundations of the Sartrean concept of Nothingness. Bergson considers Nothingness as something that is related to the function of the brain. Nothingness for Bergson is only a logical operation; he thereby reduces it to an element of consciousness relating man to the world. Bergson is firmly convinced that Nothingness does not exist as anything more than a subjective state. Nothingness is but an illusion, a word, a consequence of a lack of satisfaction. Bergson is therefore more direct than Sartre: "The concept of emptiness is born when human reflection is related to a past memory when already a new situation is in place. It is nothing else but a comparison of what is there with what could be there, in other words, a comparison of the full with the full." Bergson, *L'évolution créatrice*, p. 257. What Sartre says is not very different when he speaks about the human origins of Nothingness, but Sartre tries to recuperate the ontological weight of Nothingness, which was denied by Bergson.

8. Christian personalism at the beginning of the twentieth century attempted to avoid the dangerous consequences of this by doubling the self. Berdjajev suggested a separation of the self into two parts: the *individual*, dependent on the surrounding world, and the *persona*, independent from the material world and resembling God. The persona is free, but this freedom does not oppose the self to God. It is God that, within the self, opposes the material world: "It is within the self that the struggle between the world and God takes place." Nikolaj Berdjajev, "The Persona," in *Az orosz vallásbölcselet virágkora*, ed. Török Endre (Budapest: Vigilia, 1988), p. 217. It is through this metapsychological fiction that Berdjajev tried to save individual freedom and at the same time avoid "nihilism," which is a dangerous consequence of individual freedom. Nevertheless, he himself accepts that nihilism (in its Russian, and not Nietzschean, form) is quite close to personalism. See Nicolas Berdiaev, *L'idée russe* (Paris: Maison MOME, 1969), p. 142.

9. Torben Grodal, *Moving Pictures. A New Theory of Film, Genre, Feelings and Cognition* (Oxford: Clarendon Press, 1997), p. 257.

10. Laura Mulvey, *Visual and Other Pleasures* (London: MacMillan Press, 1986), p. 41.

11. *Il grido* provides an exception to this pattern.

12. Quoted in an interview in *L'Express* May 24, 1962.

13. Ibid.

14. Jeno Király, *Frivol múzsa*, vol. 1 (Budapest: Nemzeti Tankönyvkiadó, 1992), p. 289.

PAUL C. SANTILLI

Cinema and Subjectivity in Krzysztof Kieślowski

So far we were floating in the vast vacuum of Democritus raised high on the wings of the butterfly called metaphysics, where we even conversed with spirits. Now, the sobering force of self-knowledge is pulling back its silken wings, and once again we return to the firm ground of experience and common sense.
> Immanuel Kant, *Dreams of a Spirit Seer* (1766)

And can film do what Kant could not do?
> Stanley Cavell, *Contesting Tears: The Hollywood Melodrama of the Unknown Woman* (1995)

Near the conclusion of the *Critique of Practical Reason*, Kant remarks that if a human being were able to know with complete clarity (*Erleuchtung*) that there is a God and a soul destined for an afterlife, then "[a]s long as human nature remains as it is, human conduct would be thus changed into a mere mechanism in which, as in a puppet show, everything would *gesticulate* well but there would be no *life* in the figures."[1] He contends that our natural, sensuous desire for happiness would lead us to comply unfailingly with the moral law once we recognized "God and eternity with their awful majesty." In an interesting twist on Plato's allegory of the cave, Kant suggests that metaphysical enlightenment by itself would not free us from the domination of the marionettes casting their life-like shadows on the wall of the cave. It would rather transform us into those very marionettes! We would become mere simulacra of humans because we would operate according to our inclinations, especially our fears, and would not experience that tension between duty and sensuousness that is the very mark of our freedom and dignity. By his awesome presence and power, God would be a sort of puppet master.

Earlier in the *Critique*, Kant also made use of the marionette theater to defend his distinction between acts undertaken in the phenomenal appearance of time and the noumenal reality of freedom. If a temporal series were simply a feature of reality in itself and not a mode of sensible consciousness determining the way reality appears, then human actions would belong to a causally ordered sequence in time, and so would not be free. Kant writes: "A human being would be a marionette or an automaton…built and wound up by the Supreme Artist."[2] It is not enough for Kant that there be a self-conscious and rational "ghost in the machine" to distinguish the human being from an automaton: "self-consciousness would indeed make him a thinking automaton, but the consciousness of his spontaneity, if this is held to be freedom, would be a mere illusion." A genuine and not illusory free act must spring from the will's conformity to a moral law that transcends the spatial-temporal order. Such an act would appear to external eyes to come from nowhere; nothing in the causal temporal series of events preceding it could have predetermined it. In itself, however, it would spring from the deepest, but unseen, reality of free subjectivity.

So, human freedom in Kantian thought necessitates a gap between our experience as temporal, phenomenal beings and our inner reality as spiritual subjects of moral law. Not only are we theoretically barred by the *Critique of Pure Reason* from knowing God and our own souls as they are in themselves, but, as the *Critique of Practical Reason* suggests, we should not even *desire* to cross this "infinite gulf."[3] Penetrating the veil of phenomena may be morally disastrous. As Slovenian cultural theorist Slavoj Žižek has written, "what appears as 'essential' (moral law in ourselves) is possible and thinkable only within the horizon of our limitation to the domain of phenomenal reality; if it were possible for us to trespass this limitation and to gain a direct insight into the noumenal thing, we would lose the very capacity which enables us to transcend the limits of sensible experience (moral dignity and freedom)."[4] Kant mocks the claims of theological metaphysics to know the direct truth about the highest reality as being infected with "transcendent presumptions and theories of the supersensible" and indulging in a "magic lantern of chimeras."[5] So, Kant can think of no worse deflation of the pretensions of those who would go beyond appearance to cognize God and the soul than to compare them to the illusions of the puppet theater and the magic lantern, ancestors of modern cinema!

And yet, it could also be said that the modern cinema is itself the Kantian art form *par excellence*. One could say of movies that they are, according to Žižek, "not simply the domain of phenomena, but those 'magic moments' in which another, noumenal dimension momentarily 'appears' in (shines through) empirical/contingent phenomena."[6] When a film audience experiences images on the screen it is in no danger of taking them for agents operating in a "real" spatio-temporal continuum, for what is seen are hyper-phenomenal apparitions, less substantial than puppets. In the cinema there is no temptation to try to penetrate the veil of the phenomena to see what is really going on, behind the screen, as it were. A film director may, however, suggest that there are metaphysical and spiritual depths to the scenes being displayed, offering viewers an occasion to reflect on God, freedom, and the human soul. In this respect, a film can be taken as a philosophical act expressing ideas about the ground of phenomena, without pretending to offer a conceptual knowledge of that ground. When we watch a good film we may experience, not the rigidly determined and lifeless marionettes that we know the moving images "really" are, but rather the evocation of what may be life's "deepest essence."[7]

In what follows, I shall suggest that such metaphysical and spiritual depths infuse the films of the late Polish director, Krzysztof Kieślowski, a master at shaping the screen image to probe a reality underlying ordinary, mundane existence. Specifically, I hope to show by a study of three of his films, *Decalogue 1* (1988), *La Double Vie de Veronique* [*The Double Life of Veronique*] (1991), and *Bleu* [*Three Colors: Blue*] (1993), that Kieślowski provides a powerful testimony to, or even an argument for, the reality of a human soul. His films are artistic phenomena that have much to teach us about the human psyche, moral power, and the absolute, indirectly and discreetly without violating Kantian prohibitions against knowing being in itself. I do not want to imply, however, that Kieślowski has a distinctly Kantian view of the soul, as a transcendental ego, for example. Rather, I want to examine how his films reveal, in his words, "the secret life of people" that animates the gestures and countenances that we display to one another. I shall try, then, to indicate some of the ways Kieślowski creates a kind of cinematic iconography endeavoring to disclose "the soul on celluloid," to borrow Monika Maurer's expression.[8] To assist my interpretation of these films, I shall continue to draw on the fertile thinking of Slavoj Žižek's Lacanian approach to cinema and subjectivity, which he puts to good use in his book on Kieślowski, *The Fright of Real Tears*, and in other writings. We do not need to subscribe to Lacanian orthodoxy in order to recognize the power of depth psychology for eliciting good readings of movies like Kieślowski's that explore subtle facets of the human subject and "bear witness to the human personality."[9] Kieślowski does not ever confess to any interest in psychoanalysis, but both the thematic content and style of his films lend themselves, I think, very naturally to Žižek's unique blend of Lacanian developmental psychology and Kantian transcendentalism.

I

Kieślowski's films are not known for their plot or action. Instead, they use artful cinematography, sparse dialogue, subtle acting, and haunting musical scores to gesture toward a mysterious, noumenal order of being. In some early films, Kieślowski experiments with the fantastic to link the supersensible with spatio-temporal reality. In *Bez Konca* [*No End*] (1984), for instance, the ghost of a widow's recently deceased husband makes an appearance, and in *Przypadek* [*Blind Chance*] (1981), the protagonist,

Witek (Bogusław Linda), has the chance to live three alternative lives, much like the characters in the Tom Tykwer's film *Lola rennt* [*Run Lola Run*] (1998). But for the most part, Kieślowski sticks to a narrative realism that respects the Kantian challenge for a filmmaker to reveal a spiritual horizon in ordinary existence without indulging in fantastic visions of spirits and ghosts. Kieślowski himself has recognized the difficulty of meeting this challenge: "This goal is to capture what lies within us, but there is no way of filming it." As he said of his film, *The Double Life of Veronique*: "The film is about sensibility, presentiments and relationships that are difficult to name...Showing this on film is difficult: if I show too much the mystery disappears."[10]

A good introduction to Kieślowski's cinema is *The Decalogue*. *The Decalogue* consists of ten one-hour films made for Polish television in 1988 and represents an attempt to translate the meaning of the Ten Commandments for modern society. All ten films of *The Decalogue* are set in the same massive apartment complex in Warsaw at a time when Polish society was still suffering from the spiritual and economic deprivations of communist rule. The Polish world was, Kieślowski says, "terrible and dull," full of pitiless people, moving in a gray, robotic atmosphere alone, isolated, and lonely. Although Kieślowski's earlier films, both in the documentary and narrative genre, engaged political events in Poland, participating in what was then called "the cinema of moral concern," *The Decalogue* focuses more on the psychological and moral life of individuals, using the depressing political climate of martial law in the 1980s only as a backdrop for exploring the inner states of his characters.[11] "All my films," he says, "are about individuals who can't quite find their bearings, who don't quite know how to live, who don't really know what's right or wrong and are desperately looking."[12] Politics, he asserts, whether of the Communist Party, the Solidarity Movement, or Western liberalism, cannot answer "our essential, fundamental, human and humanistic questions."[13]

Decalogue 1 explicitly poses a philosophical question about the reality and nature of the soul. It is a meditation on what for Kieślowski would be the first of the Ten Commandments: "Thou shalt not worship false gods." This film tells of a close relation between a father, Krzysztof (Henryk Baranowski), and his young son, Pawel (Wojclech Klata). (The mother is away and indications are that it is not a good marriage.) The plot turns on Pawel's desire to use his new Christmas ice skates on a local pond and his father's caution about making sure that the ice is thick enough. Krzysztof is a professor of computer science, engaged in a project to develop software for a computer to construct poems and stories. As he explains to his university class, with his son watching from the back of the room, a properly programmed computer may have a will, aesthetic preferences, and a personality of its own. Tragically and ironically, however, his computer fails to gauge correctly the thickness of the pond's ice, which thaws because of "unexplained events," causing his son to drown while trying out his new skates.

Early in the film, Pawel comes across the corpse of a dog lying in the street and then, shortly thereafter, reads about a man's death in the obituary section of the newspaper. These experiences disturb him, prompting him to ask his father about why people die. In response, his father, Krzysztof, offers an account of death in which the human being is described as a machine. Death occurs, he says, "when the heart stops pumping blood...movement ceases, everything stops." Pawel, not quite satisfied with this, asks about some words he saw in the paper, "the deceased's peace of soul," to which his father replies: "It's a form of words of farewell. There is no soul." At the end of the film, of course, these words that reduce the human being to an automaton will come back to torment him, as the encounter with the reality of his son's drowning shatters the precious mathematical certainties by which he has structured his life. In one beautiful and haunting scene, Kieślowski suggests the dissolution of such certainties by filming a splotch of blue ink mysteriously seeping through some paper on Krzysztof's desk. There is a perfectly rational explanation for the appearance of this stain—the bottom of an ink bottle has cracked—but in this context the viewer is allowed to discern an elemental, disruptive reality lurking beneath and behind our solid, phenomenal reality. We learn as the film unfolds that at the very moment the blue ink washed over Krzysztof's desk, the ice on which Pawel was skating gave

way, causing his death. The question Kieślowski elicits in this film is how we could ever
know this deeper reality that eludes our modern
machines and scientific calculations. What in us
fails when the computer, our contemporary
"graven image" of the gods, fails?

We do have a sense from Kieślowski that the
father did not attend to his own vague intuitions
of unease about the ice, intuitions that could not
be translated into a computer program. Even
though his measurements presumably calculated the safety of the ice sheet, Krzysztof
nevertheless at one point ventures out to the
pond to feel it for himself. There he observes a
young man huddled by a fire on the side of the
pond. The man says nothing but gazes directly
at Krzysztof with an intense, questioning look.
As we watch this we have an ominous sense of
something wrong and know that Krzysztof does
as well. Viewers of the entire *Decalogue* will
recognize this silent, watchful character (Artur
Barciś) as one who appears briefly in other
films of the series, for example: as a student in
the class of a philosophy professor who earlier
in her life had abandoned a Jewish child to the
Nazis (*Decalogue 8*); as a medical intern in the
office of a doctor who makes a prognosis that
he knows is not true in order to save a fetus
from abortion (*Decalogue 2*); as a highway
worker who peers into the eyes of a young man
about to murder a cab driver (*Decalogue 5*).
Various interpretations have been given for this
character's appearance. He has been described
as an angel, a witness, and an embodiment of
conscience.[14] His appearance by the pond in
Decalogue 1 suggests that there is a gap
between what the protagonist knows and what
he is about to do, a gap that can only be closed
by an attunement to something other than what
can be gauged by a machine. Failing to heed
feelings, intuitions, and presentiments, he
misses a kind of truth about the fragile nature of
the human reality he has attempted to reduce to
computer codes—with terrible consequences.

II

Such attunement to the mystery of being that
lies below the surface of ordinary, impersonal
reality as a "shadowy double," in Žižek's
words, is treated in great depth in Kieślowski's
subsequent films, *The Double Life of Veronique*
and the trilogy, *Three Colors: Blue, White, and
Red*.[15] Kieślowski claims that *The Double Life*,
the next work I examine, is a film about "emotions and nothing else," but in fact it is a film
about the *psyche* in a broad sense and about
what Geoff Andrew has called "the unseen,
unfathomable forces—fate and chance—that
shape our lives even as we go about our banal
everyday business."[16] With a visual style that
critic Jonathan Romney has called "luminous,
numinous, and ominous," it tells a complex
story of two very young women, Veronika and
Veronique (both played by Irene Jacob), living
different but uncannily parallel lives, one in
Poland and one in France.[17] The film opens
with a voice-over announcing that these women
were born on the same day in 1968 and shows
each as a little girl being spoken to by a mother,
who later dies. They both have gentle fathers to
whom they are very close; both have beautiful
singing voices, and both, incredibly, have a serious heart condition.

The first part of the film, which is in Polish,
concentrates on moments in the last days in the
life of Veronika, a spontaneously joyful person
whom we first meet singing ecstatically in a
downpour while the rest of her chorus runs for
cover. Veronika travels to Krakow from her
hometown and wins a music competition,
allowing her to perform a celestially beautiful
piece of music. During her debut concert, as she
reaches for an impossibly high note, she per-
ishes from a heart attack. Her story closes from
the viewpoint of her glass-topped coffin; we
watch, as though from the grave, dirt being
shoveled from above onto the coffin until the
screen becomes entirely black. In that moment,
we are brought to the bedroom of the Frenchwoman Veronique, who is making love with her
boyfriend. Veronique tells her boyfriend that
she feels a deep sense of loss and sadness.
Afterward, she decides to give up her singing
career, have her heart condition taken care of,
and accept a job as a music teacher at a provin-
cial elementary school. She visits her widowed
father on occasion and seems resigned to a dull,
but comfortable, life, until she attends a marionette performance at her school.

The performance is put on in the school audi-
torium, which is filled with excited children.
The camera alternates shots of the children's

faces with the marionette show conducted by a puppet master named Alexandre Fabbri (Philippe Volter). Alexandre draws a ballerina from a black box and sets it into a dance motion. The ballerina collapses, dies, and miraculously comes to life again as an angel-like being or a large winged butterfly, to the relief of the distressed school children. Given the beauty and psychological power of this scene, one can understand what Henrich von Kleist was getting at when he observed in his 1810 essay "On the Puppet Theater" that, although the puppet is an automaton manipulated by a human master, we witness in its movements a grace and spirit that seem more soulful than those of a real human dancer.[18] Kieślowski seems also to have captured cinematically the sensibilities of Rilke's lines from the fourth Duino Elegy, *Ich will nicht diese halbgefüllten Masken, lieber die Puppe* [I won't endure these half-filled human masks; better, the puppet], and *Engel und Puppe: dann ist endlich Schauspiel* [Angel and puppet: a real play, finally].[19]

During this performance, the camera catches Veronique looking into a backstage mirror and spotting the puppet master, Alexandre, absorbed in his work. He in turn sees her looking at him and seems disturbed by that fact. Beginning with this meeting in the mirror, a relationship develops between Alexandre and Veronique. Alexandre begins to lure Veronique to him by sending her little mysterious items like a shoestring, a phone call, and a tape with train station noises. In one shot of Veronique's apartment, an orange-yellow light dances around, like an angelic visitor, apparently cast by a mirror held by Alexandre in another apartment window. It becomes clear later that this puppet master has somehow acquired knowledge of Veronique's double, Veronika, and is using this knowledge both to seduce Veronique and to fabricate a story for another of his marionette dramas. Once Veronique herself recognizes this, her relationship with Alexandre crumbles, and she returns in tears to her father's home.

How are we to understand these incidents? Although the age of Veronique-Veronika in this movie appears to be about twenty-two and although the character is played by an actress (Irene Jacob) of twenty-five, Kieślowski himself said, "I realized it's a film about a girl and not a young woman."[20] Veronique is a "girl"

who has lost her mother but who is still attached to and haunted by this absent mother. As a psychoanalyst would remind us, until she can in some way cut herself off from her mother, she cannot develop a mature subjectivity that would allow her to act as an independent ego and, among other things, have a healthy love relationship with a male. Both the death of Veronika and Veronique's encounter with Alexandre's puppets, I would suggest, represent phases of a young woman's psychological and spiritual development that provide clues to Kieślowski's understanding of the importance of the soul.

The Polish Veronika is depicted as being, despite her illness, extraordinarily buoyant, full of emotion and what Lacanians would call *jouissance*. She takes passionate delight in her lovemaking as she does with her music, but it is a dreamy, unanchored delight. She lives at the Lacanian imaginary, presymbolic, and narcissistic stage of psychological development. Reality to her is an apparition, symbolized by her train journey to Krakow where she looks at villages through the distorting glass of the train window, and then through the further deformations of a prized glass ball. When she makes love she smiles at her own photograph, which is smiling back at her. Although male figures appear briefly in her world, as a very masculine aunt, a dwarf-like lawyer, and a passerby who exposes his penis to her, they have no resonance in her being. In a way, she lives as a pure voice disconnected from her body, or as what has been called an *acousmatic*, "a voice without a bearer, without an assignable place, floating in an intermediate space."[21] Lacanians hold such a disembodied voice to be a little bit of the other or a *petite objet a*, which stands for a void left by the absent mother. We attach ourselves to such things in an effort to recover the lost reality of what we really desire, the unconditional admiring gaze of a mother who loves us and us alone. So, I believe that Veronika's devotion to her voice is a symptom of her unwillingness or inability to give up her mother. What Renata Salecl has said of vocal performances fits the case of Veronika very well: "The singer has to approach 'self-annihilation' as a subject in order to offer himself or herself as pure voice."[22] In the case of Veronika we have a girl who is pure voice because she is not yet a subject, who in fact resists subjectivization. To become a subject, she would have to, as Žižek says, "renounce…the object which vouches for the fantasmatic, incestuous link [with the mother]."[23]

The death of Veronika spurs Veronique, her double, to give up her voice to save her life. The formation of subjectivity requires us early in life to move from the narcissistic self-absorption to a self-reflective stage, in which we ourselves are split inwardly, and not magically entranced by the appearance of ourselves in others. In psychoanalytic terms it is the "father," the representative of the law and the entire sociocultural system of codes and symbols, that makes the splice (or castration) necessary for subjectivity and allows a normal, mature subject to "tarry with the negative," as Žižek puts it, and integrate oneself reflectively into a symbolic-linguistic reality.[24] Unlike Veronika, Veronique does have an encounter with a male, Alexandre, which restimulates the kind of self-reflection and sense of emptiness that the death of Veronika first awakened in her. She says to her father, "I am in love. I just don't know with what." What fascinates her from the start about Alexandre is that she is the object of his gaze first mirrored during the puppet performance. What becomes clear as their relationship develops, however, is that what she loves in him is *herself* as he looks at her, not what *he* is in himself. Each time he sends mysterious objects, she is entranced by dreamy, shapeless possibilities in her soul to which he seems to hold the key and to which these items seem to be objective correlatives. Therefore, despite her aroused subjectivity, she is still in the grip of a wounded narcissism.

Near the conclusion of the film, after she and Alexandre make love, Veronique comes into his workshop and sees two marionettes made in her exact likeness. At that moment, when she and her doppelganger are made mundanely visible to her by this fabricator, her love for Alexandre collapses and she returns to her father's home. Why? Kieślowski said that he employed the puppetmaster Bruce Schwartz to perform the dance of the dying ballerina because Schwartz does not disguise his hands when performing: "you can see his enormous paws all the time. Yet you don't notice them; you only see the dancing, the puppet dancing beautifully. That was something, which I thought was absolutely necessary. That Alexandre's hands should be

there, too, the hands of someone who's manipulating something."[25] When Veronique watches the puppet performance, Alexandre's hands are translucently phenomenal, invested with the luminous, transfiguring, and soulful possibilities she sees in the puppets themselves. When she then looks at the puppets he has manufactured to represent the two Veroniques ("in case one gets damaged," says Alexandre), they sicken her with their lifelessness, their flatness, their lack of spirit, and their raw reality. They no longer mirror her inchoate thoughts and inner longings; rather, in their naked, public state they are what they are in themselves, mere simulacra of the human soul. The marionettes are like the hands of their manipulator that have so recently caressed her; these hands are no longer part of a fantasy show, but big paws without noumenal depth. As Žižek has said in another context, "life becomes disgusting when the fantasy that mediates our access to it disintegrates, so that we are directly confronted with the Real."[26] Now the puppets are not the angelic beings drawing the soul to a mysterious kinship with noumenal depths, but Rilke's child dolls, which, he says, are "unmasked as the gruesome foreign body on which we squandered our purest affection."[27]

Veronique remains immature.[28] Unable to become a *couple*, she remains ultimately in the shadow of her *double* until she experiences a loss of her intimate fantasy. When defining the nature of fetishes in the cinema, Marc Vernet wrote that "in the heart of the desire to see and to know is the desire not to see and not to know."[29] This insight, I think, applies quite well to the psychology of this young woman who, fascinated by representations of reality that promise fantastically deep and rich experiences, prevents herself from knowing or loving the actual source of these phenomena. In the next film Kieślowski directed, *Three Colors: Blue*, the reverse could be said of its main character Julie (played by Juliet Binoche): "In the heart of the desire not to see and not to know is the desire to see and to know."

III

Blue is about a Frenchwoman who loses her husband and daughter in an automobile crash and as result of this trauma tries to commit a kind of psychic suicide by obliterating her identity and her memories. She does this by selling off her possessions, closing up her house, tearing up a musical score on which she and her husband, Patrice, a famous composer, had been working, and moving to a Paris neighborhood where she hopes she can live in anonymity. At a real estate office where she is looking for an apartment, she replies to the agent's inquiry about her occupation that she does "Nothing— Nothing at all" (the agent, by the way, is uncannily played by Philippe Volter, Alexandre in the *Double Life*). This refrain is repeated later to her mother whom she visits at a nursing home: "I'll only do what I want to now. Nothing. I don't want any belonging, any memories…no friends, no love."

For the narcissistic Veronique, the world was a mirror of her psychic need for a mother. For the traumatized Julie, the world is a representation divested of all significance and desire. This is shown brilliantly early in the film, as she lays in her hospital bed after the accident, through the use of an immense closeup of her eye that contains only the mirage images of her surroundings, including her attending doctor, who in her eye's reflection looks exactly the same as the father of Veronique. (He is indeed played by the same actor, Claude Duneton.) Her eye is a twin of the miniature television her friend, Oliver, brings her so that she can watch the funeral of her husband and daughter. In a moment of intense pathos, as Julie touches the tiny television screen depicting the two coffins, the viewer experiences a powerful overlay of Kieślowski's cross-references. The television monitor reminds us of the ending of *Decalogue 1* where the image of Pawel after his death lingers, frozen onto a television screen, of Veronika's glass-topped coffin and her treasured glass ball, of the mirror in which Veronique and Alexandre first espy each other, and now, in *Blue*, of the cold mirroring eye of Julie herself. It is as though under the impact of traumatic losses the familiar reality of the world takes on an uncanny alien aspect, or deadness, making it unreal, nothing more than a phantom. Julie cannot mourn her dead daughter and husband or cry. It is as though her eyes now are not real human eyes, but cold mirrors, like the icy surface of the fateful pond in *Decalogue 1*. The

blue tints of the cinematography itself reinforce the tones of melancholy, coolness, and boundless nothing, evoking the collapse of Julie's world.

In her act of withdrawal, not only does Julie try to strip the luminous sheen off the everyday world—highlighted by a scene where she angrily scrapes her knuckles along a stone wall—so that for her it has no significance or desirability, she also tries to remove any of her features that may arouse another subject's desire for her. If, as Levinas has suggested, we perceive infinite and incalculable depths in the face and words of another beckoning us to goodness and to love, then for Julie the trick is to present a visage that signifies nothing. In the marionette theater we are entranced by the supersensible possibilities of an apparitional automaton. We could say that Julie, suffering perhaps from what psychiatrists have called a "marionette syndrome," a complex of feelings of powerlessness, emotional rigidity, and ego alienation, wants to exhibit herself as a soulless puppet and an empty shell.[30] To her friend, Oliver (Benôit Regent), who confesses his love for her after the accident, and with whom she shares one night of kind, but dispassionate, lovemaking, she says, "I'm like any other woman. I sweat. I cough. I have cavities. You won't miss me." To love someone, one must see him or her as a kind of virtual image, disclosing and concealing depths, both inaccessible and lovely. It is that depth that Veronique believed she saw in the puppets and token signs from Alexandre. By emphasizing the repellant aspects of her flesh, Julie wishes to disenchant her own being in the eyes of her male friend and negate his desire for her. Whereas Veronique wants to be the desired object of a gaze that holds her gaze, Julie wants to deflect the gaze, to be merely a window without soul. In short, she wants to become for her fellow human being a flat automaton by stressing, paradoxically, the banal carnality of her humanity.

Julie's own elderly mother spends her days in a nursing home gazing at the most insipid images television has at its disposal. Suffering from something like Alzheimer's disease, she has lost her memory and misrecognizes her daughter, confusing her with her own sister, Marie France. She is objectively what her daughter would need to become to succeed in her nihilistic retreat from reality, a blank eye peering at a meaningless screen. But there is a gap between the mother and daughter that ensures that Julie will not be caught, like Veronique, in a nostalgic longing for the lost mother. The mother *is lost*, but she is also embarrassingly *present* precisely as one who is lost, repelling rather than inviting a psychic union or doubling, offering thereby a kind of escape from a narcissistic immaturity not available for young Veronique. Whereas Veronique was entranced by the dream that there was an other who bore her name (Veronika) to replace the mother who knew her name, Julie is compelled to accept the existence of a mother who misnames her. In this misrecognition lies hope for Julie's growth into a more complete human subject.

The awareness that she is not the beloved object of her mother's gaze parallels a truth to which she comes later in the movie. As the film unfolds, Julie, despite her resolve, begins to form attachments with her Parisian neighbors and to reawaken to the world around her. In particular, she forms a close relationship with a stripper named Lucille (Charlotte Véry, a raucous and earthy person, who embodies all the sex and erotic desire that Julie has managed to suppress. It is in Lucille's club that she sees, ironically on a television screen, a documentary about her husband, Patrice, and learns for the first time that he had a mistress. The shock of this knowledge propels her back to the world she thought she knew to seek out friends, like Oliver, to explain the affair her husband had with this young woman named Sandrine (Florence Pernel). Aware now of her own misrecognition of her married life and of fantasy elements in her construction of a happy marriage, she tracks down Sandrine, the ex-mistress, only to learn that this woman is pregnant with Patrice's child. Then, in an extraordinary and spontaneous act, Julie makes arrangements to give Sandrine and the child her house and her money. What accounts for this act?

The act cannot be interpreted simply in the words Sandrine uses: "Patrice told me a lot about you. That you are good…That you are good and generous. That's what you want to be." The cold look on Julie's face tells us that Sandrine has misread this gesture. Rather, we viewers should see it in the context of the whole film as a gesture from the depths of the empty pit into which Julie has descended, and not as an act of ordinary virtue. One can recognize such gestures in other Kieślowski films—spontaneous attempts to bear witness to the needs of another person, which seem to spring from a subjectivity that is both unlike and yet underlies ordinary human agency. A good example of this is that of the doctor in *Decalogue 2*, whose unbearable loss of his entire family during a bombing raid in World War II at first isolates and deadens him to his fellow humans, but also, in the course of time, moves him to heed sympathetically the desperate pleas of a woman who is (like Sandrine) pregnant with a lover's child and who is about to have an abortion she does not want. Lying about a prognosis in order to alter this woman's decision to have an abortion, the doctor becomes a good and faithful witness who, at least for a while, forms a connection with another soul. Likewise, in her offering to Sandrine and her child, Julie draws on her shattered life, the breakdown of *her* reality. Emerging from the dark night of her soul, she attains a degree of free subjectivity and human contact that was not possible for the narcissistic Veronique, in whom there was *no* moral capacity whatsoever.[31]

In *Three Colors: Blue*, this liberating movement out of the psyche's fathomless depths to a communion with others is magnificently captured by Kieślowski's integration of Zbigniew Preisner's musical score. While Veronique was a presence haunted by the absence of her double, Julie throughout the film is an absence haunted by a presence of musical phrases that return from her unconsciousness like powerful waves. To take one example, while she is swimming in the blue waters of an indoor pool, musical fragments from her husband's unfinished concerto wash over her as the screen image fades away completely for a few seconds. This return of repressed musical memories provokes what Jonathan Lear has called "*petits morts*," breaks in the flow of mental life and the fabric of meaning, presenting "the possibility for new possibilities."[32] Despite her conscious choice to retreat from human contact and to erase her past, there remains in Julie a powerful undercurrent of will and desire associated with the music her husband had composed. It is this periodic, resurgent lifeforce that saves her from the psychosis of a complete withdrawal from reality and actually moves her to finish the concerto herself. The music erupts with a driving Schopenhauerian energy, as though memory were an earthy, palpable thing, capable at any point of disrupting ordinary existence.

Blue concludes, as does the *Double Life of Veronique*, with an act of lovemaking. Julie returns to Oliver and accepts his profession of love. As they lie with one another, we hear a splendid concerto (scored by Preisner) and a chorus singing in Greek the words of St. Paul's "First Letter to the Corinthians." Julie's face is pressed against a window sprayed with a rain unleashed from the heavens. The chorus sings: "Though I have all faith so that I could move mountains, without love I am nothing." We then follow the camera as it traces a loop, creating a montage joining images of Julie's mother in her nursing home, Lucille at her strip club, and Sandrine in a hospital where her fetus appears on an ultrasound monitor, a television now alive with human reality. Then, as Oliver sleeps, to use the words of Kieślowski's script: "By the window we find Julie, her face in her hands. One by one, tears appear on these hands. Julie is crying helplessly."[33] Annette Insdorf has said of this final scene: "The music engenders what could be called an epiphany; as the camera embraces the characters, it equalizes, forgives, and suggests hope."[34] The last shot of the film lingers on Julie's face, giving us the opportunity to witness that this face is still haunted by death, by the infidelity of her husband, and by the collapse of her illusions. But it is also a face, just because it has been stripped of its conceits and exposed to "the zero-point of the night of the world," that can bear witness to a "mystical communion of *agape*" or something like Christian love.[35] We can say, then, that with Julie the soul of a woman has truly grown from the primary narcissism and fantasies of Veronique to a mature acceptance of reality and of the other. It is a soul whose moral power and transcendental life we have been privileged to behold, thanks to the genius of Kieślowski, as though we were indeed present at a cinematic epiphany.

IV. CONCLUSION

In an interview shortly before he died, Kieślowski said: "Film is helpless when it comes to describing the soul, just as it is describing many other things, like a state of consciousness. You have to find methods, tricks, which may be more or less successful in making it understood that this is what your film is about." He admitted that "some people may like those tricks, others may not."[36] No doubt, film is an enchanting illusion that "tricks" us into thinking that the characters and scenery are real when they are mere appearances of appearances, and no doubt film can be interpreted, like the puppet theater, to be a simplistic way to approach the human psyche in comparison to philosophy. The risk of film is the same as that of the puppet theater, or indeed any other use of icon or graven image: that one will become idolatrous, superstitious, or presumptuous rather than cautiously reflective about extra-mundane reality. Kieślowski himself planned to retire from making films, live in the country, and read favorite authors like Dostoyevsky and Dickens, who wrote the kind of literature that provided access to the immanent and transcendent dimensions of experience that he tried to recreate in his films. Unfortunately, he died of a heart attack at fifty-four, shortly after making his last film *Three Colors: Red*. I would contend that, despite his sense of disappointment with cinema, Kieślowski did succeed through his explorations of the mysterious depths of the human personality in offering to his audience an intriguing and serious philosophy of the soul.

The "tricks" that I have tried to describe here in my brief examination of some of his films— the intimations of a doubled self, cinematic cross-references, psychically charged objects, and ethereal music—do arouse in us a sense of an extra-phenomenal reality while respecting the limits of realism and the Kantian ban on direct insight into the noumenally transcendent and immanent. It is a credit to his ambitions and integrity as an artist that he was not satisfied with this and wished to do even more "to describe what lies within us."

PAUL C. SANTILLI
Department of Philosophy
Siena College
Loudonville, New York 12211
USA

INTERNET: santilli@siena.edu

1. Immanuel Kant, *Critique of Practical Reason*, trans. Mary Gregor (Cambridge: Cambridge University Press, 1997), p. 122. I thank members of the Metaphysical Society of America and members of the Philosophy Department at Penn State University for their encouraging comments on earlier drafts of this essay. Thanks also to the editors, Tom Wartenberg and Murray Smith, for their insightful suggestions.

2. Kant, *Critique of Practical Reason*, p. 85.

3. Kant, *Critique of Practical Reason*, p. 48.

4. Slavoj Žižek, *Tarrying with the Negative: Kant, Hegel and the Critique of Ideology* (Duke University Press, 1993), p. 114.

5. Kant, *Critique of Practical Reason*, p. 117.

6. Slavoj Žižek, *The Ticklish Subject: The Absent Center of Political Ontology* (London: Verso Books, 1999), p. 196.

7. Victoria Nelson, *The Secret Life of Puppets* (Harvard University Press, 2001), p. 37.

8. Monika Maurer, *Krzysztof Kieslowski* (Pocket Essentials, 2000), p. 73.

9. Slavoj Žižek, *The Fright of Real Tears: Krzysztof Kieslowski Between Theory and Post-Theory* (London: British Film Institute, 2001), p. 73.

10. *Kieslowski on Kieslowski*, ed. Danusia Stok (London: Faber and Faber, 1993), p. 194.

11. On the cinema of moral concern, see Boleslaw Michalek and Frank Turaj, *The Modern Cinema of Poland* (Indiana University Press, 1988), pp. 59–93.

12. *Kieslowski on Kieslowski*, p. 79.

13. *Kieslowski on Kieslowski*, p. 144.

14. See, for example, Maurer, *Krzysztof Kieslowski*, p. 42 and Annette Insdorf, *Double Lives, Second Chances: The Cinema of Krzysztof Kieslowski* (New York: Hyperion Books, 1999), p. 74.

15. Žižek, *The Fright of Real Tears*, p. 77.

16. Geoff Andrew, *The 'Three Colours' Trilogy* (London: British Film Institute Publishing, 1998), p. 19.

17. Jonathan Romney, review of *La Double Vie de Veronique*, *Sight and Sound* 1 (1992): 42–43. Cited in Andrew, *The 'Three Colours' Trilogy*, p. 19.

18. Heinrich von Kleist, "On the Puppet Theater," in *An Abyss Deep Enough: Letters of Heinrich von Kleist with a Selection of Essays and Anecdotes*, trans. Philip B. Miller (New York: E. P. Dutton, 1982), pp. 211–216.

19. *The Selected Poetry of Rainer Maria Rilke*, trans. Stephen Mitchell (New York: Vintage International, 1982), pp. 169, 171.

20. *Kieslowski on Kieslowski*, p. 175.

21. Slavoj Žižek, "In His Bold Gaze My Ruin is Writ Large," in *Everything You Always Wanted to Know about Lacan But Were Afraid to Ask Hitchcock*, ed. Slavoj Žižek. (London: Verso Books, 1992), p. 234.

22. Renata Salecl, "The Silence of Feminine Jouissance," in *Cogito and the Unconscious*, ed. Slavoj Žižek (Duke University Press, 1998), p. 181.

23. Žižek, *The Fright of Real Tears*, p. 51.

24. Ibid.

25. *Kieslowski on Kieslowski*, p. 181.

26. Žižek, *The Fright of Real Tears*, p. 169.

27. Rainer Maria Rilke, "Doll: On the Wax Dolls of Lotte Pritzel," cited in Nelson, *The Secret Life of Puppets*, p. 69.

28. In an odd little subplot of *Double Life*, a friend of Veronique asks her to perjure herself during a divorce proceeding by saying that she had slept with her friend's husband. Kieślowski admits that this subplot does not fit the mood or theme of the rest of the film, but he needed it because "only the soul existed for [Veronique], only premonitions, only a certain magic." So to bring her "down to earth" he decided to "have her agree…to appear in court, bear false witness against someone and in this way become a normal human being again." *Kieslowski on Kieslowski*, p. 186. But it seems to me that the scene achieves the opposite of what Kieślowski intends. Veronique so easily agrees to her friend's request because the realm of the law and the ethical are for her unreal; the moral imperative is not for her an organ of conscience or in any way constitutive of her still unfinished, girlish personality.

29. Marc Vernet, "The Fetish in the Theory and History of the Cinema," in *Endless Night: Cinema and Psychoanalysis, Parallel Histories*, ed. Janet Bergstrom (University of California Press, 1999), p. 93.

30. Reference to this syndrome can be found in Nelson, *The Secret Life of Puppets*, p. 252.

31. Space does not allow me to pursue this study of the ethical in Kieślowski's female characters, particularly in his last film, *Rouge [Three Colors: Red]* (1994). In *Red*, Irene Jacob returns to play the character of a young woman named Valentine. Valentine represents a new phase of subjectivity in Veronika-Veronique-Julie. She exhibits a natural moral grace and a Pauline spirit of love in her dealings with people, qualities that were not present in the other women.

32. Jonathan Lear, *Happiness, Death, and the Remainder of Life* (Harvard University Press, 2000), pp. 112, 115.

33. Citation from the screenplay by Krzysztof Kieślowski and Krzysztof Piesiewicz, *Three Colours Trilogy: Blue, White, Red*, trans. Danusia Stok (London: Faber and Faber, 1998), p. 98.

34. Insdorf, *Double Lives, Second Chances*, pp. 150–151.

35. Žižek, *The Fright of Real Tears*, p. 175.

36. In an interview with Geoff Andrew, *The 'Three Colours' Trilogy*, p. 82.

Is Sex Comedy or Tragedy? Directing Desire and Female Auteurship in the Cinema of Catherine Breillat

I

Over the last few years, the films of Catherine Breillat have run the gauntlet of critical reaction, from condemnation as pornography dressed up as art cinema, to acclaim for the audacity required and displayed by her uncompromising depictions of sex acts and female sexuality. Breillat has become a well-known *cinéaste* and novelist (some of her films are translations of her own novels to the screen), but has been less credited as a theorist, despite the philosophical character of interviews such as "The Absolute Opacity of Intimacy" and texts such as the preface to the screenplay of *Romance* (1999).[1] She states in the latter, for example, that what she holds dear is "making a moral cinema," but that morality in cinema is to be found not in the morality of the acts filmed, but in the moral dimension of the director's *regard* [look].[2] Breillat's contribution to feminist philosophy has been recognized, however, in a recent essay by Anne Gillain: "In effect, what Breillat advocates is a symbolic reappropriation of a feminine realm that for centuries has been dissected by the imaginary of men."[3]

   In this essay, I want to draw out the philosophical implications of Breillat's depictions of sexualities and sex acts in order to set out the female auteurship I think is proposed by her filmmaking. In arguing for Breillat's auteurship as the "symbolic reappropriation of a feminine realm," I shall be drawing in particular on the theoretical writings of Judith Butler and Luce Irigaray.

   As my title suggests, specific meanings of "tragedy" and "comedy" are in question in this

exploration of Breillat's contribution to feminist philosophy. The understanding of "tragedy" I shall use is Judith Butler's, outlined at the end of the section of Part 2 of *Gender Trouble*, entitled "Lacan, Rivière and the Strategies of Masquerade," where Butler sums up a lengthy analytic description of Lacan's concept of the Symbolic order as "[t]his structure of religious tragedy in Lacanian theory."[4] Most of the paragraph is quoted below, since it sets up the first parameter of my discussion of Breillat.

What plausibility can be given to an account of the Symbolic that requires a conformity to the Law that proves impossible to perform and that makes no room for the flexibility of the Law itself, its cultural reformulation in more plastic forms? The injunction to become sexed in the ways prescribed by the Symbolic *always* leads to failure and, in some cases, to the exposure of the phantasmatic nature of sexual identity itself. The Symbolic's claim to be cultural intelligibility in its present and hegemonic form effectively consolidates the *power* of those phantasms as well as the various dramas of identificatory failures. The alternative is not to suggest that identification should become a viable accomplishment. *But there does seem to be a romanticization or, indeed, a religious idealization of "failure," humility and limitation before the Law, which makes the Lacanian narrative ideologically suspect.*[5]

Butler expands on this interpretation of the Symbolic by describing it as a "dialectic between a juridical imperative that cannot be fulfilled and an inevitable failure 'before the law' [that] recalls the tortured relationship between the God of the Old Testament and those humiliated servants who offer their obedience without reward." This romanticization or religious idealization of humility is then glossed as Lacanian theory's "structure of religious tragedy." This structure of religious tragedy "undermine[s] any strategy of cultural politics to configure an alternative imaginary for the play of desires."[6] Cultural politics is prevented from aiming at an alternative imaginary *or* an alternative Symbolic by a certain "structuralist legacy within psychoanalytic thinking." The critique of the Lacanian Symbolic Butler begins in *Gender Trouble* is expanded to some extent in *Bodies That Matter*, in 1993, and even more so in *Antigone's Claim*. There, Butler identifies this structuralist legacy as being behind the "'position' talk within recent cultural theory," a genesis often not known to those using that theory.[7] This legacy in Lacanian and therefore feminist film and literary theory is the legacy of Levi-Strauss, and Levi-Straussian structuralist anthropology. It interdicts social and cultural change in the same way that structuralist theory revealed and exerted its separation from history and narrative. The Symbolic order of Lacanian theory *can* impose itself (it should be added, as Butler does, that whether it does this depends on who is speaking or whose pen is writing) with the force of a law that "guarantees the failure of the tasks it commands."[8] Its purposes are perhaps "not the accomplishment of some goal, but obedience and suffering to enforce the 'subject's' sense of limitation 'before the law.'"[9] Like Butler, I shall be arguing here against the force and absolutism of Lacanian Symbolic law. But my argument goes beyond Butler in that I shall be using her critiques of the Lacanian Symbolic to outline a trajectory critical of psychoanalytic film theory. This trajectory will in many ways run parallel to the critiques of psychoanalytic film theory and its "subjected" subject formulated by cognitive and other film theorists from 1988 on.[10]

Since I want to argue that Breillat's films have achieved and are achieving the female Symbolic envisaged by feminist theorists of the 1980s and 1990s, I shall now continue with recent commentary on the concept of the Symbolic order, but focus on its guise as a (or "the," clearly an important use of the definite article) female Symbolic. For some time now, a female Imaginary and a female Symbolic have been positive goals set by feminist writers not just for theory, but for society and all the cultural representations that help to constitute and sustain that society. These goals can be associated particularly with the work of Irigaray, and from a British point of view, with books such as Margaret Whitford's *Luce Irigaray: Philosophy in the Feminine* and Teresa Brennan's *Between Feminism and Psychoanalysis*.[11] Whitford in fact concentrates more on the construction of a female Imaginary than a female Symbolic, but these two things are envisaged and argued as inseparable and mutually dependent.[12] The route to a female Symbolic in Irigaray, however, depends on its proposed construction out of an un- but to-be-symbolized maternal-feminine best evinced by the mother-daughter relation and female genealogies. Chapter 4 of Whitford's *Luce Irigaray: Philosophy in the Feminine* is entitled "Maternal Genealogy and the Symbolic," and she prefaces the section of the chapter called "The Mother-Daughter Relationship" by stating that representations of a maternal line or genealogy are "the major and most significant absence in the symbolic."[13]

Irigaray's and Whitford's line of argument can be counterposed to Butler's suggestion, in *Antigone's Claim*, that a deconstruction of existing symbolic structures may be a better route to take than the construction or revelation of partially existent, excluded, or invisible ones. Butler's suggestion of this alternative route comes when, in a recognizably Derridean move on a linguistic performative, she identifies the utterance "[But] it is the law!" as that which attributes to the law the force that the law itself is said to exercise. This utterance is "a sign of allegiance to the law, a sign of the desire for the law to be the indisputable law, a theological impulse within the theory of psychoanalysis that seeks to put out of play any criticism of the symbolic father, the law of psychoanalysis itself." She continues: "Thus the status given to the law is precisely the status given to the phallus, the symbolic place of the father, the indisputable and incontestable." This statement should perhaps be read more as an implication of how the symbolic place of the father may be undone than as a suggestion that it should be. Butler proceeds carefully, using rhetorical questions to imply that accepting the law as a final arbiter of kinship life is "to resolve by theological means the concrete dilemmas of human sexual arrangements that have no ultimate normative form."[14]

The theoretical analysis accompanying Butler's reading of *Antigone* (Sophocles's play and the readings of it made by Hegel, Irigaray, and Lacan, respectively) can be set alongside the discussion in *Gender Trouble* that leads up to her identification of the structure of religious tragedy in Lacanian theory. In "Lacan, Rivière and the Strategies of Masquerade," Butler extracts two very different *tasks* (a term carrying important theoreticopolitical weight) from Lacan's analysis of Joan Rivière's famous essay "Femininity as Masquerade." Here, she says, "On the one hand, masquerade may be understood as the performative production of a sexual ontology, an appearing that makes itself convincing as a 'being'; on the other hand, masquerade can be read as a denial of a feminine desire that presupposes some prior ontological femininity regularly unrepresented by the phallic economy."[15]

In the next paragraph Butler is already concluding that these two "alternative directions…are not as mutually exclusive as they appear," but first, she suggests that the first task would "engage a critical reflection on gender ontology as parodic (de)construction and, perhaps, pursue the mobile possibilities of the slippery distinction between 'appearing' and 'being.'" In my reading of Breillat's cinema, I shall engage just such a critical reflection. By concentrating on the gender ontology that appears to govern feminine and masculine sexual identities in *Sex Is Comedy* (2002), I shall reveal the masquerade that is producing it. *Sex Is Comedy*, and especially the scene of the "deflowering" of the Actress (Roxane Mesquida) by the Actor (Grégoire Colin), appears to deal in fixed sexual identities. But the fact that a prosthetic and not a real penis is worn by the Actor for this scene is the clue to the fact that something quite different is going on—that the phallic mastery that would deflower the Actress is a masquerade, an "appearing that makes itself convincing as a 'being.'" Pursuing the philosophical possibilities of the distinction between "appearing" and "being" in *Sex Is Comedy* in this way will return me to tragedy and to comedy, since Butler states that exploiting the

potential of the distinction between appearance and being is "a radicalization of the 'comedic' dimension of sexual ontology only partially pursued by Lacan."[16] (Presumably, what Butler means by this is that her own work on the subversive or parodic activities of drag and cross-dressing gives much more attention to the cultural comedy of sexual ontology than Lacan ever did.)

II

Sex Is Comedy is, first and foremost, a self-reflexive meditation on Breillat's working methods as a director, and particularly as a director of explicit sex scenes: the film being shot, *Scènes Intimes*, resembles Breillat's previous film *A ma soeur!* (2001). In its self-reflexivity, *Sex Is Comedy* bears a resemblance to Truffaut's *La nuit américaine* (1973) and a stronger one to Abbas Kiarostami's *Through the Olive Trees* (1994), itself a meditation on his *And Life Goes On…* (1992). In a sense the film is an autofiction, in which the central character is Breillat's fictional incarnation Jeanne, impressively played by Anne Parillaud in what the actress herself says was her best experience of *being* directed since Luc Besson's 1990 film *Nikita*.[17] Breillat's interviewers in *Cahiers du cinéma* call it self-portraiture, and Breillat herself says: "To begin with, I thought I would be making a film like *La nuit américaine*. I didn't imagine the dimension of self-portraiture" (*Au départ, j'imaginais tourner un film comme La nuit américaine. Je n'imaginais pas cette dimension d'autoportrait*).[18] In my view, however, *Sex Is Comedy* is not a conventional autofiction, not any kind of autobiography—which Breillat says she hates.[19] The film does not concentrate on the character resembling Breillat, as a conventional autofiction would do, and its narrative is limited to one episode, the shooting of the film *Scènes Intimes*. The aspects of Breillat it reveals and draws out are her desire to direct and the agency with which she does so—the investment she has as a creative artist in cinema, and the transformation of her wish to convey explicit sex to audiences intelligently. This is confirmed particularly at the end of the film, when the central, most taxing scene of *Scènes Intimes* is "in the can," and Jeanne is relieved and happy, even reservedly jubilant, and is pictured energetically and warmly embracing Roxane Mesquida, also her leading actress in *A ma soeur!*.

Breillat has noted that *Sex is Comedy* "is also a comedy in the 'comic' sense of the term" (*est aussi une comédie, au sens comique du terme*).[20] (She thus distinguishes between a comedy of laughter and "comedy" as an activity involving fictional representation, the sense drawn on by Butler when she refers to the "comedic" dimension of sexual ontology.) The comedy of laughter may not be the primary sense of the word as it figures in the title of Breillat's film, but as she says, she did mean this sense to be included. Which it certainly is when the Actor in Breillat's *scène intime* trots around the set waggling the prosthetic penis manufactured for him by the props manager in order to defuse the tension created for the entire crew by intense acting and filming. (Colin wears the prosthesis both to maintain an erection and to ensure no skin contact with Roxane Mesquida, so in contrast to *Romance*, where audiences and critics speculated that sex was really going on between Caroline Ducey and Rocco Siffredi, Breillat's fictional representative assures them here that it is not.) Laughter also arises spontaneously in the opening "beach" scene of *Sex Is Comedy* from the misery of two scantily clad actors and an entire crew trying to create an atmosphere of oblivious sexual passion in a freezing Atlantic wind. To bring out the feminist theoretical implications of Breillat's play with literary or dramatic genres in her films up to *Sex Is Comedy*, I shall now briefly review the structure of tragedy in three of her earlier films, *Une vraie jeune fille* (1976), *36 fillette* (1987), and *Parfait Amour!* (1996).

Une vraie jeune fille and *36 fillette* are Breillat's two studies of adolescent femininity, both pervaded by an atmosphere of confinement, and attempted rebellion against the confinement, through underage sex. The languors of Alice's (Charlotte Alexandra) summer vacation with her parents on a rural smallholding in *Une vraie jeune fille* are if anything exceeded by the pain, mistrust, and wild behavior of Lili (Delphine Zentout) in *36 fillette*, clearly linked to undermining treatment by both her parents and physical abuse by her father. Breillat's tragedies of female desire reach their apogee in the searing irony of her title *Parfait Amour!* It has become something of a cliché to link men's violence against women to their often socially sanctioned desire to maintain power over them, but the violent death met by Frédérique (Isabelle Renauld) as her affair with Christophe (Francis Renaud) is briefly and rather desperately revived for a while after it has ended remains Breillat's most brutal illustration of the power structures women can suffer. The sense of limitation "before the law" characterizing life in the tragic Lacanian Symbolic is lived out in the claustrophobic structure of *Parfait Amour!*, in which an erotic relationship is presented as Frédérique's only route to fulfillment as a woman, and a sense of destiny if not fate hangs over the action. Frédérique does not see her tragedy coming, but the film is identified *as* the tragedy of her self-destructive passion for Christophe by its presentation in flashback. The film opens with the police taking a numb Christophe through the reconstruction of the crime, and this is followed by a sequence in which Frédérique's teenage daughter confirms the couple's mutual passion and her mother's powerlessness to escape from her relationship with her younger lover.

III

In *Romance*, both tragic and comic modes are present. Breillat says that in the opening scene, "where you see Paul (Sagamore Stévenin) all powdered up like a geisha, posing for a fashion shoot in a matador costume…it's funny" that he has to be on the tip of his toes to play the man.[21] Gender identity is revealed to be performed in its "essence," and comically so. On the real set of *Romance*, as on the fictional set in *Sex Is Comedy*, the crew laughed at the actors amid what is probably the most emotionally and dramatically intense scene in the film, the second of the two bondage scenes, of which Breillat says: "But the really funny scene is the second scene of bondage with Robert (François Berléand), that I call the 'bondage in the red dress' scene. I did it intentionally. On the set we were roaring with laughter. That's the way I wrote it. I wanted people to be able to think that a scene as weird as one about bondage and sadomasochism could be cheerful and convivial."[22]

We can now extend and deepen this examination of the interplay of comedy and tragedy in *Romance* and *Sex Is Comedy* by relating it to Butler's double reading of masquerade's part in sexual ontology. The opening shots of *Romance*, where Paul models a matador, show that masquerade in Breillat's cinema relates to masculine gender roles and identities as much as to feminine ones. A more significant instance of masquerade, however, occurs in the scenes with Grégoire Colin's prosthetic penis, where it is the phallus "itself," signifier of the "indisputable and incontestable" law of the father, whose ontological status is contested.[23] The phallus as masquerade is the point in *Sex Is Comedy* at which Breillat decisively opens up the distinction between appearance and being of masculinity in order to question the meaning and authority of the sexuality that is "taking" the virginity of an adolescent girl. The few scenes of *Sex Is Comedy* where the masquerading phallus is actually visible reveal Breillat's deconstruction of the symbolic structures of phallocentrism, a realization in images of what I suggested above is a Butlerian route to an Irigarayan female Symbolic. The scene in which Grégoire Colin comically offers his prosthesis to the assembled crew performs the "'comedic' dimension of sexual ontology" Butler finds undeveloped in Lacan, and exposes the mobility of the relationship between female auteur and male actor. This relationship is open to performative reconstruction, and by means of a close reading of the relationship between Jeanne and her unnamed male lead, I now want to link Breillat's performative cinema to the Irigarayan theory of a female Symbolic, and to the theory of female auteurship that emerges from Breillat's *mise-en-scène* of female directing in *Sex Is Comedy*.

In *Speculum of the Other Woman*, Irigaray lists a number of types of female behavior that she claims can be seen as "manifestations of a lack of an auto-erotic, homo-sexual economy" for women.[24] What women do not have is a libidinal economy prohibited by the phallocentric Symbolic: in other words, under phallocentrism, women's desire cannot circulate as effectively as men's can. As I set out earlier when referring to Whitford's reading in her chapter "Maternal Genealogy and the Symbolic," Irigaray's preferred argument for countering the negative effects of the phallocentric Symbolic on women's sexuality is the development of a "homo-sexual" (same sex) economy among women, an economy to be constructed out of female genealogies and the mother-daughter relationship. But Whitford also refers to another way of changing current sexual economies for the benefit of women's sexuality described by Irigaray: this is to create an economy "*of the death drives*," the mobilization of which is currently prohibited "for/in female sexuality."[25] Women's "nature" has been constructed by a particular symbolic organization, in which it is "used" for the representation and sublimation of men's death drives, but is unable to sublimate or represent itself.[26]

A phallocentric symbolic economy allows the representation and sublimation of men's death drives, but not the "rechannelling, metaphorization or sublimation" of women's.[27] The concept of the death drive is specific to psychoanalysis, but here I am calling on it to make an argument about sociosymbolic organization, not about the psyche.[28] As Whitford says, Irigaray's critics read her as if she were offering an alternative psychoanalytic theory, when, in fact, she is "interrogating psychoanalytic conceptualization itself."[29] She claims: "Lacanians take Irigaray to be talking about feminine specificity at the level of the drives, whereas I take her to be talking about feminine specificity at the level of the symbolic, or representation."[30]

A redistribution of the death drives of men and women would create at least the conditions of possibility for a female Symbolic. As Whitford states, the concept of the death drive is conceptualized differently by different psychoanalytic theorists, but its association with (self-) destructive impulses, with the drive to repeat and to return to immobility, and with sadism and masochism (phenomena pertinent to the sexualities of Breillat's cinema), means that the fundamental question involved is one of happiness and unhappiness, and to what degree these states are caused by social and psychic factors. "Is it the fault of society or is there something inherent in the human psyche which is an obstacle to happiness? Most people would probably say 'both,' but it is hard to determine with any precision what is 'inside' and what is 'outside.'"[31] I would endorse both parts of this estimation, which means that a reorganization of symbolic economies by means of a redistribution of the death drives entails broaching the large topic of the relationship of the psychic to the social. My contention, though, is that Breillat's representation of the directing of desire in *Sex Is Comedy* offers a *mise-en-scène* of this relationship—or if not of the relationship of the psychic to the social in its entirety, which can probably be addressed only discursively by philosophers and theorists, then of the enacting of desire (of the drives) in a context where the activity *is* representation and, importantly, artistic representation of which a woman is in charge.

To see this, consider that, from the start of filming in *Sex Is Comedy*, Jeanne is limping around the set due to a foot injury that has put her foot in plaster. The injury is shrouded in mystery and apparently symbolic of Oedipally disadvantaged femininity, since when asked, Jeanne says it is not she that has broken her ankle, but her ankle (*pied*) "that broke itself. It's the metaphor of the film" (*qui s'est cassé tout seul. C'est la métaphore du film*). As I have already emphasized, the focus of drama in *Sex Is Comedy* is the filming of *scènes intimes* between the Actress and the Actor. Interspersed with Jeanne's instruction of her actors in the movements and gestures that will produce the emotion she wants, however, are a series of *tête-à-tête* conversations with the Actor in which she coaxes, cajoles, and bullies him into a convincing performance. In these dialogues she is outspoken to the point of being insulting, and tyrannically insistent on sex being acted as *she* sees it. She bans "male larking about" (*plaisanteries d'homme*) from the sacred place that is her set, refuses the Actor's own interpretation of himself as "timid," and lambastes the "moral ugliness" (*laideur morale*) of an actor who performs with his body but not with his soul. The Actor is subjected to a demeaning comparison with the Actress, to which he retorts that she is no good (*nulle*), and that he is only interested in himself as a unique individual. This is precisely the sort of male egoism Jeanne will not indulge, and although she continues to respond to the Actor's pleas for attention (she frequently puts her arm around his waist or shoulders and walks off into the wings with him to talk things through), she will not engage in any flattery of his narcissism. She

complains to her assistant director Leo (Ashley Wanninger) that the Actor is "arrogant…terribly arrogant" (*orgueilleux…atrocement orgueilleux*), and, when the Actor apparently tries to sabotage the smooth running of the deflowering scene by turning Jeanne and her leading lady against one another, claiming that the Actress will not perform nude since it is not in her contract (in the event she complies uncomplainingly), Jeanne tells him he is egoistic, vain, irresponsible, and lacking in professional conscience. The Actor has said several times that he only puts up with Jeanne's authoritarianism because he is getting well paid, and now she throws his words back at him: "Actors are very well paid for what they do because it's very hard. There, that's it" (*Les acteurs sont très bien payés pour ce qu'ils font parce que c'est très dur. Voilà*).

The clashes between Jeanne and her male lead are an important dramatic focus of *Sex Is Comedy* but, as I have already suggested, they also illustrate the politics of desire represented in Breillat's *mise-en-scène* of female directing. Jeanne's foot injury symbolizes the disadvantage Breillat sees women directors as suffering by virtue of their sex, and Jeanne's passionate and often selfish involvement in her film (to prepare for the shooting of the deflowering scene, she expels the entire crew except Leo from the bedroom set for an hour-and-a-half, to allow her the solitary concentration she says artists and writers like her need) reveals iron will and determination. The character played by Grégoire Colin displays the anti-authoritarian attitude Breillat's fictional persona needs as a foil, but although some explanation for this is offered when the Actor mentions that his stepmother beat him as a child, he is in many ways an Everyman figure with the added sensitivity one would expect of an actor, a beautiful man who on this occasion must act out a woman's vision of male sexuality. The dialogues and relationship between Jeanne and the Actor have an unmistakably symbolic—even an allegorical—dimension. Far more than just a reenactment of a "war of the sexes," they show uninhibited female aggression toward a male "artist," an altered sexual economy in which the desire of a woman director is successfully sublimated and finds its expression in the realization of *her* film. As will be clear by now, I am suggesting that *Sex Is Comedy* dramatizes the altered economy of the death drives called for by Irigaray in *Speculum of the Other Woman*. Feminine sexualities under the sway of the death drive have figured more than once in Breillat's cinema, and particularly in the person of Marie (Caroline Ducey), the masochistic female protagonist of *Romance*. In *Sex Is Comedy*, Breillat has achieved a rare degree of reflexivity about the relationship of female sexuality to artistic creation (in this case, film directing). The relationship between female director and male actor that occurs in this context may well draw on Breillat's own experience of directing, but whether it does or not, it is fascinatingly suggestive about uncharted routes of women's desire. Rather than offering a general theory of female auteurship, it demonstrates how women may achieve auteurship, via an "autofictional" *mise-en-scène* of Breillat's own direction of desire that viewers can recognize from her previous film.

IV

The conclusion I wish to draw about Breillat's cinema, one illustrated particularly by her self-reflexive meditation on woman as director in *Sex Is Comedy*, is the following. First, although Breillat herself and some of her commentators often describe her characters' sexualities as ontologies of femininity or masculinity, and thus characterize them in very essentialist terms, the gender identities shown in her films can be understood along very different lines.[32] Images of what Butler calls "the 'comedic' dimension of sexual ontology" show that the films themselves undermine this essentialism. Using Butler's theory of gender performativity to interpret masculinity as masquerade in *Romance* and *Sex Is Comedy*, along with a discussion of Breillat's bleak depictions of women's experience of sex that draws on Butler's critique of the Lacanian Symbolic, has allowed me to pursue a reading in which I have knowingly eschewed the Irigarayan approach to the masquerade Butler suggests is essentialist.[33] I have, instead, turned to Irigaray's notion of a female order of representation—a female Symbolic order—in order to develop my reading of the type of auteurship I think is constructed by Breillat's filmmaking. Through her fictional

persona Jeanne, Breillat shows women's film directing to be a tussle and a struggle involving an altered sexual economy, a redistribution of men's and women's death drives that allows a female director's desire to be successfully sublimated in the creation of her film. Second, I have illustrated how Breillat's cinema engages in a manner that has not been observed elsewhere with the literary modes of tragedy and comedy, in the specific senses given to the terms by Judith Butler, but also more broadly, since Butler herself draws on literature to arrive at her definitions. Breillat's films often include stylistically intense *mise-en-scène*, but she is also a highly literary filmmaker, as shown in her deployment of tragic and comic registers, and by my reading of the narrative and central relationship of *Sex Is Comedy*. Breillat's contribution to film as philosophy is thus a feminist and literary mode of philosophizing that plumbs the "essences" of sexualities, exposes their thoroughgoing constructedness, and suggests new and different reconstructions of gender relations.

KATHERINE INCE
Department of French Studies
University of Birmingham
Edgbaston
Birmingham B15 2TT
UK

INTERNET: k.l.ince@bham.ac.uk

1. Christine Fiszer-Guinard, "Interview with Catherine Breillat: L'opacité absolue de l'intimité," *SITES: Contemporary French & Francophone Studies* 6 (2002): 5–12; Catherine Breillat, *Scénario: Romance* (Paris: Petite Bibliothèque des Cahiers du cinéma, 1999).

2. Breillat, *Scénario*, pp. 8, 18.

3. Anne Gillain, "Profile of a Filmmaker: Catherine Breillat," in *Beyond French Feminisms: Debates on Women, Politics and Culture in France, 1981–2001*, ed. Roger Celestin, Eliane DalMolin, and Isabelle de Courtivron (New York and Basingstoke, England: Palgrave Macmillan, 2003), p. 204.

4. Lacan's Imaginary order corresponds roughly to the exclusive relationship with the mother termed the "pre-Oedipal" stage by Freud, when the child is locked into dual, dyadic relationships despite perceiving his or her own identity as a body and his or her difference from the world around it. In Lacan's terminology, entry into the triangulated relationships of the Symbolic order is effected by an encounter with the paternal law that, crucially for Lacanian theory, involves entry into language.

5. Judith Butler, *Gender Trouble: Feminism and the Subversion of Identity* (New York/London: Routledge, 1990), p. 56, emphases added.

6. Judith Butler, *Antigone's Claim: Kinship Between Life and Death* (Columbia University Press, 2000), p. 18.

7. Ibid.

8. Butler, *Gender Trouble*, pp. 56–57.

9. Butler, *Gender Trouble*, p. 57.

10. For example, Noël Carroll, *Mystifying Movies: Fads and Fallacies in Contemporary Film Theory* (Columbia University Press, 1988); Richard Allen, *Projecting Illusion* (New York: Cambridge University Press, 1995).

11. *Between Feminism and Psychoanalysis*, ed. Teresa Brennan (London/New York: Routledge, 1989). Parts 3 and 4 of *Between Feminism and Psychoanalysis* are entitled "Towards Another Symbolic (1): The Essential Thing" and "Towards Another Symbolic (2): Beyond the Phallus."

12. Margaret Whitford, *Luce Irigaray: Philosophy in the Feminine* (London/New York: Routledge, 1991), pp. 76, 91.

13. Whitford, *Luce Irigaray*, p. 76.

14. Butler, *Antigone's Claim*, p. 21.

15. Butler, *Gender Trouble*, p. 47.

16. Ibid.

17. "Autofiction" is a neologism created by the French novelist Serge Doubrovsky in 1977 that designates a variation on fictional autobiography. 'Faction' is the nearest equivalent term in English. Hélène Frappat and Jean-Marc Lalanne, "Breillat Parillaud: Auto-frictions," *Cahiers du cinéma* 568 (2002): 36.

18. Frappat and Lalanne, "Breillat Parillaud," pp. 34, 37.

19. Frappat and Lalanne, "Breillat Parillaud," p. 36.

20. Frappat and Lalanne, "Breillat Parillaud," p. 37.

21. Robert Sklar, "A Woman's Vision of Shame and Desire: An Interview with Catherine Breillat," *Cineaste* 25 (1999): 25.

22. Ibid.

23. Butler, *Antigones Claim*, p. 21.

24. Whitford, *Luce Irigaray*, p. 96.

25. Ibid.

26. Ibid.

27. Irigaray, quoted in Whitford, *Luce Irigaray*, p. 96.

28. The death drive is a speculative concept invented by Freud in *Beyond the Pleasure Principle* in 1920, and subsequently given different formulations by analysts such as Melanie Klein. For Freud, it describes both the *Wiederholungszwang* or "compulsion to repeat," and the associated psychic drive toward stasis, or an inanimate state. The death drive is the equivalent of the Greeks' Thanatos, and *Beyond the Pleasure Principle* marks the point in Freud's thinking at which the opposition between the ego and sexual instincts gives way to the tense coupling of Eros (the libido) and Thanatos (the death drive), which between them govern psychic life.

29. Whitford, *Luce Irigaray*, p. 84.

30. Whitford, *Luce Irigaray*, p. 85.

31. Whitford, *Luce Irigaray*, p. 95. On Irigaray's symbolic politics and their relationship to the death drive, see also Whitford's "Irigaray, Utopia, and the Death Drive," in *Engaging with Irigaray: Feminist Philosophy and Modern European Thought*, ed. Carolyn Burke, Naomi Schor, and Margaret Whitford (Columbia University Press, 1994), pp. 379–400.

32. For example: "The essence of masculinity is rigidity.... The essence of femininity is subtlety." Breillat, *Scénario: Romance*, p. 13. See also Kathleen Murphy's article "A Matter of Skin...Catherine Breillat's Metaphysics of Film and Flesh," *Film Comment* 35 (1999): 16–20, 22.

33. "[M]asquerade can be read as a denial of a feminine desire that presupposes some prior ontological femininity regularly unrepresented by the phallic economy...the masquerade...is what women do...in order to participate in man's desire, but at the cost of giving up their own." Butler, *Gender Trouble*, p. 47.

JINHEE CHOI

Apperception on Display: Structural Films and Philosophy

Both filmmakers and scholars have described structural films in terms relevant and important to philosophy. P. Adams Sitney, for example, characterizes the aspiration of structural films as "the cinematic reproduction of the human mind."[1] Annette Michelson, in referring to Michael Snow's landmark structural film *Wavelength* (1967), describes Snow's camera movement as "the movement of consciousness."[2] Even Snow himself compares his project with that of philosophy, claiming: "If *Wavelength* is metaphysics, *Eye and Ear Control* is philosophy, and ↔ will be physics."[3] Snow's bold statement in no way implies that he equates his filmmaking with philosophy. Rather, Snow underscores his preoccupation with some traditional philosophical questions: reality, illusion, motion, energy, and velocity. But what, then, is the relationship between avant-garde films and philosophy? Do they merely share some interests of inquiry or does a more significant relationship exist between the two?

In this essay, I aim to delineate the relationship between avant-garde film and philosophy. Philosophers, concerned with unveiling the philosophical potential and limits of film, have primarily focused on narrative fiction film, putting aside alternative film forms or modes such as documentary or avant-garde films.[4] This may have to do with the fact that many locate the philosophical potential of film in its "narrative," which contributes to the exercising and refinement of one's moral understanding of the world.[5] By shifting the focus from narrative film to avant-garde film, we should be able to examine how the nonnarrative aspects of film may make a philosophical claim or suggest a philosophical hypothesis.

I will first examine Noël Carroll's claim that avant-garde films are not theoretical. I will argue that although avant-garde films do not advance a film theory in a strict sense, their philosophical contribution can be found in their suggestion of new philosophical hypotheses regarding the film medium itself. I will then discuss the relationship between the cognitive value and aesthetic value of avant-garde film by focusing on Kurt Kren's *TV 15/67* (1967).

I. "AVANT-GARDE FILMS ARE NOT THEORETICAL"

In his article, "Avant-Garde Film and Film Theory," Carroll classifies four different ways in which an avant-garde film relates to film theory: (1) it can demand a theory expansion; (2) it can demand a theory contraction; (3) it can exemplify a theory; and (4) it can literalize a theory.[6] A theory, for Carroll, should meet the following two criteria. A theory should first aim to provide a general framework that can be applied to a large group of films, not just to one particular film. This can be called the generality requirement. Second, Carroll claims, the validity of a theory should be tested by evidence.[7] To demonstrate its validity, a theory should be able to present a reasonable amount of evidence or data that would support the theory. This can be called the verifiability requirement.

Carroll's first two postulations about the possible relationships between avant-garde film and film theory (those of theory expansion or contraction) reflect the fact that avant-garde films often challenge existing cinematic norms and conventions. Avant-garde movements in film, as well as in other art forms, prioritize a subversion of established norms and conventions by deviating from them. Thus, an avant-garde film often provides a recalcitrant example to an established film theory and brings to the fore the necessity to modify either the theory or a common conception of the film medium.

The third relationship between avant-garde film and film theory, that of exemplification, Carroll defines as "being a sample or example of the kind of film or work of art that a given theory either endorses, implies or stipulates."[8] For instance, *Zorn's Lemma* (Hollis Frampton, 1970) may exemplify Kantian aesthetics in the sense that its structure manifests the Kantian idea of "purposeless purposiveness." The film consists of three parts. In the first part, we hear only soundtrack of a woman reciting twenty-four rhymes from the Bay State Primer. The second part of film—the major portion of the film—consists of images of words organized in alphabetical order. In this segment, each shot lasts for more or less one second (between twenty-three and twenty-five frames). As the film progresses, the words are replaced by images. In the last part of the film, we see a man, a woman, and a dog walk from foreground to far background. This last portion is also accompanied by an audio track of six women reading a text.[9] The overall structure of the film is, to a certain extent, symmetrical in the sense that the first and last portions of the film are accompanied by an audio track of female voices reading texts. The second portion of the film makes the viewer anticipate which letter will be displaced next, and as the "C" is finally substituted by images in the last cycle of the film, it provides the viewer a sense of completeness and closure. *Zorn's Lemma* invites the viewer to contemplate both the unity of the film as a whole and the diversity within each of the three parts. Carroll claims that a film like *Zorn's Lemma* can be said to be theoretical in the sense that it embodies a philosophical theory, the postulation of which provides the best explanation for the interpretation of the film. Frampton may or may not have intended to demonstrate Kantian philosophy in his film, but this postulation does illuminate both the structure and the spectatorial effect of the film.

The fourth relationship, the notion of literalization, is harder to grasp compared to the other three. As far as I understand it, a film literalizes

a theory when it evokes or aligns itself with the theory by addressing issues associated with it. For example, in *Chelovek s kino-apparatom* [*The Man with the Movie Camera*] (1929), Dziga Vertov aligns himself with proletarian ideology by depicting filmmakers as workers, ones who gather and assemble fragments of the modern world. One of the differences between exemplification and literalization, according to Carroll, is that in the latter, the theory alluded to does not necessarily provide the best explanation for the interpretation of the film in question. Carroll makes an example of Bill Brand's *Works in the Field* (1978), which evokes information theory by superimposing a random dot matrix over images from documentary footage. According to Carroll, Brand somewhat misappropriates information theory's notion of the code to underscore the idea that the editing is coded because the referents of the code in these two cases seemingly differ.[10]

An avant-garde film, in Carroll's view, cannot achieve theoretical status proper by either exemplifying or literalizing a theory. According to Carroll, even if an avant-garde film alludes to a film theory by virtue of being an exemplification of the given theory, it is still far from presenting an actual film theory. Carroll readily acknowledges that many avant-garde filmmakers themselves often propose a film theory. Maya Deren, for instance, not only directed avant-garde films of various kinds, but also purported to define her filmmaking as "vertical filmmaking," which de-emphasizes the linear logic of narrative or drama. Carroll's claim, however, is that the film in question—the film itself—cannot be characterized as proposing a theory. Such an attempt does not pass the second requirement for a theory: verifiability. In Carroll's view, an individual film cannot propose a general theory as well as provide evidence for the theory in question simultaneously. Such a theory would be either skewed or circular.

Carroll is also skeptical about the capability of avant-garde film to prove or disprove a theory by literalizing it. For example, Carroll claims that structuralist/materialist films appear to bring to the fore the idea of "active spectatorship," but these films are unable to explain a set of correlations presupposed in advancing a theory of spectatorship. This, he argues, is because a film in and of itself does not provide a reason to accept a set of binary oppositions between narrative versus nonnarrative, illusion versus anti-illusion, and passive versus active spectatorship.[11]

The way Carroll characterizes the theoretical arena of avant-garde films—or lack thereof—seemingly makes tenuous the notion of whether an avant-garde film can advance a philosophical thesis or theory. One of the assumptions underlying Carroll's claims is that in order for an avant-garde film to present a theory, the film should provide a theory as well as evidence of some sort to verify and justify that theory. It seems, however, that Carroll sets the standard too high. An avant-garde film rarely states a theory in such an explicit manner. However, this does not indicate that avant-garde film cannot make philosophical contributions, nor does this mean that avant-garde film cannot further one's knowledge. I would like to discuss two ways in which avant-garde films can make a philosophical contribution through means other than advancing a theory: (1) by revealing a new possibility of the medium and (2) by providing experiential knowledge to the viewer.

Given the nature or agenda of avant-garde film theories, especially the ones promoted by filmmakers themselves, Carroll's assessment of the philosophical contribution of an avant-garde film appears to be a bit hasty. Avant-garde film theories advanced by filmmakers themselves are often prescriptive rather than descriptive. By making a film in accordance with the theory or theoretical principles in question, filmmakers propose to adopt and explore a new kind of filmmaking. Carroll entertains such an objection. He considers the possibility of whether making an avant-garde film of a certain kind can be seen as a theoretical recommendation of that type of filmmaking. He rather quickly dismisses this objection, however, by saying, "making a flat film does not supply *a reason* for making other flat films" (emphasis added).[12]

One might argue against Carroll that while the film in question does not provide an *argument* for the adoption of the film style employed, it *reveals* a new possibility for the medium. Despite the ambiguous connotations of the term, I adopt the notion of revelation to reassess some of the philosophical contributions that avant-garde film can make. Monroe

C. Beardsley claims that the notion of revelation often connotes both the suggestion and confirmation of a hypothesis.[13] For instance, if I say, "His behavior at that party revealed something to me," I imply not only that his behavior afforded me an occasion to postulate a new hypothesis about him or his personality, but also that his behavior constituted a strong case for that hypothesis. Beardsley, however, rejects the revelation theory of the cognitive value in art as a comprehensive theory for art in general. In fiction, Beardsley believes, the revelation theory faces a problem because while fiction may suggest a hypothesis about the world, or about the reality external to an aesthetic object, fiction cannot, due to its fictive nature, confirm such a hypothesis.[14]

However, avant-garde films, especially the structural films that I focus on in this essay, do not face the same kind of problems that concern Beardsley. Structural films are mostly nonfiction films. Furthermore, the hypothesis suggested by a structural film is usually not about the world or the reality outside the film; the hypothesis often regards the film medium itself.[15] An avant-garde film may not provide ample evidence for the new hypothesis suggested, since it is only one instance, but still can confirm the hypothesis by presenting a strong case that mandates the postulation of such a hypothesis. For example, Stan Brakhage's *Mothlight* (1963), comprised of insect parts, leaves, and various debris inserted between two strips of film, refutes the idea that the film medium is a photographic record of an object or a pro-filmic event that took place in front of the camera. Objects here are literally transported into the filmstrip! In this regard, *Mothlight* does offer a case for a new hypothesis about the film medium.[16] The presentation or reception of such a hypothesis in and of itself may not constitute an act of knowledge. However, it does grant the possibility that avant-garde film can contribute to one's acquisition or expansion of a certain type of knowledge.

As I have mentioned earlier, Carroll denies the possibility that an avant-garde film can explicate any theoretical assumptions underneath a theory by literalizing it. However, Carroll's view does not imply that avant-garde film cannot further one's knowledge: especially experiential knowledge. Snow's *Wavelength* is often addressed in relation to the famous debate in film studies between Stephen Heath and Noël Burch regarding the primary source of the "subject effect," the viewer's impression that both the story world and its narration process are structured around him or her. Heath argues that the subject effect is rendered via the viewer's alignment with the narrative, while Burch claims that it derives from organized perception via a particular type of film style.[17] The cognitive value of Snow's film does not derive from the fact that it provides such a crucial test case for these film theorists (on a personal note, and for the record, after reading so much about *Wavelength*, when I first saw the film, I thought to myself, "Burch is right!").

Snow must not have made this film to prove or disprove either theory, since his film preceded both Heath's and Burch's writings. Nor did Snow make the film to *illustrate* some philosophical issues. Rather, its significance lies in the fact that a viewer comes to an understanding of the issue at stake via his or her experience of the film. An experience of the film in and of itself does not constitute knowledge (or the expansion of one's knowledge) until it is combined with the rest of one's knowledge through inference and reasoning. In Snow's case, it is not merely the viewer's experience of certain cinematic effects that furthers one's knowledge about the filmic medium; it does so because it leads the viewer to examine his or her conception of the relationship between the perceptual effects that film as a medium is capable of rendering and the cinematic mechanism that achieves such an effect. James Peterson locates the cognitive value of avant-garde films in this very capacity: their capacity for the viewer to acquire both procedural knowledge and declarative knowledge. That is, the viewer comes to an understanding of filmmakers' concerns, including theoretical issues regarding the film medium itself, via his or her experience of the film.[18]

Avant-garde films, despite their associations with film theories, rarely satisfy the two requirements Carroll set out for a theory—generality and verifiability. To grant an avant-garde film its philosophical contribution, an important distinction should be made. One should note that a philosophical claim advanced by avant-garde film is something for the viewer to *infer*

via his or her own *experience* of the film. Carroll is correct in pointing out that avant-garde film rarely presents a self-contained coherent film theory within a film itself. However, the philosophical significance of avant-garde film lies in the fact that it suggests new hypotheses regarding the film medium. That is, avant-garde film often presents a case in which the viewer must reconsider and revise his or her own conceptions of film, which can subsequently further the viewer's knowledge about the medium.[19] The film-viewing process of avant-garde films often demands philosophical reflection from the viewer, especially with regard to the film medium.

In the remainder of this essay, I will examine the relationship between the cognitive value and aesthetic value of avant-garde film. If we grant that an avant-garde film can make a philosophical contribution by suggesting a hypothesis regarding the medium, a few questions still remain. To begin, how do we evaluate the cognitive value of films? Furthermore, does cognitive value necessarily enhance the aesthetic value of a film?

II. APPERCEPTION ON DISPLAY

The heavy emphasis placed on the cognitive value of avant-garde films tends to neglect the importance of other values avant-garde films offer. In a classroom setting, students often admit that they "get it," but they still do not enjoy avant-garde films. This brings us to an important question regarding the value of avant-garde film, especially the role of cognitive value in relation to the overall value that an avant-garde film embodies. Why is avant-garde film valuable to us? What are some of the reasons to cherish avant-garde films? Does the value of avant-garde film mainly derive from its cognitive value? Does the cognitive value of avant-garde film enhance aesthetic value in any way? I will first discuss ways we can evaluate the cognitive value of avant-garde films and then examine its relation to aesthetic value.

I have suggested in the previous section that the cognitive status of avant-garde film is comprised of its capacity both to suggest a hypothesis regarding the medium and to enable the furthering of one's knowledge of the medium.

How, then, can we compare cognitive value among avant-garde films? It may be more difficult to come up with a list of objective measures to determine how much an avant-garde film expands one's knowledge, as individual viewers have different ranges of knowledge about the film medium. However, there appears to be some consensus in terms of how to evaluate the significance of a hypothesis suggested by an avant-garde film: originality and consistency.

The theoretical contribution of an avant-garde film is often measured against its originality within an historical context. That is, what is significant about an avant-garde film is not the presentation of any hypothesis, but the presentation of a *new* hypothesis and a novel possibility for the medium. For example, some may view that Brakhage's abstract-expressionist films are less original than structural films at the level of cognitive value in the sense that Brakhage's conceptions of the filmmaker as the agent behind the camera and of film as a vehicle to express and convey the filmmaker's perception or vision are rooted in romanticism, already advanced in other art forms such as poetry or painting.

Conceptual consistency provides another criterion for an evaluation of the cognitive value of avant-garde films. If an avant-garde film embodies a philosophical claim, as with any other philosophical claim, it should be consistent. A lack of consistency at the level of the hypothesis inferred not only affects the cognitive status of the film, in that it is less coherent and thus less convincing, but it also can have an impact on the aesthetic value of the film (if, by "consistency," we mean not only consistency at the level of the philosophical claim, but also consistency in the relationship between the hypothesis that the film suggests and the evidence that the film provides as an example of that hypothesis). Lack of consistency (or better coherence between hypothesis and evidence) will have an impact on the unity of the work as a whole. In my view, consistency in the latter sense (in the assertion of a hypothesis and the providing of evidence) is worthy of further examination in that it illuminates the relationship between the cognitive and aesthetic value of avant-garde film. In the remainder of this essay, I offer Kurt Kren's *TV 15/67* as a test case.

Kren, together with Peter Kubelka, is often considered to be the father of European structural film. Malcolm Le Grice praises Kren's *TV* as the first apperceptive film that transfers the primary arena of structuralist activity to the viewing of the film itself.[20] Kren's *TV* is a black-and-white silent film with a running time of less than five minutes. It consists of repetitions of five different shots—most lasting less than two seconds—intercut with short black-leader spacing. All five shots are of the same scene at a dock and are shot from approximately the same camera position. Each shot contains similar components with slight variation, as described below.

Shot 1: Through a window, we see three girls sitting on a pillar in the background with their backs to the camera. Additionally, two men sit in silhouette in the foreground, blocking more than half of the screen.

Shot 2: We see the same girls seen in Shot 1, but their positions have changed: the girls on the left and right in Shot 1 have switched their positions. The girl now on the left in this shot is standing and looking at the other two sitting on the pillar. The girl on the left then turns around and looks back toward offscreen left. We also still see the two men in silhouette in the foreground.

Shot 3: The same three girls are in the background, and we see a woman and child pass by in mid-ground. As the woman and the child walk toward offscreen right, one man in the foreground bends toward screen left and blocks most of the screen.

Shot 4: The three girls in the background watch a ship pass by in distant background. As the ship moves toward screen left, the second man in the foreground moves to left.

Shot 5: There is now only one girl on the pillar and she is looking offscreen left. A man with a child passes by toward screen left in mid-ground. The two men in the foreground are still blocking much of the screen.

These five shots appear to be simple, but each shot mirrors and complements the other by exploring different planes and differing movements in screen direction. In Shot 1, the depth of the field is established via lighting and staging. Shot 2 is a variation of Shot 1: the two girls on the left and right switch their positions, while the girl in the middle stays in the same position. Two girls are contrasted via their clothing, with one wearing a black top and a light-color skirt and the other wearing a light-color sweater and a dark-color skirt. In Shot 3, the middle ground is explored via the two who pass by outside the window. In addition, the movement of the man in the foreground contrasts with the screen direction of this couple in the middle ground. Shot 4 explores another plane—the distant background—via the movement of the ship. Shot 5 balances out Shot 2. In both shots, the middle ground is explored with figure movement, but in opposite screen directions. Among the five shots, Shot 3 is the most elaborate. In this shot, three distinct planes are explored and figure movement seems perfectly choreographed: as soon as the woman and the child walk by outside the window, the man in the foreground bends over and blocks the whole screen as if it were a wipe.

Each shot is separated by a black screen. There is a longer space after every fifth shot, which suggests the clustering of shots into five-shot sequences. Furthermore, there occasionally are even longer breaks between these five-shot sequences, which suggests an additional level of sequencing, which I identify as "stanzas." The chart below depicts the order, variation, and grouping together of shots in the film. Although the ordering may seem mathematical, it is difficult to find a strict pattern, except that the first and last sequences are transposed. In each

stanza, one shot, the first shot shown, becomes salient through repetition and builds up a visual rhythm.

One of the functions of this apparent mathematical structure, as depicted below, is to enable the spectator to reflect on his or her cognitive and perceptual processes while watching the film. First, the spectator tries to identify and differentiate the five different shots. As shots are repeated, the spectator can focus on the shots themselves, on details such as differing spatial planes, and notice the balancing and complementing of screen direction within a single shot or among shots. For instance, in the stanza dominated by Shot 3, due to the repetition of this single shot, we cannot help but notice how beautifully figure movement is arranged. In addition, the apparent systematic permutation of shots in the film engages the spectator in a mental game. After a few sequences pass, the viewer tries to predict which shot will come next. The mental game between the viewer and the film gives rise to pleasure, as well as frustration, in the viewer—depending on how close each guess is.

The aesthetic value, however, of Kren's *TV* does not lie solely in its systematic structure; consider also its poetic imagery. Other structural films often reduce visual components to abstract shapes. For example, Snow's *Wavelength* and Ernie Gehr's *Serene Velocity* (1970) feature a loft and a corridor, respectively, and the visual patterns of these two films become quite abstract, dominated by the rectangular shape of the windows in the loft or the door in the corridor. The images in *TV*, on the other hand, attract us not only as gaming elements, but as beautiful poetic glimpses—evoking Symbolist poetry's interest in the epiphany and the

FIGURE 1. Short sequences in Kren's *TV*.

12345	11345	22451	33512	44513	55313	55133	54321
	11145	22251	33312	44435	55513		
	11141	22252	33313	44434			
		22422		44144			
		23222		45555			

fleeting image as a source of insight and emotive impetus. Shot 5 certainly evokes a mood of loneliness by featuring only a girl with her back to the camera sitting in the background by herself, especially since the previous shots have all shown her in the company of two other girls. The fidgety behavior of one of the girls in both Shots 1 and 2 not only provides rhythm upon the repetition of these shots, but also conveys a sense of boredom and the mundane.

How, then, should we evaluate Kren's film? Is his film aesthetically inferior to *Serene Velocity* or *Wavelength* because his film falls short of living up to structuralist ideals and principles? Or, rather, does his film suggest a new hypothesis regarding the relationship between the representational content of photographic images and their structural system—that is, that the latter cannot completely overwrite the former? To put it differently, is Kren's film aesthetically astonishing—at least to me—despite its lack of theoretic consistency or because of its complexity? In my view, Kren's case falls under the latter.

As Le Grice notes, Kren's film is more concerned with the relationship between apparent mathematical structures, poetic images, and moods manifested in images than with pure systematic structure (the film is not governed by real mathematical formula).[21] Although Kren's *TV* invites the viewer to predict the logic of the permutation, it defies our capacity to grasp the formula. His film also resists the distinction between abstract-expressionism and structuralism—hot versus cool—in terms of their emotive register. Despite the fact that structural films were developed in reaction to abstract-expressionist filmmakers such as Brakhage, whose films manifest the presence of the romantic artist behind the camera, the images of Kren's films are in no way neutral, arbitrary, or convenient fillers for a mathematical system. Images of Kren's films are, if not hot, at least warm. The very juxtaposition between poetic images and an apparent systematic structure adds complexity to his film. Despite the simplicity conveyed through the film's short duration and use of fewer than half a dozen repeated shots, a subtle emotive register certainly lurks in and enhances the aesthetic value of the film.

Kren's film neither betrays nor fails to correspond to structuralist ideals. Rather, it makes a different philosophical claim: that is, the

photographic content of a shot can defy the mathematical structure imposed on the image. The complexity of Kren's film, which I have attempted to demonstrate above, should not, however, be confused with inconsistency or contradiction. That is, complexity in this context is not opposed to theoretical consistency or correspondence as defined above, but is rather opposed to simplicity or obtrusiveness.

Certainly, one might question to what extent I can infer such a claim from Kren's film with any authority. Although I perhaps grant such epistemic difficulty embedded in the interpretation of individual films, including this one, such a concession does not seriously damage the point that I am attempting to make here: the cognitive value of an avant-garde film can enhance the value, including the aesthetic value, of the film, but only if it is successfully manifested in the film. That is, the film in question must provide a strong case to postulate a new hypothesis. In this respect, one must suppose some sort of consistency (or coherence) between the theoretical or philosophical claim that a film embodies and the film as an instance or evidence in support of such a claim. If so, then when a student says, "I get it, but I don't appreciate the film," it means either that the film failed to provide a strong case to infer its claim—even though the claim can be detected—or that the fault lies with the student, who in fact did not "get it"!

In this essay, I attempted to examine the relationship between avant-garde film and philosophy. Against Carroll's claim that avant-garde film should be distinguished from theory proper, I have argued that the philosophical potential or contribution of avant-garde films should be found somewhere else—that is, in their ability to propose new hypotheses about the medium and to expand one's knowledge of the medium by reflecting on one's own experience of the films. In the latter half of this essay, I have examined some of the ways in which we can postulate the relationship between the cognitive value and aesthetic value of avant-garde film: the former can enhance the latter only when the claim detected in the film is successfully supported in the film and thus augments the consistency of the film as a whole. In this respect, Kren's *TV 15/67* certainly proves itself to be of high cognitive and aesthetic value.[22]

JINHEE CHOI
Film Studies, School for Studies in Art and Culture
Carleton University
Ottawa, Ontario
K1S 5B6
Canada

INTERNET: jinhee_choi@carleton.ca

1. P. Adams Sitney, *Visionary Film: The American Avant-Garde: 1943–1978*, 2nd ed. (New York: Oxford University Press, 1977), p. 370.

2. Annette Michelson, "Toward Snow," in *The Avant-Garde Film Reader*, ed. P. Adams Sitney (New York University Press, 1978), p. 175.

3. Sitney, *Visionary Film*, p. 382.

4. Andrew Light, *Reel Arguments: Film, Philosophy and Social Criticism* (Boulder: Westview, 2003); Joseph Kupfer, *Visions of Virtue in Popular Film* (Boulder: Westview, 1999); Bruce Russell, "The Philosophical Limits of Film," Special Interest Edition on the Films of Woody Allen, *Film and Philosophy* (2000): 163–167; Lester Hunt, "Motion Pictures as a Philosophical Resource," in *Philosophy of Film and Motion Pictures: An Anthology*, ed. Noël Carroll and Jinhee Choi (Oxford: Blackwell Publishing, 2005).

5. Noël Carroll, "Art, Narrative, and Moral Understanding," in *Aesthetics and Ethics: Essays at the Intersection*, ed. Jerrold Levinson (New York: Cambridge University Press, 1998), pp. 126–160.

6. Noël Carroll, "Avant-Garde Film and Film Theory," in *Theorizing the Moving Image* (New York: Cambridge University Press, 1996), pp. 162–168.

7. Carroll, "Avant-Garde Film and Film Theory," p. 163.

8. Carroll, "Avant-Garde Film and Film Theory," p. 164.

9. Peter Gidal, "An Interview with Hollis Hampton," in *Experimental Cinema, The Film Reader*, ed. Wheeler Winston and Gwendolyn Audrey Foster (New York: Routledge, 2002), pp. 274–276.

10. Carroll quickly adds two more possibilities in which avant-garde films are linked to a theory: answering and compatibility. With answering, films can answer or refer to other films. By "compatibility," Carroll refers to the fact that a film may be compatible with various theories and invites multiple readings and interpretations. Carroll, however, dismisses the theoretical potential of these two in that the films themselves constitute neither an argument nor evidence for a theory.

11. Carroll, "Avant-Garde Film and Film Theory," p. 166.

12. Carroll, "Avant-Garde Film and Film Theory," p. 165.

13. Monroe C. Beardsley, *Aesthetics: Problems in the Philosophy of Criticism*, 2nd ed. (Indianapolis: Hackett Publishing, 1981), p. 379.

14. Bruce Russell finds the philosophical limitations of fiction film for a similar reason. That is, a narrative fiction film can provide a counterexample to a philosophical thesis, but it cannot provide evidence due to its fictional nature. See his "The Philosophical Limits of Film."

15. By this I am not suggesting that all avant-garde films are only concerned with medium specificity. The counter-cultural aspect, often evidenced in punk cinema and other transgressive films, constitutes one of the most important characteristics of avant-garde cinema concerning world and/or dominant culture.

16. In my personal conversations with Carroll, Carroll has acknowledged that avant-garde films such as Ernie Gehr's *Serene Velocity* (1970) can make a philosophical claim in that they encourage the viewer to postulate that what makes film a film is its moving image.

17. Stephen Heath, "Narrative Space," *Screen* 17 (1976): 68–112; Noël Burch, "Narrative/Diegesis: Thresholds, Limits," *Screen* 23 (1982): 16–33.

18. James Peterson, "Is a Cognitive Approach to the Avant-garde Cinema Perverse?" in *Post-Theory*, ed. David Bordwell and Noël Carroll (University of Wisconsin Press, 1996), pp. 110–111.

19. I do not indicate that Carroll denies such significance. His contention is rather that such reflection does not necessarily render an original philosophical argument or claim. See Carroll, "Avant-Garde Film and Film Theory," p. 166.

20. Malcolm Le Grice, "Kurt Kren," *Studio International*, November (1975): 188.

21. Malcolm Le Grice, *Abstract Film and Beyond* (MIT Press, 1977) p. 98.

22. This essay underwent various versions, starting as a paper written for the avant-garde film class I took with Ben Singer. I thank Ben Singer for introducing me to the sheer beauty of Kren's films. I also thank Noël Carroll, Murray Smith, and Thomas Wartenberg for their suggestions on subsequent versions of this essay. Vince Bohlinger proofread this essay numerous times whenever I changed its direction. I thank him for that.

NOËL CARROLL

Philosophizing Through the Moving Image:
The Case of *Serene Velocity*

As the culture becomes more and more saturated with moving images—via television, video cassettes, DVDs, video games, computer games, and that old stand-by, theatrical movies—educators understandably attempt to harness moving-image media for their own aims. They hope to enlist the seductive potential of the moving image for pedagogical purposes. And this is as true of philosophers as it is of other educators. Thus we encounter with increasing frequency books with titles like *Philosophy and ___* where the blank is filled-in with the name of some moving-image art form, like "film" or "the movies," or, even more specifically, by the names of particular motion picture accomplishments such as *Seinfeld* (Jerry Seinfeld and Larry David, 1990–1998), *The Simpsons* (Matt Groening, 1989–), or *The Sopranos* (David Chase, 1999–). In many of the essays one finds in these volumes, and in the journal *Film and Philosophy*, individual episodes and/or movies are discussed as illustrations of various philosophical problems, dilemmas, and positions. Perhaps some science-fiction depiction of the world the day after a nuclear holocaust will be used to portray the notion of the state of nature. Or the character Data in *Star Trek: The Next Generation* (Gene Roddenberry, 1987–1994) may be discussed in order to motivate the question of whether artificial intelligences could deserve civil rights. Likewise, a film or TV program might be employed to sketch the problem of subjectivism in morality. And so forth.

Clearly, the moving image can be an educational resource for philosophers. Examples from film and television can be deployed to set up philosophical problems, to raise philosophical questions, to motivate philosophical debates, and to illustrate and thereby clarify philosophical positions for students. If for no other reason, inasmuch as the moving image is such a familiar feature of the students' environment, teachers should avail themselves of it as a way of making accessible the often alien and strange preoccupations of philosophy. However, once the moving image is admitted into the precincts of philosophy, questions, undoubtedly philosophical in nature, arise about the extent of what the moving image and its prodigious genres have to offer the field. Yes, motion pictures may illustrate philosophical positions, and that can be beneficial in the classroom. But can motion pictures contribute more to philosophy than that?

In particular, can motion pictures *do* philosophy, or can they only ever illustrate philosophy? It is one thing to provide an example of a pre-existing philosophical position that has been already authored and articulated elsewhere. It is something distinctly different to create a philosophical position. With this difference in mind, then, could there be a motion picture that we would treat as an original piece of philosophizing on a par, for example, with a text by Ludwig Wittgenstein? Or are there philosophical grounds for suspecting that such an achievement is beyond the means of the moving image? That is our question.

In this essay, I will argue that this is a live possibility, since I hope to establish that there is at least one film—*Serene Velocity* (1970) by

Ernie Gehr—that may be said, unequivocally, to be an example of doing philosophy through film.[1] I do not think that this is the only example. But one example is enough to quell skeptical misgivings about the possibility altogether of producing philosophy by means of the moving image. Furthermore, I will also discuss the ramifications that the possibility of doing philosophy in film has for the thesis that a film interpretation might be philosophical in the strong sense of being an original addition to the fund of philosophical knowledge. But before turning to that issue, I must address the reasons that philosophical skeptics advance for denying, on conceptual grounds, that what we might call "philosophical motion pictures" are feasible.

II. SKEPTICAL MISGIVINGS: ROUND 1

Initially, the question of whether a motion picture can convey philosophy seems like a no-brainer.[2] Of course, motion pictures can deliver up philosophy. Roberto Rossellini made a marvelous series of television programs of the lives of various philosophers, including Socrates, Augustine, Pascal, and Marx. As actors declaimed the historic texts of these giants, there is no doubt that philosophy was being propounded directly on film. However, the skeptic with respect to motion picture philosophizing is unlikely to accept works like Rossellini's or, for that matter, Derek Jarman's film of Wittgenstein's life, as examples of what would count as philosophy on film. For, the skeptic will argue, philosophy is not so much made in films like this as it is recounted.

That is, the question of whether the motion picture can be a vehicle for philosophy is really a question about whether the moving image can produce original philosophy and not just illustrate or recount already existing philosophy. Can motion pictures *do* philosophy? Clearly, an actor dressed up and mustachioed like René Descartes reciting his *Meditations* on camera is not authoring philosophy firsthand, but merely parroting it.

Nevertheless, it may seem that Rossellini's films—even if they are not examples of *doing* philosophy through film themselves—at least indicate for us the way in which motion pictures might be deployed in order to do so. Instead of showing actors mouthing the classic doctrines of dead philosophers onscreen, get some live philosophers to present their cutting-edge ideas to the camera: have Hilary Putnam discourse about brains in vats and their implications, or have Christine Korsgaard improvise on the Kingdom of Ends. Maybe we could film Arthur Danto developing new themes on the transfiguration of the commonplace while strolling through a gallery of nine indiscernible red paintings. Would not any of these prospective blockbusters—and a horde of easily imagined comparable ones—count as instances of motion pictures that propound philosophy, original philosophy and not reruns?

My hunch is that the skeptic will not buy these examples. For though state-of-the-art philosophy may be found *in* these motion pictures, it has not really been made *by means of* the art of the moving image—namely, by means of the characteristic expositional devices of the various motion picture genres, including their recurrent visual, audio, and narrative structures. Here, the underlying presupposition is that if we are to say that a motion picture does philosophy, it must be a case where the *art* of the motion picture contributes to the construction of the philosophy in question. Simply mechanically recording a talking head, no matter how eminent and profound, spouting philosophy, no matter how unprecedented, will not merit being called a case of a motion picture creating philosophy. For the philosophy in question is only a function of a lecture that happens contingently to be housed in a film. The philosophy is not articulated to any appreciable degree by means of the art of the motion picture. Being embodied in moving pictures adds nothing to the articulation of the philosophy at hand.

In order, then, to make it as an instance of moving-image philosophizing, a specimen must develop an original philosophical idea—rather than merely illustrate, recount, or record one— and it must do so in such a way that the art of the moving image plays some role in the articulation of the philosophical point at issue. Needless to say, the notion of the art of the moving image here is a bit hazy. However, perhaps it can be given some measure of operational specificity by stipulating that it involves the mobilization of some portion of the arsenal of expressive strategies of moving-image media *over and above* the mere capacity to record philosophical lectures.

Nevertheless, as soon as we clarify what is at stake—as we have just done—in alleging that moving pictures might make philosophy, the skeptic is ready to pounce. For if it is required that the philosophy in question be elaborated by means of the art of the moving image, then the skeptic will maintain that there are insurmountable limitations to the art of moving images such that it is not credible to suppose that it could ever really contribute to the production of philosophical knowledge.

The first skeptical objection begins by taking note that the moving image typically concerns particulars, whereas philosophy is general. G. W. Pabst's *Geheimnisse einer Seele* [*Secrets of a Soul*] (1926) was intended to be something of a primer in psychoanalysis (though one that perhaps soft pedals some of Freud's more "scandalous" claims about sexuality). The script was developed in consultation with the psychoanalyst Hans Sachs and it presumably expresses some of Sachs's own individual take on psychoanalytic theory. Let us suppose that psychoanalysis is a philosophical system, or that at least part of it is. *Secrets of a Soul* was, formally speaking, an ambitious, state-of-the-art piece of filmmaking dedicated to putting forth elements of psychoanalytic theorizing. Psychoanalytic ideas were embodied through advanced motion picture techniques of editing, composition, and special effects. Focusing on a case study, *Secrets of a Soul* illustrates certain psychoanalytic doctrines with cinematic élan.

However, the doctrines it illustrates are putatively general; maybe they are even thought to be universal. Consequently, the skeptic observes, a film about a *single* case study, even one that exploits the resources of the art of the moving image as masterfully as *Secrets of a Soul* does, could never be imagined to deliver knowledge of the general scope to which philosophy pretends, since it is based on nothing more than a single instance. That is, given the supposed particularity of the moving image, it provides insufficient evidence for the allegedly philosophical, general claims it may appear to proffer. Due to its chronic lack of the amount of evidence that it takes to justify general claims, the moving image, the skeptic surmises, is not a proper channel for conveying general knowledge.

For, typically, the moving image trades in a single case, and one case is not enough to warrant the sort of general claims that are the stuff of philosophy.

So the skeptic argues: philosophical knowledge, like all knowledge, requires, among other things, justified belief. A moving image may be capable of conveying a belief and even of promoting a general belief. However, the tendency of the motion picture toward particularity, both in its images and its stories, entails that it is highly unlikely that a motion picture could ever justify any general or universal belief of the sort to which philosophy aspires. Consequently, the art of the motion picture is an implausible source of philosophical knowledge.

Here, it needs to be said that the skeptic is willing to make one concession: a moving picture, in developing a single-case scenario, may succeed in crafting a counterexample to a philosophical claim, since one instance can unhorse a universal proposition. Woody Allen's *Crimes and Misdemeanors* (1989) may conceivably serve to refute a philosophical thesis of the order of "necessarily, crime does not pay" or "immorality can never co-exist with happiness." Nevertheless, apart from contriving counterexamples to universal philosophical claims, moving pictures, the skeptic contends, are philosophically incompetent. For in specializing in the individual case, they are deficient in the wherewithal to marshal the weight of evidence required to justify general beliefs.[3]

But maybe this objection only pertains to certain kinds of motion pictures, namely, character-focused narratives? Yet this is not the only way to promote a general conception cinematically; there are alternative ways of making motion pictures. V. I. Pudovkin's *Mekhanika golovnov mozga* [*Mechanics of the Brain*] (1926) is a celebration of Pavlovian psychology. It envisions the marriage of classical conditioning and communism as an avenue to some future social utopia. Let us assume that it, or, at least, parts of it, represent an instance of social philosophy. The film does not provide us with just one example of classical conditioning, but many, and of different orders of complexity. Would this overcome the skeptic's objection?

Probably not. For many of the "experiments" in the film were staged for the camera. They were not documentary footage—traces of actual, unstaged events—but enactments, enactments, moreover, made up in order to depict classical conditioning and its potentials in an exceptionally favorable light. Consequently, though *Mechanics of the Brain* provides many more cases than one, it is still evidentially challenged, since the "evidence" has been constructed precisely to cast to best effect the general hypothesis the film is advocating. Or, to put it less charitably, the evidence has been cooked. Moreover, when one recalls that many of the films that may be said to do philosophy are fictional—with made-up stories expressly designed to fit their general theme—one may feel compelled to agree with the skeptic that much of the evidence in fiction films is not only statistically insufficient, but arguably tainted (or skewed) to boot.

So far the skeptic has maintained that moving pictures cannot support philosophical claims because typically they are woefully short on the evidence required to substantiate general assertions and, in many cases, the "evidence," in the form of made-up examples, that they do possess has been concocted in a way that is inherently defective due to bias. In short, motion pictures are flawed evidentially.

This objection is very telling in the cases of *Secrets of a Soul* and *Mechanics of the Brain* and the kinds of theories they advertise. Yet perhaps the reason here is not one that is readily generalizable to every type of philosophy. For even if we allow that these films are in part philosophical, we must also grant that they are also presentations of theories that are largely empirical, scientific theories. The question of the evidential base of these films bears primarily on the empirical claims they make. The objections the skeptic brings against these films hit their mark so accurately because the philosophies in question, supposing that they possess philosophical dimensions, are also substantive psychological theories.

Yet these problems will not arise where the philosophical subject matter in question is not empirical, but conceptual. Here, I am not intending to claim controversially that all philosophy, properly so called, is only a matter of concepts. My argument merely requires that there be a dimension of philosophy that is duly regarded as conceptual or, at least, not straightforwardly empirical. If a motion picture were to employ the arts of the motion picture to articulate some original conceptual point, it is not clear that the sorts of skeptical misgivings rehearsed thus far with respect to the recurring lack of evidence in motion pictures would have any purchase.

Furthermore, I maintain that *Serene Velocity* is such a motion picture.

III. *SERENE VELOCITY*, META-CINEMA, AND THE NATURE OF THE MOVING IMAGE

Serene Velocity is a film by Ernie Gehr that was made in 1970. It is an example of what is often referred to as *structural film*, though I prefer to call the relevant genre minimal film because it is aligned with the fine art labeled minimalism in its (1) pursuit of reflexivity (2) through reduction.[4] That is, minimal art in general and minimalist film in particular is reflexive in the sense that its subject matter is the nature of the pertinent art form itself and/or the experiences the works in question engender. The minimalist artwork is intended to disclose essential features of the art form or medium it inhabits, and/or is designed to promote apperceptive reflection on the part of the viewer with regard to the phenomenological dimensions of his or her encounter with the work, including the way the work modulates or conditions said experience. Moreover, the minimalist work provokes reflexive reflection on itself and/or its associated experiences by employing highly reductive or limited means, such as, in the case of painting, the repetition of a single geometrical configuration or even just the presentation of a single colored shape.[5]

Given its concern with the essential features and phenomenology of art, the dominant themes of minimalism are clearly philosophical. The thinking behind minimalism is indebted to Clement Greenberg, though he himself deplored the movement. Among other things, minimalism involves the notion of an artwork as a form of critique. The artwork is thought to be an occasion for revealing the conditions of possibility of the art form or medium of which it is a member. This view has come to be referred to as modernism, and minimalism was arguably the last gesture of modernism before the advent of postmodernism with its anti-modernist and anti-minimalist agenda.

Participants in the artworld in which minimalism thrived—including artists, curators, critics, gallery owners, and informed civilians—greeted and assessed the work in question within a modernist interpretive framework. That is, they composed a community of discourse in which the artwork was expected to suggest some comment about the nature of its art form or medium and/or to promote some recognition of the way in which some typical feature or strategy of the art form shapes and conditions our experience of it. The reductive vocabulary of the minimalist artwork facilitated getting to the essence of art and/or the experience thereof by clearing away everything but the most fundamental variables. Such works were "minimal" in the sense of being honed down to the basic features the artist intended to interrogate.

Minimalism is best known as a movement in painting and sculpture, but it also found resonance in music, dance, and even theater. It was also a strong presence in the avant-garde or experimental filmworld of the late 1960s and early 1970s. Among the practitioners of this tendency were Michael Snow, George Landow (a.k.a. Owen Land), Hollis Frampton, Paul Sharits, Tony Conrad, Anthony McCall, and Ernie Gehr.

Minimalist filmmaking is a form of metacinema, producing films about film. Many of these films, in turn, were "minimal" films—films stripped down to just those elements the filmmaker thought were minimally required in order for a candidate to count as a film. The minimal film, were there such a thing, would, in other words, discover the essential cinema. A film historian might even propose that one of the preoccupations of this movement was the quest to make the minimal film, the film that would reveal the essence of film. Andy Warhol's *Empire* (1964) may be one example of this tendency; *Serene Velocity* another.[6]

Broadly speaking, minimalist films generally fall into two major stylistic categories. The first, which reminds one of gallery minimalism, comprises films that might be said to have a discernible geometrical shape. McCall's *Line Describing a Cone* (1973) proposes projected light as a constituent element of cinema. The film begins as an imageless, laserlike shaft of light hits the screen and then, over a period of thirty minutes, the initial dot widens and the projector beam overhead becomes a cone whose apex is the lens of the projector. Here, since there is so little else to attend to other than the shape of the projector's main of light, the viewer (or, at least, the viewer who is party to the minimalist language game), battening upon this simplified, legible form streaming above his or her head, supposedly educes or is reminded that the projection and shaping of light is putatively an essential feature of cinema.[7] Indeed, due to their emphasis on the shape of the hallway, many of the still frame enlargements from *Serene Velocity*, the film that concerns us, look like minimalist paintings.

The second leading strategy of minimalist filmmaking involves the creation of a highly simplified, readily identified system or procedure whose underlying principle of organization can be grasped almost immediately. A good example of the systemic approach to minimalist filmmaking is Frampton's *(nostalgia)* (1971). The film comprises a series of individual photographs of things like bathroom stalls and leftover, moldering pasta. Each photo lies on a slow-burning hot plate and gradually incinerates before our eyes. Each shot lasts just as long as it takes each photo to turn to ash. As each photograph ignites, we hear on the soundtrack a description of the photo we are about to see.

The structure or system of the film is conspicuously legible. As we watch the previously described photograph burn, we hear about the one we will see next. The effect of the time lag between the description and the image is to alert us to the categorical difference between verbal language and picturing as symbol systems. None of the descriptions ever fully prepares us for the pictures we subsequently encounter. Thus, our attention is called to the incommensurability of words and images.

Made in 1971, *(nostalgia)* was, in context, a cautionary take for the semiotics-crazy 1970s, a time when film theorists and even some filmmakers were tempted to regard film as a language. *(nostalgia)* is an intervention in that discussion that reflects reflexively on the photographic dimension of film in order to underscore an essential contrast with language. The system of the film—the sequence of word followed by image—tells the tale of the disparity between the two, serving to correct even the theoretically knowledgeable viewer's inclination to take seriously locutions like "the language of cinema."[8]

Likewise, Warhol's *Empire* may be seen as falling into the simplified-procedure category of minimal filmmaking since there is scarcely a more austere cinematic *modus operandi* conceivable than merely turning the camera on and pointing it. Moreover, *Empire* is meta-cinematic, foregrounding the recording dimension of film with a vengeance.

Gehr's *Serene Velocity* weds the two stylistic tendencies of minimal filmmaking. It has both a legible shape and a legible system. It is based on a zoom shot of an empty green institutional hallway, such as one might find in a hospital or a high school. So the film, as well as sometimes looking like a minimalist painting, has the ultimate shape of a straight line as it makes its way through the corridor. However, it is a broken straight line because of the way this zoom shot is regularly readjusted. This is where the systemic aspect comes in.

The filmmaker plays the zoom lens on his camera like the slide on a trombone—moving it forward and backward at a regular pace. As a result, the different focal lengths of the zoom shot are juxtaposed at uniform intervals to each other, resulting in different phenomenological effects. For example, when slightly dissimilar segments of the zoom shots are adjacent to each other, the screen becomes animated and the hallway appears to give birth to the impression of movement.

Here is a canonical description of *Serene Velocity* by P. Adams Sitney, the leading chronicler of the American avant-garde cinema.

The filmmaker positioned his tripod within the corridor and then proceeded to alter his zoom lens every four frames. At first the shifts are not dramatic. He alternates four frames at 50 mm with four frames at 55 mm. After a considerable period the differential increases: 45 mm to 60 mm. Thus, the film proceeds with increasing optical shocks. In this system, the zoom never "moves." The illusion of movement comes about from the adjustment of the eye from one sixth of a second of a distant image to one sixth of a second of a nearer one. Although the absolute rhythm never changes, the film reaches a crescendo because of the extreme illusion of distance by the end. Furthermore, Gehr cyclically shifts the degree of exposure of every frame in the phrases of four. In its

shape, *Serene Velocity* moves from a vibrating pulse within an optical depth to an accordion-like slamming and stretching of the visual field.[9]

Generated by a simple decision procedure, *Serene Velocity* produces a series of effects that within the context of the world of structural filmmaking and minimalist art are readily interpreted by participants in the language game of structural film as comments on the nature or essence of film. Of these, one of the most important for our purposes is the way Gehr makes the impression of movement the star of his film. As Sitney notes, at first, the film seems virtually static. One might imagine that one is watching a succession of slides rather than a motion picture. But as the zoom shots converge in configuration, apparent movement erupts from the screen where there was only stillness earlier.

The film functions, among other things, as an object lesson in the principles of animation. That is, it reminds us of how animation works and, by extension, reminds us that this is the secret behind the movement in all films. The four-frame-shot segments play the role of frames; they last long enough for us to register them as individual units. Thus, when their juxtaposition to other four-frame units bursts into tumultuous movement, the underlying dynamics of the movement in films become visually palpable. The title *Serene Velocity* itself sounds like an oblique way of recalling the process that makes movies move—that is, the movement (the velocity) comes from stillness (*serenely* still pictures).

The juxtaposition of moments of stillness and moments of movement in *Serene Velocity* invites the viewer to reflect on the difference between photography and cinematography. The difference, of course, as the film vividly demonstrates, is the possibility of movement.[10] *Serene Velocity* is the type of film that we are wont to call experimental. In this case, the label is apposite, since the film functions like a philosophical thought experiment, except rather than being articulated in words, as Danto confects his thought experiments in articles like "Moving Pictures," Gehr has literally realized this experiment in living color.[11]

Gehr has made something that everyone would be willing to agree belongs under the concept of the motion picture, if only minimally, and he has done so in a way that beckons us to notice the way in which moving pictures are categorically different from still pictures such as paintings, slides, and photographs. The distinction between motion pictures and photographs is particularly worthy of note, since it was the case in the early 1970s that many film theorists remained disposed to regard photography as the essence of cinema (was that not why it was called *film*?). Instead, Gehr proposes movement as an essential feature of cinema, one that has special pride of place for the philosophical definition of the medium insofar as it signals the very species to which films belong—*motion* pictures or, as I prefer to say, *moving* images.

Within the communicative context of minimalist art, it is more than merely appropriate to expect a film like *Serene Velocity* to suggest something about the nature of the art form or the medium to which it belongs. Clearly, the film is about movement—movement versus stillness. Since it is a film, if only minimally, it is more than likely that it is advancing movement as the minimal condition for membership in the art form to which it belongs. That is, given that everyone will agree that it is an instance of cinema, then, if we ask ourselves what about it leads us to categorize it as cinema rather than as a succession of still photographs (after the fashion of an automated slide show), we will feel compelled to say our assessment is based on the fact that it imparts the impression of movement. That, I believe, is our only recourse. Therefore, movement (or the possibility of movement) is an essential attribute of what it takes to count as an instance of film.

If the preceding paragraph is persuasive, then it would appear that *Serene Velocity* is an instance of philosophizing through moving images. Its topic, the nature of the motion picture, is unquestionably philosophical. This is surely not the only question that a philosopher may ask of motion pictures, but it is undeniably one of them. Moreover, *Serene Velocity* proposes its answer to that question by means of the art of the motion picture—by the juxtaposition of settings on the zoom lens. Indeed, the film and its argumentative purport is entirely an affair of visual invention, thoroughly without words, except for the title. It should also be

stressed that in its election of movement as an essential feature of film, *Serene Velocity* is a significant piece of *original* philosophizing. To my knowledge, the importance of movement to the conceptual analysis of cinema was not advanced and defended by means of philosophical argumentation in print until 1979 when Danto published his essay "Moving Pictures," whereas *Serene Velocity* premiered nine years earlier. Since philosophical theses, like the belief in free will, quite often preexist their philosophical articulation in the culture, in establishing when a philosophical proposal is original, we need to look to see not just when the idea was first aired, but when it is first made argumentatively compelling.[12]

Moreover, if we allow that the experimental film *Serene Velocity* is something like the celluloid equivalent or embodiment of the kind of thought experiments that philosophers of the moving image write up in their treatises, then it makes no difference that it articulates a general philosophical claim on the basis of a single case—indeed, a single case that has been expressly constructed to support precisely the conclusion that movement is an essential defining feature of all motion pictures. For the conclusion is conceptual and not empirical and, therefore, unscathed by the skeptic's misgivings regarding the evidential limitation of movies.

IV. THE SKEPTIC RESPONDS

Though *Serene Velocity* is but a single case, it may nevertheless disclose to us that the possibility of movement is a necessary criterion for our application of the concept of film. For conceptual analysis does not depend on amassing a vast selection of films and then finding their common feature by way of enumerative induction; conceptual analysis logically precedes the empirical toting up of the features of film because before we start counting, we need to define what we are counting; we need, for example, a way of sorting films from other things, like slide shows. This is the role of conceptual analysis and a single example prefabricated to zero-in on the *sine qua non* of motion pictures can direct reason to the correct conclusion. The aptness and comprehensiveness of a candidate induced in this manner is tested in the laboratory of the mind by a process of reflective equilibrium against our background of real-world experiences and our web of beliefs. Inasmuch as philosophy as conceptual analysis is not a simple empirical venture, a motion picture that qualifies as this type of philosophy would not be stigmatized by the putative evidential liabilities adduced earlier by the skeptic.

But, the skeptic will retort, philosophical knowledge of the conceptual sort is still a matter of *justified* belief. It still requires support. In the case of conceptual knowledge, the justification of a philosophical claim will come in the form of argument and/or analysis. *Serene Velocity* may evoke the belief that movement is an essential feature of film in the mind of the viewer. But, the skeptic charges, it does not substantiate that view by means of argument and/or analysis. Whereas previously the skeptic contended that the problem with delivering philosophy through film was the lack of empirical evidence, the charge now is that films lack argumentation. This, it might be added, is especially obvious in the case of *Serene Velocity*, since, as already observed, it is literally silent. Moreover, it might be added that in the case where films contain arguments, like the trial scene in King Vidor's *The Fountainhead* (1949), all the argument (and, therefore, all the philosophy) is in the speeches—that is, we may be back at the problem of the mere recording of talking heads.

The preceding objection to the philosophical status of *Serene Velocity*, however, seems to me to rest on too narrow a view of what counts as philosophical argumentation—even at the hallowed meetings of the American Philosophical Association. For a standard piece of philosophical operating equipment includes the thought experiment. Moreover, the thought experiment is patently a form of argumentation. This is obviously the case with respect to the counterexample whose task is to negate philosophical generalizations. A possible, by our lights, generally fictional (or made-up) case—say, of a jealous husband asking you where you put his revolver—is enough to undermine the universal proposition "Never lie."

Thought experiments can also be designed to reach positive philosophical conclusions. John Rawls asks us to arrive at the fundamental principles of justice by inviting us to indulge a thought experiment in which we set to determining what would count as a fair social order from behind a veil of ignorance. Rawls does not take a statistical survey of people's responses nor does he propose a deduction moving forth from first principles in order to obtain his conclusions. He encourages us to reflect on a certain array of circumstances in such a way that we will arrive at the intended result on our own through a process of reflective equilibrium.

An argument need not be spelled out deductively or inductively step by step in order to count as an argument. The thought experiment is an argumentative strategy that works by guiding the reasoning of the listener to the desired conclusion ineluctably, rather as the punch line of a joke leads the listener to its interpretation. With a thought experiment, the argument, so to speak, transpires in the movement of thought in the reader's mind and not necessarily on the page. The thought experiment engages the reflective resources of the listener—his or her beliefs about the world and his or her conceptual framework—to come to a result. Like the rhetorical question, the thought experiment is a way of advancing a conclusion and, correspondingly, it counts as a philosophical argument, generously construed. If it did not and the skeptic's assertion that philosophy requires argument is correct, much of what we now count as philosophy, motivated by argumentative thought experiments, would fall by the wayside.

But if philosophers are entitled to deploy thought experiments argumentatively in defense of their conceptual analyses, why should artists, including minimalist filmmakers, not be accorded a parallel privilege with respect to their experiments? Danto imagines a minimal film of the title page of *War and Peace* to promote his conviction that movement is a necessary condition of film.[13] Is what Danto has done in principle different than what Gehr has done with *Serene Velocity*?

Both have invented minimal films—films pared down to their putatively minimal constituents—for the purpose of probing the concept of the motion picture, and both have done so in a way that reveals that the prospect of movement is the crucial differentiae that separates the film from its near neighbors, such as the photograph. The only difference is that you can project Gehr's film, but not Danto's. So if descriptions of minimal films can function argumentatively or analytically as thought experiments that illuminate the conceptual structure of motion pictures, then there seems no reason to deny that actual experimental films may operate in the same way. Parity of reasoning requires no less. Thought-experimental films and actual experimental films ought to be on a par here.[14]

One objection that the skeptic is apt to voice is that with a philosophical thought experiment, we know what its objective is. But who seeing *Serene Velocity* has any idea of what Gehr is up to? However, the anticipated answer to this rhetorical question is not accurate. Though it may be true that most average filmgoers, accustomed exclusively to the mainstream, narrative commercial cinema, were at a loss viewing *Serene Velocity*, those who followed the conversation of avant-garde, experimental film knew right out of the gate, so to say, what was at stake in *Serene Velocity*. The situation would appear to be no different than what frequently occurs after a philosophy presentation. Someone imagines a case without announcing its point ahead of time; and everyone familiar with the context of the debate sees its putative significance, sans prefatory remarks. Conversants who know the conceptual lay of the land have no need of an advance road map; they know where they are. Ditto participants in the experimental film-world. We would not deny the aforesaid argumentative exchange was philosophical because outsiders, not party to the context of the discussion, would be apt to be mystified. Nor should we deny that prepared viewers were unaware of the point that Gehr was making in the way he made *Serene Velocity*.

The skeptic regarding the philosophical status of *Serene Velocity* may also allege that when it comes to genuine philosophical thought experiments, there is always an elucidation of its implications. However, there is no such accompanying explanation with *Serene Velocity*; it is, after all, mute. But, again, the skeptic's generalizations concerning thought experimentation here are too hasty. Wittgenstein posed thought experiments whose precise ramifications were unstated; he left them to be worked out in the minds of the audience. But they were no less thought experiments for being less than user-friendly. Nor were they something other than philosophy because they were not perspicuously transparent.

And again, philosophers in the thick of philosophical discussion constantly trade thought experiments without pedantically spelling out their thrust to others in the know. It is the thought experiment that does the philosophical work, that moves the mind of the prepared listener, and not the accompanying exegesis. Indeed, most often, the prepared listener may have no need for the exegesis.

The skeptic should not mistake the accompanying exegesis for the argument. It is the thought experiment that constitutes the argument, not the prosaic explanation of the thought experiment. The skeptic must not confuse a predilection for explicitness for argumentation. Moreover, the skeptic should also remember that a taste for explicitness over implicitness marks a difference in philosophical style and not the distinction between philosophy and something else that is supposedly not philosophy. Consequently, it is not a failure of *Serene Velocity* that it leaves implicit its relevance to the philosophical discussion to which it belongs, since the experiment that Gehr has invented is enough to move the mind of the prepared viewer to the recognition of movement as an essential feature of film.

Therefore, since the actual is possible and since there is at least one actual case of philosophizing through the motion picture, namely, Gehr's *Serene Velocity*, the option of full-blooded, genuinely philosophical moving-image artworks is a live one.[15] Furthermore, a minimal film does not argue for an essential feature of film simply by possessing one. It must make the feature salient, as, arguably, *Serene Velocity* does with respect to movement.

V. THE POSSIBILITY OF INTERPRETATION AS PHILOSOPHY

Perhaps some motion pictures are philosophical in the robust sense discussed above. That still leaves open the question of whether interpretations of motion pictures can ever be authentically philosophical in their own right.[16] Again, this would require that the interpretation not be the discovery in a film of an already existing philosophical idea that is merely being recycled in cinematic garb. The interpretation itself would have to be a contribution to philosophical knowledge

while, at the same time, being a legitimate interpretation of the motion picture in question.

Finding Friedrich Nietzsche's myth of the
eternal return embedded in *Groundhog Day*
(Harold Ramis, 1993), however interesting and
rewarding, is not philosophical in terms of creating original philosophy. Interpretively isolating the preexisting philosophy illustrated in
film is not a matter of doing philosophy, any
more than identifying various social policy
recommendations as illustrated in a film like
Sergei Eisenstein's *The General Line* (1929) is
itself an example of social planning. Furthermore, since much of the interpreting of film done
by philosophers nowadays involves claiming that
this or that film illustrates this or that philosophy,
most of it cannot be taken to be motion picture
interpretation *qua* philosophy. But might there be
an interpretation of a motion picture artwork that
would be worthy of the sobriquet "philosophy"?

Of course, answering that question will
depend on how one parses philosophy. If you
hail from a Hegelian tradition in which tracking
the state of society in terms of the play of dialectical forces is philosophical, then interpreting
the interaction and mutation of such factors as
manifested in a motion picture will count as
philosophy. However, this view of philosophy
is at least controversial, since many would contend that it does not sufficiently differentiate
philosophy from social criticism.

Perhaps a less contentious view of philosophy is that conceptual analysis is at least an
important part of philosophy, even if philosophy *tout court* involves more than just conceptual analysis. If this is granted, then perhaps
we can get a leg up on answering our question
by investigating whether a film interpretation
can ever contribute to conceptual analysis.

It seems clear that interpreting certain artworks—especially philosophical artworks—
may require philosophizing on the part of the
interpreter. Luigi Pirandello's *Six Characters in
Search of an Author* explores the categorical
differences between fictional characters and
real people, a very unique topic of philosophical
concern for the period in which the play was
written. Because of the originality of the subject
for its time, Pirandello gets at some very interesting distinctions but in language that is
perhaps predictably somewhat obscure and not
fully worked out.

There are philosophical insights in the play,
but they are often elliptical and the interpreter
needs to complete them. And that involves
expanding on Pirandello's theses philosophically
in ways that not only make them more intelligible, but that enhance the likelihood of their truth.
For example, Pirandello, through the voice of the
Father, in the "outside" or philosophical part of
the play, says that stage characters have "more
life than people who breathe and wear clothes."
Here, the interpreter needs to gloss what
Pirandello could mean by "life" here. Where the
interpreter helps Pirandello out by finding an
interpretation of his highly suggestive, intriguing, but somewhat obscure observation that is
philosophically true—such as that fictional
characters are more vivid because they are more
unified in that they are tailored expressly for the
stories in which they are found—the interpreter
is obviously doing philosophy. That is, both
Piranadello and the interpreter are cooperating in
discovering a philosophical insight; Pirandello
by initiating the thought, albeit imperfectly, and
the interpreter by fleshing it out.

In such instances, the case is strictly analogous
to that of the historian of philosophy who in
reconstructing the arguments of a past master
fills them out in ways that go beyond the letter of
text but arguably not beyond its spirit. For
instance, identifying and supplying the premises
an Immanuel Kant or a G. W. Leibniz neglected
to articulate in an argument in order to make
the argument go through, or clarifying a concept
that a Plato left ambiguous in a way that puts his
theory back in the game, are all examples of ways
historians of philosophy are typically engaged in
doing philosophy firsthand.[17] Completing the
underdeveloped or obscure philosophizing in the
course of interpreting a text like *Six Characters*
would appear clearly to be in the same ballpark.

If interpreting a play such as *Six Characters*
can be philosophical, then it is very likely that
interpreting a moving-image artwork can be as
well. Let us return to the case of *Serene Velocity*. Let us agree that it is a celluloid counterpart
to a philosophical thought experiment designed
to advance the conceptual point that an essential
feature of film is movement. I think that
everyone will agree that *Serene Velocity* calls
for an interpretation; it hardly wears its meaning
on its sleeve for the ordinary viewer. I think
that it is a fair conjecture—well warranted

hermeneutically—that Gehr intends *Serene Velocity* to provoke the philosophical insight that movement is a necessary condition of film.

However, just as the historian of philosophy may amplify or trim the arguments and/or analyses of an earlier thinker in such a way that they segue with contemporary preoccupations and discoveries, so the interpreter of *Serene Velocity* may attempt to limn the philosophical significance of the film for current debates in a way that, while consistent with and constrained by Gehr's intentions, goes somewhat beyond them. Gehr most probably regarded *Serene Velocity* as a meditation on the nature of *film*. For him, cinema was film; the motion picture was celluloid based. Since 1970, the proliferation of different technologies for producing moving images, however, has grown and continues to grow. Now it is possible to make movies without film; the prospect of completely computer-generated moving pictures is in the offing. In this context, film is coming to be regarded theoretically as just the inaugural medium of the many media that now comprise the art form of the moving image.

Given these circumstances, it is possible to elucidate the significance of *Serene Velocity* more broadly than Gehr and his informed contemporaries would have. Where they would have regarded *Serene Velocity* as a demonstration of a necessary condition of (celluloid-based) film, we may now interpret it as heralding the proposition that film itself belongs to a larger category, namely, the moving image, whose members, by definition, possess the technical possibility of imparting the impression of movement, as highlighted by *Serene Velocity*. But in doing this, we are making a philosophical move that Gehr was not yet prepared to make, even though it is not inconsistent with what he probably intended. By making such a philosophical move in our interpretation, we are obviously doing philosophy. We are going beyond the authorial meaning of the film for the sake of plumbing broader philosophical implications of the film than the inventor of the experiment ever knew.

Insofar as our explanation of the significance of *Serene Velocity* is guided by the commitment to discover what it can be elucidated to reveal of the truth about the nature of the moving image in relation to film, our interpretation should count as doing philosophy in the same vein as the contribution to philosophy of the historian who recasts certain theses of Baruch Spinoza in a way that illuminates contemporary debates about materialism. When a historian of philosophy amplifies or clarifies his or her subject's position, or teases out implications of a text that were never made explicit in the first go-around, and the historian proceeds hermeneutically with the commitment to render the pertinent philosophy true, the historian of philosophy is himself or herself doing philosophy, albeit in concert with the original author. Similarly, when in the course of unraveling the significance of a moving picture, one clarifies, qualifies, or expands on the artwork in ways that improve upon, while being conciliant with, the philosophical position toward which the auteur was reaching, the exegete is himself or herself producing philosophy.

I have argued that *Serene Velocity* is an example of philosophizing through the moving image. Specifically, it is a piece of conceptual analysis to the effect that movement is a necessary condition of film. Likewise, an interpretation of the significance of *Serene Velocity* may also involve a contribution to philosophy by refining and adjusting in philosophically pertinent respects the conceptual analysis implicit in *Serene Velocity*—for example, by qualifying Gehr's original, analytical hypothesis by noting that it is not movement *simpliciter*, but only the technical possibility of movement, that is the condition that Gehr is after, and by noting that Gehr's finding has larger implications than he might have thought: he did not merely identify a necessary condition of the film medium, but found an essential, defining feature of the larger art form of which film is but a part. In extending, modifying, and developing Gehr's original insights in these ways in an effort to account for the significance of *Serene Velocity* in the most philosophically compelling way, the interpreter does philosophy by fine-tuning the conceptual analysis Gehr initiated.

VI. SUMMARY

The primary aim of this essay has been to establish that some moving-image artworks can be philosophical in the robust sense of "doing philosophy." I attempted to defend this possibility by producing an actual example of a motion picture that meets the stringent standards for philosophy set by those skeptical about the prospects of philosophizing through the moving image. My strategy was to defeat their claims that motion picture philosophy is impossible by demonstrating that in at least one case, that of *Serene Velocity*, it has already been done. What is actual is not impossible. It is not my view that *Serene Velocity* is the only example of this sort; but one example suffices to defeat the skeptic.[18]

I have also employed the same strategy to argue for the possibility that some interpretations of moving-image artworks are philosophical in the sense of being original contributions to the corpus of philosophical knowledge. Again, I have argued this on the basis of an actual example—an interpretation of *Serene Velocity* that qualifies and expands on the conceptual analysis launched by Gehr's experiment. Of course, I do not think that this is the only case of an interpretation of a moving-image artwork that counts as philosophy, but one example is enough to defend my claim.

Though I have argued for the possibility of philosophizing through moving-image artworks and through interpretations thereof, I should add that I do not think that either of these possibilities obtain that often. It is my intuition that authentic cases are rare. I sympathize with the skeptic who suspects that most of what passes for philosophy in film is the illustration of preexisting philosophical views decanted by interpretations that locate their sources. I have not done any statistical research to prove this, but it is my impression after years of reading the relevant literature.

Lastly, I have relied on the experimental cinema to build my argument. I do not believe that this is the only place where one can find philosophizing through the moving image. It may occur in the mainstream narrative cinema and interpretations thereof as well. However, the modernist avant-garde is a natural place to look for the phenomenon, since it has declared the reflexive interrogation of its own nature— a philosophical project if there ever was one— to be its mission.[19]

NOËL CARROLL
Department of Philosophy
Temple University
Philadelphia, PA 19122
USA

1. The present essay represents a retreat from the position I have defended previously. In earlier essays I was more skeptical about the prospects for theoretical or philosophical filmmaking, especially with reference to the avant-garde tradition. I now agree that it may be possible to construct avant-garde films that make original, positive contributions to philosophy. I still do not believe—for the reasons expressed in my earlier work—that there are as many of these works as some commentators on the avant-garde appear to believe, but now I concede that there may be some, whereas earlier I was more skeptical. I should also add that my previous skepticism pertained to avant-garde motion pictures. Even then I agreed that there might be more prosaically structured motion pictures with theoretical credentials such as John Berger's TV program *Ways of Seeing*. For my earlier views, see Noël Carroll, "Avant-Garde Film and Film Theory," in my *Theorizing the Moving Image* (Cambridge University Press, 1996); "Avant-Garde Art and the Problem of Theory," *The Journal of Aesthetic Education* 29 (1995): 1–13.

2. One source of the kind of skeptical misgivings cited in this article is Bruce Russell, "The Philosophical Limits of Film," in Special Interest Edition on the Films of Woody Allen, *Film and Philosophy* (2000): 163–167.

3. Ibid.

4. For more on this terminology, see Noël Carroll, "Film in the Age of Postmodernism," in *Interpreting the Moving Image* (Cambridge: Cambridge University Press, 1998).

5. Sometimes, the images in *Serene Velocity* resemble such paintings.

6. Perhaps Warhol's *Empire* can be seen as correlated to one of the most enduring views of film—that it is essentially photographic recording.

7. Undoubtedly, the salience of the projector beam was enhanced in the days when minimalist film reigned, since most of the people in the screening room at the time were likely to be smoking.

8. Frampton also broaches this theme is his *Poetic Justice* (1972). A film of a shooting script, it ingeniously and humorously underscores the distance between the page and the screen, between reading and seeing *simpliciter*.

9. P. Adams Sitney, *Visionary Film* (New York: Oxford University Press, 1979), p. 438.

10. Perhaps the film only suggests that movement is the relevant differentiae here. However, as we reflect philosophically on the relevant difference in this vicinity, I think we should qualify this in terms of the technical *possibility* of movement, since there can be films that do not impart the impression of movement at all. I comment on the significance of this interpretive expansion on Gehr's proposal in the last paragraph of Section V of this essay. For more on films that do not impart the impression of movement, see my "Defining the Moving Image," in *Theorizing the Moving Image*.

11. Arthur Danto, "Moving Pictures," *Quarterly Review of Film Studies* 4 (1979): 1–21.

12. Of course, earlier film theorists and even ordinary folk had observed the relevance of movement to film prior to Gehr and Danto. In his 1934 article "Motion," Rudolf Arnheim invokes movement in the course of making certain medium-specificity recommendations. He writes: "Motion being one of its outstanding properties, the film is required by aesthetic law to use and interpret motion," in *Film as Art*

(London: Faber and Faber, 1958), p. 150. My point above is simply that Danto's is the first full-dress, technical, philosophical defense of the notion that movement is the defining feature of cinema and that Gehr's proposal of this hypothesis predates Danto's.

13. Ibid.

14. Let me take this opportunity to emphasize the way I think that the manner in which *Serene Velocity* leads the viewer's thinking to a philosophical point is different from the manner in which Errol Morris's *Fast, Cheap, and Out of Control* (1997) does so. Morris's film presents examples of robotic engineering and the social organization of mole rats where the massive parallel processing of dumb activities yields what appears to be intelligent behavior. The thoughtful viewer might find himself or herself contemplating the possibility that human behavior, however apparently intelligent, might also be generated in this way. That is, Morris's film may tentatively intimate something like a connectionist approach to the mind. But it does not argue for it. It is my contention that *Serene Velocity*, understood as the celluloid equivalent of a thought experiment, is an argument for a certain conception concerning the essential or minimal conditions of its medium.

15. One skeptical argument against my assertion of the minimal film as a form of philosophizing might be this: these cases are hardly interesting cases of making philosophy through film, since they cannot fail. Making a philosophical contribution is an achievement. But one cannot fail to make a film that marks some condition of film. For as long as it is a film, it will exemplify the conditions of film. If this is philosophy, it is the philosophical analog of shooting fish in a barrel.

However, it is not true that every attempt at making a minimal film will succeed. Michael Snow's *A Casing Shelved* (1970) is, I think, an attempt at meta-cinema. It is a slide of a shelf of artist's materials accompanied by a tape describing the contents of the shelf. As different objects on the shelf are mentioned, our eyes search them out. The only movement involved is the movement of our eyes. This arrangement seems to be Snow's way of suggesting that this is enough to make for a movie. However, I would argue that this "film" is not a film at all; to be a film, properly so called, requires the literal possibility of movement. Snow's embodied thought experiment, were it embraced, would turn family albums into cineplexes. Therefore, not all meta-cinematic experiments are destined to succeed.

16. The question of whether interpretations of motion pictures can be philosophical is raised in Thomas Wartenberg, "Interpreting Films Philosophically," *Film and Philosophy* 5 (2002): 164–171.

17. The historian of philosophy who first pointed out that Charles Darwin's theory challenged the teleological argument for God's existence was himself/herself doing original philosophy, since this was not an implication that Darwin himself explicitly drew from his theory in his writing.

18. See also my "The Wheel of Virtue: Art, Literature and Moral Knowledge," in *The Journal of Aesthetics and Art Criticism* 60 (2002): 3–26, and my introductions to the last two sections of *Philosophy of Film and Motion Pictures: An Anthology*, ed. Noël Carroll and Jinhee Choi (Oxford: Blackwell Publishers, 2005). As well, Tom Wartenberg explores the idea of films as thought experiments in his "Philosophy Screened: Experiencing *The Matrix*," *Midwest Studies in Philosophy* 27 (2003): 139–152.

19. I would like to express my gratitude to Sally Banes, Annette Michelson, Murray Smith, and Tom Wartenberg for their comments on an earlier version of this essay. They, of course, are not responsible for the defects in this essay; I am.

TREVOR PONECH

The Substance of Cinema

Avant-garde filmmaker Hollis Frampton once said that film art "consists in devising things to put into our projector. The simplest thing to devise, although perhaps not the easiest, is nothing at all, which fits conveniently into the machine."[1]

Frampton's arch yet earnest recipe for cinema is interesting for the ingredients it excludes. He invites the thought that cinema is defined below the level of pictorial imagery: perhaps the viewers' perceptual objects need not be moving pictures in order to be movies. Perhaps that rectangle of undifferentiated white light beamed from the projector as it gives its mechanical performance is all the audience needs to see in order to have seen a movie.

I begin by discussing two recent analytic-philosophical attempts to grasp the properties owing to which something is cinematic. One is kindred in spirit to Frampton's unruly remarks; the other, antithetical. Both try to be much more exacting about what cinema is. However, in so doing each obscures the substantive difference of cinematic from noncinematic representational systems. Hence the rest of my essay develops a third alternative. Accepting Frampton's invitation, I elaborate on the notion that cinema precedes imagery. The properties by virtue of which something is cinematic are narrowly describable structural features and physical events upon which an image might but need not supervene. These comprise what I call a stroboscopic visual display. Instantiation as this type of substantial thing is the source of a perceptual object's cinematic nature.

Several movies, plus a few "paracinematic" nonmovies, play a heuristic role in my discussion. The works selected are usually considered highly abstract. Ironically, far from trading purely in abstractions, the makers of these works undertake artistic but nonetheless practical experiments designed to uncover cinema's rock-bottom constituent elements. Using various instruments, materials, and physical magnitudes, they intuitively explore cinema's ontology. These explorations are not works of philosophy. They are hardly rigorous truth-seeking procedures providing evidence and arguments in support of their authors' conclusions. Rather, they are vehicles for their makers' philosophically pertinent ideas about cinema's nature. By putting these ideas into practice and giving them form, the artists supply us with concrete as well as conceptual resources that we can mobilize to debate and refine our ontological hypotheses.

I. ANALYTIC DEFINITIONS AND CINEMATIC ABSTRACTIONS

Noël Carroll and Gregory Currie, vanguards of analytic-aesthetic inquiry into cinema, both adopt causal approaches to defining cinema, but they identify the relevant causal chains in significantly different ways. Carroll indeed does not associate cinema with one particular etiology, opting to identify it with any underlying processes and materials capable of generating a certain result. His sense of what is cinematic is correspondingly permissive. Currie, on the other hand, accepts just one causal history as definitive, making membership in the class a lot more exclusive. How these definitional strategies handle unorthodox cinematic works—some of which flaunt the question of their ontology—is an indicator of their overall success.

Currie reserves the term 'cinema' for a group of things constituting "something like a 'natural kind.'"[2] Something belonging therein is "produced by photographic means and delivered onto a surface so as to produce, or be capable of producing, an apparently moving image."[3] When one uses a movie camera in the standard way, the mechanisms of photographic production along with the physics of optics and light naturally result in moving, pictorial images of visible objects before the camera. This much of his claim is descriptive. He admits that it also has a stipulative aspect, since he is legislating that "cinema" be reserved for only that which is made by photographic means. Ascertaining precisely the degree of similarity between such things and other imaginable as well as actual sources of items that might be called movies is a job he would rather defer.[4] When pressed, though, he is willing to pass judgment on nonpictorial, purely abstract works. Images in purely abstract works are not simply unrecognizable or unidentifiable as images of something; they are also produced by means other than photographing anything, not even a shimmer of reflected light, in the outside world. Hence formalist works like *Ballet mécanique* (Dudley Murphy and Fernand Léger, 1924) are not strictly speaking abstract. Stan Brakhage's *Night Music* (1986), made by hand-painting abstract shapes directly onto filmstrips, paradigmatically is.

Currie judges that purely abstract film stands in the same relation to cinema as setting afire a canvas prepared for painting stands to painting.[5] Such "pyro-painting" might have some artistic merit but it is not painting per se. Likewise, nonpictorial movies created entirely by nonphotographic techniques are not so much movies as they are "multifarious things you can do with the cinematic apparatus."[6]

Cinematic art, on Currie's thesis, diverges from painting in that it is necessarily imagistic and ontologically precludes genuine abstraction, construed along the lines of nondepiction combined with lack of reference. This seems more a metaphysical assumption than a description. His thesis also implies that depictive but nonphotographic animation techniques—from manually scratching pictures into the film's emulsion to digital animation—are uncinematic for all their pyrotechnics. I wonder if he has not expelled too much art from cinema, and cinema from art. I suspect, as does Carroll, that

Currie takes the etiology of one sort of movie as defining cinema in general. Thus he misses the ontologically primitive commonalities of superficially different artifacts. Or so I argue below.

Carroll realizes that choice of definitive causal conditions might say more about normative presuppositions regarding the nature of cinema than about the nature of cinema itself. His solution to this problem is anti-essentialist, ingenious, and big hearted. But I doubt it is successful.

Stated roughly, Carroll identifies as cinematic any two-dimensional image presented in a detached display, generated by a template technology, and produced by cinematic means.[7] He takes pains, though, to dissociate imagery from depiction. Indeed, he prefers "moving image" for its wider application to pictorial works (made photographically or otherwise) as well as purely abstract ones (including those made by such heteroclite methods as editing together strips of clear and opaque leader).[8]

Display detachment concerns the way cinematic and other images perforce involve spatial dislocation.[9] Just by looking at a movie image of it, I cannot orient my body in the Grand Canyon's direction. Unlike windows, mirrors, and magnifying lenses, photographically-produced movie pictures do not connect us spatially with their depicta. Say I am watching a movie at a spatial-temporal location $L1$. Following Carroll, when a display, D, at $L1$ is a photographically (or nonphotographically) generated picture of some extra-cinematic referent, S, D is detached from S's own space-time location L such that I cannot orient myself bodily and in time relative to S merely by looking D-wards at $L1$. But what if I were watching closed-circuit, live images of happenings in the room next door? As Carroll notes, background knowledge of the imagery's connection to that room, not visual experience of the image, allows one to orient one's self spatially-temporally to those happenings.[10]

A template is a physical storage, recording, exhibition, or transmission format by means of which a cinematic work is disseminated. When I watch *The Player* (Robert Altman, 1992), I could be viewing imagery produced from a DVD, videocassette, broadcast television signal, or 35 mm film print. None of these items is identical to the *work*, *The Player*, though. The work consists of story, characterization, irony, actors' performances, directorial decisions, and so forth—properties and events no traces of which are found within the template's molecules and electrons. Similarly, were my copy of *The Player* destroyed or the TV signal degraded, the work itself would not thereby be destroyed—only one particular token of its template. Moreover, screening the show requires I view a mechanical performance executed from this template. At a stage play, visiting a movie set, or attending a hockey game, I watch people as they perform their artistic or professional actions right before my eyes. When I view a play, film, or game on television or in a movie theater my proximal perceptual object, the detached display, results from something a machine is arationally "doing" in front of me. This mechanical performance facilitates my access to peoples' artistic and sporting actions, but it is not itself an artistic or sporting performance.

Finally, Carroll holds that a movie is by definition something realized by cinematic means. This claim would be no more interesting a tautology than "war is war" were it not anchored in an arresting idea: some movies contain no movement.[11] Frampton's *Poetic Justice* (1971–1972) is a film of a shooting script sitting on a tabletop; Michael Snow's *One Second in Montréal* (1969) consists exclusively of still photos. Yet these movies share with standard fare the property of having been produced by cinematic means, that is, using technologies that make a certain result, moving imagery presented in a detached display, a possibility.[12] Frampton and Snow could have employed their filmmaking means to generate moving images, had they preferred. Whereas it is categorically impossible for drawings, paintings, or photographic stills to contain moving imagery, "movement in a film image is an artistic choice which is always technically available."[13] Viewers of paintings know by looking that such works are structurally guaranteed immobile. *La Jetée*'s (Chris Marker, 1964) audience confirms that there is but one fleeting instance of movement in this work, otherwise consisting of still photographs, by watching to see if the filmmakers deviate from their aesthetic policy of immobility.

Carroll renounces any aspiration of discovering cinema's essence. He does not suppose the necessary, general features he cites jointly suffi-

cient to define what a movie is; nor does he wish to define cinema by identifying it with any actual, particular materials, processes, production techniques, causal chains, or media.[14] Still, his definition serves to group together a broad range of things by discerning their mutual difference from theater, painting, sculpture, Balinese shadow puppet plays, and so forth. At the same time, it accommodates the fact that there are many different kinds of movies and lots of ways to make them. His definition also supports my intuition that *Night Music* is as cinematic as *Gone with the Wind* (Victor Fleming, 1939). Carroll's analysis is subtle enough to allow that motion is a definitive though not universal cinematic property. On top of that, it affords an inkling, to which I will return, of a crucial structural division between display and template components.

It also turns out that Carroll is ambivalent about the necessity of a movie being imagistic. I sympathize with his doubt but it ultimately makes trouble for him. Carroll imagines a modernist filmmaker creating an underexposed film appearing pitch black under ordinary screening conditions. As this "invisible film" plays, the artist, on a voice-over soundtrack, talks of the screen being dark for half the time a movie plays.[15] Carroll notes that an actual film of this type exists, Derek Jarman's *Blue* (1993), consisting of seventy-six uninterrupted minutes of 35 mm film printed blue. He describes *Blue* as having "no images," hence being an invisible film.[16] Yet he maintains that it is nonetheless cinematic if it satisfies two conditions: being made using cinematic means and being "part of an intelligible, ongoing filmworld conversation."[17]

I am unconvinced that movies can be imageless. That claim is only as defensible as one's concept of "image." This term figures in Carroll's definition as an unanalyzed primitive. We are not told what kind of a thing it is nor what differentiates imagistic from nonimagistic items. He does allude to an image being an "intentional visual artifact."[18] But so are eyeglasses. Also, if a movie is imageless, does it therefore lack a detached display? If the answer is affirmative, the attrition rate in the list of necessary features doubles owing to the loss of an arguably integral structural element. Speaking of attrition, that cinematic works have or are generated from templates is perhaps only contingently true. In his lecture, Frampton seemed to be describing a templateless as well as imageless work. Indeed, during his presentation, he cast the beam of an empty projector onto a screen. It would be unsurprising were Carroll to treat this case as genuinely cinematic, as it is realized by cinematic means and could satisfy the psychosocial conditions of cognoscenti approval.

At least as much nothing fills Carroll's description of cinema as Frampton's. A movie, he tells us, is a possibly invisible entity resulting from an unspecified underlying cause known (knowable?) to us only by one of its contingent effects. Now *that's* cinema as pure abstraction. Notice the etiological "produced by cinematic means" condition appears to be the sole definitive characteristic exclusive to movies, although Carroll does not say so explicitly. Note, too, that, intent on defining cinema without invoking one arbitrarily privileged production mode, "cinematic means" is untheorized beyond saying that it is a technological something that can cause a certain result. This gambit resembles defining malaria as a living something potentially causing fever and death. The structure, operation, and substance of the something, of cinema, remain as obscure as if nobody cared what cinema is.

II. PROJECTABLES, VISUAL DISPLAYS, AND STROBOSCOPY

One method of exploring cinema's ontology is to do hands-on experiments designed to model one's intuitions. Instead of leaving our philosophical understanding to itself, let us take some suggestions and cautions from a few of these models.

The works I discuss are alike in at least one respect. Each treats movie making as an occasion not so much to present images of extra-cinematic depicta as to evoke the constituent physical elements of images. It is somewhat like directing one's gaze at, not through, the car windshield. More precisely, these works explicitly take as their objects three of cinema's underlying constituent physical elements: projectables, light and its characteristic cinematic behavior, and the luminescent visual display

space. The best way to explain these items and their connections is to turn directly to some film experiments.

Brakhage's *Night Music* and his earlier *Mothlight* (1963) evince unusual artistry in devising things to put into projectors. Neither was made with a camera. Both involved meticulously hand-working unorthodox filmmaking materials. Brakhage created *Night Music* by painting hundreds of film frames he mechanically duplicated then edited together. *Mothlight* is the product of putting moth wings, grass, and flowers between two strips of transparent tape, running the tape through a film-printer, then editing the resultant print. Exhibition prints of these movies are themselves worth examining.[19] *Night Music*'s individual paintings are appreciated anew when studied as still frames; *Mothlight*, which contains no frames, is seen to be as much a collage as a film print. However, making these projectables was but a step in an artistic process culminating in a cinematic object itself of focal concern to Brakhage.

Watching any movie, spectators' eyes are trained on a bounded space illuminated by a pulsating light. If, for instance, they are viewing a (super 8mm, 16mm, 35mm, 70mm) film print, a projector behind them flashes light across the screen in front of them about seventy-two times per second. During that second, around twenty-four frames pass through a gate and shutter mechanism immobilizing each one just long enough to let light penetrate it three times. The patterns, dyes, opacity, and various microphysical surface features within the frame determine what visual information is borne to the screen by each light pulse. During the milliseconds between flashes, no light at all is projected onto the screen. Hence the audience attends to a *visual display space*, the structure and visible appearance of which derives from the interaction between the *projectable* and the *stroboscopically flashing light*.

Night Music's spectators are presented with a visual display consisting of a seamless succession of colorful abstract patterns. These stream before the eyes at a furious pace. But having double and quadruple-printed frames, Brakhage keeps individual patterns within the threshold of visibility: Each lingers onscreen just long enough to be noticeable; not so long as to give a sense that the stream of visual change is ever arrested. In this way, the tempo at which one pattern gives way to the next suggests the relentless stroboscopy underlying the display's visible changes. Likewise, in *Mothlight*, moth wings and plants flutter in time with the flashing light that constitutes the visual display space. The projectable as collage is inert. It is stroboscopy and the filmstrip's mechanical advancing and stopping that reanimate the *disjecta membra*.

"Projectable" is closely related to "template," but they cannot be equated. Both concepts designate items that are not themselves perceptual objects during movie spectatorship. During *Mothlight*, we do not look at the print; watching a DVD of *The Player*, we do not look at the Mylar disk or its digital encoding. So both concepts point to a pivotal structural divide that all movies exhibit, namely: that between the visual display, which completely captures our attention as the movie plays, and the exhibition, transmission, recording, and storage vehicle by means of which the display is generated at a given place and time. However, whereas all templates are projectables, not every projectable is a template. And whereas one sort of projectable is an intrinsic property of all cinematic artifacts, no template is more than a contingent feature. The visual display is made out of light. Thus light is a cinematic primitive, a magnitude of electromagnetic radiation without which cinema cannot exist. Normally, this intrinsic projectable carries information from the template to the display. Frampton's eliminativist experiment departs from this norm by stripping cinema to the ontologically primitive. What he presented to his audience fits nobody's pretheoretical idea of a movie. By turning on an empty projector, its shutter speed set low to ensure a noticeable flicker, he nonetheless generated a stroboscopic visual display. This object has everything it needs to be an instance of cinema.

III. THE STROBOSCOPIC VISUAL DISPLAY

Visual displays are material items occurring at particular spatial-temporal locations. Turning on television, you bring one into being in your livingroom from time t until t^n, when you turn off the TV. At the theater, a display is instantiated on screen, so many meters from your eyes,

until the projector is shut down. That display is itself a spatial-temporal location, at which certain items and events arise during $t \ldots t^n$. In either case, the display is a real, substantial individual thing. It is a source of ambient energy triggering a cascade of responses in the percipient's visual system.

I agree that such displays are "detached." My reasons go a bit beyond Carroll's, though. First, D's ability to carry information about S at $L1$ does not depend on D being at $L2$. The display would carry the same information no matter where and when it existed. In other words, D being at $L2$ in itself does not mean that S exists or existed at $L1$. Contrast this situation with the following: this shadow now cast on this wall indicates the current position of the sun or some other light source. Second, the display is perceptually detached from the observer. D is located at some distance external to one's visual receptor surfaces. The display's substance, structure, and dynamics are distinct from those of the percipient's internal representational states; its visible properties are not produced by or dependent on the percipient's visual responses. One relevant upshot here is that a cinematic item cannot be a "plug-in," that is, a film-loaded prosthetic device attaching directly to your brain and letting you trip out on movie imagery with your eyes wide shut.[20] I identify cinema with the visual display. By definition, the display is an external thing, albeit one that can be represented by certain of our sensory and internal states.

Finally, the visual display is detached from the template. One's perceptual experience is of the former, not the latter. Precursors to cinema like the Phenakistoscope and Zoetrope are non-cinematic partly because they are structurally unified, the viewer's perceptual object and the exhibition or storage format being one and the same thing. The Praxinoscope, which projects a band of cartoon or photographic pictures onto an overhead screen when somebody manually cranks them past a steady beam of light, is articulated in the right way, but is as lacking in stroboscopy as the Phenakistoscope and Zoetrope. On the other hand, the peep show Kinetoscope requires looking into a box, through a magnifying lens, at a backlit filmstrip. Fully motorized, the film is continuously fed between an electric lamp and a fast shutter mechanism producing a flash of light every time a frame moves under the lens. The viewer's proximal perceptual object is the filmstrip itself. The rudimentary stroboscopic engineering seems to me to make the Kinetoscope a nonetheless genuinely pre-cinematic device.[21]

Displays are generated from various materially and technologically different kinds of templates. Indeed, displays themselves can be made of all sorts of stuff. The only limitations belong to human ingenuity and the laws of physics. Apparently, engineers can now project 2D video images onto water vapor diffused in mid-air.[22] Moreover, nothing about the concept of visual display necessitates that it be two-dimensional. Carroll defines the detached display as perforce 2D, to distinguish it from other standard modes of presenting artworks.[23] However, 3D cinema is imaginable, if not now feasible. The risk of collapsing or obscuring the distinction between visual displays and statues, standard theatrical presentations, music boxes, and the like dissolves once we recognize the display's distinctive primitive features.

I am sitting in a wooden chair crafted by a small local furniture-making company. Being made of wood is a trait that chair possesses intrinsically. It is a physical condition of the chair itself. Its location in my study to the left of a bookcase, and currently holding my body, are among the chair's broad features. These properties concern its relations to other things and parts of the world. Other of my chair's broad, relational properties are the historical properties of having been made by the atelier's artisans and demonstrating their virtuoso woodworking skills.

I take it that the visual display's narrow properties rather than its causal or psychohistorical relations to other things are the most informative when we try to define cinema. In fact, 'visual display' refers to cinema's narrow, primitive properties. Very generally, then, the visual display is a delimited area of illumination. It is visible insofar as it is the source of highly organized packages of photons projecting from a reflecting or light-emitting surface. *Pixels* and *stroboscopic motion* are two narrow, intrinsic features it possesses essentially. *Patterns* are contingent narrow properties.

'Pixel' usually denotes "picture element." I use it in a slightly adjusted but related technical sense. By 'pixels' I intend points of light. This usage converges with descriptions of movie images as constructed from separate regions varying independently in spectral distribution.[24] At a basic level of physical description, visual displays are composed of pixels. More accurately, I associate the display with a totality, namely, a field of points of light plus any unilluminated areas situated spatially-temporally between those points.

Exhibition of cinematic imagery requires light be emitted from or projected against a surface. Interrupting the flow of this light by turning off the machine is similar to closing a faucet, as the flow of imagery is thereby arrested. Contrast this situation with exhibitions of still photographic prints or painted canvases. If the salon is plunged into darkness, or light reflected from these objects is stopped from reaching our eyes, the works' visible, artistically pertinent features are not extinguished, just made harder to see. The perceptible patterns constitutive of the paper print's or canvas's image do not themselves supervene on light reflected or emitted by the image. When we watch a movie, that which we look at—the image on display as distinct from the negative image on the celluloid or the digital encoding on the DVD—is integral to a certain structure of light, not extraneous to it. Hence a pixel is any actual point of light, emitted by or projected against a screen, and consequently comprising a visible element of the cinematic image. Rather than displays being made of images, images are made out of displays.

A display is more than a field of pixels. It is also an event. At a nonmicrophysical level of description, the display and the pixels therein undergo a distinctive type of motion. Pixels flash, periods of illumination alternate with periods of nonillumination, the pixels' brightness and intensity fluctuates. Turning on a television, computer monitor, or movie projector activates, I have said, a visual display at a given location, the screen in front of you, from t until t''. There, an uninterrupted stream of changes occurs to the display's illuminated condition, achieved by the regular flashing of the pixels in a cycle of, for instance, seventy-two times a second. This is the display's stroboscopic motion. This motion is identified with constitutive, ongoing changes in the display's surface condition: the rapid onset/offset of pixels and areas of pixels. 'Stroboscopic motion' does not refer to the subjective impression of objective displacement sometimes induced by the stroboscopic flashing of lights or imagery. It signifies only the actual changes in the visual display, its transient phases of illumination. It is a property of the display itself, independent of any perceptual impact it might be calibrated to have. To date, all movies derive from stroboscopic motion. Once activated, it is by flashing at a certain frequency and degree of brightness that the visual display makes the cinematic image visible to observers.

Carroll asserts that not all movies contain motion. He is partly right. Movies necessarily contain stroboscopic motion, but not all afford impressions of objective displacement, that is, a visual experience analogous to seeing a bunny hop across the lawn while watching motion picture imagery of a bunny hopping across the lawn. That experience could never arise—no matter what "cinematic means" produced the movie—if not for the display's internal stroboscopic motion.

A clock's minute hand changes position too slowly for us to see its movement. Stroboscopic motion is similar with respect to exceeding the threshold of perceptibility. It consists of transitions between surface states normally occurring too fast to be seen. Phenomenologically, it does not seem to observers that the display is flashing. One's visual experience of the display is not *about* its stroboscopic motion. It does not represent the onset and offset of pixels any more than visual experience of the minute hand represents the event of its tiny but nonetheless real change of position. But there are usually lots of other things to look at in the display.

I use 'pattern' to refer to any of a visual display's singletons.[25] Loosely stated, a pattern is a visibly differentiated structure standing out from its background. A bit more precisely, a singleton is a perceptual target, in that it can be the object of an observer's perceptual representation. My notion of pattern includes that area of *La strada*'s (Federico Fellini, 1954) image we are inclined to call "Gelsomina wearing clown attire." Embedded in this pattern are various other singletons, like Gelsomina's eyes, the clown nose drawn onto the end of her own nose, her hat and striped vest, her hands, and so

forth. An undifferentiated, homogenous area of illumination, such as the effect created by projecting a completely blue image onto the screen, might at a global level of description constitute a pattern. Nor would I be quick to exclude unstable moiré "patterns" associated with poor television reception, and even the "snow" associated with a badly malfunctioning TV. I have no theoretical need to take any apparently borderline or question-begging cases aboard, though, since I do not maintain that anything and everything appearing in a display has to be a pattern.

Unlike my psychohistorical pattern of miscalculating my capacity to afford luxury goods, the patterns I am concerned with are not at all abstract-typical. They belong to the category of substances. Spiritual salvation, Santa Claus, the market value of John Currin paintings, and nothingness are abstract, conceptual entities. Grasping these takes reason and imagination. A substance, on the other hand, is a magnitude, a piece of stuff, or an event that can be the object of perceptual experience. It is a material, spatio-temporally localized part of the world's existing hardware. As such, it is possible to be in non-conceptual contact with it. To step on a bug requires neither a bug concept nor knowledge that you are stepping on a bug. Likewise, dogs and infant, prelinguistic children see beetles without possessing any ideas or words about beetles.

In *(nostalgia)* (1971), Frampton shows us, in separate shots, one after another still photographs being gradually incinerated on a hotplate. While looking at one photo burn, we hear a narrator's comments about the next to appear. Frampton thus provides a visual trope for an apparent consequence of the visual effervescence of cinema. If you think of movie imagery as composed of one after another still picture, then asynchrony and referential confusion are inevitable. Any given still image flashed onto the screen is gone before one can form a thought or express an utterance about it.

This remark raises the problem of individuating stroboscopically generated patterns. Within the visual display, patterns are instantiated by the onset and offset of groups of pixels. Within fractions of a second, the pixels betokening the "Gelsomina wearing clown attire" pattern vanish from the stroboscopic display space; milliseconds later this pattern is temporarily reconstituted in the display by a fresh set of pixels. And so on, until the pattern is not instantiated with the onset of the next array of pixels. The Gelsomina pattern, therefore, is a visible uniformity across pixels.

At this stage my analysis evidently comes unstuck from a basic truism, which would interpret such uniformities as nonexistent or at best abstract-typical entities, rather than substantial ones. Is not one second of Gelsomina imagery in the display merely a series of twenty-four discrete, nonidentical, still "Gelsomina" patterns disjoined by interstimulus periods, each out of sight before we can form or express and idea about it?

No. There is also a structural invariant ranging over those patterns. This particular—call it G—is no less real and substantial an individual than are you and I and our chairs. Our furniture and we are individuals by dint of being physical items existing for finite, continuous time periods at actual, contiguous spatial locations. Presumably, each such individual is a unified whole, inasmuch as it consists of parts and phases held together over time and space by various underlying physical connections, causes, and processes.[26] G is arguably more this sort of substantial entity than chimera or sheer theoretical term.

The display, I have said, is a coherent spatial location. Its parts, states, phases, and changes constitute a space—an area made of changing illumination—as unified and contiguous as that of the table at which I now sit. Therein things (pixels, patterns) and events (stroboscopic motion) occur during $t \ldots t''$. If G exists, it exists at that finite spatiotemporal location, as part of the display.

Now say that $t \ldots t''$ is greater than or equal to one second, no fewer than twenty-four Gelsomina patterns, g^1, g^2, g^3, and so forth, appearing onscreen about three times each. These are underlying parts of G, which could not exist in the display without them. Notice that $g^1 \ldots g^n$ bear a key relation: they resemble one another. That is why they are $g^1 \ldots g^n$ instead of g, e ("elephant"), f ("flower"), and so forth. To stand in a resemblance relation, they need not be identical. They only have to be relatively similar with respect to their grosser visible surface and structural features. These features pertain to an object's shape, size, color,

and texture. They include its edges and boundaries; the thickness, straightness, angularity, curvature, and junctures of its lines; distances between points on its lines; its volumetric properties; its rotation; and its luminescence. Two singletons, g^1 and g^2, are similar to the degree that they are as alike to one another as g^1 (or g^2) is alike to itself with respect to grosser visible surface and structural features. In reality, some items (g^1 and g^2) are more similar than others (g^1 and e), in the current respect. The fact of $g^1 \ldots g^n$'s degree of similarity is reflected in the display's appearance.

To the extent that every positively illuminated phase of the display during $t \ldots t''$ actually contains $g^1 \ldots g^n$, the display contains the uniformity G. G is made out of $g^1 \ldots g^n$, along with the pixels that are the display's essential narrow properties. But the display has another underlying, essential internal feature—stroboscopic motion. This physical process is central to G's existence as an individual. Although real, G is not the same kind of entity as my table or my dog. It is held together over time, at its location, not by molecular bonds or by cell division and metabolism, but by the similarity relations between $g^1 \ldots g^n$ and by stroboscopy. Stroboscopic motion is that which generates and maintains this uniformity in the display space. G exists, continuously and uninterrupted, until another stroboscopic event, from which it is absent, occurs in the display. The phase changes and discontinuities uniquely intrinsic to the visual display are neither extraneous to G's existence nor disruptive of it. They are as internal to G as molecular bonds and cellular division are to other entities, being the process keeping it on the screen.

The display plus the template-specific technologies upstream of it are machinery engineered to generate individuals like G. This singleton is often that which is on display. Not only is it presented onscreen, its description most closely corresponds to that of the content of the viewer's perceptual experience—and the referent of the viewer's thoughts and utterances. As a cinematic individual, G is not identical or reducible to any basal phase, state, or part of the display. It can have properties missing from some or all of items g^1 through g^n. It can get bigger or smaller, split in half, or metamorphose into another pattern. It can even undergo objective displacement. But that is another matter.[27]

IV. FROM ESSENTIALLY CINEMATIC ARTIFACTS TO MOVIES

Thanks to historicism's fashionability, and to their own inadequacies, essentialist definitions of cinema are in disrepute.[28] Currie's natural-kind definition does not help revive the genre, since the broad properties it identifies as definitive are merely adventitious. My essentialism seeks informative truth-conditions describing narrow, physical features not varying over time and across social contexts and being *almost* the only ones necessary and sufficient to make something a movie. It has no normative implications for how cinema should look, how best to make movies, the proper uses of the medium, or the criteria for artistic value. It succinctly indicates the underlying difference between movies and other kinds of representational systems. Its analysis is deep and precise enough to pick out shared primitive traits identifying *Workers Leaving the Factory* (Louis and Auguste Lumière, 1895), *Gone with the Wind*, *Night Music*, *Blue*, *Finding Nemo* (Andrew Stanton and Lee Unkrich, 2003), and fetal ultrasound imagery as the same type of thing.

An essentially cinematic artifact consists of a stroboscopic visual display. It does not matter what appears in that display—pictures, tetchy abstract shapes, an undifferentiated monochromatic field, words, numbers, or snowy static interference. It does not matter what template, if any, generates the display. Nor is the essentially cinematic identified with a causal chain by which the display comes into existence and acquires its visible appearance.

This definition precludes the existence of literally invisible films. Carroll's hypothetical example, the pitch black underexposed film, is not a cinematic artifact, let alone a movie, if no light is projected against the screen. Running a completely opaque filmstrip through the projector preempts the visual display as surely as putting a lead plate in front of the lens. In contrast, there is nothing invisible about *Blue* or any work in which cinema's intrinsic projectable, light, behaves stroboscopically within a display space.

My essentialism also excludes from the category of cinema such actual "paracinematic" pieces as Anthony McCall's twenty-four-hour *Long Film for Ambient Light* (1975), consisting of an empty, darkened warehouse illuminated by a bare lightbulb during the evening.[29] Jonathan Walley labels this work paracinematic because it evokes a dematerialized definition of cinema, one not limiting or reducing cinema to the traditional materials, instruments, and processes of the film medium.[30] Walley finds the paracinematic conducive to the notion that cinema is as much a conceptual phenomenon—an idea temporarily taking certain concrete forms—as a tangible one.[31] On these grounds he stakes his claim that *Long Film for Ambient Light* ought to be located within the avant-garde film canon. Granted, McCall abandons depiction to draw attention to light, space, and time—three properties necessary to cinema. But these are not nonphysical, immaterial magnitudes; nor are they exclusive to cinema; nor jointly sufficient to identify something as cinematic. McCall's artwork is about cinema without either being cinematic or embodying a cogent definition of cinema. Alas, neither Walley's credulity nor the din of filmworld discourse could turn *Long Film for Ambient Light* into an authentic member of any cinematic canon.

McCall's *Line Describing a Cone* (1973) is another of Walley's examples of paracinema.[32] This work seems without qualification a cinematic artifact. Another empty projector gig, it differs from Frampton's primarily in that the light beam widens during the thirty-minute performance and audiences are encouraged to inspect and interact with the beam itself rather than stare at the display space on a wall across the room. Yet neither Frampton's nor McCall's presentation fits the "movie" rubric. A movie is not only a stroboscopic visual display; it is one containing an image generated from a template.

No narrow, internal feature makes a visual display imagistic. Being imagistic involves relational, psychohistorical constraints. It is a broad, contingent property of a display standing in a functional relationship to plans enacted by its maker(s) or user(s). Namely, it must be intended to serve some communicative, expressive, or aesthetic purpose. The maker could aim to invite spectators to contemplate the display's purely formal, structural qualities and to explore freely its shapes, colors, and rhythmic movements. Makers also frequently use cinematic artifacts to indicate openly their own thoughts and feelings—although they need have no more expectation of audience comprehension than you do when expressing intimate thoughts to a baby or dog. Alternatively, image making can involve attempts to guide viewers to particular realizations about, for instance, what happens in a fictional story or what the maker's ostensible beliefs are regarding a given topic. In turn, these realizations might be meant to foster some appropriate response, like suspense, laughter, or belief formation. Thus the display is an image to the extent that it is a vehicle for expression and/or eliciting in a target audience some anticipated response of a kind typically associated with art appreciation.

Frampton's presentation encourages competing intuitions, his display being visually dissimilar to standard movie imagery while having at least the minimal expressive function of drawing attention to cinema's intrinsic projectable. Even were we to grant it image status and agree to call it, along with *Line Describing a Cone*, a kind of cinematic artwork, we would have no reason to call such artifacts movies. Their projectors are empty, after all.

I propose my own stipulative use of 'movie.' It is no more arbitrary than Currie's, since it helps pick out an existing class of ubiquitous items that really do differ from bare cinematic artifacts. These items are essentially cinematic because they consist of stroboscopic displays. They are movies because they contain images generated from templates. Here, a template is further described as something the structure of which makes an observable difference to the display's visible appearance. That is exactly what film prints, DVDs, videocassettes, and broadcast television signals do; projectors, television sets, satellite transmitters, and video and DVD players are correspondingly designed to be structurally coupled with these formats. During his lecture, Frampton simulated adding a template by holding a colored gel in front of the projector's lens. This gesture is functionally similar to producing an image from a template. But since nothing is loaded into the device engineered to couple the template with the display, it falls short of turning the presentation into a movie. Had Frampton projected an emulsionless, untinted, completely clear reel of film leader, that would not have been a movie, either. For nothing about the template would have made a visible difference to the display's

appearance or practical difference to its expressive potential.

The notion of imageless movies is oxymoronic. The idea of imageless displays generated from informative templates is not. Consider Ernie Gehr's *History* (1970), consisting of a depthless, textured black space in which beads of light flicker on and off in time with the projector's rhythm. Gehr made his film without a camera, exposing raw stock to dim light then making successive generations of prints. The resulting movie creates an impression of the granularity of the medium upon which photographic images are imprinted. *History* is one of Gehr's attempts to escape representational film's subordination to the photo-recorded event, affirm the material conditions of its existence, and foreground its "primordial state" as "patterns of light and darkness."[33] However, one can readily imagine a display identical in every visible respect to *History* but made without expressive intentions—the result, say, of improperly storing 16mm film stock. That artifact would be cinematic. It would be produced by cinematic means and derive from a template. It would also be imageless. Although some images are essentially cinematic, there is not anything essentially imagistic about cinema.

V. CONCLUSION

Someone might criticize my ontology of cinema for eliding crucial differences. While true, this charge signals a defect not so much in my analysis as in certain assumptions about what a proper definition of cinema ought best to do. I ignore the differences in how people perceptually, cognitively, and affectively experience films on the theater's big screen versus programs watched at home on television versus fetal ultrasound imagery viewed on the obstetrician's computer monitor. My analysis flouts major institutional, economic, and cultural differences between various modes of production and spectatorship. It is also oblivious to how speakers use the word 'cinema' and to what they variously *believe* it to mean.

Inquiry into cinema's myriad psychosocial dimensions is vital, but the immediate job of defining cinema need not involve a sweeping anthropological, historical if not historicized, enterprise. As Currie intuits, it can be more simply and elegantly done by taking advantage of the fact that there exists "something like a natural kind" that we can intelligibly use the word 'cinema' to designate. My description of this natural kind, of course, associates it with a class of artifacts. Think of it as a concise articulation of cinema's engineering specifications, one I hope is empirically grounded in uniformities across physical properties and processes of otherwise dissimilar technological artifacts. Those who say of the fetal ultrasound image, "That's not cinematic!" are reacting to the countless differences from their favored paradigm cases of cinema but are likely ignoring the underlying engineering invariants.

While their creations surely have other significant facets, Frampton, Brakhage, Gehr, and others, by modeling their artform's primitive parts and processes, provide a resource for inquiry into cinema's engineering specifications, a resource unparalleled by anything arising from philosophical discourse itself. In doing so, they remind philosophers and theorists that "the cinema" names not just a welter of cultural, human phenomena but also a unified group of tangible things—no less so than rocks, trees, and airplanes—in the world, right before our eyes.[34]

TREVOR PONECH
Department of English
McGill University
Montreal, Quebec H3A 2T6
Canada

INTERNET: trevor.ponech@mcgill.ca

1. Hollis Frampton, "Lecture," in *The Avant-Garde Film: A Reader of Theory and Criticism*, ed. P. Adams Sitney (New York: Anthology Film Archives, 1987), p. 276.

2. Gregory Currie, "Reply to My Critics," *Philosophical Studies* 89 (1998): 357. See also his *Image and Mind: Film, Philosophy and Cognitive Science* (New York: Cambridge University Press, 1995), p. 1.

3. Currie, *Image and Mind*, p. 4.

4. Ibid.

5. Currie, "Reply to My Critics," p. 357.

6. Ibid.

7. Noël Carroll, "Defining the Moving Image," in *Theorizing the Moving Image* (New York: Cambridge University Press, 1996), pp. 49–74.

8. Carroll, "Defining the Moving Image," p. 66.

9. Carroll, "Defining the Moving Image," p. 63.

10. Ibid. A larger point motivates Carroll's discussion of detached displays. He wants to demonstrate that depictive photographic images are not transparent by dint of their causal relations to their referents, as Kendall Walton, "Transparent Pictures: On the Nature of Photographic Realism," *Critical Inquiry* 2 (1984): 246–277, contends. Looking at a photographic picture of the Grand Canyon is fundamentally unlike looking at it through a window because one would need supplementary nonperceptual beliefs in order to know one's approximate location relative to the Canyon. To see something, *S*, is presumably not to need such cognitive additives in order to relate yourself spatially to *S*. Hence one does not see *S* by seeing a movie image of it.

11. Carroll, "Defining the Moving Image," pp. 64–65. See also Carroll, "The Essence of Cinema?" *Philosophical Studies* 89 (1998): 323–330.

12. Carroll, "The Essence of Cinema?" p. 329.

13. Carroll, "Defining the Moving Image," p. 64.

14. Carroll, "Defining the Moving Image," pp. 49–54.

15. Carroll, "The Essence of Cinema?" p. 329.

16. Carroll, "The Essence of Cinema?" p. 330, n.4.

17. Carroll, "The Essence of Cinema?" p. 329.

18. Carroll, "Defining the Moving Image," p. 65.

19. At <fredcamper.com/Film/BrakhageL.html> you can view frame enlargements from *Mothlight* as well as from several of Brakhage's hand-painted films.

20. I borrow this example from Currie, *Image and Mind*, p. 4.

21. Kristin Thompson and David Bordwell, *Film History: An Introduction* (New York: McGraw-Hill, 1994), pp. 3–12, give an overview of the technical developments and precursors culminating in cinema's debut. For a description of the Kinetoscope's inner workings, see David Robinson's *From Peep Show to Palace* (Columbia University Press, 1996), p. 34.

22. A pair of websites currently herald such "free-space" displays as the next big thing: <www.FogScreen.com> and <www.io2technology.com>.

23. Carroll, "Defining the Moving Image," pp. 70–71.

24. Julian Hochberg, "Representation of Motion and Space in Video and Cinematic Displays," in *Handbook of Perception and Human Performance, Volume 1, Sensory Processes and Perception*, ed. Kenneth R. Boff, Lloyd Kaufman, and James P. Thomas (New York: John Wiley and Sons, 1986), p. 224.

25. For a discussion of singletons and their role in visual perception generally, see Steven Yantis, "Attentional Capture in Vision," in *Converging Operations in the Study of Visual Selective Attention*, ed. Arthur Kramer, Michael G. H. Coles, and Gordon Logan (Washington: American Psychological Association, 1996), pp. 45–76.

26. My approach to substance concepts and individuation draws on the work of Ruth Garrett Millikan, especially her *On Clear and Confused Ideas: An Essay about Substance Concepts* (Cambridge: Cambridge University Press, 2000). My notion of an individual as a uniformity persisting through some course of events derives from Jon Barwise and John Perry's analysis of this primitive in their situation semantics theory; see their *Situations and Attitudes* (MIT Press, 1986), pp. 7–9.

27. My "Cinematic Motion" (in preparation) reopens the question of whether this phenomenon is real or illusory, and whether it is a narrow or response-dependent property of movies.

28. Carroll discusses medium essentialism's failings—especially its tendency toward prescription and its inability to countenance technological and artistic innovation—in "Defining the Moving Image."

29. For a description of this work, see McCall's "Two Statements," in *The Avant-Garde Film*, p. 252.

30. Jonathan Walley, "The Material of Film and the Idea of Cinema: Contrasting Practices in Sixties and Seventies Avant-Garde Film," *October* 103 (2003): 20.

31. Walley, "The Material of Film and the Idea of Cinema," p. 23.

32. McCall, "Two Statements," p. 251.

33. Ernie Gehr, "Program Notes for a Film Screening at the Museum of Modern Art," in *The Avant-Garde Film*, pp. 247–248.

34. My thanks to Murray Smith and Tom Wartenberg for helpful comments on, and good questions about, the ideas expressed in this essay.

WHITNEY DAVIS

The World Rewound: Peter Forgács's *Wittgenstein Tractatus*

A right hand glove could be put on the left hand, if it could be turned around in four-dimensional space.
Ludwig Wittgenstein,
Tractatus Logico-Philosophicus, 6.36111

When I came home I expected a surprise & there was no surprise for me, so, of course, I was surprised.
Ludwig Wittgenstein, *Culture and Value*, 52e

In his study of the "ontology of film," *The World Viewed*, Stanley Cavell writes that "Wittgenstein investigates the world ('the possibilities of phenomena') by investigating what we say, what we are inclined to say, what our pictures of phenomena are, in order to wrest the world from our possessions so that we may possess it again."[1] Cavell's remark specifically concerns Ludwig Wittgenstein's *Philosophical Investigations*, but it points to a deep theme in Wittgenstein's entire body of philosophical work. How and why do we seem to know the world with a kind of familiarity, clarity, and certainty despite its contingency and ambiguity? How might we understand the world "again," or afresh, in light of seeing its contingency and ambiguity as such—if we can do so at all? What would things look like on the other side, as it were, of the conventional habits of seeing that we ordinarily bring to them? To "possess the world again"—although Cavell does not pursue the matter, it is worth asking how we might take the suggestion attributed to Wittgenstein (like Cavell, a fan of Hollywood cinema) quite literally in the case of film. How might film—which *already* presents us with a picture of phenomena—help us possess the world *again*? In what way can it suggest that

things might be seen to be quite different from what they are shown—and therefore seen—to be?

Peter Forgács's film *Wittgenstein Tractatus* (1992) is an elusive, often cryptic, montage of ordinary but often suggestive and unsettling images—all or almost all of them derived from sequences of historical "found footage"—accompanied by voice-overs, subtitles, and interleaved titles entirely drawn from writings by Wittgenstein. The principal themes of the film could be approached by way of a number of art-theoretical or film-critical frameworks. For example, Forgács appears to be interested in *Wittgenstein Tractatus* (as he has been in other films as well) in certain classic texts of iconography, such as Erwin Panofsky's studies of the layering of the habitual, expressive, and conventional meaning of motifs, and of film theory, such as André Bazin's account of cinematic encounters with the ambiguity and inexhaustibility of the world.[2] *Wittgenstein Tractatus* seems to contain references to both writers, and both Panofsky's and Bazin's approaches to visuality and pictoriality—and therefore to painting and to cinema—would help explicate Forgács's ideas and practices as a filmmaker in this and his other films.[3] I will not pursue these contexts here. In this essay, I will focus on the philosophical point of reference indicated in the very title of *Wittgenstein Tractatus*. The film presents itself explicitly as an engagement with Wittgenstein's *Tractatus Logico-Philosophicus* of 1921.

The precise nature of this engagement requires exploration. It would not be enough to say that the film sets forth the propositions of

Wittgenstein's *Tractactus*—although it certainly does do this insofar as Wittgenstein's words appear throughout the film and the film deploys Wittgenstein's ideas about the triangulation between picturing, language, and the world. I will suggest that the film *philosophizes* along Wittgensteinian lines in a way that discourse—the spoken or written word, including Wittgenstein's words—cannot do, and for the very reasons suggested by Wittgenstein in the *Tractatus*. To be specific, *Wittgenstein Tractactus* conducts philosophy in the way the *Tractatus Logico-Philosophicus* suggests philosophy might be possible (a suggestion that Wittgenstein's text finds its own means of stating substantively and indicating discursively) but cannot itself *show* us or *do* for us—even if such a showing constitutes the very nature of language as Wittgenstein understands it. In the end, then, the film is not so much an illustration of Wittgenstein's ideas about language (although it is that) as it is an exemplification of language itself in its "Wittgensteinian" nature: in its particular effects, the film *is* language *as* pictorial—what Wittgenstein *says* about language made filmically into the world-showing we can now *see* it to be. In this sense, Forgács's film does not so much supplement Wittgenstein's philosophy as complement it in a manner that helps complete it in the essential but specifically nondiscursive recursion required by the philosophical insight itself—an intuition about philosophical representation that Wittgenstein himself (a mechanical engineer, architect-builder, sculptor, and film buff, as well as a teacher and writer) seems to have taken seriously throughout his own life. Indeed, at several points in his life it would seem that Wittgenstein embraced the notion that he could and should, perhaps that he must, carry out his work of thinking—his philosophy—in nondiscursive media and practices of making and living.[4]

Needless to say, my own remarks on this matter must translate the filmic philosophy relayed in *Wittgenstein Tractactus* back into discourse, in part by relating it to Wittgenstein's *Tractactus*—trying to suggest *in* language what should be conceived as the essentially visual-pictorial constitution *of* world-knowledge. Striking and obvious structures and effects in the visual-pictorial field, of course, can only be indicated clumsily—and by way of highly rhetorical devices—in speaking about them. But if language or world-knowledge is essentially pictorial or has an essential pictoriality, it follows that the philosophy of language must, in the end, address picturing and perhaps might or must do so precisely *as* a picture—as a painting, film, or other nondiscursive pictorial representation *of* language *as* pictorial. In so doing it might be able to show not only what language speaks *about* but also *how* it does so—to show what language *is* in speaking of a world at all. I will begin my description of these interrelations by addressing the ways the visual-rhetorical structure of *Wittgenstein Tractactus* finds a filmic complement for the discursive-rhetorical structure of the *Tractatus Logico-Philosophicus*. This will enable me to suggest, in turn, how the kind of world-view presented in *Wittgenstein Tractactus* might be the kind of view that would best *enable* the philosophy of the *Tractatus Logico-Philosophicus*: making us *see* the limits of the language that are the "limits of my world," as the film tries to do, is to help us to see that the limits of my world are the limits of my language's picture of it. We might conclude that for Forgács something like the visual-pictorial world-experiences relayed to us filmically in *Wittgenstein Tractactus* might have suggested Wittgenstein's own "picture theory of meaning" as it was discursively proposed in the *Tractatus Logico-Philosophicus*.

I. REWORLDING

Like the text of Wittgenstein's *Tractatus Logico-Philosophicus*, Forgács's film has been divided into seven parts. There is no continuous narrative in the film. But it has a rigorous structure; it becomes increasingly obvious—and increasingly subtle—on repeated viewings of the film. Each part of the film has been constituted from found footage (film footage not shot by the filmmaker himself, and typically derived from archives) showing seemingly ordinary people engaged in seemingly mundane activities. Each shot lasts only a fraction of a minute and sometimes only a few seconds. Each shot tends to depict a single, simple event: for example, a woman walks toward us with a dog on a leash; an elderly man gets ready for bed; a man seats himself at a café table and tips his hat to the camera. (The latter shot might well be a nod of the hat to Panofsky's famous iconological paradigm of the man in the street tipping his hat to us; as in the case of the observer in the example discussed by Panofsky, the viewer of this shot in the film cannot quite tell—cannot quite be sure—what the man "means" by what he does. Throughout the film, similar questions arise.[5]) The identification of these people and the places and times depicted—that is, the historical origin of the found footage—remains uncertain throughout the film. The usual location seems to be Hungary before or after—or before and after—World War II, although one series of shots has been taken in ski country (the Austrian Alps? Switzerland?) or Scandinavia (Wittgenstein's house in Norway is explicitly recalled in this part of the film). The seventh and last part of the film includes several shots set in Budapest in the 1950s: horse-drawn carts mix with trams and taxis in the streets and television has appeared in the home.

Preceded by a short pause separating it from the previous part, each one of the seven parts begins and ends with a freeze-frame of the initial shot or the final shot in the sequence of shots in that part. As we watch, the frozen image comes together like a jigsaw puzzle or mosaic being assembled (at the beginning of the part) or comes undone like a jigsaw puzzle or mosaic being pulled apart (at the end of the part). As each piece of the puzzle floats into the frame or floats out of it, building up or reducing the whole image, we see the fragment of the image from both or maybe all sides—our "front" and its "back" (though in reality we cannot see what is in back of what we are in front of) or maybe all the way round. As the film unfolds—and as we can rewind it to pull apart the image that has been put together or to put together the image that has been pulled apart— we come to see that these framing sequences thematize the most general visual interests, and most prominent filmic effects, of the entire montage of shots.

The seven parts of the film are roughly equal in duration—about three or four minutes each for a total running time of thirty-two minutes. Whatever the image track might show us, each part of Forgács's film quotes—in interleaved titles, in voice-overs, in overlaid titles and images—from individual passages in the corresponding part of Wittgenstein's text; that is to say, the first part of the film quotes from the *Tractatus* 1–1.121, the second part of the film quotes from the *Tractatus* 2–2.225, and so on.[6] In the film this complex stratigraphy of words and images to some extent replicates the labyrinthine lemmata of the *Tractatus*—although in the end, as the film tells us in quoting Wittgenstein's words, *der Gegenstand ist einfach*—"the object is simple" (2.02).[7]

When Wittgenstein's words are quoted in the film, sometimes Forgács displays Wittgenstein's numeration of the lemmas of the text (for example, 1, 1.1, 2.02, 4.002, 5.634, 6.36311, and so on). Provided with this information, we can see that as the film unfolds it goes "deeper" into Wittgenstein's text and its nesting of propositions—further and further into its special and specific derivations. And it would seem to travel certain tracks within the text. The first part of Wittgenstein's *Tractatus* consists simply of seven sentences numbered 1, 1.1, 1.11, 1.12, 1.13, 1.2, 1.21—sentences therefore indicated to have different levels or degrees of conceptual scope or "logical importance" (*logische Gewicht*), as Wittgenstein tells us in his footnote to 1, even if "all propositions are equally valuable" (6.4). The entire seventh part of the *Tractatus*, by contrast, is only one short sentence in length—as it were one-seventh the discursive size of the first part (even if its claim is the broadest of all). But in Forgács's *Tractatus*, the first and the seventh parts of the text receive nearly as much film time as the second through the sixth parts of the text, which occupy several dozens of pages of printed text. This is certainly as it should be. The movement from 1 to 7 (and equally important the movement from 7 to 1) is the burden of Wittgenstein's text: although we do not quite follow a series of syllogisms, we can "read" from statements that appear to be more general and comprehensive to statements that appear to be more narrow and derivative— and vice versa. As Wittgenstein says at one point, this lemmatic labyrinth of sentences might be regarded as a "ladder" (*Leiter*) (6.54). This has usually been taken to mean that the reader can discard it once the ladder has been climbed—that is, once the text has been read and understood. To some extent, Wittgenstein clearly intended his metaphor to be taken in this sense. But a ladder can—and sometimes must—be used to climb *down*, or to climb up and down again, and to move between or around various lower and higher levels of a structure. It is unclear whether Wittgenstein expected that his text *could* be fully understood in ordinary discursive terms; what the reader supposedly will attain on understanding the text—after climbing the ladder—has been a matter of considerable debate. Certainly, most readers' experience of the text of Wittgenstein's *Tractatus* involves a complicated peregrination—moving back and forth and around an array of propositions (however they are sequenced and hierarchically ordered as a text) that can be read in several ways or even, in a more literal sense, in more than one direction.

Consider, for example, the first sentence of Wittgenstein's text, that is, the first of the seven most important lemmas (1): *Die Welt ist alles, was der Fall ist* [the world is all that is the case]. A more literal translation—"The world is all, what the case is"—relays a crucial connotation that tends to be lost in the published English translations. For Wittgenstein it is not only that the world is "everything that is the case"—a kind of impersonal general logicity characterized preeminently by its truth, however that might be defined or constituted. In his formulation Wittgenstein manifestly avoided the predicative structure absorbed into the English translation so that he could emphasize what we might call a juxtapositive relation between the world and our representation of it: *die Welt* and *der Fall* occupy grammatically parallel positions in the statement of what is. All the world is/what the case is: *der Fall* was Freud's and the common word (obviously well known to Wittgenstein) for a "case" (as in a Freudian "case history" or a legal case) or better for an "affair"—as in those things and events, *Gegenstände*, however "simple" (*einfach*—single, homely, ordinary), pictured and preserved in found footage, and whether or not they might be a "case in point"—*ein vorliegender Fall*—of a general truth "in any case," *auf alle Fälle*. *Ein Fall* is also, of course, a falling—an actual waterfall or any kind of general failure or downfall. Indeed, Wittgenstein's verbal formulation of his first sentence would seem to have been carefully crafted precisely to permit the parallelism and potential recursion suggested in the argument as it will be developed in the further

propositions of the text: the world is all what the case is; the case is all what the world is.

Most important, Wittgenstein's verbal formula—and not only as a logical or philosophical argument but also as an experience of *reading* or even *seeing* that tries to enable us to read or to see *differently*—encourages us to start (and also to end) with "what is the case," what it is we see when we ask what the world is—even though asking what the world is (what we see) might challenge our view of what is the case. As the linguistic structure (if not the argumentative substance) of the first sentence of the text might suggest, we are embedded in a continuous inescapable loop in which our representation or picture of the world, our image-statement of what is the case, recurs or threads through itself; though the world can perhaps be seen differently at different times and in different contexts, it is always seen as what is (seen as…) the case. What is the case in or as the world, then, must be contingent on the seeing—what we might call our use of pictorial techniques, habits, and motifs or (following Panofsky) our iconology. As such, of course, the world could readily be (seen to be) otherwise in the same way that a picture—after a change of pictorial techniques, habits, and motifs—might be different from what it is initially seen to be and indeed seen to show: if what we take to be the case about the world is somehow revisioned or repictured or (to draw the metaphor from Wittgenstein's own favorite medium) refilmed, the world itself must be changed in the same sense in which we would say that apples painted by Paul Cézanne and by Henri Matisse, even if both painters had used the very same real apples as models, show us quite *different* apples. This notion—this feeling we have in relation to pictures and our world-picture as such—seems to be captured in an enigmatic proposition quoted by the film at one point: "Feeling the world as a *limited* whole—it is *this* that is mystical" (6.45, emphasis added). At the same time as the picture gives "all that is the case" (that is, the world) to us, we can feel (if we cannot actually see) the contingency of the picture, the fact that as a picture it must have certain limits—a particular degree of resolution, certain occlusions or foreshortenings, and select devices of framing and focusing. We might suspect that the world continues beyond or behind these limits of the picture: as we might say, the world is "out there." Nevertheless, we cannot speak about this "out there" readily or even coherently because our world-picture, our language, does not show it. Our awareness of this presence of the world outside—if we can come to have any such awareness *within* the picture-seeing that gives us the world—remains a "mystical" one.

How can we revision, repicture, or refilm the world when all of the world—what the world *is* for us—is constituted *by* the picture that we make and use to see it? Forgács's film recalls and reiterates the quasi-palindromic linguistic, logical, and structural devices of Wittgenstein's own text (read as much for its literary or imagistic force as for its substance) in order to *visualize* or *picture* Wittgenstein's understanding of the world imagined in the propositions of the *Tractatus*—namely, as visualized or contingently pictured—in a way that might be unavailable to its standard written exegesis. Although the standard written exegesis can say that the world—the world as a picture or as pictured—might be different, it cannot see this world if it is a world outside its own pictorial purview, showing what this world would be; as logical or discursive language, the text cannot reverse or invert itself—except perhaps palindromically—without falling into an unintelligibility or chaos (*der Fall*) that will not permit us to see and to show any world (*eine Welt*) at all. Here, film as a mode of picturing can advance philosophy—especially and specifically Wittgenstein's philosophy of language. In particular, I think, and precisely as *film*, it can—though it need not always—demonstrate the contingency of world-picturing: it can show the possible inversions or reversals of world-picturing suggested in the first sentence of the *Tractatus* and carried throughout its philosophy as its own world-picture.

II. *ÜBERWINDEN*

To help bring out the possibilities—and difficulties—for a specifically filmic presentation of Wittgenstein's philosophy, and especially in relation to its discursive representation, it is worth recalling Max Black's remarks on the order or sequential logic of Wittgenstein's text; Black's well-known commentary can stand for the wider reception and understanding of the *Tractatus*—a reception or understanding addressed and challenged by the film.[8] Black begins with Wittgenstein's title in translation ("probably suggested by Spinoza's *Tractatus Theologico-Politicus*, it is said to have been proposed for the English edition by G. E. Moore").[9] He ends with Wittgenstein's final sentence (that is, 7)—*Wovon man nicht sprechen kann, darüber muß man schweigen* [What we cannot speak about we must pass over in silence]. Black here recalls the more euphonious—and more famous—English translation by C. K. Ogden: "Whereof one cannot speak, thereof one must be silent."[10] Both English translations, however, lose an echo in the German—"whereof" or "about what" one cannot speak, one must be silent *darüber*, "over it" or "over there." Wittgenstein had summoned this connotation in the immediately preceding remark when he asserted that his reader must "overcome" (*überwinden*) the philosopher's sentences or propositions in order to see the world rightly (6.54). "Over there"—where we cannot speak about the world, even if (or maybe precisely because) we *see* it—we must be silent.

This picture of things (for the text represents what it imagines the world to be) tends to be occluded when it is said, as Black himself does at the very beginning of his commentary, that "Wittgenstein treats the famous concluding remark [that is, 7] as summarizing 'the whole sense of the book.'"[11] This is certainly what the English translation of Wittgenstein's Preface says: "The whole sense of the book might be summed up in the following words: what can be said at all can be said clearly, and what we cannot talk about we must pass over in silence." With the exception of the substitution of *reden* (to talk) for *sprechen* (to speak), the word Wittgenstein actually uses in 7, the final phrase of this remark in the Preface does reproduce (though it textually anticipates) the text of 7. But in his Preface, Wittgenstein himself does not say, as the English translation would have it, that 7 "sums up" the "whole sense of the book." Rather, he says: *Man könnte den ganzen Sinn des Buches etwa in die Worte fassen: Was sich überhaupt sagen läßt, läßt sich klar sagen; und wovon man nicht reden kann, darüber muß man schweigen* [One could *comprehend* the whole sense of the book *somewhat* in the words: ...] (emphasis added). Taking him at his word, then, the single sentence of the seventh part of the text cannot be so much a conclusion—in the sense of a derivation—or a *full* summary as simply one part of a serviceable understanding of what the entire book says. The *other* part asserts that what one can say in general—for example, 1 to 6—can be "clear" (*klar*); *where* we cannot speak clearly, *there* we must be silent.

As Wittgenstein says in his penultimate remark in the text (6.54), his sentences (*Sätze*) can "at the end be known as nonsensical" (*am Ende als unsinnig erkennt*): after going "through" them and "on them" and "over them" (*durch, auf, über*), one can "get out of them" or even "dismount" or "alight from" them (*hinaussteigen; steigen* refers not only to climbing but also to riding). In parenthesis, Wittgenstein adds that the reader *muß sozusagen die Leiter wegwerfen, nachdem er auf ihr hinaufgestiegen ist* [he must, so to speak, throw away the ladder after he has climbed up it]. This English translation conflates *hinausgestiegen*, Wittgenstein's initial word, and *hinaufgestiegen*, his parenthetical elucidation; *steige aus* and *steige auf*—in the metaphor of a *Leiter*—would have to be climbing down (the other side?) and climbing up (whatever side one is on?), respectively. According to the translation, a reader must "transcend these propositions"—the sentences of the text. Wittgenstein actually says, however, that *Er muß diese Sätze überwinden*—one must *overcome* these sentences—literally, one must "overwind" or "twist over" them. In this *Überwindung* we might be able to *see* the world clearly.

Wittgenstein's last sentence (from the point of view recommended in the text it could also be the *first* sentence) prompts the question with which Black completes his own commentary: "Is the 'Tractatus' self-defeating?" Black assumes a series of propositions that one might take to develop in sequential consequentiality *from* 1 *to* 7, for he wants to rescue Wittgenstein from the charge that his text fails itself (*ein Fall?*)—that 7 *does not* follow from, and even undoes, everything leading up to it from 1 onward.[12] Even if Black thinks Wittgenstein does not contradict himself, he has to assume a text in which contradiction could be a feature of its sentences in total relation to one another. This does not always sit easily, however, with

the lemmatic conformation of the text. Presumably, a sentence numbered 1.2 has "equal value" to a sentence numbered 4.2, and a sentence numbered 1.21 or 4.21 can be regarded as stating an aspect—or pursuing a particular implication or giving a partial elucidation—of 1.2 or 4.2, even though it would seem to have less scope or generality. Nevertheless it does not follow that 4.2 derives—as aspect, implication, or elucidation, let alone as logical consequent—from 1.2 through any number of intermediate sentences, even though 1.11 "follows" or better flows from 1.1, which "follows" or flows from 1. To "read" the first part of the *Tractatus*, for instance, one could read:

1—1.1—1.11—(1.1)—1.12—(1.1)—1.13—(1)—1.2—1.21.

But with equal cogency one could also read:

1.11—1.12—1.13—1.1—1.21—1.2—1.

To ask how sentences ordered in this way might conclude in an argumentative sequence, and especially what they might prove or how they might be "summed up," does not seem apposite to the assertion of 7 itself—"whereof we cannot speak, thereof we must remain silent." 7 seems explicitly to draw our attention to the fact, obvious throughout the series of sentences flowing to this point, that there are many gaps—as it were "nothing there" over there—in their representation of a world said to have this very structure (see especially 2–2.225). More important, the text offers a showing (but cannot be a telling) of something endless or infinite, or maybe nothing endless and infinite, extending in all directions before and after and around and between all the sentences actually given. In the first short part of the text alone, for example, there is a 1.11 but no 1.111, a 1.2 and 1.21 but no 1.22 (though there is a 1.12), a 1.1 and a 1.2 but no 1.3, and so forth. To notice these gaps or places of no-speaking or (from another point of view) to make these discoveries—here is a density of elucidatory representation, there is a thin overlay of general understanding, and "over there" we cannot speak, like a blank space on a map—we must continually *read back* through or *rewind* the text: after absorbing 1.13 following 1.12 following 1.11, we reconsider 1.1 (and maybe even 1) before flowing to what follows *it*, namely, 1.2.

III. REWINDING

The particular directionality or orientation— and the general reversibility—of world-perspectives lay at the heart of Wittgenstein's philosophy and his constructive practice in written and other media.[13] As film, and precisely as film, Forgács's representation turns out—we can use that verb advisedly—to be peculiarly capable of instating, of "doing," the philosophy that it engages.

Like Wittgenstein's text, Forgács's film has constant refrains. Two ubiquitous motifs complement one another visually and relay the fundamental theme of changing and even reversing direction. First, we are constantly presented with shots and scenes of people going in a particular direction—taking a road, following in line, making or pursuing a track. For example, the first part of *Tractatus* opens with a shot of the wheel of a cart or a carriage, seen from above, churning over muddy ruts in a road ("the world is all that is the case" (1)).[14] Next we see the cart trundling along the road itself, running through a flat farmland, then poled across a river by a ferryman; an intervening shot shows a rower in a single scull rowing downstream ("the world is the totality of facts, not things" (1.1)). Second, these motifs are frequently followed, or inflected, by shots or scenes of a person or people dancing or otherwise "going or turning around." Different people doing different kinds of dances appear throughout the film. For example, the first part of the film ends with a brief shot of a man walking in a circle upside down on his hands followed by a scene of a group of men and women dancing in a round with joined hands (again, we're told, "the world is the totality of facts, not things" (1.1)). As these descriptions suggest, both motifs—going somewhere in particular, going round and round—embed images of going backward (the rower sits facing away from the direction in which he is rowing) or being upside-down (like the man walking on his hands). More important, then, the motifs support the film-philosophical investigation of Wittgenstein's world-picture— his claim that if the world is everything that is the case (in our picture of it), it could also be otherwise (in another picture or from another "point of view"). As the film goes on—as it unwinds before our eyes—the viewer becomes

increasingly aware of the possibility, the possible fact, that these people could change their direction or orientation or even reverse or invert it: that what they are shown to be doing could seem to be "going the wrong way" or "being wrong way up"—at least from *our* point of view as viewers of the world in which *they* are pictured for us, and granting that from *their* point of view, presumably, they could be "doing it right."

The middle sequences in the first part of the film announce Forgács's Wittgensteinian direction of approach—even though it will take the entire duration of the film to secure the viewer's sense that it has been seen there at all. After the sequence of the carriage traveling the road and ferried across the river in the first part of the film, we see a striking scene of a dying pig rolled over and over on itself in its own blood and feces, prodded first by a human leg and foot encased in a polished jackboot and then by a leg and foot wearing a heavy workboot. (In the fourth part of the film, Forgács briefly repeats a segment of this shot; the voice-over quotes Wittgenstein's remark that "the horrors of hell can be experienced in a single day."[15]) The owners of the boots are not shown and we are left to speculate on their historical Austro-Hungarian or other identity; in other films, Forgács has proffered scathing condemnation of German and Austro-Hungarian Nazism and Soviet-satellite Communism alike. In the succeeding sequences in the first part, we see a group of dancers (the dance seems to reverse itself partway through) and then a group of people—clearly they are friends if not relations or lovers—seated in row in a mountainside meadow, relaxing and having a meal. The camera pans from left to right across the group, showing each person in turn—smiling, smoking, looking at the camera, looking elsewhere. Then it reverses itself, though whether the person originally holding the camera has simply panned back or whether the filmmaker using the footage has "rewound" it partway through remains an open question. (It is difficult to resolve this matter even after repeated viewings of the film. The very fact that the film includes instances of the image-track as it were "going backward," being played in reverse, makes it difficult to decide whether what seem to be continuous sequences of filmed events "going forward"—whether or not they include a *filmed* action of "looking back"—belong to the original participants, to the original wielder of the camera, to the film artist using the found footage, or even to ourselves, the latest viewers of the footage as reworked by the artist. It seems to be important to Forgács to create this proliferating doubt—this sense that things are not what they seem or are said or shown to be and that who or what is doing the looking, saying, or showing itself is hard to pin down.) Either way, however, when the camera returns to where we thought it began "seeing" the scene it now reveals two women, one leaning intimately against the other (are they strangers? sisters? dear friends? lovers?)—women we *did not* see in the initial scan, even though one of the other women in the group (we have seen *her* twice) appears to have been looking right at them. ("How hard I find it to see what is right in front of my eyes."[16]) Though it is hard to tell, this group of men and women appears to be the same as the group of people dancing hand in hand, already noted, that concluded the first part of the film ("the world is the totality of facts, not things"(1.1)). We would need nothing more than all this—neither the brief closeups of Wittgenstein's face (taken from well-known portrait photographs) nor the occasional overlays of his handwritten texts nor the quotations from his writings—to grasp that the film tries to show (though it would be difficult or impossible to "speak" or discursively to describe) the contingency of the depicted world or to show the world *as* a picture, specifically, a *film*-like-picture in which its contingency and reversibility can be shown.

In the final shot of Forgács's *Tractatus*, closing the seventh part of the film, a middle-aged man dressed in a street suit approaches a small round table in what seems to be an outdoor café. We do not recognize the man—he has not appeared earlier in the film—and the scene gives us few clues to his identity. He seats himself facing the camera, tips his hat toward it, and blows his cigarette smoke sideways out of his mouth—almost as if trying not to blow it in our eyes and almost as if we are in his way. It appears that he does not know and maybe does not want to know the person behind the camera. The tip of the hat seems sardonic; indeed, we feel the force of the man's exhalation between pursed lips—almost hear the vigorous *hppphhh.*

Just before the shot begins, a title gives us the full text of the final lemma of Wittgenstein's *Tractatus*: "What we cannot speak about we must pass over in silence." The silence denoted here is not the silence of a silent movie or the found footage in Forgács's film, in which we do not hear the filmed human beings saying anything. Rather, the film investigates what "we must pass over in silence"—it might be unspeakable—in the fact that "what can be *shown* cannot be *said*" (4.1212). It is the easiest thing in the world to miss what the film shows in what it cannot say about the world, about "everything that is the case"—to overlook the fact that the world it depicts, and because it depicts it, might be entirely otherwise at the same time as it is nothing other (and for us can be nothing other) than what it is. In Forgács's hands, this insight becomes beautiful and optimistic even as it might also be ominous and horrifying.

In this respect *Tractatus* belongs to Forgács's broader project—especially in his films confronting the historical destruction of central European Jewry—to figure the consubstantiality between everyday human happiness and an unsayable—and in some or many historical cases an unspeakable—futurity and fatality shown to be entirely outside it, turning everything upside down or inside out. The film repeatedly proffers a formal congruence between the two motifs already noted; as the film unwinds before our eyes, we come to see that they are the same thing viewed "from within" or from one side and "from without" or from another side. On the one side, people join hands and dance side by side or in a line or in a circle. On the other side, the dying pig rolls over on itself in its own blood and waste, prodded by booted human feet. (Once or twice the film seems to solicit us to wonder whether we see the *same* boots on the dancers *and* the torturers—but we would have to rewind and replay to be sure. And even then, I think, we would not be *entirely* sure—no matter what we thought we had finally been able to see.) In the opening shot in the fifth part of the film, a dying rabbit, neck or back seemingly broken, crawls round itself in a backward circle as if trying to put its head back on ("the limits of my language are the limits of my world" (5.6); "whatever we see could be other than it is" (5.634)). As suggested already, however, it is the easiest thing in the world to miss the deeper visual fact—distributed throughout the film—that an essential two-wayness or multisidedness and inherent reversibility, what I might call a kind of necessary contingency, characterize the whole human dance itself: if it is not the *Totentanz* or Dance of Death, then maybe it must be, or will be; and if it is a *Totentanz*, then maybe it will not be or need not be. (In one of the series of enigmatic shots closing the last part of the film, a Death-like figure—a street hawker in black cloak and skull mask—wears a placard that says the same thing, "The Invisible Man Returns," whether he is coming or going.[17]) In *Wittgenstein Tractatus*, it is the essence of the world we are in that we are never quite sure whether we are seeing things "going forwards" or "going backwards" or "right way round," whether there is a "change of direction" in the middle of things or "another side" to them, whether things are "going the right way" or "going the wrong way," what exactly and whether anything will "turn out." "I am my world—the microcosm" (5.63): a woman enters a swimming pool—she is walking backward facing us—she comes around in a circle, always facing us—she steps out of the pool. At any point has she turned around to go another way? Or is she always turning around and backing up and going another way *as* she goes her own way? ("The limits of my language are the limits of my world" (5.6).) Toward the very end of the film, an elderly couple prepares a bedroom for use and the old man undresses and goes to bed reading his newspaper ("the world is independent of my will" (6.373)). Is he going to die? The camera seems to go "in" to a photograph in the newspaper and there to see scenes shown to be televised (a ping-pong game!)—and then to come back out again (*hinausgestiegen*) into the bedroom, where the old man's wife now dances with a younger female companion—and touches hands with the old man sitting by her side. Have we gone back in time? Forward? In and out of different but interconnected worlds? Are we somewhere else altogether? Having a dream? ("Death is not an event of life: we do not live to experience death" (6.4311); Wittgenstein's text continues, though it is not quoted in the film: "Our life has no end in just the way in which our visual field has no limits.") The final

fact of the matter always seems to be at, or perhaps just over, the horizon of what we see—the very edge, or just beyond the edge, of what seems to be shown to be going on.

At points in the film we certainly *do* see that what is said in a *language* of describing the world is not at all what is shown—what is actually going on in what is depicted. For example, the early shot of a rowing man—because he is seated backward, he seems to be going forward in reverse—finds a supplement in a later closeup, seemingly drawn from the same or a similar sequence, of the action of rowing. On a shot of an arm and hand pushing the oar up, over, down, and around, Forgács has superimposed a notation of a movement *going in the opposite direction*. The contradiction in representations is actually quite hard to see—"how hard it is to see what is right in front of my eyes"—and a viewer could easily overlook it. (At a recent screening, several well-prepared observers of the film—even after multiple viewings, replayings, and rewindings—had some difficulty seeing the effect.) The cumulative effect of all the footage in the film provokes a sense in us that something is not yet wholly aright in what we have seen in relation to what has been said. In setting up this effect (there are many like it throughout *Tractatus*), Forgács is not especially interested in routine conflicts between natural language (spoken and written) or other notations on the one hand ("saying") and pictorial representation or depiction on the other ("showing"). He is interested in the fundamental contingency and irreducible ambiguity of anything being on this hand or that hand—it is the rower's (or the viewer's) right or left, up or down, this way or that—in the first place.

As I have stressed, Forgács deploys an essential logical property of the picture-world of cinema to show the contingency of the world-picture—perhaps most visible to us at the "edge" of the picture or at the points where its limits and reversals and inversions become palpable. It is clear at points in the film that in making it Forgács has *actually* replayed the rewound footage, as it were running its backward forward—even though we think we are seeing something "going on" in one and the same continuous way. In one notable sequence, we see a man dancing and leaping in a circle; the footage clearly speeds up (that is, fast-forwards) at a certain point and at another point—even though everything seems to be one continuous shot—seems to be playing (though now at expected or "normal" speed) in rewind. This next-to-final shot in the second part of the film, like earlier shots, explicitly deals with pictures—"it is impossible to tell from the picture alone whether it is true or false" (2.224)—and implicitly with our world *as* a picture ("we picture facts to ourselves"). In another shot, a young woman standing behind a fence bordering the track at a train station looks one way, then the other: is she really doing this, or has the film "rewound" her movement? Is she expecting something to arrive from *both* directions—or do we see something like a reversal of her single and directed expectation? Or is everything an effect, a trick, of the found footage—or of its manipulation by the film—or of our viewing? Similarly, a man and a girl standing at the fence—they seem to be strangers to one another—seem to look toward the same point between them, though there is not anything there, then to look in opposite directions. Are they waiting for the same thing, or has the film, rewound-replayed, shown that they could be waiting for different things—or vice versa? ("What is thinkable is also possible" (3.02).) In the third part of the film, we see a series of shots of a group of people in a bright snowy landscape—they are skiing—they put on lotion, they rub the snow into their mouths, they stretch: "Their inner life will always be a mystery." Or yet again, a man fires a revolver while a female companion clutches his arm (they seem to be at a house party in a country chateau, as if in a scene from *Rules of the Game* (Jean Renoir, 1939)); we see him pull the gun from his coat, extend his arm, a flash—and then the whole movement in reverse. Did he really "pull" the gun on someone or something? Or did he fire it and put it away? We are never quite sure—even if and perhaps especially when we rewind and replay—that we are seeing something all the way through, or the same thing different ways through, or different things the same way through, or the same thing both ways, or different things the same way. The film asks us to rewind and replay *as* the indefinitely extended condition of coming around to understand things next time around: maybe *then* we will see, maybe *there* things will turn out differently.

In much of *Tractatus* it is as if the very same things are simultaneously being seen, or could be seen, from the *other side* of the film stock—the "found footage"—actually projected before us. Thus in the end *Tractatus*, like other films by Forgács, tends to ask us what side we are really on. To some extent this question in the film is ordered and proposed as a formal or structural matter—a problem for and in speaking, seeing, and showing. But it is palpably connected, albeit in an enigmatic and elusive way, to immediate questions of our moral, social, and cultural affiliations, allegiances, identifications, and commitments—of our "side" or "sides." These commitments inherently contain the possibility of "being on another side," "changing sides," and so forth. But at the same time they can also appear to be the "only way to look at things." In this respect, *Tractatus* offers a meditation on the perceptual and cognitive conditions of possibility of the concrete psychic and political histories explored more explicitly and in relation to particular historical events in other films by Forgács, notably the dislocation and destruction of central European Jewry—recorded and remembered in found footage—and the rise of fascism and other totalitarian ideologies. I cannot take up this matter in any detail here, but it is worth remarking that *Wittgenstein Tractatus* does not have a readily apparent *political* perspective in the narrow sense; its images are too laconic—too ambiguous and multisided—for any overt commitment to a "side" or a "direction" to be easily inferred by the viewer. To be sure, the film appears to be sympathetic toward—to identify with—ordinary human beings conducting their ordinary affairs or (as Wittgenstein might say) simply "going on," and to some degree it mourns the fragile existence (and seemingly the loss) of these people and their worlds. These people do not have to be dead for us to mourn them; as in other films by Forgács, *Wittgenstein Tractatus* pursues a proleptic or anticipatory mourning: *we* already know—and in watching the film we dread to see—their destruction in advance. Do *they* also know—do they dread—it too? As in other films by Forgács, the simplest and most mundane activities—a glance, a gesture, a word—seem to contain movements of shattering consequence; they seem to relay forces of world-historical change, of everything turning entirely inside out or upside down, that are so vast and pervasive and yet so subtle and impalpable that we cannot quite see them as they occur all around us and they cannot quite be named or spoken about. In such a world, in a world where the unspeakable might occur because it is not *sayable*, perhaps it is necessary to "take sides" in order to see and to say anything at all—even though this, in itself, might be the same thing as being utterly unable to see things in any other way and as saying things that in the end must result in something unspeakable. It is this horrifying yet inescapable framing condition and structural consequence of moral identification, cultural affiliation, and political commitment as such—rather than any particular historical identification, affiliation, or commitment—that concerns Forgács: things cannot be otherwise.

When a man walks from left to right in front of us, swinging his arms left and right, his right arm swinging before him is on *our* right, and it is also on *his* right. But if we mimic his action, walking left to right in front of him and swinging our right arms ahead of us, from his point of view *our* right is *his* left. Is it all the same to him and us? When a man lifts his hat up and down to us, his hat goes up for him *and* for us. But *his* "up"—is it a friendly greeting? a neutral, official courtesy? an obsequious obeisance? an irritated put-off? a sardonic put-on? a hostile condescension?—is not necessarily ours in its "meaning." *Wittgenstein Tractatus* exposes such coincidences—they might or might not be congruences—in their unavoidable recursion, asymmetry, and intransitivity. To understand the man we must know what it is like *for him* to tip his hat in the way that he does—even though we are on the other side. Is he friendly? Indifferent? Is he hostile? To discover this we feel we would have to lift our hat, and purse our lips, and vigorously blow our cigarette smoke sideways—just as he does. But to do this *just like him*, to feel and to understand the gesture as he does and as it were from within, we would already have to know what he is doing within his own world, his way of seeing and his picture of things—that is to say, we would already have to be "on his side." No mere rewinding and replaying (a mechanical *Überwindung*) can get us "over there" (*darüber*) (the man's "inner life will always be a mystery"); we can show this place only as

another side of where *we* are. Like Wittgenstein before him, then, Forgács admits a leap of faith: since what I see could be entirely otherwise, what I see—it is how things *must be* for me, the "totality of the facts" (1.1), the "limits of my world" (5.6)—partakes of the "mystical" in the fact that it exists at all in the seemingly solid and certain way that it does for me (*Nicht wie die Welt ist, ist das Mystische, sondern daß sie ist* [It is not *how* the things are in the world that is mystical, but *that* it exists] (6.44)). In his filmic repossession of the world—rewound—Forgács's found footage, sometimes unsettling, often ambiguous, is always sacramental: "Feeling the world as a limited whole—it is this that is mystical" (6.45).[18]

The happenstance incidence, the astonishing preservation, the manifest unlikeliness of the found footage as such—in its blithe and deadly existence it is a reminder of everything that could have been pictured that was never actually filmed—becomes a total representation of consciousness as such. In *my* world it is the greatest surprise of all that the world—everything that is the case, my affair, my failure (*alles was der Fall ist*)—is not a surprise at all, for it would be a surprise beyond measure—certainly unsayable, maybe unspeakable—that the world *is* a surprise. As Forgács shows, however, it is there *in* the world at the press of a button.[19]

WHITNEY DAVIS
Department of History of Art and Center for
  New Media
University of California at Berkeley
Berkeley, CA 94720
USA

INTERNET: wmdavis@Berkeley.edu

1. Stanley Cavell, *The World Viewed: Reflections on the Ontology of Film*, enlarged ed. (Harvard University Press, 1979), p. 22.
2. Erwin Panofsky, *Studies in Iconology* (Oxford University Press, 1939), and *Meaning in the Visual Arts* (New York: Doubleday, 1955); André Bazin, *What Is Cinema?*, trans. Hugh Gray, 2 vols. (University of California Press, 1967–1971).
3. For the terms, see Whitney Davis, "Visuality and Pictoriality," *Res* 46 (2004): 9–31.
4. For Wittgenstein's activities in nondiscursive media—they might be taken to be philosophical activities—see especially Paul Wijdeveld, *Ludwig Wittgenstein, Architect* (MIT Press, 1994).

5. See Panofsky, *Studies in Iconology*, p. 3. Panofsky provided a largely positive, albeit hermeneutic, answer to the question of the meaning—habitual, expressive, and cultural—of the man's gesture. According to Panofsky, we have a method of understanding him—of interpreting the material, the traditional, and the conventional aspects of his behavior and in so doing of localizing it historically and understanding it culturally. This ordinary method of negotiating the world visually and pictorially can be formalized as *Kunstwissenschaft*—a discipline that, as it were, retraces the ordinary functions of human consciousness in making sense of things we see around us in the world. It would take me too far afield to consider the similarities and differences between Panofsky's iconology and Wittgenstein's picture theory of meaning (as well as Wittgenstein's later doctrine of language games woven into a natural and cultural "form of life"). There is no evidence that Panofsky read Wittgenstein's *Tractatus*—though there are some striking similarities in their phrasing—in the same way, for example, that there is clear evidence for Panofsky's sustained engagement with the writing of Martin Heidegger in the 1920s. Panofsky responded to many of the same philosophical and ideological currents that shaped Wittgenstein's thought in the 1920s and before.

6. Forgács's film also sometimes quotes from writings by Wittgenstein other than the *Tractatus Logico-Philosophicus*, namely, the short remarks and fragments (mostly written in the 1930s and 1940s) selected by Georg Henrik von Wright from Wittgenstein's *Nachlass*, edited by Wright in collaboration with Heikki Nyman and first published in 1977 as *Vermischte Bemerkungen*. I have quoted them from the revised edition of the original German texts selected by von Wright, edited by Alois Pichler, translated by Peter Winch under the English title *Culture and Value: A Selection from the Posthumous Remains* (Oxford: Basil Blackwell, 1998). The textual origins of these particular remarks are nowhere cited in the film. If the film does not exclusively quote from the text of the *Tractatus*, it is, however, certainly about the philosophical perspective of the *Tractatus*.

In Forgács's original version of *Wittgenstein Tractatus*, the quotations from Wittgenstein, whether written or spoken, are given in Hungarian translation. To my regret I cannot evaluate this translation or Forgács's use of it. In the English-language version, also produced in 1992, many of the Hungarian titles (whether interleaved or superimposed) have been preserved, but English titles have been added. Naturally, this addition changes the sequence and layering of certain pictorial images in relation to accompanying text. Moreover, the Hungarian voice-over has largely been replaced by an English voice-over spoken by Forgács himself. (At a few points in the film there are brief passages spoken by a female voice, as if to recall Wittgenstein's strange and self-revealing comment—cited in the film itself—that there might be "something feminine about this way of thinking," namely, the way of thinking recommended by Wittgenstein in the *Tractatus* and elsewhere. In the English-language version of the film these phrases have been left in the original Hungarian.) For obvious reasons, the Hungarian version of the film offers a more tightly coordinated representation than the English version, but as I do not know Hungarian, I am not able to comment on particular differences between the two versions of the film.

7. The purity and sophistication as well as the psychological and literary suggestiveness of Wittgenstein's German, like Freud's, can hardly be appreciated in another language. Unless otherwise indicated, I have quoted from the German text of Wittgenstein's *Tractatus* published with a facing English translation by David F. Pears and Brian F. McGuinness (2nd imprint with corrections, Oxford: Basil Blackwell, 1963), which differs in small ways from the German original of 1921. This translation replaced an earlier and influential translation by C. K. Ogden (assisted by Frank P. Ramsey) published in 1922 and corrected in 1933—the translation used by Forgács in preparing the English version of his film.

8. Max Black, *A Companion to Wittgenstein's "Tractatus"* (Cambridge: Cambridge University Press, 1964).

9. Black, *Companion*, p. 23.

10. Black, *Companion*, p. 377. As noted, it is this translation that is used in the English version of the film.

11. Black, *Companion*, p. 23.

12. See Black, *Companion*, pp. 378–386.

13. The film makes explicit reference to the house Wittgenstein built for himself in Norway—we see an image of his hand-drawn sketch (bearing various directional and cardinal indications) of the house and site—and makes many references to the operation (again in terms of the direction and possible reversal of movement) of the mechanical devices that had fascinated him ever since he "had been a student of engineering at Manchester University." Photographs and discussions of these artifacts and activities can be found in Wijdeveld, *Ludwig Wittgenstein, Architect*.

14. These quotations refer to the quotations from Wittgenstein's *Tractatus* or other writings that the film offers alongside the image track in the interleaved or superimposed titles or in the voice-over. For reasons of space, in the present discussion it is not possible to distinguish between these various methods of quotation; in a fuller consideration it would be important to differentiate between the quotations from Wittgenstein's texts that are "spoken" by a human voice and those meant to be "read" (by our eyes) as part of the image track—the pictured world. This play between speaking and showing or pictorially displaying enriches the film's philosophical presentation of this very relationship understood philosophically. The full calibration of image- and soundtracks—and of saying and seeing and of picturing and hearing (both visual scenes and spoken words)—is extremely complex. The film aims to *show* the dense nesting of seeing and speaking.

15. Wittgenstein, *Culture and Value*, p. 52e.

16. Wittgenstein, *Culture and Value*, p. 44e.

17. Although it is one of the few examples of writing or "speaking" captured in the film's found footage, and obviously a consequential one for that reason, the placard is not, unfortunately, readable to the English-speaking viewer of Forgács's film. According to Forgács (personal communication), the street hawker is advertising the American film—it was the sequel to the original *Invisible Man*, released in 1940 starring Vincent Price—on the Nagy Korut (Grand Boulevard) in Budapest, where one could find the seven major cinemas of the city. Though presumably the street hawker is supposed to look like the bandaged Invisible Man, he is dressed in the traditional garb of Death as we would see it in medieval or Renaissance woodcuts.

18. Wittgenstein writes *begrenzte*—bounded, fenced, frontiered, framed. My world is "limited" by my language, by the structure of the visual field, and by the logical/mystical configuration of "facts" or propositions—pictures of what is that could be otherwise.

19. The ideas developed in this essay germinated while I was a scholar in residence at the Getty Research Institute in Los Angeles from 2001 to 2002, along with

Peter Forgács and other scholars and artists, to study the topic of "Reproductions and Originals." I am especially grateful to Forgács for several discussions about his work, and to Thomas Wartenburg and Murray Smith for their detailed, incisive, and challenging comments. Steven C. Seid of the Pacific Film Archive at the University of California at Berkeley helped with surprisingly tricky technical issues.

Contributors

RICHARD ALLEN is Associate Professor of Cinema Studies at New York University and author of a forthcoming book entitled *Hitchcock's Romantic Irony: Storytelling, Sexuality, and Style* (Columbia University Press). He is co-editor of *Film Theory and Philosophy* (Clarendon, 1997) and *Wittgenstein, Theory, and the Arts* (Routledge, 2002). His most recent publication is an anthology entitled *Hitchcock: Past and Future* (Routledge, 2004).

NOËL CARROLL is Andrew Mellon Professor of the Humanities at Temple University and a former president of the American Society for Aesthetics. His influential books on the philosophy of film include a three-volume series: *Theorizing the Moving Image* (Cambridge University Press, 1996), *Interpreting the Moving Image* (Cambridge University Press, 1998), and *Engaging the Moving Image* (Yale University Press, 2003).

JINHEE CHOI is Assistant Professor of Film Studies at Carleton University. She is the co-editor of *Philosophy of Film and Motion Pictures* (Blackwell, 2005) with Noël Carroll. Her articles on the philosophy and aesthetics of film have appeared in *The Journal of Aesthetics and Art Criticism, The British Journal of Aesthetics*, and *Asian Cinema*.

WHITNEY DAVIS is Professor of History and Theory of Ancient and Modern Art at the University of California at Berkeley, where he is also Chair of the Department of History of Art and Director of the Film Studies Program. He is the author of several books on prehistoric, ancient, and modern archaeology and art theory, and is currently completing two books, *The Archaeology of Standpoints* and *Art and Analogy: Culture and Forms of Likeness*.

DAN FLORY is Assistant Professor of Philosophy at Montana State University, Bozeman. He has published essays on film aesthetics and Classical philosophy. Currently President of the Society for the Philosophic Study of the Contemporary Visual Arts, he is completing a book entitled *Philosophy, Black Film, Film Noir*.

CHRISTOPHER GRAU has a B.A. from New York University and an M.A. and Ph.D. from Johns Hopkins University. He is currently Assistant Professor of Philosophy at Florida International University in Miami. Chris has previously taught at Brooklyn College, Dartmouth College, and Johns Hopkins University, and is the editor of the anthology *Philosophers Explore "The Matrix"* (Oxford University Press, 2005).

LESTER H. HUNT, Professor of Philosophy, University of Wisconsin—Madison, is the author of *Nietzsche and the Origin of Virtue* (Routledge, 1991) and *Character and Culture* (Roman &

Littlefield, 1997), in addition to articles on ethics, political philosophy, literature, and film. He has also taught at Carnegie-Mellon University, the University of Pittsburgh, and Johns Hopkins University.

KATHERINE INCE is Senior Lecturer in French Studies at the University of Birmingham, England. Her book on the filmmaker Georges Franju has just been published (*Georges Franju*, Manchester University Press, 2005), and she has written a study of the performance artist Orlan, *Orlan: Millennial Female* (Berg, 2000). She has also co-edited books on women's erotic writing, Beckett, and Duras, and is now editing a volume on authorship in contemporary French cinema.

ANDRÁS BÁLINT KOVÁCS is Head of the Film Department at Eötvös Loránd University, Budapest and Director of the National Audiovisual Archive. He is also the artistic advisor for Béla Tarr's production company. His many books include *Les Mondes d'Andrej Tarkovsky* (L'Age d'Homme, 1987) and *Tarkovszkij* (Helikon, 1997). His latest book, *Mapping Modernism*, will be published by the University of Chicago Press.

PAISLEY LIVINGSTON is Professor of Philosophy at Lingnan University in Hong Kong. He has published books and essays on various topics in aesthetics and film studies. His most recent book is *Art and Intention* (Clarendon, 2005).

STEPHEN MULHALL is Fellow and Tutor in Philosophy at New College, Oxford. His research has focused on Wittgenstein, Heidegger, Kierkegaard, political philosophy, and the philosophy of religion. His book *On Film* (Routledge) was published in 2002. Other recent publications include *Philosophical Myths of the Fall* (Princeton University Press, 2005) and a second edition of the *Routledge Guidebook to Heidegger and "Being and Time"* (Routledge, 2005).

TREVOR PONECH, Associate Professor of English at McGill University, Montréal, is the author of *What Is Non-Fiction Cinema?* (Westview, 1999). He is currently at work on *Invisible Cinema*, a study of the metaphysical and ontological assumptions underlying contemporary analytic-philosophical and cognitive film theories.

PAUL C. SANTILLI is Professor of Philosophy at Siena College in Loudonville (Albany), New York. His prior writings on Kieślowski include an article published in *Film and Philosophy* and a recent essay delivered at the University of Notre Dame. He has also published work on genocide, ancient philosophy, and ethics. He is presently composing a series of papers on the idea of horror.

DANIEL SHAW is Professor of Philosophy and Film in the Department of Communication and Philosophy at Lock Haven University of Pennsylvania. He is the managing editor of the print journal *Film and Philosophy*. He is co-editor of the recent book *Dark Thoughts: Philosophic Reflections on Cinematic Horror* (Scarecrow, 2003), and has published many articles in the areas of aesthetics, existentialism, and film. He is presently writing a textbook on ethics and film.

MURRAY SMITH is Professor of Film Studies at the University of Kent, UK. He is the author of *Engaging Characters: Fiction, Emotion, and the Cinema* (Oxford, 1995) and *Trainspotting* (British Film Institute, 2002), and the co-editor of *Film Theory and Philosophy* (Oxford University Press, 1998) and *Contemporary Hollywood Cinema* (Routledge, 1998). He has published widely on the relationship between ethics, emotion, and films, including essays in *The Journal of Aesthetics and Art Criticism* and *Cinema Journal*.

THOMAS E. WARTENBERG is Chair of the Philosophy Department at Mount Holyoke College, where he also teaches in the Film Studies Program. He is the author of *Unlikely Couples: Movie Romance as*

Social Criticism (Westview, 1999) and *The Forms of Power: From Domination to Transformation* (Temple University Press, 1990), the editor of *The Nature of Art* (Wadsworth, 2001), and the co-editor of *Philosophy and Film* (Routledge, 1995) and *The Philosophy of Film: Introductory Text and Readings* (Blackwell, 2005).

GEORGE WILSON is Professor of Philosophy at the University of Southern California. He is the author of two books: *Narration in Light* (Johns Hopkins University Press, 1986) and *The Intentionality of Human Action* (Stanford University Press, 1989). He has written articles on the philosophy of language, theory of action, and film studies.

Selected Bibliography

Allen, Richard, and Murray Smith, eds. *Film Theory and Philosophy*. Oxford: Clarendon Press, 1997.

Allen, Richard, and Malcolm Turvey, eds. *Wittgenstein, Theory and the Arts*. London: Routledge, 2001.

Andersen, Nathan. "Is Film the Alien Other to Philosophy?: Philosophy *as* Film in Mulhall's *On Film*." *Film-Philosophy* 7 (2003), available at <http://www.film-philosophy.com/vol7-2003/n23anderson>. Reprinted in Special Interest Edition on Philosophy and Science Fiction, *Film and Philosophy* 9 (2005): 1–11.

Arnheim, Rudolf. *Film as Art*. London: Faber and Faber, 1958.

Astruc, Alexandre. "The Birth of a New Avant-Garde: La Camera-Stylo." In *The New Wave*, ed. Peter Graham, pp. 17–23. New York: Doubleday, 1968.

Baggini, Julian. "Alien Ways of Thinking: Mulhall's *On Film*." *Film-Philosophy* 7 (2003), available at <http://www.film-philosophy.com/vol7-2003/n24baggini>. Reprinted in Special Interest Edition on Philosophy and Science Fiction, *Film and Philosophy* 9 (2005): 12–23.

Bazin, André. *What Is Cinema?* 2 vols. Trans. Hugh Gray. University of California Press, 1967 and 1971.

Bergson, Henri. *Creative Evolution*. Trans. Arthur Mitchell. New York: Modern Library, 1944.

Brooks, Cleanth. "The Heresy of Paraphrase." In *The Well Wrought Urn*, pp. 157–175. London: Methuen, 1968.

Butler, Brian. "Transgression: Ordinary and Otherwise." *Film and Philosophy* 5/6 (2002): 180–183.

Carroll, Noël. *The Philosophy of Horror, or Paradoxes of the Heart*. London: Routledge, 1990.

——. "Avant-Garde Art and the Problem of Theory." *The Journal of Aesthetic Education* 29 (1995): 1–13.

——. "Avant-Garde Film and Film Theory." In *Theorizing the Moving Image*, pp. 162–168. New York: Cambridge University Press, 1996.

——. "Art, Narrative, and Moral Understanding." In *Aesthetics and Ethics: Essays at the Intersection*, ed. Jerrold Levinson, pp. 126–160. New York: Cambridge University Press, 1998.

——. "The Wheel of Virtue: Art, Literature and Moral Knowledge." *The Journal of Aesthetics and Art Criticism* 60 (2002): 3–26.

Cavell, Stanley. *The Claim of Reason*. New York: Oxford University Press, 1979.

——. *The World Viewed: Reflections on the Ontology of Film*. Enlarged ed. Harvard University Press, 1979.

——. *Pursuits of Happiness: The Hollywood Comedy of Remarriage*. Harvard University Press, 1981.

——. *Themes Out of School: Effects and Causes*. San Francisco: North Point Press, 1984.

——. "What Photography Calls Thinking." *Raritan* 4 (1985): 1–21.

——. *Contesting Tears: The Hollywood Melodrama of the Unknown Woman*. University of Chicago Press, 1990.

Chatman, Seymour. *Coming to Terms: The Rhetoric of Narrative in Fiction and Film*. Cornell University Press, 1990.

Constable, Catherine. *Thinking in Images: Film Theory, Feminist Philosophy, and Marlene Dietrich*. London: BFI, 2005.

Currie, Gregory. *Image and Mind: Film, Philosophy, and Cognitive Science*. New York: Cambridge University Press, 1995.

Danto, Arthur. "The Artworld." *Journal of Philosophy* 61 (1964): 571–584.

——. "Moving Pictures." *Quarterly Review of Film Studies* 4 (1979): 1–21.

——. *The Transfiguration of the Commonplace: A Philosophy of Art*. Harvard University Press, 1981.

——. "Philosophy and/as Film and/as if Philosophy." *October* 23 (1982): 4–14.

Deleuze, Gilles. *Cinema 1 and 2*. Trans. by Hugh Tomlinson and Barbara Habberjam. University of Minnesota Press, 1986 and 1989.

Diamond, Cora. "Missing the Adventure: Reply to Nussbaum." In *The Realistic Spirit: Wittgenstein, Philosophy, and the Mind*, pp. 309–318. MIT Press, 1991.

Eisenstein, Sergei. *Selected Works*. Vol. 1, *Writings, 1922–34*, ed. and trans. by Richard Taylor. London: BFI, 1988.

——. *Selected Works*. Vol. 2, *Towards a Theory of Montage, 1937–40*, ed. Michael Glenny and Richard Taylor and trans. Michael Glenny. London: BFI, 1991.

——. *Selected Works*. Vol. 3, *Writings, 1934–47*, ed. Richard Taylor and trans. William Powell. London: BFI, 1996.

——. *Nonindifferent Nature*. Trans. Herbert Marshall. Cambridge: Cambridge University Press, 1987.

Epstein, Jean. *L'intelligence d'une machine*. Paris: Jacques Melot, 1946.

Falzon, Christopher. *Philosophy Goes to the Movies: An Introduction to Philosophy*. London: Routledge, 2002.

Fleming, Bruce E. *Art and Argument: What Words Can't Do and What They Can*. Lanham, MD: University Press of America, 2003.

Flory, Dan. "Black on White: *Film Noir* and the Epistemology of Race in Recent African American Cinema." *Journal of Social Philosophy* 31 (2000): 82–116.

——. "Race, Rationality, and Melodrama: Aesthetic Response and the Case of Oscar Micheaux." *The Journal of Aesthetics and Art Crticism* 63 (2005): 327–338.

Freeland, Cynthia A. "Art and Moral Knowledge." *Philosophical Topics* 25 (1997): 11–36.

——. *The Naked and the Undead: Evil and the Appeal of Horror.* Boulder: Westview, 2000.

Freeland, Cynthia A., and Thomas E. Wartenberg, eds. *Philosophy and Film.* New York: Routledge, 1995.

French, Peter. *Cowboy Metaphysics.* Lanham, MD: Rowman and Littlefield, 1997.

Gibson, John, and Wolfgang Huemer, eds. *The Literary Wittgenstein.* London: Routledge, 2004.

Gilmore, Richard. *Doing Philosophy at the Movies.* SUNY Press, 2005.

Granger, Herbert. "Cinematic Philosophy in *Le Feu Follet*: The Search for the Meaningful Life." *Film and Philosophy* 8 (2004): 74–90.

Grau, Christopher, ed. *Philosophers Explore the Matrix.* New York: Oxford University Press, 2005.

Hunt, Lester. "Motion Pictures as a Philosophical Resource." In *Philosophy of Film and Motion Pictures: An Anthology,* ed. Noël Carroll and Jinhee Choi, pp. 397–406. Oxford: Blackwell, 2005.

Iampolski, Mikhail. "The Logic of an Illusion: Notes on the Genealogy of Intellectual Cinema." In *Camera Obscura, Camera Lucida,* ed. Richard Allen and Malcolm Turvey, pp. 35–50. Amsterdam University Press, 2003.

Irwin, William, ed. *The Matrix and Philosophy.* Chicago: Open Court, 2002.

——. *More Matrix and Philosophy.* Chicago: Open Court, 2005.

Jarvie, Ian. *The Philosophy of the Film: Epistemology, Ontology, Aesthetics.* New York: Routledge & Kegan Paul, 1987.

Kellner, Douglas. "Aesthetics, Ethics, and Politics in the Films of Spike Lee." In *Spike Lee's "Do the Right Thing,"* ed. Mark A. Reid, pp. 73–106. New York: Cambridge University Press, 1997.

Kitcher, Philip, and Richard Schacht. *Finding an Ending: Reflections on Wagner's "Ring."* Oxford: Oxford University Press, 2004.

Kupfer, Joseph. *Visions of Virtue in Popular Film.* Boulder: Westview, 1999.

Leavis, F. R. "Literary Criticism and Philosophy: A Reply." *Scrutiny* 6 (1937): 59–70.

Light, Andrew. *Reel Arguments: Film, Philosophy and Social Criticism.* Boulder: Westview, 2003.

Litch, Mary. *Philosophy Through Film.* New York: Routledge, 2004.

MacDonald, Scott, ed. *A Critical Cinema: Interviews with Independent Filmmakers,* 4 vols. University of California Press, 1988, 1992, 1998, 2005.

Merleau-Ponty, Maurice. "The Film and the New Psychology." In *Sense and Non-Sense,* trans. Hubert L. Dreyfus and Patricia Allen Dreyfus. Northwestern University Press, 1964.

Michelson, Annette. "Toward Snow." In *The Avant-Garde Film Reader,* ed. P. Adams Sitney. New York University Press, 1978.

——. "The Wings of Hypothesis: On Montage and the Theory of the Interval." In *Montage and Modern Life: 1919–1942,* ed. Matthew Teitelbaum. MIT Press, 1994.

Mulhall, Stephen. "Picturing the Human (Body and Soul): A Reading of *Blade Runner.*" *Film and Philosophy* 1 (1994): 87–104.

——. *On Film.* New York: Routledge, 2002.

——. "Ways of Thinking: A Response to Andersen and Baggini." *Film-Philosophy* 7 (2003), available at <http://www.film-philosophy.com/vol7-2003/n25mulhall>. Reprinted in Special Interest Edition on Philosophy and Science Fiction, *Film and Philosophy* 9 (2005): 24–29.

Nussbaum, Martha. *Love's Knowledge: Essays on Philosophy and Literature.* New York: Oxford University Press, 1990.

Plantinga, Carl, and Greg M. Smith, eds. *Passionate Views: Film, Cognition, and Emotion.* Johns Hopkins University Press, 1999.

Porter, Burton. *Philosophy Through Fiction and Film.* Upper Saddle River, NJ: Pearson Education, 2004.

Read, Rupert, and Jerry Goodenough, eds. *Film as Philosophy: Essays on Cinema After Wittgenstein and Cavell.* New York: Palgrave, 2005.

Rothman, William, and Marian Keane. *Reading Cavell's "The World Viewed": A Philosophical Perspective on Film.* Detroit: Wayne State University Press, 2000.

Russell, Bruce. "The Philosophical Limits of Film." Special Issue *Film and Philosophy* (2000): 163–167.

Ryan, Michael, and Douglas Kellner. *Camera Politica: The Politics and Ideology of Contemporary Hollywood Film.* Indiana University Press, 1988.

Scruton, Roger. "Philosophy and Literature." In *The Politics of Culture and Other Essays,* pp. 80–87. Manchester: Carcanet Press, 1981.

Sitney, P. Adams. *Visionary Film.* New York: Oxford University Press, 1979.

Singer, Irving. *Three Philosophical Filmmakers: Hitchcock, Welles, Renoir.* MIT Press, 2004.

——. *Reality Transformed: Film as Meaning and Technique.* MIT Press, 1998.

Small, Edward S. *Direct Theory: Experimental Film/Video as Major Genre.* Carbondale: Southern Illinois University Press, 1994.

Smith, Joseph H., and William Kerrigan, eds. *Images in Our Souls: Cavell, Psychoanalysis and Cinema.* Johns Hopkins University Press, 1987.

Smith, Murray. *Engaging Characters: Fiction, Emotion, and the Cinema.* Oxford: Clarendon Press, 1995.

——. "Film and Philosophy." In *The Macmillan Encyclopedia of Philosophy.* Macmillan, forthcoming 2006.

Smith, William. *Plato and Popcorn: A Philospoher's Guide to 75 Thought-Provoking Movies.* Jefferson, NC: McFarland & Co., 2004.

Stoehr, Kevin, ed. *Film and Knowledge: Essays on the Integration of Images and Ideas.* McFarland & Co., 2002.

Stroud, Scott R. "The Twain Shall Meet: The Philosophical Narratives of the *Bhagavad Gita* and *The Thin Red Line.*" *South Pacific Journal of Philosophy and Culture* 5 (2001): 94–113.

Taylor, Clyde. *The Mask of Art: Breaking the Aesthetic Contract—Film and Literature.* Indiana University Press, 1998.

Walton, Kendall. *Mimesis as Make-Believe: On the Foundations of the Representational Arts.* Harvard University Press, 1990.

Wartenberg, Thomas. *Unlikely Couples: Movie Romance as Social Criticism*. Boulder: Westview Press, 1999.

——. "Interpreting Films Philosophically." *Film and Philosophy* 5 (2002): 164–171.

——. "Philosophy Screened: Experiencing *The Matrix*." *Midwest Studies in Philosophy* 27 (2003): 139–152.

——. "Looking Backward: Philosophy and Film Reconsidered." *Film and Philosophy* 8 (2004): 138–141.

——. "Film as Argument." *Film Studies: An International Review* 8 (Summer 2006).

Wartenberg, Thomas, and Angela Curran, eds. *The Philosophy of Film: Introductory Text and Readings*. Oxford: Blackwell, 2005.

Wellek, René. "Literary Criticism and Philosophy." *Scrutiny* 5 (1937): 375–383.

Wilson, George. *Narration in Light*. Johns Hopkins University Press, 1986.

Wittgenstein, Ludwig. *Philosophical Investigations*. Trans. G. E. M. Anscombe. New York: MacMillan, 1953.

——. *Tractatus-Logico Philosophicus*, published with German text and facing English translation by David F. Pears and Brian F. McGuinness. Oxford: Basil Blackwell, 1963.

——. *Culture and Value: A Selection from the Posthumous Remains*, ed. Alois Pichler. Oxford: Basil Blackwell, 1998.

Yeffeth, Glenn, ed. *Taking the Red Pill*. Dallas: Benbella Books, 2003.

Žižek, Slavoj, *The Fright of Real Tears: Krzysztof Kieslowski Between Theory and Post-Theory*. London: British Film Institute, 2001.

Žižek, Slavoj, ed. *Everything You Always Wanted to Know about Lacan But Were Afraid to Ask Hitchcock*. London: Verso Books, 1992.

Index